Presidential Elections
Strategies and Structures
of American Politics
Tenth Edition

Nelson W. Polsby
Aaron Wildavsky
University of California, Berkeley

CHATHAM HOUSE PUBLISHERS
SEVEN BRIDGES PRESS, LLC
NEW YORK • LONDON

Seven Bridges Press, LLC
135 Fifth Avenue, New York, N.Y. 10010

Publisher: Robert J. Gormley
Managing editor: Katharine Miller
Project manager: Electronic Publishing Services Inc., N.Y.C.
Cover design: Andrea Barash Design
Cover art: Henry Fong
Printing and binding: Victor Graphics, Inc.

Library of Congress Cataloging-in-Publication Data

Polsby, Nelson W.
    Presidential elections: strategies and structures of Americn
Politics / by Nelson W. Polsby, Aaron Wildavsky.—10th ed.
        p.   cm.
    Includes bibliographical references and index.
    ISBN 1-889119-26-1 (pbk.)
    I. Presidents—United States—Election.   I. Wildavsky, Aaron B.
II. Title
JK528.P63   2000
324.973—dc 20   9532493
                                                              CIP

Manufactured in the United States of America
10 9 8 7 6 5 4 3 2 1

To our grandchildren:

Benjamin Polsby Stern

Eva Miriam Wildavsky

Aaron Alexander Wildavsky

Edward Polsby Stern

Saul Abraham Wildavsky

Contents

Tables, Figures, Boxes

Preface

This is the 10th edition of *Presidential Elections*, the second edition to appear since the death of Aaron Wildavsky on 4 September 1993. Changes in the text reflect the ongoing march of events in the world of American politics, and new scholarship about voters, parties, candidates, and journalists in presidential elections. There is much continuity as well, in which Aaron's contribution can plainly be seen. The most important element of continuity in this book is what has proven to be its sturdy theoretical foundation, which has helped to organize each edition of this book since the first edition in 1964. The substance of this theoretical foundation can be summarized as follows: A lot of what goes on in a presidential election can be understood if we think of these activities as strategic choices by actors who operate in a world that is partially manipulable—that is where strategies come in—and partially structured by elements that are more or less given. The main structural influences on actors' strategic choices are (1) the rules and regulations governing nominations and elections and (2) principles of behavior governing how voters involve themselves in the process. Thus we draw attention to politicians' choices in the light of evolving structures of politics—political parties, primary elections, national conventions, campaigns and their organizations—and the emerging study of the behavior of masses of voters.

This edition sticks to this theme and explains the strategic choices of actors differently situated—Democrats, Republicans, incumbents, challengers, journalists, delegates, and voters—by seeking to understand the ways in which their world is organized and their choices framed by incentives and prohibitions, habits, customs, regulations, and opportunities.

The aim, as always, is to help readers understand what presidential elections are all about, not to make predictions or advise people how to vote. In the spirit of previous editions, this edition of *Presidential Elections* seeks to be useful to readers no matter what their political preferences. While Aaron and I did not always agree about party politics, I hope in this edition to continue to uphold his life-long commitment to political enlightenment as a necessary attribute of a self-governing society. It will serve our purposes very well if our readers take knowledge from this book that will help them understand their political world a little better, and perhaps even find encouragement to participate in it with greater confidence and skill.

Acknowledgments

Writing this book with Aaron Wildavsky eight different times was a lot of fun, and it is a pleasure to remember his vitality and intelligence, still visible in these pages.

I record with sorrow also the loss of our dear friend and distinguished publisher, Ed Artinian, who died on 7 September 1997. Ed made Chatham House a very special home for political scientists, and gave an inimitable personal touch to the craft of publishing. I remember with great affection Ed's telephone call a few days after I had sent him the manuscript of the ninth edition of this book. He had read it carefully and had some queries and suggestions. Overall, he was enthusiastic: "It is just like Aaron talking to me," he said.

In this edition, I see that I am falling more and more under the influence of a younger generation of scholars, a few of whom have worked side by side with me in its preparation. In particular I am grateful for the collaboration of Jonathan Bernstein, an original, perceptive, and fruitfully opinionated student of politics. Jonathan and I were thoughtfully backstopped by Thad Kousser and Kathryn Pearson. Samantha Luks and Ben Highton helped with statistical work. I thank also for continuing conversation shaping my understanding of parties and elections Bill Mayer, Leon Epstein, Austin Ranney, John Zaller, Herb McClosky, Jack Peltason, David Brady, Susan Rasky, Jack Citrin, Bruce Cain, Jerry Lubenow, Michael Baruch Grossman, Ray Laraja, Byron Shafer, and Ray Wolfinger, as well as other devoted members of the political junkies' seminar which meets periodically here at the Institute of Governmental Studies under the leadership of Jonathan Bernstein.

Finally, I offer heartfelt thanks to Caren Oto and to the superb librarians and staff of IGS, where I found a happy academic home for ten good years.

Nelson W. Polsby
Berkeley, California

PART I

The Strategic Environment

The strategies of all the participants in presidential elections are to a certain extent constrained, and to a certain extent driven, by the ways in which actors are situated with respect to conditions that are for them given and hard to manipulate. Here are some examples: the rules governing how votes are counted, the sequence in which primary elections occur, the accepted practices of campaign journalism, whether candidates are incumbents or challengers, and the habits of voters. All these conditions need to be taken account of by participants and need to be understood by observers.

CHAPTER 1

Voters

IN 1996 MORE THAN 96 million Americans voted in the presidential election. Millions more who were old enough to vote—over 100 million in 1996—did not. Parties and candidates depend on voter turnout. So it is important for them to know why some people show up at the polls and why others do not. In two respects, Americans are different from citizens of other democracies. A smaller proportion of Americans will vote in any given election than citizens of other democracies, but Americans collectively vote much more often, and on more matters, than anyone else. Voting behavior is one of the most carefully studied of all political actions. Who votes? Who doesn't vote? What motivates voters? All these questions are the subjects of extensive study.

Why People Don't Vote

A lot of elections, not just presidential elections but also state and local and congressional elections, take place in the United States. Americans are noted for their lukewarm levels of participation as compared with voters in most Western European democracies. Table 1.1 compares the turnout of Americans in presidential elections, when U.S. turnout is highest, to typical turnout figures in parliamentary elections in other democratic countries. Why don't Americans vote more, or at least more like Europeans? In some respects, to be sure, the elections being compared really are not comparable. Parliamentary elections in many places—for example, the United Kingdom—require voters to do only one thing: place a single X on a ballot to fill an office more or less like that of a U.S. representative in Congress. Who ends up running the government in these countries depends on how many parliamentarians of each political party are elected (in the United Kingdom from over 600 constituencies), and so most voters cast party-line votes and do not much care about the identity of individuals on the ballot.[1] Ballots in U.S. presidential elections are longer and more complex: they require voting for president, vice-president, members of the House, senators (two-thirds of the time), frequently various

TABLE 1.1   RANKING OF COUNTRIES BY TURNOUT

1. Australia*	93.8	13. Norway	84.0
2. Belgium*	93.4	14. Israel	79.7
3. Austria	90.5	15. Finland	77.6
4. Italy*	90.5	16. Canada	75.5
5. Iceland	90.1	17. United Kingdom	75.4
6. Luxembourg	87.3	18. Portugal	72.6
7. New Zealand	87.2	19. Japan	71.4
8. Sweden	86.0	20. Spain	70.6
9. Netherlands	85.8	21. Ireland	68.5
10. Denmark	85.7	22. France	66.2
11. Greece*	84.5	**23. United States**	**52.8**
12. Germany	84.3	24. Switzerland	46.1

SOURCES: Thomas T. Mackie and Richard Rose, *The International Almanac of Electoral History*, 3d ed. (Washington, D.C.: CQ Press, 1991). Compulsory voting information from G. Bingham Powell, "American Voter Turnout in Comparative Perspective," *American Political Science Review* 80 (March 1986): 38, and Raymond Wolfinger, David Glass, and Peverill Squire, "Predictors of Electoral Turnout: International Comparison," *Policy Studies Review* 9 (Spring 1990): 561.

NOTES: These figures refer to voting turnout for the country's most recent national election as of 1989. The format used in this table is the most common representation of comparative voting turnout, but the turnout numbers are in fact deceptive. In this comparison, U.S. turnout is calculated as a percentage of the voting-age population, while turnout elsewhere is calculated as a percentage of registered voters. This difference artificially deflates the U.S. number because it includes noncitizens and other ineligible but age-eligible citizens (e.g., convicted felons in some states), and simultaneously inflates some of the other nations' score because their denominators do not include all "age-eligible" residents (e.g., guest workers) but only registered voters. See Box 1.1 (p.22) for a table that standardizes the denominator for all countries.

*Indicates nations where voting is compulsory.

state offices, local offices, ballot propositions, and so on. American ballots therefore demand quite a lot of knowledge from voters. In general, Americans do not invest their time and energy in becoming knowledgeable about all the choices they are required to make.[2]

But voters do turn out for presidential elections more conscientiously than for elections in years when there is no presidential contest, so the complexity of presidential elections is pretty clearly not a deterrent to voting (see table 1.2). To the contrary, the added publicity of a presidential contest obviously helps turnout, as do the greater sums of money spent by political campaigns in presidential elections, and the fact that the level of campaign activity by activists and interest groups is greater in presidential elections.[3]

TABLE 1.2   VOTER TURNOUT IN PRESIDENTIAL AND MIDTERM ELECTIONS (IN PERCENTAGES)

Year	Presidential elections	Year	Midterm elections
1960	65.4	1962	49.2
1964	63.3	1966	49.3
1968	62.3	1970	48.4
1972	57.1	1974	39.5
1976	55.2	1978	39.0
1980	54.3	1982	41.6
1984	55.2	1986	37.2
1988	50.1	1990	33.1
1992	55.2	1994	37.4
1996	48.9	1998	36.1

SOURCES: 1960–1986: Walter Dean Burnham, "The Turnout Problem," in *Elections American Style,* ed. A. James Reichley (Washington, D.C.: Brookings Institution, 1987), 114; 1986–1996: *Statistical Abstract of the United States 1997* (Washington, D.C.: Government Printing Office, 1997), 289; 1998: "1988 Turnout Resumes Downward Trend," Committee for the Study of the American Electorate, 8 February 1999.

A favorite explanation of low American turnout (low by the standards of Western democracies) is that Americans are unusually disaffected from politics and that abstention from voting is their method of showing their disapproval of, or alienation from, politics. Scholars have been deeply interested in the subject of political alienation, but they have shown that this explanation of low turnout is improbable or at best incomplete.

There are several elements to their demonstration. First, scholars note that the constellation of sentiments associated with alienation—disaffection, loss of trust in government, and so on—are stronger, on the whole, in many countries where turnout is relatively high. Americans do not express especially negative feelings toward government. On more measures than not, Americans are actually more positive about government than citizens of other democratic nations (see table 1.3, p.6).

Americans are also comparatively high in other forms of political participation: discussing politics with others, trying to persuade others during elections, working for candidates or parties of their choice, expressing interest in politics. Within the United States, people who don't like or don't trust government vote about as frequently as people who do.[4] And electoral turnout does not appear to fluctuate with well-publicized manifestations of ill-will (see table 1.4, p.7).

A better explanation for what really divides Americans who vote from those who don't is registration: people registered to vote tend to vote roughly at Western European rates of participation. But people not registered cannot vote legally, and so it is important to know that registration to vote is more difficult in most parts of the United States than in the democracies with which the United States is compared. In America, permanent registration does not come

TABLE 1.3   COMPARATIVE ALIENATION: UNITED STATES AND EUROPE (IN PERCENTAGES)

Country	Political interest index[a]	Political activity index[b]	Political efficacy[c]	Trust government all or most of the time[d]
United States	48 (1)	24 (1)	59 (2)	34 (9)
West Germany	41 (2)	15 (6)	33 (7)	52 (5)
Netherlands	36 (3)	17 (2)	37 (6)	46 (7)
Austria	32 (4)	12 (7)	N.A.	55 (4)
United Kingdom	32 (4)	11 (8)	42 (4)	40 (8)
Finland	29 (6)	17 (2)	N.A.	50 (6)
Switzerland	29 (6)	16 (5)	N.A.	76 (1)
Italy	18 (8)	17 (2)	39 (5)	14 (12)
Greece	N.A.	N.A.	N.A.	62 (2)
Denmark	N.A.	N.A.	N.A.	56 (3)
France	N.A.	N.A.	N.A.	33 (10)
Belgium	N.A.	N.A.	N.A.	20 (11)

SOURCES: Samuel H. Barnes and Max Kaase et al., "Political Action: An Eight-Nation Study, 1973–1976," Inter-University Consortium for Political and Social Research Codebook, cited in Raymond E. Wolfinger, David P. Glass, and Peverill Squire, "Predictors of Electoral Turnout: An International Comparison," *Policy Studies Review 9* (Spring 1990): 557; Commission of the European Communities, *Euro-Barometre*, no. 17 (June 1982): 25; and 1980 *National Election Study Codebook* 1:614, variable 1030, cited in Wolfinger, Glass, and Squire, "Predictors of Electoral Turnout."

NOTES: The number in parentheses following the percentage is the country's rank on that question.
N.A. = data not available.
a. Scores are the mean of the percentage of respondents who said they (1) were very or somewhat interested in politics; (2) often read about politics in the newspapers; and (3) often discussed politics with others.
b. Scores are the mean of the percentage of respondents who said they (1) often worked with others in their community to solve a local problem; (2) often or sometimes attended a political meeting or rally; (3) often or sometimes contacted public officials; and (4) often or sometimes worked in behalf of a party or candidate.
c. Scores for the Europeans are the percentage of respondents who agreed that "people like yourself can help to bring about a change," and for the Americans, the percentage who disagreed with the statement, "People like me don't have any say about what the government does."
d. Percentage of respondents who agreed that they could trust their government all or most of the time.

automatically as an attribute of citizenship, as it does in most countries. Instead, prospective voters are required to take positive steps to sign up on a voting roll maintained in the locality where they wish to vote. Normally, you vote where you live, and because Americans change where they live quite a lot—about one-third of Americans change their local address every two years—a lot of reregistering is required.[5]

TABLE 1.4   ALIENATION AND U.S. VOTER TURNOUT (IN PERCENTAGES)

	Voters	Nonvoters
How much money do the people in government waste?		
None or some	59	41
A lot	61	39
How much of the time can you trust the government to do what's right?		
Always or most of the time	59	41
Some or none of the time	61	39
Is the government run by a few big interests or for the benefit of all?		
For the benefit of all the people	61	39
For the benefit of a few big interests	61	39
Are most of those running the government smart, or do many not know what they are doing?		
Are smart	61	39
Don't know what they are doing	60	40
Are the people running the government crooked?		
Hardly any or not many are crooked	64	36
Quite a few are crooked	57	43
The federal government in Washington is doing a:		
Good job	60	40
Fair job	64	36
Poor job	66	34
How much attention does the government pay to what people think?		
A good deal or some	67	33
Not much	58	42
How much does having elections make the government pay attention to what the people think?		
A good deal	65	35
Some	65	35
Not much	53	47

SOURCES: Chart adapted from Raymond Wolfinger, David Glass, and Peverill Squire, "Predictors of Electoral Turnout: An International Comparison," *Policy Studies Review* 9 (Spring 1990): 555. Data from The Vote Validation Study of the University of Michigan Center for Political Studies, *The American National Election Study,* 1980.

The fact that there are so many different local jurisdictions and variations in registration requirements, state by state, is a result of the size and diversity of the United States, and of our federal heritage, in which the national government established by the U.S. Constitution arrived later on the scene than the original state governments. The Constitution says eligibility to vote in national elections is determined by state laws governing eligibility to vote for the most numerous house of the state legislature.[6]

Voting itself takes place not on a holiday, as in some countries, or over a weekend, but on a regular workday—for presidential elections, customarily the first Tuesday after the first Monday in November. Presidential primaries take place, state by state, on a series of dates, usually but not always on Tuesday, stretching from February or March to June. These primary dates change every four years and may or may not be combined with a state's other primary elections. History, geography, and custom thus play a significant part in determining contemporary patterns of turnout.

There is no convincing evidence that the basic human nature of Americans differs from that of citizens of other democratic lands. But the United States has organized itself differently—state by state rather than as a unitary nation—to do political business. Entitlements to vote are recorded in a more decentralized fashion than in most democracies and require more work on the part of the prospective voter, and that seems better than any other explanation to account for the lower level of turnout in American presidential elections.

Turnout: Why People Do Vote—A Theory of Social Connectedness

This still leaves open the question why the millions of Americans who do vote in presidential elections bother to do so. This is a matter of some interest to candidates and their managers. Even though in recent years some local elections and a few congressional elections have turned on a handful of votes, it cannot possibly be that millions of voters have convinced themselves to vote in presidential elections because each of them personally believes he or she will materially affect the actual outcome of the election. Oddly enough, the more votes being aggregated in an election and the more voters expected to turn out, the larger the proportion of those eligible who actually show up, so that presidential elections regularly inspire higher turnout than midterm elections for Congress. But as the psychologist Paul Meehl once figured the odds, the chances that a particular voter could actually affect the outcome of a presidential election are pretty slim. Far more likely, that voter would be struck by lightning going to or from the polling place.[7]

Why people vote is, after years of investigation, still a bit of a mystery. Scholars who try to understand human motivations have put forward the argument that voting must in some way or other make people feel good, or better, at least, than if they did not vote. Or that voters somehow calculate that the benefits of voting exceed the costs.[8] Our best guess is that the decision to vote is on the whole not rationally calculated but is a more or less standing decision or habit that citizens fall into as they adopt other forms of social participation in the course of becoming integrated into the ordinary social life of their communities.[9]

Essentially, voting seems to make sense mostly as an act of social participation or civic involvement. There are by now a great many studies of voting and nonvoting, and in general voters are people connected in various ways to the larger society or to their local community, and nonvoters are not. Thus people who are settled in one place vote more than people who move around. Married adults vote more frequently than unmarried. People who belong to civic organizations or interest groups vote more than nonjoiners. Voting participation generally increases with age until late in life, when social participation of all sorts drops away—frequently as the result of the loss of a spouse. The young, many of whom are unsettled and unmarried, vote much less than their elders, but as they settle down, they begin to vote. The better educated vote more than the less well educated. People who identify with one or another political party vote more than those who claim no party affiliation or loyalty.[10]

Residence, family ties, education, civic participation in general, and party identification all create ties to the larger world, and these ties evidently create social habits that include turning out to vote. Families of government workers—a special sort of interest group—also participate at extremely high levels.[11] Perhaps these voters are voting because they perceive a monetary incentive to do so. Typically, however, their votes have little or no direct impact on their salaries. But they may feel keenly the centrality of civic involvement in their lives.

If voting were in general a rationally calculated business, we conjecture that large numbers of the most well-educated and sophisticated citizens would become free-riding nonvoters, since showing up is hardly worth the effort given the next-to-zero probability that any single vote would affect the outcome. Yet it is precisely those citizens best equipped to see the logic of the free ride—the well educated—who vote the most conscientiously.

This reasoning also gives a basis for the view that political life is significantly organized according to the group affiliations of voters. Foremost among the groupings that matter to voters are the political parties, organizations that specialize in political activity. Two such organizations, the Democratic Party and the Republican Party, more or less monopolize the loyalties of American voters.

In the Minds of Voters: Party

Most people vote according to their habitual party affiliation.[12] In other words, because they always support a particular party, many people will have made up their minds how to vote in 2000 before the candidates are even chosen.[13] These party regulars are likely to be more interested and active in politics and have more political knowledge than people who call themselves political "independents."[14] But party regulars rarely change their minds. They tend to listen mostly to their own side of political arguments and to agree with the policies espoused by their party. They even go so far as to ignore information that they perceive to be unfavorable to the party of their choice.[15]

Thus party identification is important in giving a structure to voters' pictures of reality and in helping them choose their preferred presidential candidate. But where do people get their party affiliations? There seems to be no simple answer. Every individual is born into a social context and consequently inherits a social identity that may contain a political component. People are Democrats or Republicans, in part, because their families and the other people with whom they interact are Democrats or Republicans.[16] Most individuals come into close contact predominantly with affiliates of only one party.[17] Just as people tend to share characteristics with their friends and families, such as income and educational level, religious affiliation, and area of residence, they also tend to share party loyalties with them.[18]

Of course, we all know of instances where this is not so, where people do not share various of these status-giving characteristics with their parents and at least some of their friends. In these circumstances, we would expect political differences to turn up when there are other kinds of differences. But by and large, voters retain the party loyalties of the primary groups—people they interact with directly—of which they are a part.

Parties as Aggregates of Loyal Voters

The overall result is to give each of the major political parties reservoirs of voting strength they can count on from election to election (see table 1.5). Since the 1860s, when the Republican Party was organized, Republicans traditionally have done well in the small towns and rural areas of New England, the Middle Atlantic states, and the Midwest. They draw their support from people who are more prosperous and better educated than Democratic supporters, occupy managerial or professional positions or run small businesses, live in or move into the well-to-do suburban areas, and are predominantly Protestant. Democrats traditionally draw great support from the large cities. Wage earners, union members, Catholics, African American voters, and many of the descendants of the great waves of immigrants entering this country in the latter half of the nineteenth century—Jews, Irish, Poles—all contribute disproportionately to the Democratic vote.[19]

But why did these particular groups come to have these particular loyalties? We must turn to history to find answers to this question. Enough is known about a few groups to make it possible to speculate about what kinds of historical events tend to align groups with a political party.

Here are a few examples. From the Civil War until the era of George Wallace and Barry Goldwater—about a century—the historically "Solid South" was overwhelmingly Democratic in its presidential voting. For all those years, resentment against the harsh Reconstruction period (1864–1877), when the

TABLE 1.5 POLITICAL AFFILIATION (IN PERCENTAGES)

	Republican	Democratic	Independent
National	29	38	33
Male	30	36	34
Female	28	40	32
White	32	34	34
Nonwhite	11	65	24
Black	9	71	20
Hispanic	23	52	25
College graduate	36	32	32
College incomplete	33	34	33
High school graduate	28	38	34
Less than high school graduate	21	50	29
East	24	41	35
Midwest	30	32	38
South	32	40	28
West	32	39	29
19–29 years	29	33	38
30–49 years	29	37	34
50–64 years	28	42	30
65 and older	33	43	24
Boomer (26–46)	29	36	35
Income $40,000 and over	35	32	33
Income $25,000–$39,999	32	34	34
Income $15,000–$24,999	26	41	33
Income under $15,000	23	51	26
Protestant	34	36	30
Catholic	26	42	32

SOURCE: *Gallup Poll Monthly,* July 1992, 49.

former confederate states were governed under the leadership of the national Republican Party, was reflected in the election returns. Less well known is that the South was not unanimous in its enthusiasm for the Civil War in the first place or in its resentment of Reconstruction. In many states of the Old South there were two kinds of farms: plantations on the flat land, which grew cash crops, used slaves, and, in general, prospered before the Civil War; and subsistence farms in the uplands, which had a few or no slaves and, in general, were run by poorer white people who had little or no stake in the Confederacy and opposed secession. This latter group formed the historical core of mountain areas that year after year, well into the latter half of the twentieth century, voted Republican in presidential elections. These areas were located in western Virginia and North Carolina, eastern Tennessee and Kentucky, and southeastern West Virginia.[20] Since the 1960s, through a combination of white Republicans migrating in, black Democrats migrating out, and conversion from Democratic to Republican of conservative white southerners, the once solidly Democratic South has become a lot less Democratic and a lot more Republican.[21]

The voting habits of African American citizens, where they have voted, have been shaped by several large events. The Civil War freed them and made them Lincoln Republicans. The reaction to Reconstruction in the South disenfranchised them because a century ago most of them lived in the rural South well within the reach of Jim Crow laws.[22] The growth of American industry brought many African Americans north.[23] This took them away from the most severe legal impediments to citizenship but did not always lift their burden of economic destitution or relieve them of racial discrimination. The effects of the Great Depression of 1929 on African American voters in the North brought them into the New Deal coalition, and the northern African American voter has remained overwhelmingly Democratic ever since.[24] In the South, especially after the Voting Rights Act of 1964 was enacted by bipartisan congressional majorities during the Democratic presidency of Lyndon Johnson, newly enfranchised African Americans also voted Democratic. As these voters have observed Democratic politicians espousing causes in which they believe, they have maintained their high levels of support.

If the historical events of the Civil War in the 1860s and the depression of the late 1920s and early 1930s shaped the political heritage of some people, for others the critical forces seem less dramatic and more diffuse. It is possible to see why the poor become Democrats, for the Democratic Party since the 1930s has been welfare minded; but why do the rich lean toward the Republicans? Undoubtedly, in part, this is a negative reaction to the redistributive aspirations of some New Deal programs and the inclination of Democratic presidents to expand the role of government in the economy. But in all probability it is also a positive response to the record of the congressional wing of the Republican Party, which so thoroughly dominated the post–Civil War era of industrial expansion in the 1890s and on up until the election of 1932. In this era, Republican policies vigorously encouraged, and to a degree underwrote, risk taking by private businessmen, granted them federal aid in a variety of forms (notably, tariffs), and withheld federal regulation from private enterprise.[25]

Sometimes party affiliation coincides with ethnic identification because of the political and social circumstances surrounding the entry of ethnic groups into the country. A dramatic example is the rapid influx since the 1960s of Cuban refugees—many of them well-to-do and solidly middle class or above—from the communist regime of Fidel Castro into southern Florida. Unlike Hispanic voters elsewhere in America, for these Cuban refugees and their families opposition to communism is extremely salient, and they favor the Republican Party. By contrast, the descendants of the Cuban cigar makers who settled many decades ago in the Tampa area, on Florida's west coast, vote more according to their pocketbooks and their union loyalties and are predominantly Democratic.[26]

In the cities of the Northeast, politics was dominated by the Republican Party and by "Yankees" (Protestants of British ancestry) of substance and high status during the decades following the Civil War. During these decades, thousands of Irish people—many of them fleeing the potato famine of the mid-nineteenth century and rule in Ireland by the English and Scots-Irish cousins of Yankee Americans—streamed into this area. The Democratic Party welcomed them; the Republicans did not. In due course the Democratic percentage of the two-party vote began to increase, and Irish politicians, who uniquely among newer immigrants already knew the English language, took over the Democratic Party.[27] In the Midwest, events such as American involvement in two wars against Germany under Democratic auspices in many cases shaped the political preferences of Americans of German descent toward the more isolationist Republicans.[28]

These are a few examples of the ways in which group membership and historical circumstances have given voters special ties with particular parties. Once voters have such ties, a great deal follows. Merely to list the functions that party identification performs for voters—reducing their costs of acquiring political information, telling them what side they are on, organizing their information by ordering their preferences, letting them know what is of prime importance—is to suggest the profound significance of parties for voting behavior. Politics is complex; there are many possible issues, relevant political personalities, and choices to be made on election day. Voters who follow their party identification can simplify their choices and reduce to manageable proportions the time and effort they spend on public affairs simply by voting for their party's candidate. Voters with strong party identifications need not puzzle over each and every issue. They can, instead, listen to the pronouncements of their party leaders, who inform them what issues are important, what information is most relevant to those issues, and what positions they ought to take. Of course, citizens with greater interest in public affairs may investigate matters for themselves. Even so, their party identification provides them with important guidance in learning about the issues that interest them as well as the many matters on which they cannot possibly be well informed. All of us, including full-time participants such as the president and other leading politicians, have to find ways to cut information costs on some issues.[29] For most of the millions who vote, identification with one of the two major political parties performs that indispensable function most of the time.

Ideologies, Candidates, and Issues in the Minds of Voters

Another method of reducing the costs of information may be for voters to have or acquire a more or less comprehensive set of internally consistent beliefs, sometimes known as an *ideology*. How do ideologies structure political beliefs? Voters or party activists may be conscious of having an ideology and thus adopt views consistent with their position; they can use ideological labels as a shortcut in decision making, or at least they can think of one issue as related to another. There is some evidence that relatively small numbers of voters are fully consistent in their ideological thinking; a larger minority make use of various forms of group references when expressing preferences for a particular candidate, and an even larger group makes use of ideological labels.[30] Labels such as left and right and liberal and conservative, while commonly used in political discourse, sometimes work and sometimes do not in structuring attitudes. If we talk about social welfare or economically redistributive issues, these labels serve reasonably well in sorting people out: left for, right against. But some issues are harder to fathom. What would be the "conservative" position on abortion, for example, when conservative libertarians are pro-choice and other conservatives pro-life?[31]

Specific candidates of special attractiveness or unattractiveness may under certain circumstances sway voters to desert their habitual party in a presidential vote. The extraordinary elections of President Eisenhower (1952, 1956) are examples of this. His appeal to Democrats was quite amazing. This was possible partially because these Democrats did not perceive Eisenhower as a partisan figure but rather as a nonpartisan hero of the recently concluded World War II (1941–1945). It is not surprising, then, that Eisenhower's personal popularity did not greatly aid other Republicans who ran with him, or the Republican Party, once he no longer headed the ticket. The candidacy of George McGovern in 1972 had the opposite effect; it propelled Democrats out of their party.[32]

Scholars have pointed out that in recent presidential elections even successful candidates carry a burden of negative evaluations. This negativity may be a consequence of the rise to prominence in the nomination process since 1968 of primary elections—a strenuous gauntlet in which prospective candidates of the same party must run against one another in different states for many weeks during the early months of the election year. These elections produce a lot of bad-mouthing. As a result, in the general election the nominees usually have no "coattails" helping candidates of their party for other offices farther down on the ballot. High negative ratings for all surviving candidates also mean that they will be unable to lure voters for positive reasons away from the expression of their habitual party loyalties in the general election. But negative ratings may push voters to desert their party because they have heard so much bad publicity.[33]

Particular issues have much the same occasional effect as candidates on voters' loyalties.[34] This is true because for an issue to change a voter's voting habit, it has to reach a high degree of salience for the voter. Voters must know about the issue; they must care about it at least a little; and they must be able to distinguish the positions of the parties and their candidates on the issue. Data from public opinion polls tell us that most people are not well informed about the details of issues most of the time.[35] All but major public issues are thus eliminated for most people as important in influencing their vote. Even these major issues may enter the consciousness of most people in only the most rudimentary way.

Once voters have some grasp of the content of a public policy and learn to prefer one outcome over another, they must also find a public leader to espouse their point of view. Discerning differences on policy issues between parties is not always easy. Party statements on policy may be vague because leaders have not decided what to do. Leaders may deliberately obfuscate an issue for fear of alienating interested publics. They may try to hold divergent factions in their parties together by glossing over disagreements on many specific issues. Even when real party differences on policy exist, many voters may not be aware of them. The subject may be highly technical, or the time required to master the subject may be more than most people are willing to spend. By the time we get down to those who know and care about and can discriminate between party positions on issues, we usually have a small proportion of the electorate. The proportion of ideologically sophisticated voters appears to be no larger than 30 percent.[36]

What can we say about these people? Their most obvious characteristic is interest in and concern about issues and party positions. These are precisely the same people who are most likely to be strong party identifiers. Party loyalty thus works against the possibility that voters will shift allegiance just because of a disagreement on one or two issues.[37] Voters who pay only a moderate amount of attention to politics are most likely to be affected by new information on issues. This is because the most attentive are generally committed to a party and that party's position, whereas the least attentive are unavailable to persuasion: since they don't take in political information, they cannot be influenced by it. This leaves the middle group as most open to persuasion. Not being intensely partisan, they are not previously committed, but they learn enough so that it is possible for them to be swayed by new information about issues and by campaigns.[38] The number of issue-oriented "independents"—people who care about public issues but have no consistent party preference—is very small. Most people who call themselves independents actually lean toward one or another of the two major parties.[39] So purely issue-oriented people are not numerous and may be distributed on both sides of major policy questions in such a way that gains and losses balance out and the total number of votes gained or lost by the impact of any specific issue is minute. This is even true of such issues as the Vietnam war, which from 1968 to 1972 was of tremendous salience to many Americans.[40]

Even these changes may not amount to much if other issues are also highly salient to voters and work the other way. For if voters were willing to change their votes on one particular issue, why should they not switch their support back because of another? There usually are many issues in a campaign; only if all or most of the issues pointed voters in the same direction would they be likely to switch their votes. What is the likelihood that parties will arrange their policies along a broad front, forcing large numbers of weak identifiers or "independent" voters from or into the fold? It is low, but not nonexistent. In 1964 the Republicans, led by Barry Goldwater, likely did so. In 1972 the Democratic candidate, George McGovern, "was perceived as so far left on the issues that his Republican opponent, Richard Nixon, was generally closer to the electorate's average issue position on 11 out of 14 separate issues."[41]

Issues that arouse deep feelings can alter longer-term voting patterns, but this usually occurs when one party gets very far out of step with the preferences of voters. In the 1930s and 1940s this happened to the Republicans on the issue of welfare programs.[42] When voters perceive a vast chasm separating them from one of the candidates, as they did with Goldwater and again with McGovern, the importance of issues relative to party is bound to grow. The research group at the University of Michigan's Center for Political Studies estimated that in 1972, party identification and issue differences each accounted for approximately one-third of the total vote. In this election Richard Nixon received almost all Republican votes (94 percent), two-thirds of independent votes (66 percent), and nearly half the votes of people calling themselves Democrats (42 percent). This was a better showing among Democrats than Dwight D. Eisenhower managed in his landslide year of 1956, when he garnered 28 percent of the Democratic vote. Why did this happen? Because Nixon's 1972 opponent, George McGovern, "was seen as quite distant from the population's policy preferences." The Michigan group concluded that "a candidate such as McGovern who may represent only one segment of the national policy preference spectrum may capture control of a political party that shares his policy preferences but cannot go on to win an electoral victory under contemporary conditions of polarization."[43] In short, when voters disagree with a candidate and know that they disagree with him, they are likely to vote against him. Candidates and their campaigns work hard to evoke this knowledge. It leads to a lot of negative campaigning, much of which works uphill against party habits and the disinclination of voters to pay much attention to the content of campaigns.

When voters wish to reject the current presidential administration, yet they are not sure the other party's policies are better, they may nevertheless decide to vote negatively. Stung by "stagflation," a politically deadly combination of high inflation and unemployment, and dismayed over what they perceived to be President Carter's lack of leadership, many voters in 1980 chose Ronald Reagan despite uneasiness about Reagan's conservative issue positions. They may have thought that under the current conditions of uncertainty about the economy, a new administration would do better. When unemployment rose in 1981 and 1982, President Reagan's popularity dropped, and Republican congressional candidates suffered. Economic recovery brought Reagan renewed support and a resounding victory in 1984. Figure 1.1 shows how closely the vote for the president's party tracks the performance of the economy.[44]

News of an economic turnaround came too late to save George Bush in 1992. He lost despite his tremendous popularity two years earlier at the time

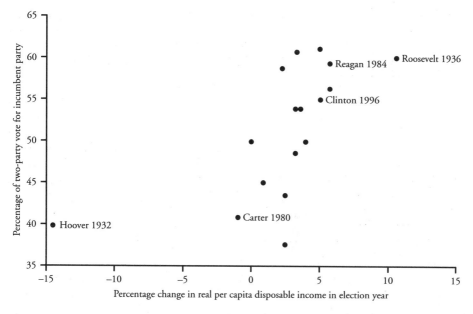

FIGURE 1.1   IMPACT OF CHANGE IN DISPOSABLE INCOME ON VOTING

SOURCES: Economic data: 1932–1968, *Historical Statistics of the United States: Colonial Times to 1970* (Washington, D.C.: Bureau of the Census, 1975), 225; 1972–1992, *Statistical Abstract of the United States* (Washington, D.C.: Bureau of the Census, 1994), 451. Electoral data: 1932–1988, Michael Nelson, ed., *Congressional Quarterly's Guide to the Presidency* (Washington, D.C.: CQ Press, 1989); 1992, *Statistical Abstract of the United States* (1994), 269.

of the Desert Storm operation (January 1991) when he orchestrated the defense of Kuwait against Iraqi aggression. But in the fall of 1992, Bush fell victim to negative retrospective evaluations of his performance on domestic matters and to popular feelings that he did not show enough concern about the economy. Even so, he won 89 percent of the votes of Republicans, as usual benefiting from the greater party loyalty of Republican voters.[45]

So while candidates matter sometimes, and issues matter sometimes, and both are capable of affecting who wins, for most voters party matters almost all the time. Activating party loyalties is the most important electoral strategy at the disposal of candidates.

Changes in Party Identification: Social Habit Versus Contemporary Evaluation

Thus far we have considered factors that cause voters to deviate in voting from their underlying party allegiance. Under what conditions do they actually change their party identification?

The prevailing model of party identification holds that it is a strong social habit. It begins early in life, is remarkably stable, resists short-run political forces, and changes only through reaction to long-lasting and powerful political events, such as the Great Depression of the 1930s. This view was authoritatively propounded in 1960 by the authors of *The American Voter*. At its core is the idea that party identification constitutes a strong emotional bond and is therefore "firm but not immovable."[46] This leaves at least a little room for candidate and issue-related changes and for a more active evaluative role on the part of voters. One study shows that those who change party from one election to the next generally are sympathetic to some key policies of their new party. "Standpatters," in contrast, are in general sympathy with major policies of their party.[47]

Whether the citizen seeks a party in accordance with his independently arrived at beliefs or is taught what to believe by party allegiance cannot be determined from evidence now available. Almost certainly, both processes are having an impact on the electorate. One synthesis that combines long-term habit with more contemporaneous evaluations concludes that "there is substantial continuity in partisanship from one point in time to the next" and that party identification "can be interpreted as the individual's accumulated evaluation of the parties."[48]

In addition to massive tidal waves that change the party preferences of large numbers of voters, there are also squalls that affect the life experiences of smaller numbers of individuals and lead a relatively few voters to alter their party identifications from time to time. Since these eddies in the larger flow of events lack a common origin, they usually cancel one another out in their net effects. Thus the picture of relatively stable partisanship overall can be reconciled with a more complicated picture of occasional individual change. The thinking and feeling individuals who change parties once in a while and the large masses of people who are caught up in infrequent movements away from or toward certain parties are galvanized by their reactions to shared experiences. Thus individuals whose partisanship was not firmly fixed early in life, perhaps because politics was seldom discussed in the home, may develop party identifications in their twenties or thirties. They adjust their party loyalties to their policy preferences or to the views of the groups with which they associate. But they do not make these adjustments often. As Charles Franklin tells us, "citizens remain open to change throughout life, though as experience with the parties accumulates, it is accorded greater weight."[49]

Is party identification a durable standing decision to vote a certain way, as the authors of *The American Voter* put it, or, as Morris Fiorina says, a "running tally of retrospective evaluations of party promises and performance"?[50] Scholars find that citizen assessment of party performance on major dimensions of public policy—war and peace, employment, inflation, race—do matter.[51] Nevertheless, most changes of party identification involve switching in and out of the independent category rather than between the parties.[52] Donald Kinder sums up:

Party identification is not immovable: it both influences and is influenced by the performance of government, by policy disagreements, and by the emergence of new candidates....The loyalty citizens invest in party is at least partly a function of what governments and parties do, and what they fail to do....We should not press this too far, however. Although party identification does respond to political events, it does so sluggishly. It is one thing for Republicans to feel less enthusiastic toward their party after a period of sustained national difficulty presided over by a Republican administration; it is quite another to embrace the opposition. The latter seldom happens. In this respect the running balance sheet metaphor is quite misleading. The strongest message of the evidence reviewed here may be the durability of party identification, how difficult it is to budge people from their commitment to party.[53]

Has there been a decline in party identification? From 1952 to 1964, the overall level of party identification among voters remained stable. From 1964 onward, many more Americans identified themselves as independents. Indeed, by 1974 self-styled independents outnumbered Republicans five to three and came near to the number of Democrats. It is important to distinguish, however, between "pure" independents, who exhibit no party feeling, and partisan independents, who lean toward the Democratic or Republican Party. Almost two out of every three people who call themselves "independents" say that they are closer to one party than to the other, and they do not all lean the same way.[54] These partisan independents are far more knowledgeable and participate much more actively in politics than pure independents, who do not lean; they also show a far greater tendency to vote, and they give large proportions of their vote to the party toward which they lean. In short, independents who lean toward a party behave almost the same as strong partisans and not at all like truly independent voters. By separating party identification into seven categories rather than three, table 1.6 (p. 20) shows that the number of pure independents is only 12 to 13 percent, not the 35 percent often cited.[55]

People are a lot more stable in their party identifications than in the policy preferences that are sometimes held to underlie party allegiances.[56] But there have been massive defections of identifiers from the major parties in presidential voting in some elections. From 1952 to 1968, Democrats defected about twice as often as Republicans (19 percent to 10 percent). Since 1972, Republican defection rates have stayed about the same, but Democratic defections have increased (to a mean of 24 percent), and they remained at high levels through 1988. That included the election of Jimmy Carter in 1976: Carter received the votes of 77 percent of Democrats and only 9 percent of Republicans. Recent elections, however, have been different. Clinton, after losing about a quarter of Democratic voters in 1992, lost only 15 percent of those voters in 1996. Republicans, for the

TABLE 1.6   PARTY IDENTIFICATION, 1952–1996 (IN PERCENTAGES)

	Democrats			Pure	Republicans		
	Strong	Weak	Independent	Independent	Independent	Weak	Strong
1952	22	25	10	6	7	14	14
1962	23	23	7	8	6	16	12
1972	15	26	10	13	11	13	10
1982	20	24	11	11	8	14	10
1992	17	18	14	12	13	15	11
1996	19	20	14	9	11	15	13

SOURCES: Bruce E. Keith, et al., *The Myth of the Independent Voter* (Berkeley: University of California Press, 1992); Harold W. Stanley and Richard G. Niemi, *Vital Statistics on American Politics 1997–1998* (Washington, D.C.: CQ Press, 1998), 108.

first time, were slightly less loyal than Democrats, with defections totaling 27 percent in 1992 and 20 percent in 1996.[57]

So party as a value and an orientation point may be less important than it once was, but it is still very important. Most people, especially most voters, since those without any party preference are not likely to vote, identify with or lean toward one party or the other. There are always defections, however, and the parties cannot automatically count on all their identifiers to give them unqualified support in every election. Party identification does not translate automatically into party-line voting. Voters may tend to be loyal, but they can also be driven away.

A Central Strategic Problem: The Attentiveness of Voters

A remarkably consistent picture emerges from the study of American voters over the past several decades:

1. Most voters have a party allegiance, which determines their vote most of the time. The strategic implication for presidential candidates is that there is such a thing as a party base. Major-party candidates must mobilize this party base so that the party faithful turn out, and they must strive to minimize defections; the overwhelming evidence is that efforts in this direction will be rewarded.

2. In any election, the number of voters making a judgment to desert their customary party of preference will ordinarily be small. If there is a tide of such evaluations in a single direction, this can be decisive for the outcome. Mostly, these tides are expressed as decisions to move from partisan loyalty to weaker loyalty, from weak loyalty to neutrality or to a weakened resolution to vote at all.

3. Most citizens are not well informed about the substantive details of politics or attentive to politics. The world that politicians inhabit of public policy and of contention over issues is only dimly perceived by ordinary voters. A strategic implication is that politicians must expend resources and work very hard to give meaning to the choices that voters ordinarily make according to party habit. For a candidate to become visible as an individual to voters is a difficult task. Much of the activity in an election year is understandable in the light of the fact that voters are not attentive to the details of politics or ideologically consistent in their views or spontaneously eager to change their habitual orientations to politics; politicians must therefore strive to capture their attention.

4. Voters participate mostly in accordance with their social loyalties and involvements. They retain and sometimes exercise their capacity to make contemporary judgments on issues. Either way, their behavior is importantly influenced by the ways in which they are organized into groups, especially political parties.

Box 1.1 Registration and Voting

THE AMERICAN SYSTEM of voter registration is at least partially responsible for low levels of voting by Americans. One study shows that the level of voter registration is easily the greatest influence on the percentage of the population that actually votes (accounting for 80 percent of the variance). This is far greater than any other single factor usually cited in studies of voting by those registered and, in fact, greater than all such factors put together.[1]

Unlike the citizens of foreign democracies in which the government takes responsibility for registration (see table 1), Americans must prepare for the eventual vote by taking the initiative to register before the election, at a time in the political cycle when political information and interest are at a low point. Since interest and information are important factors, the level of registration can be advanced or retarded by altering the time of year when voter registration rolls are closed or by changing the physical ease of reaching a registration point, and practicing political leaders are well aware of this. As Stanley Kelley and his collaborators observe, "Local differences in the turnout for elections are to a large extent related to local differences in rates of registration, and these in turn reflect to a considerable degree local differences in the rules governing, and the arrangements for handling, the registration of voters."[2]

Some areas of the United States make it far easier to register by allowing election-day registration. Table 2 shows that the consequences for voting turnout are impressive. In 1980 Minnesota voters turned out at a rate nearly 20 percentage points above the national average. When citizens are registered, they turn out to vote.[3]

While the rest of the United States (except Maine) now lags behind the Minnesota performance, there was once a time—in an era when the impact of the president was remote, mass communication absent, and electronic voting equipment unheard of—when more than 70 percent of potential (not just registered) voters turned out in presidential elections. In the election of 1876, 82 percent of the possible voters (men only, of course) turned out for the nation as a whole. Soon thereafter, however, harsh registration restrictions were introduced, cloaked in rhetoric about stopping corruption but aimed at keeping down the vote of "undesirable elements" (immigrants and black voters). As Kelley et al. observe: "Turnout in presidential elections in the U.S. may have declined and then risen again, not because of changes in the interest of voters in elections, but because of changes in the interest

**TABLE 1 TURNOUT OF REGISTERED VOTERS, UNITED STATES COMPARED
TO OTHER DEMOCRACIES**

Country	Turnout percentages	Compulsory voting	Eligible required to register
Australia	93.8	Yes	Yes
Belgium	93.4	Yes	Automatic
Austria	90.5	No	Automatic
Italy	90.5	Yes	Automatic
Iceland	90.1	N.A.	N.A.
Luxembourg	87.3	N.A.	N.A.
New Zealand	87.2	No	Yes
United States	**86.8**	**No**	**Yes**
Sweden	86.0	No	Automatic
Netherlands	85.8	No	Automatic
Denmark	85.7	No	Automatic
Greece	84.5	Yes	Automatic
Germany	84.3	No	Automatic
Norway	84.0	No	Automatic
Israel	79.7	No	Automatic
Finland	77.6	No	Automatic
Canada	75.5	No	Yes
United Kingdom	75.4	No	Automatic
Portugal	72.6	N.A.	N.A.
Japan	71.4	No	Automatic
Spain	70.6	No	Automatic
Ireland	68.5	No	Automatic
France	66.2	No	No
Switzerland	46.1	No	Automatic

SOURCES: Thomas T. Mackie and Richard Rose, *The International Almanac of Electoral History,* 3d ed. (Washington, D.C.: CQ Press, 1991). Compulsory voting information from G. Bingham Powell Jr., "American Voter Turnout in Comparative Perspective," *American Political Science Review* 80 (March 1986): 38, and Raymond Wolfinger, David Glass, and Peverill Squire, "Predictors of Electoral Turnout: An International Comparison," *Policy Studies Review* 9 (Spring 1990): 561.

demanded of them....[Not only are] electorates...much more the product of political forces than many have appreciated. But also ... to a considerable extent, they can be political artifacts. Within limits, they can be constructed to a size and composition deemed desirable by those in power."[4]

Continued

TABLE 2   **TURNOUT IN STATES WITH ELECTION-DAY REGISTRATION (1996)**

State	Percentage of the voting-age population who voted	Where to register
Maine	64.5	Registrar of Voters, Board of Registration, Justice of Peace, Notary Public
Minnesota	64.3	At polls on election day, City Hall, City Clerk, County Auditor
Wisconsin	57.4	Election day at polls with identification, Municipal Clerk or Board of Election Commissioners in counties where registration is required
North Dakota	56.3	No registration required
All United States	49.0	

SOURCE: Richard M. Scammon, Alice V. McGillivray, and Rhodes Cook, *America Votes 22* (Washington, D.C.: CQ Press, 1998), 1.

Whether an expanded electorate would have any direct effect on primaries and delegate selection would depend on the particular enrollment plan adopted. At one extreme, if enrollment were held every four years in October and provided for continuation on the rolls only if the registrant voted in each election held in the district—state and municipal elections, as well as federal—reform would have little direct effect. If the canvass occurred in the spring, however, and registrants had to vote only once every four years to stay on the rolls, there would be a significant addition to the presidential electorate. Some have argued that this portends new strength for activists unconnected with parties, since this new group of voters would be far less tied to any political organizations than the already enfranchised groups. In general, however, nonvoters have preferences for candidates much like those who vote.[5]

The major limiting factors of this potential electorate are legal requirements concerning residence, age, literacy, criminal conviction, mental incompetence, and U.S. citizenship. The most notorious of these restrictions has been the residence requirement. In a nation noted for the geographic mobility of its population, a majority of states required, as recently as 1972, one year within the state, three months within the county, and thirty days within the precinct to vote in any election, including presidential. In 1972 the Supreme Court ruled that thirty days was an ample period of time for the state of Tennessee to register its voters and declared its existing six-month state residency requirement an unconstitutional denial of equal protection. In two subsequent *per curiam* decisions, the court held that an extension to fifty days was permissible under certain conditions, but that this time period represented the absolute limit.[6]

In an important study, Squire, Wolfinger, and Glass show, first, that the extraordinary mobility of Americans leads to low voting turnout, and, second, that countering this effect would dramatically increase turnout. In order to vote in the United States, a citizen must register. But to stay registered, the citizen must live in the same place. Yet something like one-third of all adults change their home address every two years. If all movers were registered in their new residences, perhaps by using the post office change-of-address form for that purpose, as Wolfinger suggests, these scholars estimate that national turnout, the proportion of eligibles who vote, would increase by 9 percent. They also conclude that "expanding the voting population in this way would produce no consequential advantage for either party."[7]

A number of other major groups are now kept out of the potential presidential electorate. In most states rules for absentee voting have recently loosened considerably. But in states that limit absentee ballots to travelers and shut-ins, many depart or become ill too late to take advantage of this opportunity.[8] Aliens, legal and illegal, are not allowed to vote. Finally, in most states, convicted felons are permanently stripped of their voting rights. These three groups are not insignificant in size. William Andrews, in 1960, calculated that they contained nearly 8 million potential voters.[9] As the number of aliens and of ex-felons has increased markedly since 1960, the figures today would surely be even larger.

Notes

1. Stanley Kelley Jr., Richard E. Ayres, and William G. Bowen, "Registration and Voting: Putting First Things First," *American Political Science Review* 61 (June 1967): 362. More recent and equally comprehensive studies of this subject leading to similar results are found in Raymond E. Wolfinger and Steven J. Rosenstone, "The Effects of Registration Laws on Voter Turnout," *American Political Science Review* 72 (March 1978): 22–45. The general outline of this argument has been known in this country for at least 50 years. For

Continued

example, in 1924, Harold G. Gosnell wrote, "In the European countries studied, a citizen who is entitled to vote does not, as a rule, have to make any effort to see that his name is on the list of eligible voters. The inconvenience of registering for voting in this country has caused many citizens to become non-voters." *Why Europe Votes* (Chicago: University of Chicago Press, 1930), 185. See also Raymond E. Wolfinger and Steven J. Rosenstone, *Who Votes?* (New Haven: Yale University Press, 1980).

2. In Richard A. Ayers, "Registration 1960: Key to Democratic Victory?" (unpublished senior thesis, Princeton University, 1964), cited in Kelley, Ayres, and Bowen, "Registration and Voting," 375, the author notes the correlation between convenience of registration and percent of the vote for the Democratic party as proof of the Chicago Daley machine's awareness of this phenomenon. By making registration extremely convenient, the state of Utah has succeeded in getting nearly total registration. See "Registration Procedures in the State of Utah," *Election Laws of the Fifty States and the District of Columbia* (Washington, D.C.: Government Printng Office, June 1968), 247–48. Similarly, Edmond Costantini and Willis Hawley estimate that turnout in California could be raised by more than 5 percent simply by keeping registration open until the last week before the election ("Increasing Participation in California Elections: The Need for Electoral Reform," *Public Affairs Report* 10, Bulletin of the Institute of Governmental Studies June, 1969). A 1968 registration figure of 97.8 percent was attained by holding registrations open until the Wednesday before the election (when political interest, which would stimulate voters to register and the party activists to get them registered, is highest) and by having publicized locations in every district.

3. Kelley, Ayres, and Bowen, "Registration and Voting," 373. See David Glass, Peverill Squire, and Raymond Wolfinger, "Voter Turnout: An International Comparison," *Public Opinion* 6 (December/January 1984): 49–55.

4. Kelley, Ayres, and Bowen, "Registration and Voting," 374–75.

5. See John R. Petrocik, "Voter Turnout and Electoral Preference: The Anomalous Reagan Elections," in *Elections in America,* ed. Kay Lehman Schlozman (Boston: Allan & Unwin, 1987), 261–92; and Benjamin Highton and Raymond E. Wolfinger, "The Political Implications of Higher Turnout," paper delivered at the meeting of the American Political Science Association, Boston, September 1998.

6. *Dunn v. Blumstein,* 405 U.S. 330 (1972); *Marston v. Lewis,* 410 U.S. 759 (1973); and *Burn v. Forston,* 410 U.S. 686 (1972).

7. Peverill Squire, Raymond E. Wolfinger, and David P. Glass, "Residential Mobility and Voter Turnout," *American Political Science Review* 81 (March 1987): 45–61. The quote is from p. 61. In an earlier study, Wolfinger and Rosenstone found that the effect of registration laws has been to depress voting turnout in national elections by approximately 9 percent. Yet even if relaxation of voter registration restrictions brought about a corresponding expansion in the electorate, they conclude that the impact on electoral outcomes would be "wholly insignificant," since "the ideological composition of the expanded electorate would be virtually identical to the actual electorate in 1972." Wolfinger and Rosenstone, "The Effects of Registration Laws on Voter Turnout," 41; see also their response to a challenge to their conclusions in "Comment," *American Political Science Review* 72 (December 1978): 1361–62.

8. California voters may now vote by mail for any reason, and increasingly are doing so. A quarter of the votes in 1998 were cast by absentee ballot; *California Statistical Abstract 1998* (Sacramento: 1998), 182; see Martha Walrath-Riley, "New Absentee and Mail-in Ballot Campaigns: The Winning Edge," *Campaigns and Elections* 5 (Spring 1984). Oregon has taken voting by mail even farther, making some elections—including presidential primaries—entirely vote-by-mail. See B. Drummond Ayres Jr., "Voter-Friendly Rules Upset Democrats," *New York Times,* 17 January 1999, 12.

9. William G. Andrews, "American Voting Participation," *Western Political Quarterly* 19 (December 1966): 643.

CHAPTER 2

Groups

The Presidential Vote as an Aggregation of Interest Groups

IN EACH ELECTION, members of the various groups that make up the American voting population turn out to vote, dividing their loyalties in varying ways between the major parties. Turnout varies enormously among different groups in the population, rising with income, occupational status, education, and age (for the details, see Appendix B, p.324). Since Republicans are disproportionately located in the high-turnout groups and Democrats in the low, this tends to give Republicans electoral advantages that in some measure, varying from election to election, make up for the preponderance of Democrats in the potential electorate.

The two major parties are somewhat differently constituted as voting blocs of interest groups. Democrats appeal to identifiable segments of the population—notably disadvantaged minorities—that have specific programmatic interests. That is the Democratic base, and Democrats win presidential elections by activating their interest groups and persuading them to turn out. This is not always easy, since many groups that characteristically do not turn out—the poor, the less well educated, newer ethnic groups such as Hispanics, the less well socially integrated—tend to favor the Democratic Party when they do vote.

Republicans win presidential elections by doing slightly better than Democrats and better than usual for Republicans among the big battalions: aggregates of voters not necessarily organized as self-conscious groups, such as white voters (87 percent of the electorate in 1992), voters in their middle years, those with some college or more, and Protestants. In years when Republicans do slightly less well among these very large segments of the population, Democrats win (see table 2.1).

Democrats maintain a strong electoral base among groups that for one reason or another can be considered less well off or out of the mainstream: black voters, Catholic ethnic voters, union households, gay voters. Even in years when Democrats lose the presidency, they tend to do quite well with these

TABLE 2.1   **REPUBLICANS WIN BY DOING WELL WITH LARGE GROUPS**

	Percentage of 1996 electorate	*Republican percentage of group vote*					
		1976	1980	1984	1988	1992	1996
Whites	83	52	56	64	57	40	48
Employed	—	51	54	60	56	38	—
Married	66	—	—	62	57	41	48
Moderates	47	48	49	53	49	31	33
Suburbs	39	—	55	61	57	39	42
Republicans		lost	won	won	won	lost	lost

SOURCE: "Portrait of the Electorate," *New York Times,* 10 November 1996, 28.

groups (see table 2.2). Note, for example, the strong Democratic vote of these groups even in Ronald Reagan's landslide year of 1984. On the whole, no large interest groups vote as overwhelmingly Republican as African Americans vote Democratic. Several other groups vote nearly as lopsidedly for Democrats.

The differences in the ways the two major parties are constituted as voting coalitions give a clue to the differences in the ways they approach public policy-making. Democrats are more overtly distributive in their concerns, Republicans more concerned with overall principles that apply in a blanket way to the entire population.[1] Republicans figure, rightly, that policies that yield evenhanded opportunities for all will not greatly disadvantage their well-situated clientele; Democrats figure, rightly, that their relatively disadvantaged clientele will be less well served by blanket policies that take no special account of them.

The comparatively particular and group-specific orientation of the Democratic Party is reflected in much folklore and research proclaiming the relative fragmentation of the Democrats. Republicans are far more united by ideological agreement and are better able to sustain a united front in most arenas than

TABLE 2.2   **THE DEMOCRATIC PARTY BASE: SMALLER, LOYAL GROUPS**

	Percentage of 1996 electorate	*Democratic percentage of group vote*					
		1976	1980	1984	1988	1992	1996
Blacks	10	83	85	90	86	82	84
Hispanics	5	76	59	62	69	62	72
Jews	3	64	45	67	64	78	78
Union household	23	59	49	53	57	55	59
Family income under $15,000	11	58	51	55	62	59	59
Big cities	10	—	—	—	62	58	68
Democrats		won	lost	lost	lost	lost	lost

SOURCE: "Portrait of the Electorate," *New York Times,* 10 November 1996, 28.

their Democratic counterparts. Republicans occupy a narrower range of the ideological spectrum than Democrats. This relatively strong signal over a narrower band has its payoff in the greater voting loyalty of Republican voters, that is, in their disinclination to defect in presidential elections. But for most of the past half-century they have not been the majority party; the Democrats, who stand for a greater variety of things, are the larger of the two major parties and have remained so even in periods when the Republicans, because they were far more effective in mobilizing their voters, won presidential elections with some regularity.[2]

In the 1990s, and especially after the midterm elections of 1994, in which the Republicans did remarkably well, it appeared that the gap between the two major parties was beginning to narrow significantly. It was too soon to say, however, whether Republicans would maintain their near-parity with the Democrats over a longer period, or even take the lead.

To determine the contribution that a particular group makes to one side or the other, it is necessary to know three things: how big the group is, how many of its members actually vote, and how devoted its members are to one party or another. For example, let us look at the votes of poor people—defined as those whose incomes were below $3,000 through 1980, $5,000 in 1984 and 1988, and $7,000 thereafter. As table 2.3 shows, the contribution of the poor to the total Democratic vote has fallen from 28 percent in 1952 to only 7 percent in 1996.[3] This trend can be accounted for in any, or all, of three ways: (1) more of the nonpoor voted Democratic in recent years, diluting the contribution of the poor; (2) fewer poor people voted Democratic in recent elections; (3) the poor declined as a percentage of the overall population.

Most people have overlapping characteristics. Thus a single individual can be white, female, Catholic, and a union member all at the same time. It would be useful to try to identify the contribution of each attribute alone. By separating subjective identification with the working class from being a union member, scholars have shown that belonging to a union creates a strong push toward Democratic allegiance. Being Jewish, being black, and being female propel people toward the Democrats. So too does being Catholic or working class. The pro-Democratic tilt of these latter groups, however, has declined since the 1950s.[4]

While the poor have not been an important part of the Democratic coalition in recent years, African Americans have established themselves as a substantial component: from 5 percent to 7 percent in 1952–1960 to 12 percent in 1964, and 19 percent in 1968. In 1972 the percentage rose again, to 22 percent. In 1976 their contribution fell for the first time, reaching 16 percent, largely as a result of the return to Democratic voting of many other voters who had defected in 1972. In 1980 the African American percentage of Democratic voters was again at 22 percent, and in 1984 it went up to 25 percent, where it has remained with only slight changes since. In 1992 a quarter of Bill Clinton's

TABLE 2.3 WHERE THE VOTES CAME FROM, 1952–1996

	Democratic Coalition:						Republican Coalition:					
	P	B	U	C	S	CC	NP	W	NU	P	NS	NCC
1952	28	7	38	41	20	21	75	99	79	75	87	84
1956	19	5	36	38	23	19	84	98	78	75	84	89
1960	16	7	31	47	27	19	83	97	84	90	75	90
1964	15	12	32	36	21	15	89	100	87	80	76	91
1968	12	19	28	40	24	14	90	99	81	80	80	92
1972	10	22	32	43	25	14	93	98	77	70	73	95
1976	7	16	33	35	29	11	97	99	80	76	74	98
1980	5	22	31	31	39	7	98	90	80	75	66	96
1984	10	25	30	39	32	7	97	96	83	69	72	92
1988	11	24	26	32	27	—	95	97	84	70	75	—
1992	7	25	22	35	29	—	96	93	85	68	71	—
1996	7	22	27	41	33	—	96	97	87	77	69	—

SOURCES: 1952–1984: Robert Axelrod, "Presidential Election Coalitions in 1984," *American Political Science Review* 80 (March 1986): 281–84. 1988–1996: National Election Studies.

P/NP	Poor/Nonpoor (income under/over $3,000 before 1980, $5,000 before 1988, $7,000 since)
B/W	Black and other nonwhite/White
U/NU	Union member/Nonunion
C/P	Catholic and other non-Protestant/Protestant
S/N	South/North (figures since 1988 exclude border states)
CC/NCC	Central cities/Not in central cities (of 12 largest metropolitan areas)

votes were supplied by African American voters, and in 1996 they supplied 22 percent of his votes. The African American population has remained a relatively constant 11 percent of the total population. Black voters' vastly increased contribution to the Democratic vote since the 1960s has been the result of a near doubling of their turnout throughout the nation, of their high loyalty to the Democratic Party, and of fluctuations in Democratic voting by white voters.

While union members and their families made up a third of all Democratic votes in the 1950s, their contribution fell slightly to 28 percent in 1968 and rose again to average 32 percent in 1972, 1976, and 1980. In 1996 they supplied 27 percent of the Democratic vote. They are important to the Democratic Party because between a quarter and a fifth of all adults are in union families, their turnout is reasonably good, and they vote more Democratic than other people. Although only half of union members voted Democratic in 1980, the overall defection among other Democrats that year was so great that union members still voted 9 percent more Democratic than others. Whereas union families contributed four times as many votes as African Americans to the Democratic Party in 1960 (25 percent of the total), union families contributed only slightly more Democratic votes (30 percent) in 1984 and in 1988 (26 percent), slightly fewer (22 percent) in 1992, and a little more in 1996.

Catholics comprise roughly a third of the population and provide a third of all Democratic votes. In 1952 and 1956, southerners voted about 10 percent more Democratic than the rest of the country. In more recent elections they have been slightly more Republican than other people, though they moved back to the Democrats in 1976 and 1980, when a southerner headed the Democratic ticket. They gave a quarter of their votes to the third-party movement of George Wallace in 1968. African American southerners stayed with the Democrats in that year, but white southerners split their presidential vote among all three parties. Since 1984 the Republicans have received very strong support from southern whites.[5]

A major change can be observed in the votes of young people, that is, those under thirty years of age. Until 1972 they were not part of any party coalition and their low turnout reduced any impact that their 18 percent of the voting-age population might have given them. Because the voting age has since 1971 been lowered to eighteen, and because of the baby boom after World War II, their proportion of the voting-age population has increased to 28 percent, and in the 1970s there was much talk of young people as a separate voting block. Since then, as the baby boomers have aged, young people have decreased as a proportion of all voters; they comprised 17 percent of all voters in 1996. Are they now making a big difference?

"Whatever else young voters are," Raymond Wolfinger tells us in a well-advised note of caution, "they are not harbingers of future outcomes."[6] The reason is that most of the time people under thirty do not divide their vote differently from the rest of the population. The belief that the youth vote was pro-Democratic began in 1972, when it was close to being true, but it has not been particularly true since 1976. A similar tale, only in the opposite, pro-Republican direction, has been told of the big youth vote for Ronald Reagan in 1984. Actually, as table 2.4 shows, the youth vote did not differ from other age groups in that year, while in 1988 and 1992 Michael Dukakis and Bill Clinton both received their strongest support from the oldest and the youngest

TABLE 2.4 **VOTE FOR DEMOCRATIC PRESIDENTIAL CANDIDATE BY AGE GROUP, 1964–1996**

Age	1964	1968	1972	1976	1980	1984	1988	1992	1996
18–29	72	38	47	51	34	40	47	43	53
30–44	69	47	34	48	37	42	45	41	48
45–69	70	37	31	52	37	39	42	41	48
60+	59	40	29	50	47	39	49	50	48

SOURCES: For 1964–1980, National Election Studies of the University of Michigan Center for Political Studies; for 1984–1996, network exit polls reported in Harold W. Stanley and Richard G. Niemi, *Vital Statistics on American Politics 1997–1998* (Washington, D.C.: CQ Press, 1998), 116–17.

voters. In 1996 Clinton did slightly better among the youngest voters than he did with any other age cohort.

The Republican coalition appears to be constituted as follows: White people, who comprise almost 90 percent of the U.S. population, vote anywhere from 3 to 5 percent more Republican than the whole population. The comparatively small size of the black population means that even in 1960, when Richard Nixon got about a quarter of the black vote, 97 percent of his total came from whites; 99 percent of his vote came from whites in 1968, and 98 percent in 1972. Ninety-eight percent of Ronald Reagan's votes in 1980 came from whites. If one can conceive of nonunion families and Protestants as "groups" in the usual sense, they make up about 75 percent of the population and vote 5 percent more Republican than the nation as a whole. The Republican Party gets its vote, then, from white people, nonunion members, and Protestants outside the central cities—and since 1964 from southern whites. Although Republicans received 60 percent majorities or better from all these groups in 1972 and 1984, they were able to attract at most 53 percent from any of them in 1976 and no more than 56 percent in 1980. In 1992 and 1992, defections to Bill Clinton and Ross Perot held Republicans to under 50 percent in most of these groups, making victory impossible.[7]

Variations among Interest Groups

Interest groups are collections of people who are similarly situated with respect to one or more policies of government and who organize to do something about it. The interest groups most significant for elections in our society are those having one or more of the following characteristics:

1. They have a mass base, that is, they are composed of many members.

2. They are concentrated geographically, rather than dispersed thinly over the entire map.

3. They represent major resource investments of members—such as bicycle producers, whose entire livelihoods may be tied up in the industry involved, as against the consumers of bicycles, for whom investment in a bicycle is not anywhere near as important.

4. They involve characteristics that give people status in society, such as race or ethnicity.

5. They evoke feelings about a single issue that are so intense as to eclipse the concerns of their members about other issues.

6. They are composed of people who are able to participate actively in politics; that is, people who have time and money to spare.

Interest groups having these characteristics matter most in presidential elections because these characteristics are most likely to claim the loyalties of large numbers of voters and form the basis for the mobilization of their preferences and their votes. Moreover, they reflect the fact that America is organized into geographic entities—states, congressional districts—as the basis of political representation.

Interest groups may be more or less organized and more or less vigilant and alert on policy matters that concern, or ought to concern, them. They are not necessarily organized in ways that make them politically effective; very often, the paid lobbyists of interest groups spend more time trying to alert their own members to the implications of government policies than they spend lobbying politicians.[8]

In American politics, interest-group activity is lively and can be found nearly everywhere, even when it is not particularly effective or meaningful in terms of policy outcomes. In presidential elections three characteristics of interest groups are especially important. First, membership in these groups may give voters a sense of affiliation and political location. In this respect, interest groups act much the way parties do, helping to fill in the voter's map of the world with preferences, priorities, and facts. Interest groups act as intermediary agencies that help voters identify their political preferences quickly by actively soliciting their members' interest in behalf of specific candidates and parties and, more important, by providing still another anchor to voters' identities. This helps voters fix their own position quickly and economically in what otherwise would be a confusing and contradictory political environment. Second, interest groups frequently undertake partisan political activities; they may actively recruit supporters for candidates and aid materially in campaigns.

Third, interest groups may influence party policy by making demands of candidates with respect to issues in return for their own mobilized support. The extent to which interest groups can "deliver" members' votes, however, is always a problem; to a great extent interest-group leaders are the prisoners of past alliances their group has made. This means that they may not be able to prevent their followers from voting for their traditional allies even when group leaders fall out with politicians. In 1993 labor union leaders vowed revenge on Democratic members of Congress who voted for the North American Free Trade Agreement (NAFTA);[9] but in the 1994 election, 63 percent of union families still voted Democratic in House races, as they had in 1980, 1986, and 1988. This was only one point worse than in 1984 when Walter Mondale, a conspicuous friend of labor, headed the Democratic ticket.[10]

Various ethnic votes, the farm vote, the labor vote, the youth vote, the consumer vote, and many other "votes" are sometimes discussed as though they were political commodities that could be manipulated easily in behalf of one or another candidate. This is not as easy as it sounds. When the analysis of election statistics and opinion polls was an esoteric discipline, forty or fifty years ago, most politicians could only evaluate intuitively claims to guarantee group support or threats to withdraw it, and no one could tell with any certainty whether these claims had substance. The development of the craft of public opinion analysis now makes it easier to assess these political claims.

The usual argument is that if one or another candidate captures the allegiance of a particular bloc, that bloc's pivotal position or large population in a state will enable the fortunate candidate to capture all of the state's electoral votes and thus win the election. A classic example of this style of argument was a memorandum by Ted Sorensen in 1960 aimed at big-city political leaders, which claimed that John F. Kennedy's Catholicism would be a distinct electoral asset, rather than the mild liability it actually turned out to be.[11] Of course no one combination of states totaling more than a majority of electoral votes is more critical, valuable, or pivotal than any other such combination. In a fairly close election the shifting of any number of combinations of voting blocs or states to one side or the other could spell the difference between victory and defeat.

There is little doubt that under some conditions and during some elections some social characteristics of voters and candidates may have relevance to the election results. Finding the actual conditions under which specified social characteristics become relevant to voter choice is difficult. We know that in a competitive political system various participants (parties, political leaders) back candidates with the hope of capturing the allegiance of various groups. Rarely is it wise to appeal to one group alone; in a very large electorate, one group will not be enough to win. Many different groups exist, with all sorts of conceptions of policy, and each individual voter will embody many social characteristics that are potentially relevant to his or her voting decision. While some people may be so single-minded that they have only one interest that is important in determining their vote—race, religion, ethnic background, income, feelings about gun control or abortion or the State of Israel or the environment—most of us have multiple interests. Sometimes these conflict. Ecological interest groups, for example, may have less success in mobilizing voters in areas where environmental concerns are believed to conflict with employment opportunities than in areas where the two do not compete. The worse the economic conditions, the sharper the perceived conflict. Concern about increasing unemployment may influence how some voters feel about governmental support of the unemployed. Much depends on the tides of events, which may bring one or another issue to the forefront of the voters' consciousness and incline them toward the candidate they believe best represents their preferences on that matter.[12]

One of the largest groups of all, women, provides an example of a group membership whose meaning may be changing. At one time gender could not be shown to have a strong partisan effect; what weak tendency existed at the time of *The American Voter* (1960) showed women as slightly more Republican.[13] In 1980, however, women were substantially less pro-Reagan than were men[14] and thus made up a much larger part of the Democratic than of the Republican coalition (see table 2.5). Throughout 1981, differences between men and women appeared in public opinion polls that asked about party identification, and it became commonplace to refer to President Reagan's "gender gap."[15] Yet the *New York Times* midterm 1982 election-day surveys showed only small differences between men and women voters.[16] In 1984 women voted 6 to 9 percent less for Reagan, depending on which exit poll you believe. Women cast a majority of their votes for Reagan, but Reagan's margin among women was smaller than it was among men, so women kept a distinctive orientation, which appears to favor liberal Democrats more than conservative Republicans. In 1988 the gender gap was only four points according to the Gallup poll, six or seven points according to the National Election Survey, CBS/*New York Times,* and NBC/*Wall Street Journal,* or ten points according to CNN/*Los Angeles Times* figures.[17] In 1992, 58 percent of Bill Clinton's vote came from women, but only 52 percent of Bush voters were women. In 1996 the gender gap widened. Among women, Clinton won a sixteen-point landslide, but Bob Dole actually maintained a slim plurality among men.

The case of the "women's vote" should alert us to some of the complexities of group interest. Not all women are the same: richer women are more Republican and poorer women more Democratic, just like men. In addition, single women, whether never-married, widowed, or divorced, are more Democratic than married women.[18] Group memberships do not necessarily

TABLE 2.5   THE GENDER GAP: VOTES IN PRESIDENTIAL ELECTIONS BY SEX

	Democratic		*Republican*		*Independent**	
	Male	Female	Male	Female	Male	Female
1960	52	49	48	51		
1964	60	62	40	38		
1968	41	45	43	43	16	12
1972	37	38	63	62		
1976	53	48	45	51	1	0
1980	38	44	53	49	7	6
1984	36	45	64	55		
1988	44	48	56	52		
1992	41	46	37	38	22	16
1996	45	54	44	39	11	7

SOURCE: Harold W. Stanley and Richard G. Niemi, *Vital Statistics on American Politics 1997–1998* (Washington, D.C.: CQ Press, 1998), 111–15.

*Independent Candidates were: George Wallace in 1968; Eugene McCarthy in 1976; John Anderson in 1980; Ross Perot in 1992 and 1996.

organize voters along a single dimension. The "interests" of a given group may be of greatest interest to only a subset of members. Thus the Equal Rights Amendment, a "women's issue," was of greatest importance to highly educated women. A difference between men and women may also reflect not failure in appealing to one but success at appealing to the other. Thus there can be "women's" issues such as abortion and "men's" issues such as gun control for hunters, and what can be read as a defection of women from the Republicans may equally mean a defection of men from the Democrats.[19] Moreover, a difference in one election may or may not prefigure a permanent difference in basic coalitions.[20]

Democrats have a problem with white males and Republicans have a problem with women in general. There is no doubt about the numbers, only about the explanation. It is possible that the egalitarian bent of the Democratic Party has attracted women and repelled men. The argument for this view would be that Democrats include women among the deprived minorities for whom affirmative discrimination is in order, leaving white males above the poverty line as the residual category who must help all the rest. The Republican Party's emphasis on opportunity rather than on more equal outcomes, by contrast, leaves the existing status or privileges of white and more affluent males untouched. In a corresponding manner, white women of low income may see the Democratic Party as providing them with concrete benefits, while middle- and upper-middle-income women, many of them influenced by the feminist movement, may see Republicans as opposed to their views on social issues, such as affirmative action and abortion. As Ethel Klein says, "surveys indicate that women tend to be more liberal than men on a variety of issues, including defense, environmental protection, social services, women's rights, and economic security."[21] Women are more concerned with egalitarian issues—fairness to the poor, unemployment—and less likely than men to support defense spending.[22] If defense spending is seen as taking away from social welfare, the contrast increases.

"Special" Interests and Public Interest Groups

Is there any difference between interest groups, as we have described them here, and the "special" interests that attract so much criticism? Not as far as we can tell. Americans have always organized themselves into interest groups. Groups may have interests that are broad or narrow, but it is hard to see why interests that are narrow, and therefore presumably more "special," are any less legitimate than broad interests, which presumably require more common resources to satisfy. The language of political competition in American elections frequently requires political actors to disparage the claims of others by labeling them "special" interests and therefore somehow not worthy of consideration. "We" are presumably "the people" and "they" are "special interests." But of course the "people" have interests too. In a democracy, leaders are supposed to inform themselves about and sympathize with the policies that people want. Paying attention to these concerns of the people looks to us very much like attending to the needs of special interests.

The rise of rhetoric stigmatizing interests as "special" interests is in part the result of the rise of vocal and deeply concerned groups claiming to represent the "public" interest rather than the private or pecuniary interests of their members. Although interest groups in the past have differed over policy, they have not (at least since the acceptance of industrial unions in the 1930s and African American organizations in the 1960s) denied the rights of opponents to advocate their policy preferences. But, in one significant respect, that is no longer true. "Public interest" lobbies have attacked the legitimacy of "private interest" groups. Political parties, labor unions, trade associations, and religious groups are examples of such private interest groups, intermediary organizations that link citizens and their government. Many are indeed "special interest" groups—groups, that is, with special interests in public policy. Part of the program of public interest groups such as Common Cause or Ralph Nader's various organizations is to reduce the power of private, special interests and substitute their own services as intermediary organizations. Typically, public interest groups have fewer—sometimes vastly fewer—members than private interest groups.[23] They rely on the mass media or mass mailings to carry their messages to the population at large, and their success is an indication of the extent to which American voters now rely on mass media rather than group membership to obtain their political orientations and opinions.

A remarkable example of the ways in which the mass media have to a certain extent transformed the interest-group environment of elections is the rise of radio talk shows as instruments for the crystallization of political opinions. Radio talk show hosts with compelling personalities—the conservative Rush Limbaugh seems to have been the most popular recent example—can over a relatively short period of time mobilize strong expressions of opinion by many listeners and callers, in effect creating interest groups out of thin air by giving voice mainly to exasperated antigovernment and other negative sentiments. Limbaugh has an estimated 12 million listeners each day. His books have sold millions of copies.[24] Political leaders and opinion leaders who write for the news media are increasingly persuaded that he and others like him have touched a chord of real feeling in the American populace.

Laws have been passed and constitutional amendments proposed by public interest groups that restrict the amounts of money unions and corporations can contribute to political campaigns and use in lobbying. On the whole, however, these laws have been unsuccessful in curbing interest-group activity. What has happened is that interest groups have found new ways within the law to advance their interests. One such device is the political action committee (PAC), an organization devoted to the disbursement of campaign money from interest groups to candidates. From 1974 to 1982 the number of political action committees organized by business and unions more than quadrupled, increasing from 608 to 2,601; in the next six years, PACs of all types (including those unconnected to business and unions) rose to a total of 4,268 in 1988. (See table 2.6.) The number dropped slightly to 4,079 in 1996. The bulk of the original increase was accounted for by the rise in corporate PACs from only 89 in 1974 to 1,812 in 1984, but the number of these corporate PACs has been stable in the last fifteen years, reaching a total of 1,765 in 1992.[25]

PACs are created to collect and disburse political contributions. They must contribute to more than one candidate, and the amount they may give to any one candidate is limited. In 1976 amendments to the Federal Election Campaign Act enabled individual companies or labor unions to establish multiple PACs, thus multiplying the amount of money they could funnel to any single candidate. Surprisingly, corporate PACs have not favored Republican

TABLE 2.6 THE RISE OF POLITICAL ACTION COMMITTEES (PACS), 1974–1996
(NUMBER OF PACS, BY TYPE)

	Corp.	Labor	Prof. groups	Cooper-atives	Corp. with-out stock	Non-connected*	Total
1974	89	201	318	—	—	—	608
1975	139	226	357	—	—	—	722
1976	433	224	489	—	—	—	992
1977	550	234	438	8	20	110	1,146
1978	785	217	453	12	24	162	1,360
1979	950	240	514	17	32	247	2,000
1980	1,206	297	576	42	56	374	2,551
1981	1,329	318	614	41	68	531	2,901
1982	1,469	380	649	47	103	723	3,371
1983	1,538	378	643	51	122	793	3,525
1984	1,682	394	698	52	130	1,053	4,009
1985	1,710	388	695	54	142	1,003	3,992
1986	1,744	384	745	56	151	1,077	4,157
1987	1,775	364	865	59	145	957	4,165
1988	1,816	354	786	59	138	1,115	4,268
1989	1,796	349	777	59	137	1,060	4,178
1990	1,795	346	753	58	139	1,115	4,192
1991	1,738	338	742	57	136	1,083	4,094
1992	1,735	347	770	56	142	1,145	4,195
1993	1,789	337	761	56	146	1,121	4,210
1994	1,660	333	792	53	138	963	3,993
1995	1,674	334	815	44	129	1,020	4,016
1996	1,642	332	838	41	123	1,103	4,079

SOURCE: Harold W. Stanley and Richard G. Niemi, *Vital Statistics on American Politics 1997–1998* (Washington, D.C.: CQ Press, 1998), 94.

Nonconnected PACs do not have a sponsoring organization.

campaigns as much as might be expected. Instead, the predominant trend in congressional elections has been to support incumbents over challengers, and since nationwide at all levels of government—even after the Republican landslide of 1994—there are more Democratic than Republican officeholders, Democrats have managed partially to offset the Republican preferences of corporate donors.[26]

While an individual citizen is still prohibited from contributing more than $25,000 to federal candidates during any given year, the Supreme Court decision in *Buckley v. Valeo* (1976) removed any such restrictions from PACs. Thus, "a corporate or union political action committee can collect donations and contribute an unlimited sum of money to unspecified numbers of candidates or committees so long as no single contribution exceeds $5,000."[27] In addition, once a PAC "contributes to five or more federal candidates, [it] can make unlimited independent expenditures on behalf of candidates or parties" (e.g., advertising on behalf of a candidate independent of that candidate's campaign in print or electronic media).[28] Not surprisingly, prospective presidential candidates themselves now organize PACs as a way of developing political alliances.

The rise of PACs to prominence is an ironic result of misplaced idealism. In the 1950s, reformers thought that it would be a good idea if local parties, which were held together mostly on jobs and sociability, were employed for more idealistic uses. It was thought that the replacement of a politics of patronage with a politics of issues would lead to a form of responsible party government in which informed activists could hold public officials accountable for their policy positions.[29] As government grew, however, two things happened: Business corporations, concerned about what government was doing to them, founded or reinvigorated their own interest groups, and other citizens formed and joined new groups to press their particular concerns. Instead of the integration and strengthening of parties that results in party government, parties were weakened. The weakening of parties facilitated fragmentation into a system dominated by what are called "single-issue special interest groups," groups such as those concerned to support or oppose gun control or abortion. The emphasis on issues has led to fragmentation, manifested in the explosive growth of political action committees.

A second irony is that the PACs, now a leading source of political finance, were created in response to congressional efforts to restrict the role of money in elections. In 1943 Congress, following up an earlier law against corporate spending, forbade direct spending on elections by labor unions. Soon thereafter, the more militant of the union federations, the Congress of Industrial Organizations (CIO), formed a political action committee financed by a separate fund collected from its membership, as well as a National Citizen's Action Committee to solicit contributions from the community at large. When the labor federations merged in 1955, the new AFL-CIO created its own Committee on Political Education (COPE) to collect and inject money into campaigns. COPE is commonly regarded as the model of the modern PAC.[30]

But that was only the beginning. Government intervened again in 1971, 1974, and 1976 with the passage of the Federal Election Campaign Act (FECA) and subsequent amendments. By limiting the amount of money any individual or company could contribute, FECA reduced the role of large contributors and at the same time gave incentives for the formation of groups of small contributors. Once the courts decided that money raised and spent in politics was protected under the First Amendment as a necessary adjunct to political speech and expression, the way was open for committees to proliferate, all concentrating on the issues and candidates of their choice.[31] PACs became a rival to political parties in support of candidates but without obligations to govern or to appeal broadly to electorates. Another round of governmental intervention is being proposed as a further remedy for the ills caused by the last round of intervention, with PACs, which flourished as a result of the last round of reforms, now cast as the problem that must be addressed.

Public interest lobbies, which represent not direct material interests as corporations and unions do but "issue" interests such as tort reform and reform of voting laws, have also sought to weaken the power of party leaders and strong party identifiers and to strengthen citizens who are weakly identified with parties and who emerge briefly during a particular election campaign or in response to a current issue. The emphasis on ease of entry into internal party affairs—more primaries, more conferences, more frequent and more open elections to party bodies—given the fact that party membership occurs in the first place by self-activation, leads to the domination of parties by activists who have time and education and are able to take the trouble to go to meetings. What kinds of people have these characteristics? Among others, they are the middle- and upper-middle-class professionals who predominate in supporting Common Cause, Nader's Raiders, and other public interest lobbies. Thus, among interest groups, if money matters less as a resource, business matters less; if time and talk and education matter more, ordinary workers matter less. As leaders of labor, business, and the parties lose power, organizers of public interest lobbies gain. These public interest lobbies are not necessarily all on one side of the ideological spectrum. People who defend corporate capitalism as well as those who attack it can organize in the public interest. And they do.

Two advantages have helped public interest groups expand their influence. One is a product of modern technology and the other has been generated by government. The use of computerized mailing lists has permitted these groups to tap contributions from large numbers of people who do not otherwise participate directly in group activities but receive mail and thus become privileged spectators to group leaders' battles over public policy. This opportunity for vicarious participation not only produces ready cash but also simplifies somewhat the tasks of leadership. Instead of having to satisfy an active membership that might make diverse or contradictory demands, only the top leadership of public interest groups need be consulted. Leaders of public interest groups are frequently poorly paid, accepting low income as a sacrifice for their cause, but they exercise strong influence on the groups they lead.

The second advantage is that people who contribute to public interest groups are entitled to count these monies as tax deductible. When the group wishes to undertake activities incompatible with eligibility for deduction, it often establishes a separate educational or litigating arm that can receive non-tax-deductible contributions. Without tax deductibility, the survival of some of these groups would be in doubt. The tradeoff is that they are required to engage in educational activities rather than overt lobbying, even though this may be a distinction without a difference. In addition, some of these groups achieve a status as legally authorized intervenors before regulatory commissions, a role that entitles them to payment for their activity. In this sense, public interest groups are sometimes partially subsidized by government.

Political Parties as Organizations

A third aspect of the social framework, along with voters and interest groups, that will help us account for the strategies of participants in presidential elections is the nature of political parties in this country. Here we discuss parties as organizations rather than as symbols for voters.

Party organizations are composed of three basic groups. First, professional employees of the party at the national and state levels staff the party offices and perform tasks on behalf of the party. Second, candidates and elected officials affiliated with the party carry the party label when they run for public office. Third, party activists are involved in party activities such as fund raising and getting out the vote, but not as candidates or full-time employees of the party. Each group plays a different role in party activities, and sometimes their interests conflict.

The primary goal of party professionals is to run an organization that will maintain or increase the power of the party. We define power in this situation as the ability to influence decisions made by government. Parties obtain this power by helping to elect individuals affiliated with their organization and through control of the appointive jobs (patronage) elected officials ordinarily bestow on members of their own party.[32] For party representatives—candidates and elected officials—and party activists, however, increasing the power of the party as an organization is often a secondary goal; other interests may be more important.

Candidates and elected officials are managing their own careers; their primary goal is most often personal success, both in the campaign and in governing. It used to be true that elected officials depended heavily on parties for the achievement of both these goals, but this dependency has in recent years decreased. This can be observed in such matters as the decline in the effect of "presidential coattails," whereby a popular president brings supporters out to vote who also vote for other candidates of his party. Voters are now more willing to "split tickets"—vote for representatives of different parties for different offices—and they are also more likely to view candidates as individuals than simply as representatives of a given party. Candidates for Congress, for example, usually build up their own political bases separate from support for the party and rely on these personal constituencies when running for reelection.[33]

On the national level, the rise of the primary system as a means for selecting presidential candidates (see table 2.7) has meant a corresponding decline in the candidates' reliance on traditional party organizations. In order to win a party's nomination at the convention, presidential hopefuls used to court the leaders of state party delegations, forging relationships with these party professionals to secure the votes of the state's delegates. In modern campaigns, state party bosses do not decide how their delegations will vote; instead, state delegates are pledged to candidates according to the results of the primary election's popular vote. Aspiring presidential nominees thus spend time in states courting primary voters, not party officials, and their success is more closely tied to their personal charm and charisma than to the support of the local party boss. To be sure, candidates still covet the support of party officials, but now those endorsements are tools to raise money (which is used to advertise to primary electorates) and to impress reporters (in order to obtain favorable coverage, and therefore win votes in primaries).

Thus, party professionals cannot always count on their party's candidates to share the goals of the central organization. What might be the most effective strategy for a candidate to adopt in a given campaign or legislative situation may

TABLE 2.7   THE GROWTH OF PRESIDENTIAL PRIMARIES

	Democrats		Republicans	
	Number of primaries	Percentage of delegates selected in primaries	Number of primaries	Percentage of delegates selected in primaries
1960	16	38.4	15	38.6
1964	16	41.4	17	45.6
1968	17	48.7	17	47.0
1972	23	66.5	22	58.2
1976	30	76.1	29	70.4
1980	35	81.1	36	78.0
1984	30	67.1	29	66.6
1988	37	81.4	38	80.7
1992	40	88.0	39	85.4
1996	35	70.9	43	85.9

SOURCE: Harold W. Stanley and Richard G. Niemi, *Vital Statistics on American Politics 1997–1998* (Washington, D.C.: CQ Press, 1998), 60.

not fit with the party's overall plan or policy platform. Conflicts are certain to arise. Aware of this, party organizations have developed strategies aimed at keeping candidates and elected officials loyal to their goals.

Most significant is the fund-raising that party organizations perform on behalf of affiliated candidates. The Republican National Committee (RNC), under Chairman William Brock, began in the late 1970s to raise large sums of money from a broad network of individual donors to provide aid to state parties and to help candidates and state parties professionalize their operations.[34] The Democratic National Committee (DNC), more haltingly and less successfully, began to follow suit. In 1983 and 1984 the Republican Party raised $289 million; the Democrats $84.4 million. In 1987 and 1988, the Republican Party raised $257.5 million, while the Democratic Party raised $116.1 million. In 1991 and 1992, the RNC and DNC raised $272.9 million and $163.9 million, respectively. This process was accelerated when the Supreme Court ruled in the case of *Colorado Republican Campaign Committee v. Federal Election Commission* in June 1996 that the First Amendment protected the right of political parties to campaign on behalf of its candidates and policy positions. In 1995 and 1996, the Republican Party raised $416.5 million, and the Democratic Party raised $221.6 million.[35]

Conflicts can also occur between party professionals and party activists—those individuals who make up the volunteer force of the party and a portion of the delegates to the national conventions. Party activists are often primarily concerned with questions of policy; these individuals we refer to as "purists." Purists wish their views to be put forth by the parties without much equivocation or compromise, and although they otherwise seek to win elections, they do not care to do this at the expense of self-expression.[36] In the purist conception of things, a party convention, rather than being a place where a party meets to choose candidates who can win elections by pleasing voters, becomes a site for passing resolutions and for finding a candidate who will embody the message delegates seek to express. In short, purists support parties of advocacy.

Party professionals are in no way indifferent to questions of policy, but as noted earlier, their primary concern is usually getting their candidates into office and keeping them there. Party leaders are neither for nor against policies in the abstract; they are concerned with policies as a means to the end of office-holding. If new policies help win elections, they are for them; if they help lose elections, they are against them. If officeholders are popular, party leaders have to accept them; if they are unpopular, threatening to bring the party into disrepute, party leaders will turn against them.

This attitude shapes the way in which parties behave. On the one hand, they must satisfy their activists and interest-group supporters by committing, or appearing to commit, to policies of concern to them. On the other hand, they are trying to lure enough people uncommitted on these policies in order to win the election. In a close election, the ability of a party to increase its support within one critical electoral group from, say, 20 to 30 percent may be crucial, even though that group still votes overwhelmingly for the opposition. The strategic implications of these remarks color all of national campaign politics: when they are trying to win, the parties try to do things that will please the groups consistently allied to them without unduly alienating other voters.

The temptation for political parties to avoid specific policy commitments in many areas, therefore, is very great. The American population is so extraordinarily varied—crisscrossed by numerous economic, religious, ethnic, racial, sectional, and occupational ties—that it is exceedingly difficult to guess at the total distribution of policy preferences in the population at any one time. Even where issues like Social Security and unemployment compensation appear to be settled, many questions—whether benefits should be taxed or the rules of eligibility altered—remain. It is even more difficult to predict how these aggregations of actual and potential interest groups might react to shifts in party policy positions, and still more hazardous to prophesy what different policy commitments might do to the margin of votes required for victory. This pervasive problem of uncertainty makes the calculations of gain from changes in policy questions both difficult and risky and suggests that the interests of parties and candidates frequently are best served by vague, ambiguous, or contradictory policy statements that will be unlikely to offend anyone. The advantages of vagueness about policy are strengthened by the facts that most citizens are not interested in policy or are narrowly focused on a few issues and that only a few groups demand many specific policy commitments from their parties and candidates.

Despite all this, political leaders and parties do, at times, make policy commitments that are surprisingly precise, specific, and logically consistent. Thus we must go beyond our consideration of why the parties sometimes blur issues and avoid commitments to ask why they often commit themselves to policies more readily than their interest in acquiring or retaining office would seem to require.

Part of the answer may arise from the fact that the parties depend on their party activists and that many of these activists, especially the purists among them, demand specific policy commitments from the party. The activists are the heart of any party organization; they are the volunteers for campaigns, the people who stimulate participation in their communities, and most likely they are the party's strongest supporters and most dependable voters. Unlike most voters, who are otherwise largely disengaged from politics, activists are likely to have elaborate political opinions and preferences. Their desire to make these preferences internally consistent and consistent with the preferences of their party certainly lead to demands on the party leadership for policy positions that are reasonably clear and forthright.[37]

Furthermore, the interest groups most closely allied with each party make policy demands that parties must to some extent meet. Even more than voters, who are generally interested at most in only a few specific policies, interest-group leaders and their full-time bureaucracies are manifestly concerned citizens and often party activists as well. If they believe that the interests they represent are being harmed, they may so inform their members or even attempt to withdraw support from the party at a particular election. Should voters find that groups with which they identify are opposed to the party with which they identify, they may temporarily support the opposition party, or they may withdraw from participation and not vote at all. Consequently, the party finds that it risks losing elections by ignoring the demands of interest groups, especially those that are part of the party base. The demands of many of these groups conflict, however. If unions object to the advocacy of antipollution devices on automobiles because they increase costs and decrease car sales, for example, labor and ecology groups cannot both be equally satisfied. If the costs of increasing worker safety compete with the costs of welfare payments, both cannot be obtained at the same level. Therefore, the parties may attempt to mediate among interest groups, hoping to strike compromises that, though they give no one group everything, give something to as many groups as they can. The increasing number of single-issue groups makes mediation more difficult. Jimmy Carter, Walter Mondale, and Geraldine Ferraro discovered this when Catholic bishops, who wanted a strong antiabortion stand, rejected their efforts to remind them of a common interest in social welfare policies.

The contradictory pulls of vagueness and specificity are well exemplified in Jimmy Carter's successful 1976 campaign. He slid by such potentially divisive issues as amnesty for draft evaders or resisters—"a classic example of how to say something and not piss off people," as his press adviser Jody Powell put it—by saying he preferred pardons, which implied wrong had been done but had been forgiven. On the proposed B-1 bomber, Carter campaigned by saying the decision should be made by the next president, leaving listeners to guess what he might do. On abortion, he was personally opposed but fudged on the role of government. This led a Carter speechwriter to quit with a public blast, declaring, "I am not sure what you believe in other than yourself." Yet time after time, as in his proposal for a more progressive income tax or for a ten-cent-a-gallon duty on imported oil, candidate Carter was attacked when he became specific. His poll taker, Pat Caddell, attempted to resolve the dilemma during the campaign:

> We have passed the point when we can simply avoid at least the semblance of substance. This does not mean the need to outline minute, exact details. We all agree that such a course could be disastrous. However, the appearance of substance does not require this. It requires a few broad, specific examples that support a point.[38]

In addition to the distinctions between professionals, candidates, and activists, party organizations are further divided between state organizations and national organizations, and this division provides additional occasions for conflict and disunity. The national organization concerns itself primarily with national elections, and thus is interested above all in promoting unity and support for national party candidates. State organizations devote themselves primarily to state elections, pursuing state party interests, and to a decreasing extent, building a state base for national party activities.

On most matters the national party organizations have difficulty producing uniformity among the states because parties are regulated primarily by state, not federal, law. Furthermore, state organizations follow no single organizational pattern. Sometimes elected state chief executives run them; sometimes they are run by coalitions of party chieftains representing the local organizations of several large cities or counties. Sometimes party officials and elected officials work cooperatively; sometimes they work at cross-purposes. Sometimes the state may have little party organization or significant activity at all in one party, sometimes in both. The best evidence suggests the number of states with permanent headquarters with professional staff who recruit candidates, raise money, and help campaigns is growing.[39] State party chairs now have seats on the national committees. They mediate between national rules and state practices. They are conduits for the growing services—recruitment, polling, fund-raising, issue development, vote mobilization—provided by the national parties.

What at the national level used to be a loose federation of state parties is slowly being converted, by changes in party rules and by judicial decisions, into a somewhat more centralized structure. Thus our national parties combine elements of both decentralization and centralization. The most obvious indicator of continuing decentralization is that national parties are organized on a geographical basis with the state units as the constituent elements. The party organizations from different states meet formally by sending delegates to national committee meetings, and most important, by coming together at national conventions to nominate a president. The strongest indicator of nationalization is the guidelines set out at the national level, which especially for Democrats are becoming increasingly important in determining who these delegates will be.[40] Still, it is the states who choose their representatives to national party bodies; the national committees and conventions do not choose officers of state parties. On the Democratic side, until recently, the permanent national party organization was not in a position to help the state parties, having neither the funds nor the personnel nor the contacts to contribute substantially to the nomination or election of candidates for Congress or local offices, who must run within state boundaries.[41] Now, following the lead of the Republicans, the Democratic National Committee and the Democratic Congressional Campaign Committee and Senatorial Campaign Committee provide some campaign services.[42] The Republican National Committee and the National Republican Campaign Committee have sizable staffs who maintain lists of effective campaign managers, consultants, poll takers, and accountants, going so far as to buy blocks of services that then can be allocated to close races. The Republicans, Paul S. Herrnson finds, are "much more effective in targeting their campaign management services to competitive candidates than the Democratic Party organizations."[43] In addition, under the law parties may spend independently.

On the other hand, when and where they are strong enough, state parties have substantial powers enabling them to share in making national policy and to be influential in the nomination and election of senators and congressmen. The states have their own sources of patronage, as well as a share in federal patronage through their members of Congress and senators. The very fact that the states are each separate constitutional entities engenders a drive for autonomy as those who hold places of prestige and profit in the state governments and parties seek to protect their jurisdictions, much as the framers of the Constitution hoped they would. This is federalism and it is much more than a legal fact. The states have great vitality because there are distinct, numerous, and vigorous ethnic, religious, racial, and economic groups that are disproportionately located in specific geographic areas that demand separate recognition. State organizations, therefore, become infused with the purposes of groups that use their state parties for the recognition and enhancement of their separate identities and needs. Italian Americans in Rhode Island, Jews and African Americans in New York, dairy farmers in Wisconsin, labor unions in Michigan, wheat growers in Kansas, gay rights advocates in California, and many others form the building blocks of unique political cultures state by state and make the idea of an uncentralized party system a reality.[44]

Each of the state parties is composed of different people with somewhat different interests to protect and demands to make. Control over state parties must be exercised from within each state, since the various states do not control one another and the national party exercises only partial control. This is the essence of what is meant by a decentralized party system in which power is dispersed among many independent state bodies. Efforts, which in recent years have been quite successful, to centralize control of the criteria for delegate selection to national conventions may lead state parties to adopt two sets of rules, one for state and local nominations and another for federal. This will lead to even greater fragmentation of the American party system.

Third Parties

The unusual success of Ross Perot in 1992 in attracting votes added a dimension to the calculations of candidates of the two major parties because each had to figure out whom the third candidate hurt the most. It is somewhat misleading to refer to candidates such as Perot as constituting third parties, since the organizational basis of his candidacy was a membership organization geared to his candidacy alone. This differs from a proper political party, which also runs candidates for lesser offices.

In 1992 Perot was using his enormous financial resources to support only one candidacy, his own, supplemented by a last-minute choice of Admiral James Stockdale as a vice-presidential running mate. There was no contest among alternatives or any decision-making process that might have led to the selection of somebody other than Perot as the candidate of his front group, United We Stand America. So he was not the founder of a third party so much as a self-promoter.[45]

In many states of the union, presidential candidates from minor parties appear on the ballot, although it is rare for voters to vote for them. In New York City a bona fide third party, the Liberals, has run candidates for local political office for a very long time, and many voters in the city vote on the Liberal line, usually for the Democratic presidential candidate, who customarily receives the endorsement of Liberal Party leaders.[46] Third party candidates have a long record of occasional success in other races; the most prominent current example is Reform Party candidate Jesse Ventura, who was elected governor of Minnesota in 1998. In recent years, however, such successes have been individual efforts, without long-term consequences in those states.

The Perot candidacy was kept afloat initially by the novelty value of his appearance on the scene. Journalists were impressed by his willingness to spend large amounts of his seemingly unlimited personal fortune in his own behalf, purchasing the services of such established campaign managers as Hamilton Jordan, Jimmy Carter's former chief of staff, and veteran Republican consultant Ed Rollins. So Perot was taken "seriously" by the news media, and this as well as his television advertisements kept his candidacy afloat for a while. In the end, he attracted a substantial number of votes, and so it is worthwhile to consider what unusual factors might have set his candidacy apart from other recent third-party candidates.

Unlike George Wallace in 1968 or Strom Thurmond in 1948, Perot's candidacy had no particular regional base. This precluded the possibility of his winning votes in the electoral college, which requires candidates to come first in a state. A Texan, Perot was thought to be just barely plausible as a winner there in a three-way race. This would not have been a negligible achievement, given the size of the Texas electoral vote, but at a maximum it would have spoiled the result for one or the other of the major parties rather than contribute to a likely winning coalition for Perot. It was assumed that the main loser would be George Bush, whom Perot gave signs of personally disliking.[47]

Thus it was something of an anomaly that the Bush campaign calculated that Perot was hurting Clinton more and took steps behind the scenes to assure that Perot would be treated as a serious contender by being included in the national debates organized by the bipartisan Commission on Presidential Debates. Until this eccentric decision, Perot's public opinion ratings had more or less tracked those of independent candidate John Anderson in 1980 (see figure 2.1, p.50), who, after a favorable spurt of early publicity, faded when President Carter

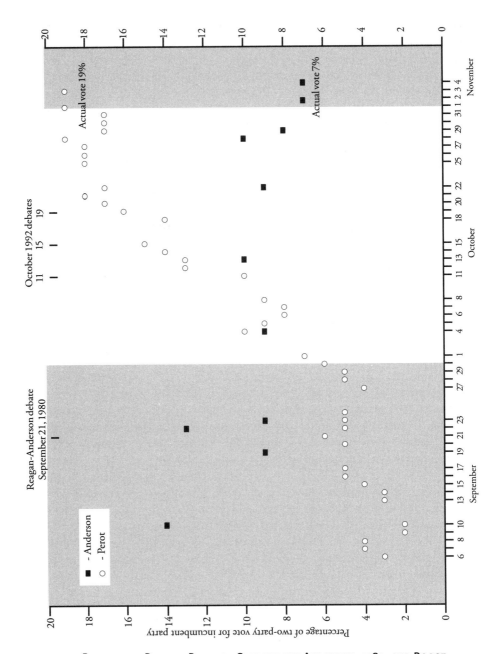

FIGURE 2.1   DEBATES DIMINISH SUPPORT FOR ANDERSON, 1980, AND BOOST PEROT, 1992

SOURCES: Perot data: Peter Goldman, Thomas M. DeFrank, Mark Miller, Andrew Murr, and Tom Mathews, *Quest for the Presidency, 1992* (College Station: Texas A&M University Press, 1994), 733-34; Anderson data: Roper Center, "Public Opinion On-Line," various issues.

refused to accord him parity in the debates of that year.[48] As John Zaller shows, press coverage of Perot became quite negative after he was in the race for a while, and so the decision in the Bush camp to refuse to participate in the debates without Perot was a major factor in keeping Perot's candidacy alive.[49]

Perot ended up with an extraordinary 19 percent of the popular vote, drawn from disgruntled voters from many segments of the population, and about equally from both major-party candidates.[50] His vote was not widely interpreted as approval of Perot so much as a visible place to park the negative feelings that the campaign had generated about both major candidates.

Thus third candidacies can be seen to have a significant role in presidential elections. They can act as spoilers if they draw votes disproportionately from one major side or the other. They can focus discontent. They can raise issues.[51] But because of the rules for counting votes in the electoral college, the electoral system is stacked strongly against third-party candidates actually winning.[52]

CHAPTER 3

Rules and Resources

Rules: The Electoral College

AMERICAN PRESIDENTIAL ELECTIONS are not decided directly by popular vote. Instead, popular votes are collected within each state, and each state casts all of its electoral votes for the candidate receiving the most individual votes within the state. This "winner take all, loser take nothing" approach is called a "unit rule."[1] Later in this book we consider whether votes ought to be counted in this manner. For the moment, however, we concentrate on how the electoral college works, and why it matters.

Each state is allowed as many electoral votes as it has senators and representatives in Congress. Thus, all states, no matter how small, have at least three electoral votes. This means that sparsely populated states are overrepresented by the electoral college. In 1992, 241,620 Alaskans influenced the disposition of three electoral votes, which gives a ratio of one electoral vote for every 80,540 voters. In New York, on the other hand, 6,321,620 voters went to the polls and voted for thirty-three electors, a ratio of one electoral vote for every 191,564 voters. In California, 10,018,581 voters for fifty-four electors produced a ratio of one electoral vote for every 185,529 voters.[2] One might conclude, therefore, that each Alaskan had about two and one-half times as much influence on the outcome as each Californian. But this is not entirely valid.

Why not? Because of the unit rule, which provides that the candidate having the most votes in a state receives the entire electoral vote of the state. This means that each Alaskan was influencing the disposition of all three of Alaska's electoral votes, and each Californian was helping to decide the fate of all fifty-four of California's votes. Ask any politician whether he or she would rather have three votes or fifty-four—the answer is immediately apparent. Thus the Californians get more attention, which means the candidates may promise more to California voters even though each one of them does not matter so much. In fact, the present method of electing the president tends to give greater power to the large, populous states, not the small or empty states, because the large states can deliver to the winner large blocs of the votes needed to win.

Although it was true in the past that presidential nominees tended to come from big states, this is no longer the case. The reason is that politicians, specifically the leaders of state parties, no longer control the nomination process. When they did, the size of the electoral vote in a candidate's home state mattered to their calculations. Ordinarily, a candidate could be expected to carry his home state and therefore the bigger the state, the better. Since the reforms of the 1970s, however, candidates are selected by a series of primary elections in which whatever it is that sways primary election voters matters most of all: favorable publicity, not too much competition from others running in the same race, and ideological agreement with large clumps of voters. These are some but probably not all the factors that may matter. One result is to depress the influence of electoral college vote-counting rules. How votes are counted by the electoral college matters less to the political calculations of participants in the nomination process because, on the whole, it is more important for candidates to be popular in states that pick their delegates early in the election year than for them to be popular even in the largest states. This is a significant example of the way in which changing the rules of the game changes the chances for success of each and every player.

Once the party nominations are made, however, the varying strength of states in the electoral college matters for the strategies of nominees. They concentrate their campaigns in the big population centers, and as politicians know, they stand or fall on the big-state votes.[3] In 1976, as it happens, Jimmy Carter and Gerald Ford used strategies that emphasized seven of the same states— New York, New Jersey, Pennsylvania, Ohio, Illinois, Michigan, and California—with Carter adding Indiana and Ford including Texas.[4] In other years, different candidates see different states as winnable. But the reason the battleground is so frequently identified as the big states that might go either way is the unit rule of the electoral college.

Thinking about Resources

In thinking about resources and their importance, it is necessary to distinguish between conditions that exist for the official candidates of the two major parties after they are nominated and the situation of prospective candidates who want the nomination during the prenomination period. Individual candidates before the nomination are pretty much on their own, and the way they look at resources is quite different from the way successful party nominees do.

There are many resources that, at any given time, may be disproportionately available to Democrats and Republicans, or to different candidates. Possession of the presidential office, skill in organization, knowledge of substantive policies, a reputation for integrity, facility in speechmaking, ability to devise appealing campaign issues, personal wealth, stamina—all can be drawn on to good advantage in a presidential campaign. More resources are available to parties and candidates than any one book could deal with exhaustively. But some resources obviously are going to be more important than others, and the importance of different resources varies from occasion to occasion. It would be sensible to regard as especially important those resources that one side monopolizes—such as the presidential office—and those resources that can be easily converted into other resources, or directly into public office—such as money, which can be used to buy competent staff, newspaper space, television time, and so on.

Although political resources are distributed unequally between the parties, in a competitive two-party system such as ours the inequalities rarely run all in the same direction. Sometimes Republican candidates reap the benefits; sometimes Democrats do. One result of these inequalities of access to different resources is that different strategies are more advantageous to each of the two parties, as we see when we examine the effects on election strategies of three resources commonly held to be extremely important: money, control over information, and the presidential office.

Resources: Money

Presidential campaigns are terribly expensive. Radio and television appearances, newspaper advertising, travel for the candidate and his or her entourage, mailings of campaign material, buttons and placards, maintaining a network of campaign offices, taking polls, and raising money itself—all cost a great deal of money.[5] It is estimated that the various party committees (the Republican and Democratic national committees, the House and Senate campaign committees of both parties, and various ad hoc volunteer committees that spring up in each campaign) at the national level spent approximately $20 million in 1960, roughly $100 million in 1972, $299 million in 1984, and $880 million in 1996.[6] Substantial sums were also spent by state and local organizations on behalf of the presidential candidates. Total political costs for all candidates at all levels of government amounted to something like $200 million in 1964, $425 million in 1972, $1.8 billion in 1984, $3.2 billion in 1992 and $4 billion in 1996 (see table 3.1).[7] How do candidates for the presidency manage to raise these sums in their quest for office?

In answering this question, we draw a sharp distinction between the prenomination period, when hopeful candidates are on their own and when finding money may prove to be a severe problem for some of them, contrasted with after the party nominations take place, when large amounts of public finance, soft money, and other factors come into the picture, shrinking the problem of the availability of money to manageable size for most party nominees.

TABLE 3.1   POLITICAL SPENDING IN ELECTION YEARS (IN MILLIONS OF DOLLARS)

	Presidential election spending	Total U.S. political spending
1960	30	175
1964	60	200
1968	100	300
1972	138	425
1976	160	540
1980	275	1,200
1984	325	1,800
1988	500	2,700
1992	550	3,220
1996	700	4,000

SOURCE: Herbert E. Alexander, "Financing the 1996 Election," in Regina Dougherty, ed., *America at the Polls 1996* (Storrs, Conn.: Roper Center for Public Opinion Research, 1997), 142–45.

NOTE: Presidential election spending includes prenomination, convention, and general election costs.

RAISING MONEY IN THE PRENOMINATION PERIOD

The primary source of money for a candidate seeking a party's nomination for president is the individual contributor. Party committees, an important source of income for candidates in the general election, do not give money to candidates for their presidential nomination, except, as Frank Sorauf points out, afterward, to help the successful candidate pay off debts incurred during the nomination campaign.[8] The Federal Election Campaign Act amendments of 1974 (FECA) created a system of public funding in which a candidate for nomination who has established eligibility (by raising at least $5,000 in contributions of $250 or less from individuals in twenty states or more) will receive public funds matching all individuals' contributions up to $250. This provision thus doubles the value of individuals' contributions up to $250, encouraging candidates to target individual contributors.

Political action committee (PAC) contributions are not eligible for matching, nor do they help a candidate qualify for eligibility for matching funds. This makes PAC contributions less attractive to the candidates than those coming from individuals. In any event, most PACs prefer to avoid prenomination campaigns and the high-risk politics associated with them and instead, when they give at all, give later on in the process.[9] The result is that PAC contributions to candidates for nomination are negligible, around one percent of the money candidates secured in the 1996 election.[10]

The FECA also limits to a maximum of $50,000 the amount candidates accepting federal matching funds may contribute to their own campaign from their own assets or from those of their immediate family. Since almost all candidates seek federal funds, this limit has effectively limited the influence of personal wealth in campaigns—the notable exception, of course, being Ross Perot, who did without federal funds and spent $68.4 million of his own fortune in his unsuccessful bid for the presidency in 1992.[11]

The importance of raising money early in the electoral cycle is heightened by FECA rules. Candidates may begin to collect matchable contributions starting on 1 January of the year before the election year; the FEC, however, will not release matching funds until 1 January of the election year. Therefore, the more money a candidate raises in the year before the election, the larger the boost given to the campaign by the sudden influx of matching funds in the short period in the election year before the first primaries and caucuses.[12] Successful early fund raising not only helps bring in matching funds, it can deny funds to other candidates. In planning the 1992 campaign, for example, the Bush campaign scheduled a $25 million fund-raising blitz in 1991, even though they did not expect any serious primary opposition. The plan was to take advantage of a Treasury Department ruling that gives campaigns raising the earliest contributions first access to the pool of matching funds, should that pool run out.[13]

Bush had other advantages by virtue of his incumbency. He was able to attract to his reelection campaign some of the most prominent Republican fund raisers, such as Peter Terpeluk, a Washington lobbyist, Donald Bren, a Southern California developer, Lodwrick Cook, chair of ARCO, and Henry Kravis, a Wall Street investment banker. Confident that President Bush would be renominated, they organized fund-raising events in late 1991 that raised more than $1 million each. In the early stages of the 1991 campaign, the Bush organization already had thirty-eight national finance vice-chairs.[14]

As a challenger in 1992, Bill Clinton was critical of such practices. As an incumbent in 1996, Clinton was, if anything, even more adept and innovative at turning the Presidency into a fund-raising tool. As Alison Mitchell reported in the *New York Times:*

> Mr. Clinton and Mr. Gore presided over unpublicized, small gatherings aimed at rewarding the largest donors with access to the highest echelons of power. Donors who gave roughly $50,000 or $100,000 to the Democratic Party could have dinner with the President in small groups of 10 or 20 in luxurious Washington hotels near the White House: the Jefferson, the Hay-Adams, and the Carlton....Others were escorted in small groups to the Map Room in the White House residence for an hourlong coffee with Mr. Clinton. Democrats say the President was host at an average of two White House coffees a week this [election] year for a mix of political activists and large donors....Mr. Clinton occasionally played golf with a potential donor while other large givers were taken on overseas trips or invited to State Dinners. Some stayed overnight in the Lincoln Bedroom.[15]

Candidates may enjoy access to various natural constituencies. For example, then-Governor Clinton used his connections in Arkansas to raise over $2.5 million in 1992, a remarkable harvest from a state with a population of only 2.3 million. One event in Little Rock in late 1991 raised almost $1 million. Many local businesses helped organize Clinton fund raising, no doubt mindful of the governor's control over the state's bond market, pension funds, and other regulated businesses. The Worthen National Bank of Arkansas established a credit line worth $3.5 million for the Clinton campaign. This helped tide the campaign over when allegations about Clinton's marital infidelity and draft dodging arose.[16]

Paul Tsongas found in 1992 that despite his strong connections to the Greek American fund-raising network Michael Dukakis had built during the 1988 election, the perception after 1988 was that a Greek American could not win. They were "traumatized," said Tsongas, and "for every dollar that Michael got, I get 10 cents." Tsongas's estimate was accurate: by September 1991, he had raised only $800,000, compared to the $8.1 million raised by Dukakis at the same point in the previous election cycle.[17]

THE BEVERLY HILLS PRIMARY

Candidates must go where the money is. For Republicans, this means to Texas for oil money, to New York for corporate and Wall Street money, and to California. Democrats follow much the same track. Both parties raise more in New York, Washington, and Los Angeles than in any other metropolitan areas. Looking at it in smaller units, the three most generous zip codes in the nation during the 1996 election cycle (and five of the top ten) were all found in New York City, on Manhattan's East Side. One especially well-documented path leads Democrats to the movie colony. For Democrats, Beverly Hills' famous 90210 zip code ranks fourth in generosity, with Century City in Los Angeles ranking fifth.[18] Jimmy Carter, for example, took this path in 1976 when he emerged as the Democrats' surprise nominee. Warren Beatty organized a fund-raising reception for Carter and invited Faye Dunaway, Robert Altman, Paul Simon, Diana Ross, Sidney Poitier, Cybill Shepherd, and Hugh Hefner.[19] In 1991 most of the Democratic candidates visited early: Clinton in October and November, at events hosted by television producers Linda and Harry Thomason, Sony Pictures Entertainment chair Peter Guber, and former Columbia Pictures president Dawn Steel. Bob Kerrey arrived in November, for a fund raiser organized by Fox chair Barry Diller, a contact he had made through his highly publicized romantic relationship with actress Debra Winger. Tom Harkin benefited from events organized on his behalf by Roseanne and Tom Arnold, Ed Asner, David Crosby, and Steve Allen. Even Jerry Brown, despite his $100 contribution limit, held an event in Hollywood with actress Talia Shire and actor Martin Sheen present. The event, raising $40,000, was the Brown campaign's most lucrative.[20]

In the financial environment created by FECA, many candidates have resorted to campaign techniques designed to reach large numbers of individuals outside the traditional mechanism of fund-raising events. Particularly important has been the use of direct-mail campaigns. Traditionally the preserve of congressional candidates within their districts, the process of direct-mail solicitation was modernized by William Brock, Republican national chair in the 1970s. Brock used computers to generate lists of proven and potential contributors to the Republican national party organization. By the late 1970s, direct mail was bringing in 75 percent of the RNC's receipts, and it did not take the Democrats long to catch on.[21] Although direct-mail solicitation seemed to have fallen off a little as a source of fund raising for the national parties by the late 1980s, it had nonetheless taken off as a means of fund raising for candidates in the prenomination phase of the process. Michael Dukakis raised $2.4 million in direct-mail contributions in 1988, and although one-third of this amount went toward paying for setting up his mail campaign, matching funds brought net receipts up to $3.4 million.[22] In 1992 Patrick Buchanan ran an extremely successful direct-mail campaign, with initial response rates of almost 14 percent for an average contribution of nearly $62, compared to more typical success rates of 3 percent and contributions of $20. Overall, Buchanan raised more than $4 million from direct mail, 85 percent of which was eligible for matching.[23]

Other creative campaign techniques besides direct-mail solicitation were used in 1992. Paul Tsongas, for example, ran a full back-page advertisement in the *Boston Globe* the week after his victory in the Democratic primary in New Hampshire, asking for contributions to his campaign. The ad cost $18,000 and raised $108,000.[24] Jerry Brown established a toll-free telephone number for people to call and make pledges to his campaign and used unconventional means to promote this device: an appearance on syndicated disc jockey Howard Stern's talk show, for example, was particularly successful in yielding calls to the phone banks. The telephone campaign raised nearly $5.2 million and stimulated matching funds of $4.2 million. Despite its success, Brown's telephone campaign also illustrates one of the major difficulties inherent in attempts to raise money directly from a mass public, namely expense. A Brown adviser estimated that the campaign lost roughly one in every two potential contributors because of overcrowded telephone lines. At its peak, the Brown campaign could afford only 80 people staffing the lines, compared to the average of 3,000 operators used for the telemarketing of consumer goods.[25]

Why Do They Need It?

Candidates for nomination accepting matching funds are limited in their expenditures to an amount fixed by FECA in 1974 and adjusted for inflation every four years, plus an additional 20 percent of that sum to cover fund-raising costs: $30.9 million plus $6.2 million in 1996. (This is the equivalent of $10 million plus $2 million in 1974.) Second, they are limited in their expenditures in individual states to amounts fixed by FECA and adjusted for inflation: either $618,200 or 50 cents per voting-age person, whichever is greater, in 1992 (up from $200,000 or 16 cents per voting-age person in 1974). Expenditures made by candidates in order to comply with the election law, known as compliance costs, are exempted from spending limits. [26]

The overall spending limits have placed increasing pressure on candidates. As Anthony Corrado notes, the cost of basic campaign essentials, such as air travel, direct mail, and television airtime, has grown at a rate far beyond the inflation of the consumer price index since 1974.[27] The pressure of a spending limit also interacts with peculiarities in the timing of the nomination process: early primary or caucus victories are important beyond the number of voters involved. Thus in the early races candidates typically spend whatever it takes to stay visible. Ford and Reagan in 1976, Reagan again in 1980, Mondale in 1984, and Bush in 1988 all had to scale back significantly on staff and other expenditures late in their nomination campaigns because of overspending in the earlier parts of the campaign.[28] In 1996 Bob Dole secured the nomination early but used practically all of his allowable spending to do so. Dole had only $1.2 million to spend between May and August, an amount that could hardly cover office rent and salaries, let alone such tangible products as polls or campaign ads. Bill Clinton, an incumbent unopposed for renomination, was nevertheless legally able to spend up to the pre-nomination limit as he saw fit—and unlike Dole, he did not need to use the money in the early delegate selection contests. Instead, Clinton spent his money in the spring and early summer, while the Dole campaign was silent.[29]

Research indicates that FECA state-by-state limits on spending are not important overall—the number of states in which candidates spend even 75 percent of the state limit remains in single figures even in highly competitive nomination campaigns.[30] The two earliest races, in Iowa and New Hampshire, take place in states so small that very low spending limits are applicable. In 1984, for example, the New Hampshire limit was $404,000, the lowest possible, matching the limit for the insignificant caucus in Guam and only 7 percent of the much later and therefore far less important California primary.[31] As a result, candidates seek loopholes, such as renting cars in Massachusetts or buying television time in Boston (whose stations reach four-fifths of the New Hampshire population), and charging these expenditures against the much larger Massachusetts spending limit.[32]

Another loophole, used to circumvent national and state spending limits, is the precandidacy political action committee. This is a PAC sponsored by the candidate, which, unlike a candidate's campaign committee, may receive contributions and incur expenditures without respect to FECA limits. This is because under the law as it has been implemented by the Federal Election Commission's rulings, establishment of such a PAC does not imply a declaration of candidacy for the presidency, whereas establishment of a campaign committee does.[33] This method of getting around spending limits was hit upon accidentally when Ronald Reagan's campaign committee reconstituted itself as a PAC in order to spend the $1 million surplus left over from his unsuccessful bid for the 1976 Republican nomination.

By 1988 nine of the major-party candidates were sponsors of such a PAC.[34] The number of precandidacy PACs fell in the 1992 campaign. Alexander and Corrado identify unusual circumstances that led to the dip in candidate PACs, namely President Bush's high popularity in the year before the election, which depressed all prenomination activity.[35] No such circumstance applies in 2000, and candidates were quick to exploit the potential of precandidacy PACs prior to the election year.[36]

The accumulation of money interacts with the events of the nomination process. As a candidate's defeats add up, credibility slips, and fund raising falls. Tactical considerations become more and more important as dwindling resources limit the number of races that can be contested. For example, by 3 March 1992, the date of several primaries, Bob Kerrey was forced by financial desperation to ignore the Maryland primary, to limit expenditures in Colorado to one thirty-second advertisement, to rely on his presence in Georgia to generate enough free press coverage to make up for his lack of any paid airtime, and to hope that $6,600 spent on radio ads in Idaho might influence the outcome in the state's low-turnout caucus. Not surprisingly, none of these tactics paid off, and Kerrey withdrew from the race two days later.[37]

Kerrey's dilemma points to another tactical choice that the candidates must address: the extent to which the campaign will allocate expenditures to television and radio advertisements, or to setting up the kind of organization designed to support the presence of a candidate actively campaigning in a state or to campaign actively on his behalf. Obviously, candidates would like to be able to establish both types of campaigns in a state. Consider the position of Paul Tsongas in 1992. Having expended most of his available resources on his New Hampshire victory, he lacked the money to develop organizations in the 3 March primary states. He decided, therefore, to concentrate on Maryland, combining television ads with active campaigning and winning with 40 percent of the vote. A television presence alone, by contrast, was not enough to prevent solid defeats at the hands of Clinton in Georgia and both Clinton and Brown in Colorado.[38] In 1996 only Bob Dole was able to raise enough money to withstand setbacks without ending his campaign. By contrast, Lamar Alexander's fund-raising efforts were helped when he was perceived to have done well in the Iowa caucuses, but he could not raise money quickly enough to compete in the states after the New Hampshire primary; he had used all of his resources in those two early contests.[39] All candidates, winners or losers, face the same choices. They face the same demands on a limited pool of resources and must make the same sorts of decisions.

RAISING AND SPENDING MONEY IN THE GENERAL ELECTION

After the nominations, full public funding is available to the major-party candidates, under FECA, if they want it—and no major party candidate has turned down public funding. Candidates are given $20 million in 1974 dollars—$61.8 million in 1996—from the pool created by the federal income tax checkoff introduced by FECA. In return, candidates must accept limits on their expenditures to this amount, with three exceptions. First, there are the "coordinated expenditures" permitted to the national party committees—two cents per voting-age person in 1974, a total of $12.3 million in 1996. Second, the candidates may raise funds from private contributions under FECA limits, or from their own pockets subject to a limit of $50,000, in order to pay the compliance costs incurred in following the law. In 1992 compliance costs came to $4.3 million for Bush, and $6 million for Clinton.[40]

The third sort of spending permitted outside the limits imposed by acceptance of public funding is by far the most significant: the phenomenon known as "soft money." This is money raised by the national party committees and then transferred to state and local parties or candidates. Although originally not permitted under FECA's 1974 amendments, soft money was allowed by further amendments in 1979 in order to restore to state and local parties the campaign role that the 1974 amendments had denied them.[41] The parties argued that the 1974 reforms had the unfortunate consequence of threatening traditional, grassroots styles of campaigning: for example, registration drives or neighborhood leafleting. At first, that was the the main use of soft money. In 1996, however, the Clinton campaign discovered a new loophole in the law that made soft money (and hard money raised by the parties) even more crucial. Under the law, parties are allowed to use soft money to fund "issue" television ads. The only requirement is that the ads do not specifically urge anyone to vote for a candidate. Typically, the ads discuss the strengths of one candidate or the deficiencies of an opposing candidate on one issue or a set of issues, but avoid referring to any upcoming election. Both major parties used this tactic, but the Democrats had a crucial advantage: they knew who their nominee would be long before the conventions met or even before anyone had voted in the presidential primaries, and could construct a campaign around the themes he was using as president. The Democrats spent some $34 million on such ads in the year before their convention, mainly in twelve states expected to be crucial to a Clinton

Box 3.1   Party Expenditures and Funding in General Elections

TABLE 1   PARTY EXPENDITURES IN GENERAL ELECTIONS

	Democratic percentage of two-party vote	Democratic percentage of two-party expenditures
1932	59	49
1936	62	41
1940	55	35
1944	52	42
1948	52	39
1952	44	45
1956	42	41
1960	50	51
1964	61	37
1968	49	35
1972	37	33
1976	50	47
1980	45	38

SOURCES: U.S. Bureau of the Census, *Statistical Abstract of the United States 1981* (Washington, D.C.: Government Printing Office, 1981), 478; and Herbert E. Alexander, *Financing the 1980 Election* (Lexington, Mass.: Lexington Books, 1983), 109.

COMPARABLE FIGURES FOR years following 1980 are not available. Note that the table includes prenomination and general election expenditures. In 1984, when the Republicans had a strong, unopposed incumbent, they spent less than half of what Democratic candidates did prior to the convention. In the general election, however, Republicans spent more than Democrats by a large margin—$78.4 to $53.9 million—when "soft" money (money controlled by state and local parties, governed by state and local law, but spent in coordination with the candidate) and independent expenditures are taken into account.

In 1988, when both parties had competitive nomination battles, Republicans outspent Democrats in the prenomination period by a margin of $109.9 million to $83.5 million. In the 1996 general election campaign, the GOP slightly outspent the Democrats when all sources are considered.

TABLE 2   FUNDING FOR THE GENERAL ELECTION, 1996 (IN MILLIONS OF DOLLARS)

	Dole	Clinton
Limited funds		
Federal funding	61.8	61.8
National party	12.3	12.3
Unlimited funds		
Soft money	110.7	95.4
Total	184.8	169.5

SOURCE: Anthony Corrado, "Financing the 1996 Elections," in Gerald M. Pomper, ed., *The Election of 1996: Reports and Interpretations* (Chatham, N.J.: Chatham House, 1997), 150–55.

On the state level the story may be different.[1] In congressional elections, which are generally far less visible to voters than presidential elections, money is frequently more scarce and may help to determine the chances especially of a challenger, as funding is needed to overcome the advantages of incumbency, while contributors do not want to fund likely losers.[2]

Notes

1. Murray Levin and George Blackwood, *The Compleat Politician* (Indianapolis: Bobbs-Merrill, 1962), 227–43.
2. Gary C. Jacobson, *Money in Congressional Elections* (New Haven: Yale University Press, 1986).

victory. The Republicans waited until May 1996 to begin their issue ads in support of the Dole candidacy.[42]

Neither the expenditure nor the raising of soft money is federally regulated. The states do place limits, but these tend to be far less stringent than those that fall under FECA. National party committees and the presidential candidates are free to channel soft money they have raised to the state and local parties, and to coordinate its expenditures with their own spending of "hard" money. Thus the candidates often bring their fund-raising teams from the nomination races into the general election campaign, and they are free to raise soft money from wherever they want, with no limits on the size of the contribution. In the last three presidential elections, soft money has been raised in increasingly visible and competitive ways. In 1992 the Republicans claimed 198, and the Democrats 375 individuals who gave or raised soft money totals of at least $100,000. Although Clinton placed a limit of $100,000 on contributions from individuals and refused to accept soft money from PACs, corporations, or labor unions, these sources had already contributed large amounts to the Democratic National Committee, mainly for the purpose of financing the national party convention. Bush placed no limits and did not back away from accepting corporate money if offered.[43] In 1996 both parties raised over $100 million in soft money. About half of that was transferred directly to the state and local parties; the rest was spent in joint activities with the state and local parties, donated to state and local candidates, or spent on party-building activities not directly affecting the 1996 elections. Both sides received large donations. The large tobacco company Phillip Morris donated $1.6 million to the Republicans (and $400,000 to the tobacco-bashing Democrats), while the Association of Trial Lawyers gave $361,000 to the Democrats (and $157,000 to the trial-lawyer-bashing Republicans).[44]

The rise of soft money shows how difficult it is to regulate money in elections. On the one hand, it constitutes a loophole, returning "big money" to presidential campaigns and raising anew the question of the motives of contributors prepared to give large sums of money to politicians. Soft money has also undermined the campaign cost-limiting rationale of the FECA by allowing candidates to spend huge amounts above the legal limit; in 1996 the candidates spent well over twice the FECA limit for the year. It also creates a gray area within which the application of campaign finance law becomes uncertain: for example, should a presidential candidate be allowed to speak at a soft-money fund-raising event? Such an appearance appears to be exactly the sort of private fund-raising activity that, by accepting public funding, a candidate has agreed not to engage in.

But soft money also addresses a real problem: how to energize voluntary "party-building" activities and create an incentive for the parties to encourage citizen participation. In order to qualify as a soft-money expenditure, any campaigning by the national committees or the candidates' personal committees has to be undertaken in conjunction with volunteer-based state and local party organizations. This is an incentive that would not, and did not, arise without soft money. Almost all hard-money expenditures go directly to advertising, travel, and other direct campaign costs associated with the candidate personally.[45]

Soft money has become such an important part of presidential campaign financing that it has fundamentally changed the basic rules instituted in 1974. From that point through about the 1984 election, campaigns were basically waged using public money. Now, public money serves as a floor, not a ceiling. That is, while both major party candidates are guaranteed a sizable nest egg, any candidate who chooses to run a campaign using only public money would be at a severe disadvantage.

DOES MONEY BUY ELECTIONS?

The millions of dollars spent on American elections (see table 3.2) inevitably raise serious questions about the relationship between wealth and decisions in a democracy. Are presidential nominating and electoral contests determined by those who have the most money? Do those who make large contributions exercise substantial or undue influence as a result? Is the victorious candidate under obligation to "pay off" major financial contributors? Do those who pay the piper call the tune?

This was certainly the reasoning that inspired the post-Watergate political reforms of the mid-1970s, which attempted to take money as an influence out

TABLE 3.2   PRESIDENTIAL SPENDING: 1960–1996 (ADJUSTED FOR INFLATION, 1960=100)

	Actual spending	Consumer Price Index (1960 base)	Adjusted spending
1960	30	100.0	30.0
1964	60	104.7	57.3
1968	100	117.5	85.1
1972	138	141.2	97.7
1976	160	192.2	83.2
1980	275	278.1	98.9
1984	325	346.8	93.7
1988	500	385.4	129.7
1992	550	446.9	123.1
1996	700	499.6	140.1

SOURCE: Herbert E. Alexander, "Financing the 1996 Election," in Regina Dougherty, ed., *America at the Polls 1996* (Storrs, Conn.: Roper Center for Public Opinion Research, 1997), 143.

NOTE: All spending figures are in millions of dollars and include prenomination, convention, and general election costs.

of presidential elections.[46] Before these elaborate limitations were established, however, the evidence was slight that presidential elections were unduly influenced, never mind "bought," by monied interests. In the general election, that is, after the primaries, Republicans did spend more than Democrats in most places, but the difference was not as overwhelming as some would suppose. The Democratic percentage of major-party postnomination expenditures from 1932 to 1980 varied from a low of 33 percent in 1972 (when McGovern lost) to a high of 51 percent in 1960 (when Kennedy won); the average was about 41 percent.[47] Although the Johnson forces spent more money in 1964 than Kennedy's had in 1960 (the Democrats in 1964 managed to spend $12 million), Goldwater's campaign spent $17.2 million, significantly more than Johnson's.[48] Total expenditures of both parties were high in absolute terms, but outlays per voter per party were quite modest, running in the 1972 election to about $1.31 for each of the 76.02 million voters.[49] One of the startling facts of the 1988 election was that, in contrast to all other presidential campaigns of this century except 1960, the Democratic candidate, Dukakis, managed to outspend the Republican by a substantial (though not, evidently, electorally significant) margin.[50]

The most obvious and most important conclusion in our view is that even in the era when the parties were free to spend whatever they could raise and were not subjected to the limitations of the party finance law, money did not buy election victories. The candidates and party with the most money did not always win. Otherwise, Republicans would have won every election but two in the past fifty years, and we know, in fact, that Democrats won ten of the seventeen presidential contests from 1932 to 1996 and seven of the eleven from 1932 to 1972. Nor does there seem to be a correlation between the amount of money spent and the extent of electoral victory in national elections.[51] In 1968, for example, the Republicans outspent the Democrats by more than two to one, yet they won the election by a mere 500,000 out of the 72 million votes cast. One would expect that money would flow into the coffers of the party believed to have the best chance of victory. Yet with the possible exception of 1968, there does not seem to have been a single presidential election in this century that any competent observer believes would have turned out differently if the losing candidate had spent more money.

No one doubts that money is important; parties and candidates, not to speak of ordinary mortals, can hardly function without it. If a candidate could not raise any money, or only a pitifully small amount, he or she would be dreadfully handicapped and might not be able to run at all. But this situation has never arisen (although Humphrey in 1968 came close) after the national convention has made its choice. The first part of our explanation, therefore, is that the differences in spending ordinarily have not been so great as to give any major-party nominee an overwhelming advantage. As long as the poorer candidate could raise the minimum amount necessary to mount a campaign, that is, to hire employees, distribute literature, go on radio and television a few times, get around the country, and so on, he could do most of what he had to do. Thus, even before the 1974 law eased the financial burdens of both major parties, spending more than the minimum amount necessary to run a campaign did not confer significant advantages. Like other goods, money is subject to diminishing returns. People may get tired of being bombarded with literature and harangued by speakers. The candidates sometimes worry about overexposure lest they go the way of certain television celebrities who were seen once too often. Accusations of "trying to buy the election" may arise if too much time is taken on television. Indeed, there may be resentment if favorite programs are taken off the air to accommodate candidates who seem to have had more than their say. We know that many voters are relatively impervious to bombardment by the opposition, and all the leaflets in the world will not make them change. The actual result of an extensive assault by the richer party may be to give those who oppose that party additional reasons to intensify their opposition.

Given the necessary minimum amount of money, the less affluent candidate in the general election can count on a good deal of free publicity. Presidential campaigns are deemed newsworthy by the news media and are extensively reported. While Democrats may get somewhat less space than Republicans in the shrinking number of newspapers that openly display their partisanship in their news columns, they still get some, and they do better in the magazines and on the air. To some extent the candidates can make news. John Kennedy's grappling with the religious issue, Walter Mondale's choice of a woman as his running mate, Dwight Eisenhower's dramatic promise to go to Korea, Jimmy Carter's efforts to rescue the hostages in Iran or to negotiate them out, and George Bush's pledge "Read my lips, no new taxes" all made headlines at little or no financial cost. The television debates in 1960 and regularly since 1976 all ran without significant monetary costs to the candidates and attracted millions of viewers, numbers far in excess of the usual political broadcasts for which fees had to be paid.

Money makes a greater difference at the prenomination stage than later on. Having money early to aid in making a good showing helps raise money to sustain oneself throughout the primaries. Eisenhower and Taft each spent about $2.5 million on their nominating campaigns in 1952.[52] McGovern spent $12 million in 1972 on the way to his nomination.[53] Jimmy Carter spent $12.4 million in 1976 and, as an incumbent president, $19.6 million in 1980.[54] In 1984 Walter Mondale spent $26.2 million, while Ronald Reagan, despite the lack of serious competition for the Republican nomination, spent $25.9 million.[55] In 1988 the winning nominees had more money to work with than their rivals; Bush spent $27.7 million, and Dukakis spent $28 million.[56] By 1 January 1988, the Dukakis campaign had raised more than twice as much as any other Democratic candidate, an advantage difficult to overcome in the front-loaded primary system.[57] Of course, inflation explains much of this growth in spending. The candidate who wishes to enter primaries and conduct a national drive to obtain delegates may be dissuaded through lack of the minimum amount necessary to get started. The press will not "take seriously" a candidate who cannot qualify for federal matching funds.

Money, however, is only one factor. Having money manifestly does not guarantee victory in primaries. In 1984 there was a negative relationship between Gary Hart's spending and his share of the vote. Hart was most successful in those states in which he was outspent by Walter Mondale. In contrast, Hart lost four of the five major states in which he outspent Mondale by two to one or more.[58] Michael Robinson notes that "Hart had little money to spend when he was winning; he had plenty of money to spend as he lost. Spending and winning are unrelated; it is the 'drunken sailor' syndrome in presidential politics, spending what you have, regardless."[59] One can always argue that a small sum at a critical moment, if only one knew beforehand, might have been crucial. "If I'd only known then what I know today," Morris Udall lamented to an interviewer, referring to his decision to stop advertising during the last week of the 1976 campaign in Wisconsin, where he lost by 5,000 out of 670,000 votes.[60] Since Udall came in second six times, losing three times to Carter by a tiny margin, any number of "it might have beens" (including an entry by Senator Henry Jackson into New Hampshire, which could have prevented Carter from getting started) might well have made the difference. Thus it cannot successfully be argued that a candidate who ran so long and so often in so many primaries lost only because he lacked money for a week.

Skill and strategy in using resources matters as much as having them. Witness a memorandum written to Morris Udall by his campaign manager: "We've got a reputation, frankly, as the sloppiest campaign in memory. No one knows who is in charge."[61] In 1976 Birch Bayh's indecision about entering primaries, Henry Jackson's taking Pennsylvania for granted, Hubert Humphrey's waiting until the California primary, when it was too late, Jimmy Carter's failing to see Maryland was not for him and getting involved in a pointless scrap with Governor Jerry Brown of California, all this and more mattered. It also mattered that Carter's strategy of running early and everywhere was a good strategy that paid off. Carter not only was able to run because he could raise money, but he was able to raise money on the strength of his early victories.

It is exceedingly difficult to get reliable information on an event that involves a decision not to act, such as a political candidate's decision not to run because he could not raise the money. There is only a little literature on this subject, mostly news stories announcing early decisions not to run. But undoubtedly there have been some prospective candidates whose inability to raise cash has proved fatal to their chances of being considered for the nomination. In 1995 Richard Cheney, Jack Kemp, Bill Bennett, Dan Quayle, and conceivably others might have run if more money had been available to them.[62] Whether their failure represents an inability to satisfy the monied classes or to convince enough people that their candidacies were serious and worthy is difficult to say in the abstract. A more important question concerns whether there has been systematic bias in favor of or against certain candidates that consistently alters the outcomes of presidential nominations. We can immediately dismiss the notion that the richest person automatically comes out on top. If that were the case, Rockefeller would have triumphed over Goldwater in 1964 and Nixon in 1968, and Taft over Eisenhower in 1952. In 1976 Ronald Reagan's personal wealth eclipsed Gerald Ford's, as in 1980 Edward Kennedy's did Jimmy Carter's. Nevertheless, in both these instances, the incumbent president beat the challenger. Indeed, for candidates who accept public funds, the maximum personal contribution allowed is now $50,000. In 1988 only three candidates came close to this limit, and three others made loans of a similar size to their campaign organizations. Richard Gephardt's $50,000 must be compared with the $7 million or so that his campaign consumed. Of the $27.7 million spent by George Bush to win the Republican nomination, only $2,000 came out of his own bank account.[63]

Perhaps the best test of the proposition that the richest candidate will win was found in the Republican nomination contest in 1996. Rather than relying on a mixture of small contributions and matching public funds, as every major candidate for the nomination had done since the 1974 FECA regime came into effect, publisher Steve Forbes decided to spend his own money in an effort to secure the Republican nomination. Under the Supreme Court decision in *Buckley v. Valeo* (1976), candidates may spend as much as they want of their own money in self-promotion. Many wealthy state-level candidates have taken advantage of that ruling, but Forbes was the first candidate for a major party presidential nomination to do so. Certainly, self-financing helped Forbes. Other than money, the only obvious resource he brought to the campaign was a mild case of name recognition, since his family's name is in the title of their magazine. It was his ability and willingness to spend vast sums of money—over $40 million, almost as much as nominee Bob Dole and far more than any other candidate for the nomination—that convinced the press to treat Forbes as a serious candidate, despite his late entry, lack of organization in Iowa or New Hampshire, and absence of normal qualifications such as previous elective office or substantial public service. The money was not, however, capable of buying Forbes the nomination. In the critical states of Iowa and New Hampshire, he failed to finish among the top three candidates. While he did win two primaries (one, in Delaware, by default since he was the only candidate to campaign there), he never really threatened to win the nomination.[64]

What does the case of Steve Forbes tell us about the political efficacy of personal wealth? Money could not buy him the nomination. Moreover, even the money he did spend was radically insufficient to do the job. As William G. Mayer put it, for Forbes to be even somewhat competitive, "he had to spend *enormous* amounts of money. Dropping a few million bucks here and there over a large state like New York just would not do it. Forbes absolutely needed to blanket the airwaves with his commercials, as he did in Iowa, New Hampshire, Delaware, and Arizona."[65] If this is correct, then to compete in the delegate-rich large states, Forbes would have had to spend hundreds of millions of dollars. Even then, his saturation spending only succeeded when the competition did not devote their own resources to the state, an unlikely possibility in large states.

This is not to say self-financing cannot have an effect on nomination politics. Forbes was certainly able to buy attention, if not approval, for his main campaign issue, the flat tax. His negative ads may well have hurt Dole in Iowa and New Hampshire. In addition, Forbes may have simply been the wrong billionaire; a self-financed candidate with additional assets, such as experience in elective office, might do better in the future. But that underscores the point that money itself is only one of the resources important to electoral politics.

The ability to raise money is a matter not only of personal wealth but also of being able to attract funds from others. Does this mean that only candidates attractive to the wealthy can run? The question is not so much whether it helps to be rich but whether candidates who favor the causes of the rich have the advantage over those who favor the poor. There is little evidence to support such a view. Given the nature of the American electorate, no candidate would openly admit to being the candidate only of the rich. Candidates holding a variety of views on economic issues, most of which are highly technical, manage to run for the nominations of both parties. In 1995 Republicans from all parts of the political spectrum launched presidential bids, from Arlen Specter and Lamar Alexander to Pat Buchanan and Bob Dornan. At the same time, Steve Forbes's first-choice candidate, Jack Kemp, declined to run.[66] If candidates are generally chosen from among people who differ only a little on most substantive issues, the reason is not that the rich are withholding their money from the more radical candidates. Rather, it is that the distribution of opinions in the electorate renders the radicals' cause hopeless. Our conclusion is that it is nice to be rich; some candidates who lack funds are disadvantaged in the early going. From the standpoint of the total political system, however, the need for money does not appear to bar nonrich candidates who are otherwise acceptable to the electorate.

REFORM

Four broad issues are raised by the ways in which money is acquired and spent in presidential elections. The least troublesome is the issue of public disclosure of campaign financing. In federal campaigns, all contributions in excess of $200 and expenditures by candidates and committees in excess of $1,000 must be publicly reported under the Federal Election Campaign Act of 1971 (FECA). The availability of this information led Common Cause in 1972, and others since, to compile and publish lists of contributors to congressional campaigns. These compilations document the unsurprising news that some senators and representatives attracted donations from contributors having business before the committees on which they sat, and that some Senate and House races attracted money from sources far away from the state or district concerned. As well they might; a few hundred thousand dollars invested in Delaware or South Dakota could help elect a sympathetic congressman or senator making decisions affecting the whole nation as readily as several million dollars invested in New York or California.[67]

When these contributions are matters of public record, voters can decide for themselves whether or not their representatives are still able to represent them adequately. Against this clear public gain must be weighed the possible chilling effects of publicity on the financial angels of small, unpopular parties. Safeguards against this difficulty are not at present in the law, and so far First Amendment protections of free speech have not been successfully invoked against disclosure on the grounds that disclosure inhibits political expression by chilling support for unpopular parties.[68]

A second feature of FECA are the provisions for public financing of presidential election campaigns. Among the policy issues raised by public financing are: How much should minor parties get? Should not some method be found so that people rather than legislatures allocate public funds to the parties of their choice? In view of the nearly $100 million spent by the major-party candidates in 1972, the last presidential year before public finance went into effect, was not $90 million twenty years later too low to provide adequate political communication in a nation as large and diverse as the United States? A comparative study by Howard Penniman suggests that, contrary to popular opinion, American elections actually cost less per voter than those of other democracies.[69] Although actual spending in 1988 showed a considerable 54 percent jump from the previous presidential election, the trend over time is less disturbing: real campaign spending in 1988 was four times the 1960 figures, and spending adjusted for inflation actually fell in the 1992 cycle, before rising by 12 percent in 1996.

Related to this last question is, of course, the question whether private expenditures should be prohibited where public expenditures are used. Any limitation on campaign expenditures limits political communication, a class of speech that one would think would be especially protected by the First Amendment. In practical terms, limits on campaign spending constitute an incumbent's protective device, since challengers almost always have a greater burden of making their names known. When expenditures are limited, political competition is inhibited. At present, however, the courts have held that Congress can set expenditure limits as a condition of accepting public subsidy but not when politicians are spending their own personal money, which it is their unlimited right to do.[70]

The final issue raised by recent legislation is the issue of limitations on contributions. Here, once again, a First Amendment problem is encountered, since voluntary political contributions of their own money by citizens as a means of political advocacy can readily be construed as an exercise of free speech. Against this must be weighed a general public interest in seeing to it that politicians are not unduly influenced by people who have large financial interests. May it not be that those who contribute or raise money in large amounts thereby gain influence not available to others? Aware that the answer to this question is not a simple one and certainly does not dispose of the First Amendment problem, we would say, "Yes, but not overly much." As one fund-raiser said of Washington: "This town works on personal relationships. Any time there's an opportunity to develop those relationships, it's a plus. The most anybody figures they can get in this business is access. You can't buy a vote. What you can do is say, 'Listen, I've helped you.'"[71]

What contributors or fund-raisers (the financial middlemen) get to begin with is access to centers of decision making. That is why a lot of PAC money goes to incumbent legislators. Control over money certainly makes it easier to get in the door and present one's case. Persons of wealth, however, are likely to have substantial interests that would provide them with good access whether or not they made contributions. If no significant interest feels disadvantaged by what these contributors want, the contributors may well be given the benefit of the doubt. But in matters of great moment, where the varied interests in our society are in contention, it is doubtful whether control over money goes very far with a sitting president. There are many reasons for this.

In the first place, a candidate is likely already to be publicly committed on many issues. Suggestions that he or she change a position during the campaign are likely to be met with little favor. If the matter is important enough to be mentioned, it has to be considered in relation to its vote-getting potential. Forced to make a choice, nominees are far more likely to prefer votes to dollars. Even if a miscalculation is made in public, candidates generally prefer not to reverse their field and appear vacillating and inconsistent. Money may be given in the expectation of future favors. To spell this out in detail would amount to bribery, however, and is likely to be rejected outright as illegal.[72] The common sense of the candidates would most likely forbid such a thing. If not, their advisers would no doubt argue that the consequences of discovery are much worse than any possible benefits. Thus, any strings attached to a gift are likely to be vague and cloudy, subject to all sorts of interpretations. When they are not, the risks of exposure are so great that the costs of corruption are as likely to be as high for the contributors as for the public.

Once a president assumes office, he or she is in a much stronger bargaining position. The president can do more to affect contributors' fortunes than contributors can do to affect the president's. A president may at that point refuse to acknowledge any alleged agreement on policy concessions in return for contributions. Wealthy contributors frequently give to both parties and, in any event, are often found on opposite sides of public issues. For candidates to give in to one of them may simply incur the wrath of others.

A decline in contributions from one source may be made up by funds from another. The president's need to gain or maintain support from voters, the limits placed on the president's powers of decision by what Congress, bureaucrats, and interest groups will accept, and his or her own preferences all place drastic constraints on benefits contributors get from campaign contributions. In brief, money becomes much less important to the things a president needs to do while in office. Contributors may be heard to complain in the hurt tones of steel magnate Henry C. Frick, who, after visiting Theodore Roosevelt at the White House, said, "We bought the son of a bitch and then he did not stay bought."[73] The foregoing analysis should help to explain why presidential politicians do not "stay bought," at least on public policy matters, whatever their debt to their financial supporters.

It would be amazing if the exponential growth in the governmental regulation of private industry did not lead the business community to seek advantages or selective forms of relief. The fact is that what government does—an airline route or a television license here, a tax ruling or an import quota there—can have an enormous impact on the fortunes of private people. Business people, as we learned from investigations of the fund-raising practices of the Nixon Committee to Reelect the President, believe they must act defensively. They may give to a campaign fund not so much to steal a march on their competitors as to make sure they are not left behind. Thus, for example, airlines may give to protect their routes.[74] Because government power is so pervasive, business people, not knowing when or where they may need a friend, frequently give to the campaigns of both parties. Deregulation makes this less necessary. So does public financing of elections.

Resources: Control Over Information

Political information is so easy to acquire during a presidential election campaign, it is hard to identify anybody as actually controlling the spread of information. There are, however, features of the overall system by which information is manufactured and distributed in the United States that materially affect the fortunes of candidates and the ways in which they are perceived by electorates.

Campaign professionals generally divide sources of information into free media and paid media. Free media consist of publicity that candidates do not have to pay for, as the result of news coverage. Patterns of news coverage matter enormously to candidates, and they spend great effort conforming their campaigns to the professional practices of the news media, both print and television.

News organizations customarily assign experienced journalists to campaigns they judge to be "serious," and so in the first instance aspiring candidates must contrive to be taken seriously. This usually means being a well-known public figure and hiring a staff of campaign professionals recognized by journalists as capable. Thus, even receiving free coverage usually requires money, and sometimes quite a lot of money. Television ordinarily covers debates among candidates. Appearing in debates is one good way for candidates to get publicity while keeping costs down, and being included in debates is a mark of credibility for candidates, a sign that they must be taken seriously.

Paid media refers mostly to television and radio advertisements, which campaigns must produce and place on the air more or less as though they were commercial advertising. Advertising is a form of information that uninvolved observers, such as a normal American electorate, frequently find credible.

What constitutes information varies with the various stages of the process, as we discuss in chapter 4. Traditional news media topics include horse-race information, estimating which candidates are ahead and which are behind, thereby keeping a running tally on the viability and hence the seriousness of different candidates. The news media also cover what they call "the issues," which may be, variously, topics of public policy brought up or emphasized by one or more candidates and social and political issues of the day.

In all these matters, the news media generally maintain a rather close consensus about who is serious, who is ahead, what issues are important. This consensus arises from the sharply competitive conditions under which individual news organizations exist, from the shared perspective that arises because journalists from different organizations hang around together as they cover the travels of campaigning candidates, and because they keep close track of one another's product. Because television producers watch the other networks and read the newspapers, and print media keep an eye on what's on television, there is a tendency for their stories to converge.

NEWSPAPERS

As we scan the major information media, it appears that, generally speaking, newspapers are somewhat more partisan in their straight news coverage than are most radio and television stations. A political party that feels discriminated against over the air can complain to the Federal Communications Commission, which may take such complaints into account when the offending station's broadcast license is up for renewal. This makes station management jumpy and is a strong incentive for balanced coverage.[75] There is no such legal limitation on the freedom of newspapers and magazines to be one-sided in the presentation of the news, and indeed, it has again and again been discovered that the print media avail themselves rather extensively of this freedom. Many newspapers enjoy monopoly positions in their communities, and much of the detailed political information available comes from the press. For these reasons, the character of press coverage of presidential elections is a matter of strategic importance.

Historically, partisanship in news coverage has generally tended to favor the side most often endorsed editorially by the press, namely, the Republicans. Repeated studies have shown that the Republicans usually are the favorite party of newspaper executives, who determine editorial policy in most newspapers. They have also shown that whatever biases exist in news reporting— for example, in placing stories in papers, in location and size of headlines—systematically have favored the Republicans.[76] The election of 1964, when newspapers gave a slight edge to President Johnson, provided an exception; in 1968 and thereafter newspapers returned to form except in 1992, when Clinton did better than Bush. Dole received more endorsements than Clinton in 1996.

But endorsements mean less and less; the days of the crusading editor who owned the paper and used it as a vehicle to propagate his or her own political doctrines are largely gone. In our time, newspapers with substantial circulations are much more likely to be part of corporate chains devoted primarily to making money for their stockholders.[77] The costs of publication are high. In order to show a profit, a paper must have a high circulation and a good deal of advertising. This is difficult to achieve in the midst of competition among several papers and with television and accounts for the trend toward the consolidation of newspapers. Reader attention is gained by emphasizing human-interest stories—sports, crimes, local personalities, and the high jinks of movie stars. Especially outside the major metropolitan areas, political news, though it does have a place, is downplayed because most readers are not terribly interested in politics. An excessive emphasis on public affairs, therefore, is unlikely as long as appeal to readers is a prime consideration. This certainly has drawbacks for civic education. But for present purposes, it means that the possibilities for political propaganda are much less than they otherwise might be, because public affairs do not get much space.[78] Advertising is gained by convincing advertisers that it will pay them in increased sales. The periodic appeals of conservatives requesting business people to place or withhold advertising as a form of political coercion usually fall on deaf ears because the motives of those who pay are commercial rather than political. Both the paper and its advertisers are likely to shy away from political controversy; controversy tends to make enemies rather than friends and is commonly believed to be bad for business. The result is that much of the time newspapers are bland. Such political opinions as they do express are watered down so that they will not give offense. Their opinions, far from being their central concerns, tend to be sporadic and aimless, rather than representative of a coherent political ideology.[79]

These tendencies are strengthened by a prevailing belief that papers ought to be nonpartisan in their news stories and present both sides of the issues of the day. However much the norm of impartiality may be honored in the breach, it provides a standard that to some extent holds down partisanship. More than that, the belief that newspapers should report what happens rather than editorialize in their news columns has many other attractions for editors. It enables them to avoid the hostilities engendered by political controversy; it lessens problems of editorial judgment, thus decreasing their workload; it enables them to select items that they think will enhance their readership; it provides editors with a defense against the charge of giving too much prominence to causes and candidates that may be unpopular with advertisers or influential readers. The norm of impartiality, however, leaves the papers open to manipulation by political strategists who can create sensational news stories. During the heyday of Senator Joseph McCarthy, for example, journalists slowly became aware of the extent to which they aided him by publicizing his charges because they were "news" rather than ignoring or carefully evaluating them.[80] During presidential campaigns, application of the same standard gives candidates opposed by newspapers the opportunity to enter at least some of its news stories because whatever they say is "news." If they should be incumbents, their exposure will be greater because presidents of the United States get attention for the smallest things they and their families do.

The desire to cut costs has at least one favorable consequence for increased impartiality in news stories. There is today a growing reliance on material put out by the giant news services, the Associated Press, the *New York Times,* Knight-Ridder, *Los Angeles Times,* and *Washington Post* services. These newsgathering agencies serve a wide clientele having a broad spectrum of opinions. They therefore endeavor to prepare stories that will prove acceptable to various shades of opinion.[81] Presenting what happened with a minimum of slanted commentary is a good way to do this, though the wire services are by no means perfect in this respect. The final product, however, is closer to the canons of impartiality than would be the case if each paper prepared stories in accordance with its editorial position.

While it remains true that candidates favored by newspapers receive better treatment and somewhat greater coverage than others, there is one compensating factor in presidential campaigns. Although the papers are generally conservative and Republican, political correspondents are comparatively more liberal and Democratic.[82] Most of the same standards of professional practice that constrain right-wing partisanship by publishers also damp down left-wing partisanship by journalists. As Michael Robinson has shown, while reporters may lean to the left, it is hard to find this bias in their copy.[83] Hard, but not impossible. Overt expressions of partisan bias are regarded as unprofessional in news columns and may even be veiled in articles labeled "analysis." In at least two ways, however, news coverage that has a differential impact on the fortunes of candidates can be observed in contexts that are formally understood to be neutral territory.

In the first place, it is permissible under standard journalistic norms to entertain a general pro-underdog bias. Journalists pride themselves in their calling to "comfort the afflicted and afflict the comfortable." Comforting any sizable body of afflicted persons may be well beyond the capacities of the news media.[84] It is far easier to afflict the comfortable, since this merely entails maintaining a pro forma skepticism about the presumably self-interested pronouncements of incumbents of high office. Incumbents escape this presumption only rarely. In the early stages of a foreign crisis, when there is a rally-round-the-flag effect, incumbents are permitted the luxury of being described as speaking in behalf of all the people. As George Bush discovered in 1991, this does wonders for their public opinion ratings. Ordinarily, however, Americans are instructed by the media to take their leaders' views with a grain of salt.[85]

Second, and more fundamentally, illustrating Bernard Cohen's observation that the news media tell their consumers what to think about, there is the issue of "framing." How issues are framed matters over the long run because frames determine the terms within which alternative solutions are debated, and indeed they frequently serve to define the very nature of the problem.[86] Thus whether or not environmental degradation, global warming, carcinogenic cranberries, inadequate schooling, unemployment, and inflation are seen as problems at any given time is not entirely controlled by scientific measurements of the underlying phenomenon in question.[87] In part, their status as problems is determined by how people feel about them, and these feelings are in turn partially determined by how the news media write about them. Thus the very problems our leaders are called on to solve may differ from era to era according to ebbs and flows of public attention to them. Politicians work hard to seize control of this public agenda and have a considerable impact on its contents.[88] So, too, do the autonomous decisions of journalists, who give and withhold credibility to leaders according to their own collective judgments about issues and the seriousness with which politicians are addressing them.

Experimental studies, which tend to focus the attention of respondents far more than the real-world experience of television does during an election campaign, demonstrate that exposure to media stimuli does have effects on political attitudes.[89] Insofar as media stimuli reach ordinary voters, we would expect their effects to be negative toward incumbents and front-runners and positive toward those perceived to be underdogs.

In 1960 John F. Kennedy, who was popular with reporters, got some favorable extra attention. Richard Nixon, who was not so popular with them, quite understandably complained.[90] By 1968 Nixon was a battle-scarred veteran who could watch with grim satisfaction as the press pursued the early Republican front-runner, the relatively inexperienced George Romney. Jules Witcover comments:

> Romney, Nixon reasoned correctly, had not yet learned the lessons about the press that Nixon's experience had taught him, and even if he had, he could not go into hiding. A moratorium on politics by a former Vice-President, Presidential candidate and conspicuous globe-trotter would make little difference, since his face and his views already were widely known in the country; Romney, however, needed exposure in large doses on the national scene if he hoped to graduate to the status of a national candidate. That exposure, Nixon was confident, would be Romney's down-fall.... Meanwhile, Nixon himself could sit back, let Romney's destruction happen, and emerge all the stronger by virtue of the contrast between the way he and Romney conducted themselves in the pre-election year shakedown.[91]

In 1972 Nixon carried his strategy of avoidance even further, programming himself into local television spots in key places around the country and totally bypassing exposure to possible hostile questions from national news correspondents.[92] He used the norm that the president's statements are news to get the coverage he wanted. Ronald Reagan, with his affable personality and long experience in show business, did exceedingly well with the men and women of the media as a candidate in 1980. Jimmy Carter's efforts to portray Reagan as insensitive to poor people or a warmonger were contradicted by Reagan's media coverage. By comparison, President Carter had far less favorable press notices. In 1984 underdog Walter Mondale got much better press coverage than incumbent Ronald Reagan, but this apparently made little difference to the voters.[93]

Are ordinary citizens actually influenced in their opinions and voting choices by the newspapers they take? The fact that a newspaper enters a home is no guarantee that its political news and editorials will be read. Most people pay little enough attention to politics; they often read nothing or just scan the headlines without carrying away much of an impression. Analyses of tons of newspaper clippings showing political propaganda by the press mean very little if these stories are never read.

When stories and editorials are perused with some care, the reader's perception of what has been written may differ markedly from the writer's intentions. An editorial may not be clear in intent, particularly if it is hedged by qualifications or watered down to minimize offense, as it often is. Frequently, readers pay attention only to those parts of the piece that substantiate their own opinions. Opinion studies have demonstrated the remarkable capacity of people to filter out what they do not wish to hear and come away with quite a different impression than an objective analysis of an editorial or article would warrant. Indeed, the reader may interpret the story to mean precisely the opposite of what it intends. A criticism of Harry Truman for being vituperative, for example, could be taken—as it now generally is, with the hindsight of history—as a commendation of his fighting spirit. A condemnation of Jimmy Carter for being obstinate could emerge as praise for his high principles.[94] Ronald Reagan's "detachment" could be seen by some observers as incompetence, by others as being above politics.

Stories and editorials may also be interpreted as they were meant to be and still be rejected as invalid. There is a great deal of suspicion of the press in the United States.[95] Party identification is so powerful that it is likely to overwhelm almost anything a paper says. Obviously millions of citizens have no difficulty voting Democratic while reading Republican newspapers. Group loyalties are another force that may lead to the rejection of opinions in newspapers. Face-to-face groups in unions, on the job, or in fraternal, religious, and ethnic organizations may generate opinions of their own. If these differ from those in the newspaper, members of the group are provided with a defense against the persuasion of the press. Group pressures of this kind are likely to be far more influential than what is written in a paper. The group may also reinforce what the paper says, but this represents an intensification rather than a change of opinion.[96]

Consider a puzzle concerning the political impact of the *New York Daily News,* a tabloid with superb coverage of crime and sports and great photographs that in the 1930s and 1940s had a circulation in the millions. If those who read the *News* all through those years had voted against Franklin D. Roosevelt, as the paper repeatedly recommended in vitriolic terms, Roosevelt certainly would never have carried New York City by the huge margins he did. At the same time, it seems strange that so many people who not only voted for but revered FDR in New York continued to read a newspaper whose editorials bitterly attacked their hero. The Democratic readers of the *News* apparently managed to get the best of both worlds. They read the paper they liked and voted for the man they favored without noticing the apparent contradiction. For them, perhaps, there was no contradiction. They either did not pay attention to the editorials, or they blocked out the unfavorable ones completely, or they interpreted them to mean something favorable to FDR. Voting studies document instances where people who wanted to vote for Harry Truman in 1948 convinced themselves that the incumbent president was against price controls; some people who preferred Dwight Eisenhower in 1956 apparently had no difficulty in believing that he favored medical care for the aged.[97]

Let us consider the case of the opposite of the *New York Daily News,* the upscale *New York Times.* After the *Times* came out for John F. Kennedy in the closing weeks of the 1960 presidential campaign, various political pundits speculated on the probable impact of this endorsement by so august and respectable a source. The standard theory about voting behavior would lead us to be wary of claiming much influence for the *Times,* not because its readership is too indifferent to heed a call to reason, but because of the kind of people who read this paper. One has to be terribly interested in politics to read through the *Times* as far as the editorial page. Precisely because of this interest, *Times* readers are likely to identify with a political party and to resist changing their allegiance. An endorsement from the *Times,* therefore, is targeted to people who are very hard to influence. Voters who are vacillating, doubtful, uninformed, and unable to make up their minds are far more likely to read comic books or listen to talk radio than to wade through the *New York Times.*[98]

One newspaper that may have more impact is the *Manchester Union Leader.* This paper has neither the resources nor the circulation of national papers such as the *New York Times* or the *Wall Street Journal.* But its location—New Hampshire, site of the nation's first presidential primary—and its unabashed partisanship have made the *Union Leader* a force to be reckoned with in presidential elections. The paper's attacks on front-runner Senator Ed Muskie (and his wife) helped derail Muskie's 1972 campaign. In 1980, after an upset victory by George Bush in the Iowa caucuses, Ronald Reagan's candidacy appeared to be in serious trouble. David Moore argues convincingly that the *Union Leader* played a key role in Reagan's recovery and his victory in the New Hampshire primary. Moore finds that readers of the *Union Leader* were much more favorably disposed toward Reagan, by a margin of 35 to 40 points, than nonreaders. This pattern held true regardless of the voter's ideological predisposition. But it is not surprising given the stories the Bush-bashing *Union Leader* was running.[99] This illustrates a difference between primary and general elections. In primaries, when party loyalty is no help in sorting out the choices, cues from the news media may matter. In general elections, where choices are better structured and candidates represent different parties, the news media are less influential.

No doubt the monopoly position of most newspapers in local communities makes the dissemination of opposing views more difficult than it might be in the presence of competition from a newspaper of a different outlook. But there are ways of getting around this. Other publications may enter the home—magazines and pamphlets that are religious, ethnic, union, fraternal, and even political in their origins—and these may contain contrary notions of public policy and candidate preference. So may nationally circulated newspapers such as *USA Today* and the *Wall Street Journal.* True, only a relatively few persons read a second newspaper or the political magazines, but these people are likely to be opinion leaders, people who take an active interest in public affairs and from whom others seek advice. The availability, therefore, of alternative voices expressing many shades of opinion permits opinion leaders to receive and then disseminate on a personal basis information that may counteract whatever is in the local newspaper. There is also the pervasive influence of television, which has put so many afternoon newspapers out of business and is now the favorite means by which citizens inform themselves of the rudiments of the daily news.[100] Finally, there are political talk shows on the radio and cable television, a wholly new medium of political communication that has sprung up in recent years.

What, then, is the significance of newspapers in presidential campaigns? We have suggested that the press is by no means immensely influential. Its major importance probably lies in two directions: presenting basic information about the candidates and the campaign to its readers and intensifying the predispositions held by people who tend to agree with the paper's preferences. Under some circumstances, also, a united press can force politicians to pay attention to a particular range of issues. Candidates would undoubtedly rather have the press on their side than against them. But they can and do win in the face of opposition from the press.

It may be that under some conditions the newspapers people read frame their attitudes toward parties and that this has some effect on their opinions and voting choices.[101] One study, by Robert S. Erikson, suggests that when a newspaper in a monopoly position endorses a presidential candidate, that endorsement slightly influences the prevailing trend. Erikson found no influence by the press in 1968, a close election, but some in the polarized contests of 1964, when the usual Republican predominance lessened, and of 1972, when it intensified. The press matters more, it appears, as a conveyer of information during landslides, when its effect on the outcome matters less.[102]

Whatever impact the press has varies enormously with circumstances. Against well-known and immensely popular presidents (such as Franklin Roosevelt in 1936 or Ronald Reagan in 1984) with publicity resources of their own, the impact of the press may be negligible. Against a less-well-known candidate, such as Adlai Stevenson in 1952, the attitudes communicated by the press—say, aloofness, overintellectuality, indecisiveness—may be more significant. Yet we know from voting studies that in 1952 Stevenson was favorably regarded by Democrats who identified him with his party.[103] The sheer number of different issues that may become relevant during a presidential campaign may either neutralize or intensify the influence of the press, depending on whether they are "pocketbook" issues that are grasped with relative ease by voters or "style" issues that owe their existence as issues to the attention paid them by the mass media.

TELEVISION

As a news medium, television reaches more voters than the newspapers. As an advertising medium, it soaks up enormous amounts of the money allocated to candidates under the law. As a medium of political influence, television makes a considerable difference.

Television news coverage plays a significant role in determining who wins the nominations in the first place. Early in the nomination process, when there are many prospective candidates, those candidates who are taken seriously by the news media, and especially by television, have a much better chance to survive the primaries and caucuses. Because the delegates to national party conventions are picked mostly by primary electorates, favorable exposure to mass electorates through the mass media—expensively by buying advertisements or inexpensively by receiving news coverage—is absolutely necessary for hopeful candidates.

There is a tendency, brought on by the brisk competition among the three major television networks, for television news to deal rather ruthlessly with candidates, declaring them "winners" and "losers" with great rapidity on primary election nights, based on projections from early returns and exit polls. The competitive pressure to see a pattern even when the outcome is not terribly clear is overwhelming. Thus, on the night of the early-bird Iowa caucus in 1976, Jimmy Carter was proclaimed a big winner for bagging 29 percent of the vote. This was more than any of his rivals—the next in line was Birch Bayh with 11 percent—but far less than the 39 percent that went to uncommitted delegates. In 1988 Richard Gephardt, who led a large field of Democrats with 31 percent of the votes in Iowa, was much less lucky than Carter. The networks were more interested in Pat Robertson's unexpectedly strong showing on the Republican side.[104]

Television journalists, in common with their colleagues in print, make every effort to nail down "expectations" against which the performance in early primaries of candidates can be measured: Lyndon Johnson, as a write-in candidate, beat Eugene McCarthy in New Hampshire in 1968, but because McCarthy did so much better than "expected," his strong showing dominated the news and shortly drove Johnson out of the race altogether. Likewise, Gary Hart did unexpectedly well in 1984 in Iowa, and John Glenn did unexpectedly badly.

So television interacts powerfully with the delegate-selection process—especially early on, before popular images of the various candidates are fully established—and makes a difference to political outcomes. The media want excitement; that is what sells newspapers and captures viewers for the television news. From this need to compete follows a proclivity to adopt a horse-race metaphor and before election evening to overemphasize the closeness of races. Even when the results of surveys appear conclusive, the media suggest the race is still open. A close race keeps the adrenaline flowing. So, according to the study by C. Anthony Broh, reporters do what they can to hype up the contest. They

(1) avoid predictions if they are definitive; (2) avoid reporting percentages if they are not close; (3) report the attitudes and preferences of subgroups that cast doubt on the outcome; (4) compare polls to a time period that can demonstrate a narrowing or constantly close gap between the candidates; (5) report voter reaction to spectacles of the campaign; (6) distort results that do not generate excitement; and (7) question the validity of polls that show a wide gap. Furthermore, they interpret methodological ambiguities involving undecided voters and sampling error in ways that maximize shifts in campaign support.[105]

Decisions favoring horse-race excitement and sensationalism eventually produce premature closure on apparent winners, not only on primary election nights, but also later on in the course of interpreting to viewers what has happened. Consequently, the news media tend to start bandwagons early in the election season and hasten the outcome of nomination processes.

Building bandwagons, however, conflicts with the recent tendency of print and media journalists to give severe scrutiny to people in (or who might get in) public office. So early front-runners, like Republican George Bush in 1980 or Democrat Gary Hart, before his flame-out in 1988, are in some jeopardy.

The influence of media coverage on primaries is illustrated by the Mondale-Hart-Glenn rivalry of 1984. In the Iowa caucuses on 25 February, attended by around 85,000 people, Mondale got 45 percent to Hart's 16 percent, McGovern's 13 percent, and Glenn's 5 percent. Despite Mondale's huge victory and the relatively small number of people who voted—Hart got just 12,600 votes—the media made the nominating contest into a two-man race. Glenn suffered a near knockout blow. Hart's media coverage, with hardly a negative voice, rose dramatically, while Mondale's shrank. After Hart's victory in the New Hampshire primary, where he got most of the votes of Democrats who made up their minds after the Iowa caucuses, Hart briefly became the front-runner. At once, as Gary R. Orren reports, "in a daily series of biting critiques... all three networks attacked Hart's credibility." On 13 March, "Super Tuesday," with four state caucuses and five primaries, amid generally mixed results, Hart received 35 percent and Mondale 31 percent of the popular vote. Yet "the media message was that this was a Mondale victory, or at least a split decision." Apparently, Mondale was helped by no longer being considered the front-runner.[106] Voting results were less important than the media interpretation of these results.

After the nominations are made, if equal-time provisions of the Federal Communications Act are waived by a special act of Congress, as they sometimes are, the networks are able to give or withhold legitimacy to third-party candidates more or less at will. This greatly affects the capacity of such candidates to mount a credible challenge to the candidates of the two major parties. For example, in 1980 John Anderson lost ground steadily after he was excluded from the televised debate between major candidates, more or less at Jimmy Carter's insistence. In 1992, at the insistence of the Bush campaign, Ross Perot was included in debates on the same basis as the two major-party candidates. His ratings flourished.

Because they lend themselves easily to television coverage, primary elections and other "open" delegate-selection mechanisms that lead to pledged delegates receive a lot of attention from television journalists.[107] This, among other factors, makes it hard for state party leaders to maintain control over party nominations. In effect, the news media have been a major influence in transferring power over the nomination process from state party leaders to candidates and primary electorates.[108]

As an advertising medium, television has gained greatly from the laws requiring a strict accounting of candidate expenditures. Compared to the numerous decentralized commitments of money that might occur in a grassroots campaign, it is relatively easy to keep close watch over expenditures by buying television time for the presidential candidate's campaign. This has tended to centralize campaigns and to make candidates increasingly dependent on television to carry their message. No wonder, then, that public relations specialists and experts in the use of television have increasingly turned up on presidential staffs since the days when actor-director Robert Montgomery coached candidate Eisenhower.[109]

Newspapers, magazines, and television stations do not conspire together (or within their own industries) to control the outcomes of nominations and elections. Because print and electronic media journalists share similar biases, being far more liberal and suspicious of authority than the general public,[110] and because they face similar institutional imperatives to converge on a coherent horse race, no conspiracy is required to create a correspondence of views. Similarly, although they try, candidates do not succeed in molding or manipulating the media to their liking. What we see most often is behavior that is not essentially manipulative or conspiratorial but interactive. The media and the candidates depend on each other for news to report and for favorable reporting to such a degree that each anticipates the actions and reactions of the other.

Candidate choices continuously interact with media interpretations. R. W. Apple's *New York Times* story on the 1976 Iowa caucuses was widely credited with making Carter a front-runner. Coverage of the 1984 Iowa caucuses, as we have seen, was equally important.[111] For all we know, had there not been numerous network and newspaper polls before the 1976 Republican convention showing Ford ahead, Reagan might have been able to maneuver better against a background of uncertainty. Knowing that dramaturgical stereotypes (who the good guys are, who the leaders are, who's out in left field, and so on) tend to persist and that the front-runner of today may be carried along only by early exposure, journalists may seek to resist the obvious.[112] This, however, is hard to do, because it must be done within certain rules of the news-gathering business. Newspapers and television news programs require headlines and leads. Ignoring an act can be as dangerous as attending to it, since under- and overexposure may be evident only in retrospect. Since they need news, the media are swept along by the tide of events to which they contribute and in which they swim, very much like the rest of us.

Incumbency as a Resource: The Presidency

The presidency is one resource that, in any given election year, must of necessity be monopolized by one party or the other. A president seeking reelection enjoys many special advantages by virtue of incumbency. To begin with, a president is much better known than any challenger can hope to be. Everything a president does is news and is widely reported in all the media. The issues to which presidents devote attention are likely to become the national issues because of their unique visibility and capacity to center public attention on matters they deem important. To this extent, presidents are in a position to focus public debate on issues they think are most advantageous. Presidents can act and thereby gain credit. If they cannot act, they can accuse Congress of inaction, as Truman did in 1948 and Ford did in 1976. Since Truman won and Ford lost, this strategy, like all strategies in an uncertain world, evidently has mixed effects.

Faced with a crisis in foreign affairs, and there are many, a president can gain by doing well or by calling on the patriotism of the citizenry to support its chief executive when the nation is in danger. But if the problem lingers, as the Vietnam war did for Lyndon Johnson and the Korean war did for Truman, the continuing crisis soon becomes a lasting liability. A significant example of a foreign crisis took place during the 1980 campaign, when Iranian "students" seized the American embassy in Teheran on 4 November 1979, taking American diplomats hostage just as Edward Kennedy announced that he would run for the Democratic nomination against incumbent president Jimmy Carter. Before the hostage crisis began, Kennedy was outdistancing Carter in the polls by 54 percent to 31 percent (with 15 percent undecided). In the crisis, voters, including Democrats, rallied around the flag, and Carter's ratings shot up to 48 percent, with 40 percent for Kennedy and 12 percent undecided. Carter announced that he would suspend active campaigning, and he used his crisis responsibilities as a reason to refuse to meet his rival in debate. He continued to campaign from the White House rose garden, however, and with great success.[113] Unfortunately, the crisis dragged on too long, and after he had disposed of the Kennedy challenge, President Carter's popularity suffered a serious decline, reverting to its precrisis level. Thus this episode also shows that presidents cannot count on continued popularity if their policies do not appear successful to the electorate.

As the symbol of the nation, the president can travel and make "nonpolitical" speeches to advance his or her candidacy subtly, while opponents can be made to seem open to charges of blind partisanship in troubled times. Should opponents claim that they can do a better job, the president can respond that he or she has had experience in a job for which there exists no completely appropriate prior training. Moreover, as Nixon did in 1972, presidents can campaign by doing their jobs, while challengers, as George McGovern discovered, have to manufacture policy positions that may dissolve on close scrutiny or criticism.

The life of the incumbent is not necessarily one of undiluted joy. If the economic situation worsens, if terrorists strike, if a race riot erupts, if another nation is lost to hostile forces, whether communist or fundamentalist, the incumbent president is likely at least over the long run to be blamed. Whether really to blame or not, presidents are held responsible and have to take the consequences. Herbert Hoover felt deeply the sting of this phenomenon when the people punished him as incumbent president for the Great Depression.[114]

Incumbents have a record; they have or have not done things, and they may be held accountable for their sins of omission or commission. Not so the candidates out of office, who can criticize freely without always presenting realistic alternatives or necessarily taking their own advice once elected. The "missile gap" of John Kennedy's 1960 campaign turned out to be something of a chimera after he got into the White House, and he never found it possible to act much differently about the situation concerning Quemoy and Matsu islands near mainland China than did Dwight Eisenhower, despite their over-publicized "differences" about this question during the campaign. Richard Nixon could complain about the problem of "law and order" in 1968 without promising anything more concrete than a new attorney general, which any new president would have appointed anyway.

In 1980 candidate Reagan said "ask yourself if you are as well off today as you were four years ago" and voters, for the most part erroneously, responded as Reagan hoped, in the negative.[115] Candidate Reagan was able to blame "stagflation," the unwelcome combination of high inflation and unemployment, on President Carter. The considerable Republican losses in the 1982 congressional elections, combined with the ability of Democrats to blame the Republican president for unemployment, placed Reagan in the same difficult defensive position his predecessor had been in a few years earlier. Reagan's popularity returned with economic recovery but, as the Iran-*contra* affair showed, even an alleged "Teflon" president has difficulty escaping blame when things go wrong on his watch. The incumbent is naturally cast as the defender of his or her administration and the challenger as the attacker who promises better things to come. We cannot expect to hear the person in office say that the opposition could probably do as well or to hear the challenger declare that he or she really could not do any better than the incumbent, although in a political system that encourages moderation and has enormous built-in inertia, such as the American system, both statements may be close to the truth.

While opponents can to some extent permit themselves to be irresponsible or carried away by exuberance, presidents cannot detach themselves from office while campaigning, and they must recognize that other nations are listening when they make statements. The president's very superiority of information may turn out to be a handicap, if he or she cannot make certain statements or reveal sources for statements without committing a breach of security. Opponents can attack the incumbent's record, but the incumbent may have difficulty finding a comparable record to assail on the other side—unless, of course, a challenger succeeds at making his or her own proposals the issue. Barry Goldwater and George McGovern managed to do this, more or less across the board, on many issues. Walter Mondale's promise of higher taxes provided ammunition for President Reagan's 1984 reelection campaign.

Barring catastrophic events—depression, war, scandal—the president's power is most certainly strong enough to assure renomination within the limits imposed by the anti-third-term (the Twenty-second) amendment to the Constitution. This is not merely because the presidency is the greatest, most visible office in the land, with claims on the loyalty of many, if not all, potential rivals. The party can hardly hope to win by repudiating the president. To refuse the incumbent the nomination would, most politicians believe, be tantamount to confessing political bankruptcy or ineptitude. The fact that primary voters, not politicians, now make the relevant decisions lends a note of uncertainty to what used to be a sure thing.

This rule was bent but not broken in 1980 by Edward Kennedy's prenomination opposition to Carter and in 1976 by the Reagan challenge to Ford. Nor was it broken in 1968. The challenges of Eugene McCarthy and Robert Kennedy to Lyndon Johnson in that year demonstrated that the costs of party insurgency are high: not only do insurgents rarely win their party's nomination; their party also usually loses the election in years when party insurgency is strong. It was not only that Senator Edward Kennedy sought to take the nomination away from Jimmy Carter in 1980, but also that he persisted right up through the convention, refusing to give Carter his wholehearted endorsement, that hurt the Democrats. Consequently candidate Carter was unable to focus on his Republican opponent as early as he would have liked.

The decline of the influence of state parties in national conventions and the rise of primary elections makes presidents less influential than they once were. Presidents have a harder time controlling primaries than influencing party leaders, and this affects presidential power over conventions. Overt attempts to designate a successor make less sense for an outgoing president in a system dominated by primaries, for the risks of failure are high.

Incumbency as a Liability: The Vice Presidency

The incumbent president does have some advantages; it is the incumbent vice president who is seeking to succeed an incumbent president of the same party who suffers the most, as Nixon discovered in 1960 and Humphrey in 1968, and Albert Gore may discover in 2000. A vice president suffers from the disadvantages of having to defend an existing record and of being a new face. A vice president may find it difficult to defend a record he or she did not make and may not wholly care for. He or she cannot attack the administration in office without alienating the president and selling their party short, and a vice president cannot claim to have experience in the presidential office. This is the most difficult strategic problem of all for candidates.[116]

George Bush in 1988 was the first vice president to succeed a retiring president of his own party since Martin Van Buren succeeded Andrew Jackson in 1837. Why, despite the historical rarity of the event, did Bush win? He obtained the nomination of his party largely, it appears, because primary voters in the Republican Party considered him the logical successor to Ronald Reagan, and Reagan was extremely popular at the end of his second term. This may help also to explain why Bush won the election. At least three theories—all of them meritorious—have been invoked to explain his success.[117] They refer, respectively, to peace and prosperity, to the conduct of the campaign, and to structural properties of the parties and the nominating process. The first theory is refreshingly straightforward. It says, simply, that if nothing is badly disturbing the electorate, then incumbents will do well. George Bush was of course not an incumbent president, but as the sitting vice president he was as close to an incumbent president as it is possible to be without actually being one. In the election, most incumbents, whether they were Democrats or Republicans, did extraordinarily well for all offices, as they do in conditions of peace and prosperity. Most, of course, were Democrats. Those scholars who use fancy models to attempt to forecast elections have, on the whole, employed assumptions stressing such variables as the condition of the economy somewhat in advance of the election, and they all produced numbers suggesting a Bush victory.[118] Indeed, some of them did so even during the spring and summer months when Michael Dukakis was leading George Bush by a wide margin in the public opinion polls. The second theory also seems to us entirely plausible. It points out that Vice President Bush ran an effective campaign and Governor Dukakis did not. Jerry Roberts of the *San Francisco Chronicle* gave an excellent summary of professional opinion on this subject, noting the following features of the Dukakis campaign:

> A fatal reluctance to respond to Bush's bare-knuckle attacks. The Republican hit Dukakis as weak on defense and soft on crime, attacking him over the Pledge of Allegiance, prison furloughs and the death penalty. By the time Dukakis fired back in late fall, it was too late. Many voters by then believed the attacks because they had gone unanswered.

A failure to find a consistent campaign theme. Running against peace and prosperity, Dukakis tried campaigning on competence, the middle class squeeze and the unfairness of Bush's attacks before settling on traditional Democratic economic populism in the closing weeks of the race.

A disastrous media campaign. Matched against Bush's state-of-the-art television commercials—which meshed precisely with the message he was delivering on the campaign trail—Dukakis' shifting set of ads had little impact. They were produced by a series of media specialists and drafted by committee, and were criticized as confusing, obscure and without much content.

"We absolutely should have won this race," said California Democratic Party Chairman Peter Kelly. "What happened was George Bush defined Mike Dukakis before Dukakis defined himself."[119]

It is possible to dwell too long on particulars of the 1988 campaign. There is unusually strong agreement among campaign professionals that Dukakis campaigned badly in the general election. This overlooks the fact that he did well enough in the primary season and in dealing with Jesse Jackson thereafter and in his vice presidential pick of the magisterial Senator Lloyd Bentsen. There is, likewise, strong agreement that the Bush campaign was well tailored to make the best of the vice president's chances, conveniently overlooking the selection as vice presidential candidate of Senator Dan Quayle. So if we accept the professional assessment of the effects of the campaign—as on the whole we do—we must do so in the face of the fact that every winning campaign looks better in retrospect and every losing campaign looks worse than it probably was.

Of the third theory we are especially fond. It helps understand not only the election of 1988 but the entire set of presidential elections over the past thirty years, where Republicans have been so successful. And not only presidential elections, but also the great and persistent anomaly in the American political system in which Republicans frequently succeed in presidential elections, and at the same time, Democrats (until 1994) dominate overall, as measured by electoral success at all other levels, party identification, and party registrations. Republican gains in the 1990s put them on an even footing, but were nowhere near the large Democratic advantages that survived even the Nixon landslide in 1972 and the Reagan landslide in 1984.

Essentially, the argument is that after the drastic reforms of the presidential nominating process that took place in the wake of the chaotic 1968 Democratic National Convention, the system changed radically from a coalition-building regime to a factional-mobilization regime. Over the long run this harms Democrats and helps Republicans in the general election because the Democrats, although they are the larger of the two parties, are also far more factionally fragmented and therefore greatly disadvantaged in a long nomination process in which there are no incentives or occasions for coalition formation. Because the Republicans are much more easily mobilized and coordinated through their basic ideological similarities, the lack of coalition-building incentives harms them less.[120]

Bush nevertheless also had to contend with the disadvantages of the vice presidency, and this must undoubtedly be on the mind of Vice President Gore during the 2000 election cycle. Thomas Riley Marshall, the genial Hoosier who was Woodrow Wilson's vice president, once observed that the office he had in the Capitol was so little protected from tourists that they used to come by and stare at him like a monkey in the zoo. "Only," he complained, "they never offer me any peanuts." This is the way vice presidents have viewed their constitutional office, not just its physical setting, for a long time. "Not worth a pitcher of warm spit" was the bowdlerized version of John Nance Garner's rueful conclusion in the mid-1930s. "A mere mechanical tool to wind up the clock" was the way the first vice president, John Adams, described himself. "My country has in its wisdom contrived for me the most insignificant office that was the invention of man."

The main constitutional function of the vice president is to wait. As Mr. Dooley once said, "Every morning it is his business to call at the White House and inquire after the President's health. When told that the President was never better, he gives three cheers and departs with a heavy heart."[121] Clearly this is not much of a job for a major political leader who is used to active leadership. Yet suppose a sudden tragedy should befall the president. Can we afford in the inevitable days of uncertainty that follow such an event to replace the president with anything less than a major political leader who can step into the breach immediately, do the president's job, and do it well? This is the first and fundamental dilemma of the vice presidency and, as the quotation from John Adams amply testifies, it has been with us since the founding of the Republic. From this dilemma flow the problems characteristic of the modern vice presidency.

We can date the modern vice presidency from 12 April 1945, the day Franklin Roosevelt died. The next day his successor, Harry S Truman, remarked to some newspaper reporters: "Boys, if you ever pray, pray for me now. I don't know whether you fellows ever had a load of hay fall on you, but when they told me yesterday what had happened, I felt like the moon, the stars, and all the planets had fallen on me." Truman had been a respected but not a leading senator before he assumed the vice presidency. In his three months in that office, Vice President Truman saw President Roosevelt only a few short times. As vice president he had not been told of the Manhattan Project to build the atomic bomb. Sticking closely to the duties prescribed under the Constitution, Truman had spent most of his time on Capitol Hill, presiding over the Senate. His knowledge of the affairs of the executive branch and of foreign and military operations was the knowledge of an experienced legislator and not the inside information routinely available to top policy-makers in the Roosevelt administration. Truman wrote later, "it is a mighty leap from the vice-presidency to the presidency when one is forced to make it without warning."[122]

Since Harry Truman made the leap in the waning days of World War II, the world has grown more complicated, and so has the presidency. Efforts have accordingly been made to update the vice presidency to meet modern conditions. The vice president now sits with the National Security Council as a matter of right; under President Eisenhower, the vice president attended all meetings of the cabinet at the president's invitation and presided in the president's absence. In addition to his Capitol Hill quarters, Vice President Johnson had a suite of offices in the Executive Office Building adjacent to the White House. For a while, President Nixon moved Spiro Agnew to an office down the hall from his own. Nelson Rockefeller was not only made head of the Domestic Council by President Ford, but also was allowed to bring in his own people as top staff assistants in this presidential agency. Vice President Mondale, with an office in the White House only a few doors away from the Oval Office, was given an unprecedented full, though junior, partnership by President Carter. Vice President Bush's relations with President Reagan were complicated by worries among the Reagan staff about Bush's future ambitions, a common enough difficulty between presidents and vice presidents, somewhat exacerbated in this case by their differences in age and in political outlook. But Bush kept the White House office, and he played a part in foreign policy. Vice President Gore's role constitutes a return to the modern trend. By all accounts, he is more active, influential, and trusted even than Mondale was.[123]

In return for continuous exposure to the entire range of problems confronting the government, vastly improved access to the president, and a closer view of the burdens of the presidency, the modern vice president must also carry some of these burdens. Which burdens are carried, how many, and how far are up to the president. Withholding cooperation would impair the vice president's relationship with the president. This would be bound to affect his or her capacity to fulfill the constitutional obligation of the vice presidency, which is to be genuinely prepared in case of dire need.

Vice President Gore comes closer than any vice president in history to being second in command in a president's administration. More often, the vice president is entirely removed from any chain of command in the government. This guaranteed the independence of the vice president in the days of Aaron Burr, John C. Calhoun, Charles Dawes, and other free spirits who have occupied the office. Today, the situation is quite different: it is much easier for other high members of a president's administration to maintain independence from the presidency. Top administrative officials can constitute a loyal opposition on government policy within the executive branch because their obligations run in at least three directions: upward to the president, downward to the agencies whose programs they supervise within the administration, and outward to the clientele their agencies serve. Political executives serve the president best who serve their clients with devotion and promote the interests of their agencies with vigor. Executives know, moreover, that if in the process they conflict too much with presidential plans or priorities, the president can always fire them. If the president fails them in some serious way, they can resign, as Attorney General Elliot Richardson did when President Nixon ordered him to remove Special Prosecutor Archibald Cox during the memorable "Saturday Night Massacre" of October 1973, or as Secretary of State Cyrus Vance did from the Carter administration in 1979 over the aborted rescue mission to Iran.

Vice presidents can hardly fulfill their constitutional responsibilities by resigning, nor, in midterm, can they be dismissed. They have no anchor in the bureaucracy, no interest-group constituency. Thus, uniquely in the executive branch, modern vice presidents must discipline themselves to loyalty to their president. This sometimes has painful consequences for vice presidents, especially when they attempt to emerge from the shadow of the president and run for the presidency on their own. The worst modern case was probably Vice President Hubert Humphrey's difficulty in persuading opponents of the Vietnam war that he had deeply disagreed with President Johnson's policies, as he had privately done, while publicly defending them. Even after four years out of office, Walter Mondale found himself criticized for President Carter's perceived failures. Vice President George Bush was alternately attacked as servile and insufficiently loyal.[124] Like Humphrey and Nixon before him, Bush found it difficult to run independently on his own record.

There seems to be no way for vice presidents to avoid the dilemmas built into the office. Unless scrupulously loyal, they cannot get the access to the president that they need to discharge their constitutional function; when loyal to the president, they are saddled, at least in the short run, with whatever characteristics of the president or the administration's program that the president's enemies or their own care to fasten on them. A vice president sits there in the limelight, visible, vulnerable, and for the most part, powerless.

From 1836 until 1960, when Richard Nixon was nominated, no incumbent vice president was put forward for the presidency. Since 1960, many vice presidents—Humphrey, Ford, Johnson, Rockefeller, Mondale, Bush, Quayle, Gore—have tried for the presidency. It may be that the name recognition of vice presidents or, as Howard Reiter suggests, the decline of the ability of party leaders to select their own candidate, has made vice presidents leading candidates for the presidency.[125] Some—Truman, Johnson, and Ford—became presidents before seeking election as their party's presidential nominee, but the others did it on their own. Now even defeated vice presidential candidates, from Lodge to Muskie to Shriver to Mondale and Dole, launch their own presidential nominating efforts four years later.

As long as vice presidents have some chance eventually to run for the presidency, as they do at present, and are not arbitrarily excluded from further consideration as independent political leaders in their own right, there will be plenty of takers for the vice presidential nomination. This contributes to the strength of political parties. Vice presidential nominees can balance tickets, help to unite a warring party, and campaign effectively with party workers and before the public—as, for example, Senator Lyndon Johnson did with conspicuous success in the election of 1960, and George Bush and Walter Mondale did in 1980, and Lloyd Bentsen and Al Gore did in 1988 and 1992. Thus, vice presidential nominees can help elect a president. It is after the campaign is over that the vice president's problems begin.

Convertibility of Resources

Clearly, the social framework within which presidential election strategies must be pursued distributes advantages and disadvantages rather importantly between candidates and parties. We have attempted to explain why the unequal distribution of key resources such as money and control over information do not necessarily lead to election victories for the parties and candidates who possess and use most of these resources. Might there not, however, be a cumulative effect that would greatly assist those who possessed both more money and more control over information? This effect may exist, but it could not be of overwhelming importance, since the Democrats, who are usually disadvantaged in both respects, have won more than half the elections since 1932. We can suggest a few reasons for Democratic strength despite these disadvantages. First, the Democrats are able to convert other resources into money and control over information, thereby narrowing the gap during campaigns. Second, the Democrats have superior access to other important resources, which may counter the Republican superiority in money and control over the media of information.

Once the Democratic Party assumed the presidency in 1933 and held it for twenty years, it was able to use the resource of official position to collect campaign funds because contributors wanted access to the winner. The Democratic candidate could also get greater news coverage because the incumbent president's activities are newsworthy no matter what his or her party. The alliance of the Democrats with the large industrial unions has, at times, meant that the party has received contributions in the form of personal electioneering, for which the Republicans had to lay out cash or do without. The superiority (perhaps the mere existence) of Democratic organizations in cities of large populations with strategic impact on the electoral college has sometimes led to the availability of election workers who did not have to be paid in cash—at least not in cash the presidential candidate had to raise during the campaign. Public funding has brought expenditures in the general campaign to a fairly even level. The fact that Democrats still maintain a lead over Republicans in party identification is perhaps the most effective resource in the Democratic arsenal.

These Democratic assets are still important, but in each case the Democratic advantage has declined. The Republicans have controlled the White House (and the benefits that entails) for twenty of the past thirty-two years. Unions and urban political organizations are less important and smaller than they once were and are facing difficult times. The assistance they can offer the Democrats is limited. Finally, the Democratic edge in party identification has shrunk in recent years. The Democrats' ability to counter Republican assets has eroded.

PART II

Sequences

The next two chapters follow the chronology of the election year, first dealing with processes leading up to the nominations of major candidates, then discussing the course of the campaign leading up to election night. Many of the moves that actors execute take on meaning when they are viewed in the light of their activities at different stages of the nomination and election process.

CHAPTER 4

The Nomination Process

Once upon a time, presidential nominations were won by candidates who courted the support of party leaders from the several states. These leaders appeared at the national convention usually as heads of delegations representing their state parties. That system is history. Now, nominations are won by accumulating pledged delegates in a state-by-state march through primary elections and delegate-selection caucuses—a time-consuming, complicated, and costly process.[1]

For a party with an incumbent president running for reelection, the rules for the selection of a nominee are not terribly important. Ordinarily, challenges to a sitting president from within his own party are doomed to failure. The ground rules governing nominations are, however, extremely important in shaping the behavior of candidates and activists from any party with no incumbent. In 2000 this means both the Republicans and the Democrats, since President Clinton cannot succeed himself for a third term.

Some of these rules have been put in place as the result of national campaign finance laws. Others were enacted by the Democrats to govern their own procedures. Since these rules required changes in state laws governing the selection process, on the whole they apply to both parties.

1. All Democratic convention delegates must be selected within a three-month period (which three months to be determined by the Democratic National Committee), and each individual state must set candidate filing deadlines thirty to ninety days before the election.[2] This means candidates must contest primary elections because delegates are chosen in those elections: they are no longer "beauty contests" functioning merely as signals to party leaders about which candidates have the support of voters.[3]

2. Candidates of either party may be eligible for federal funding of their primary expenses of more than $10 million each if they can raise at

least $5,000 cash in each of twenty or more states before the primary (only the first $250 of each contribution being eligible for matching).

3. In the Democratic Party, any candidate in a statewide primary or caucus who receives more than 15 percent of the vote obtains a proportionate share of the delegates per congressional district.

4. The Republican Party has no such nationally mandated minimum threshold. States may choose proportional representation, winner-take-all, or some combination. Republican delegates are apportioned to each state by a formula that gives added weight to states that voted Republican in the last presidential, congressional, and gubernatorial elections. Thus, Republican candidates for the nomination have an incentive to win in states that go Republican in national and state elections; but each state has its own rules apportioning delegates to candidates. Some states, such as California, are winner-take-all for Republicans.

5. Democratic elected officials (members of Congress and governors) as well as officials of the Democratic National Committee have automatic seats as delegates and voting rights in the convention and are not required to pledge their support to any candidate as a condition of delegate status. This accounted for 15 percent of the Democratic delegates in 1996. Democrats also require state delegations to be evenly divided between men and women.

6. Since 1976 the position of state party leaders has been reduced to making deals to support one or another candidate at the time of the state primary or caucus—not at the national convention, which is much too late. Thus the candidate's job is to attract support from state party leaders by looking like a probable winner as early as possible.

The rules are important; they drive the strategies used by candidates. The most important imperative under the rules, as they have existed since the 1972 election, is that candidates compete in procedures that differ from state to state under which delegates are chosen by large statewide electorates. This contrasts sharply with the procedures used in an earlier era, in which candidates focused on members of the state party hierarchies, who usually chose the delegates. The rules of delegate selection and fund-raising now require candidates to obtain a broad base of support within states (for delegates) and across states (for money). Especially on the Democratic side, where delegates are allocated in proportion to the support each candidate demonstrates at the polls, candidates must compete for delegates more or less everywhere to stand a chance of reaching 50 percent plus one at the convention. Proportionate rules for counting votes encourage Democrats to enter more primaries because there are delegates to be had even if one does not win a majority. Primaries also generate attention, which means more people will be enticed out of the woodwork to make financial contributions, which the government will then match.

Before the Primaries

The first overall constraint on the system is that the more people you have to convince, the longer it takes. The nomination process has become very long, giving early starters an advantage. The second overall constraint is that the more restrictions placed on the expenditure of money, the harder it is for newcomers to attract public notice to get into the race. This, too, dictates an earlier start to the campaign. Anybody whose name is known ahead of time—a movie star, a sports figure, an incumbent of high office—gets a boost.

Among the axioms of conventional wisdom to bite the dust in 1972 was the notion that an early announcement of candidacy was a sign of a weak candidate and that it therefore behooved front-runners to avoid an early disclosure of their plans, with all the inconvenience and running around that an active campaign entails. This coyness destroyed the chances of the 1972 early Democratic front-runner, Senator Edmund S. Muskie. In 1976 this lesson was greatly reinforced when Jimmy Carter, an outsider, parlayed early, narrow wins in Iowa, New Hampshire, and Florida into the presidency. Thus the congressional elections of 1978 were barely over before a variety of Republicans announced their candidacies for the 1980 race and began to qualify for federal support. Two Democratic candidates qualified for the 1984 federal subsidy by the end of the first week of 1983.[4] By June 1987 seven candidates were campaigning for the 1988 Republican nomination and seven for the Democratic,[5] and the Democratic front-runner, Gary Hart, had already been sidelined because of publicity surrounding charges of adultery.[6] By March 1995 there was enormous activity among Republican hopefuls. Bill Bennett, Richard Cheney, Jack Kemp, and Dan Quayle had already declared themselves out of the competition, mostly because they did not believe they could raise the $20 million in early money that was generally regarded as the minimum required to run a serious campaign. Senator Phil Gramm of Texas, flush with contributions, tossed his hat in the ring, as did Lamar Alexander, former governor of Tennessee, Pat Buchanan, and Senator Richard Lugar of Indiana. Senate Majority Leader Bob Dole and California Governor Pete Wilson hovered on the brink of an official announcement, as did three or four others.[7]

Similarly, by March 1999 the campaign was already well underway. On the Democratic side, Vice President Al Gore and former New Jersey Senator Bill Bradley had formally organized their campaigns, while four other potential candidates (House Minority Leader Richard A. Gephardt, Nebraska Senator Bob Kerrey, Senator John Kerry of Massachusetts, and Senator Paul Wellstone of Minnesota) had already publicly announced they would not make the race. On the Republican side, ten candidates were actively campaigning, including the two front-runners in public opinion polls, Texas Governor George W. Bush and former Cabinet Secretary Elizabeth Dole. Others had already chosen not to make the race, including Senator John Ashcroft of Missouri and former Governor Pete Wilson of California. Two, former Tennessee Governor Lamar Alexander and publisher Steve Forbes, had barely ended their unsuccessful campaigns from 1996 before they began seeking the 2000 nomination. Alexander and former Vice President Dan Quayle ran full campaigns only to drop out, defeated, by the end of September 1999—several months before the first votes were to be cast in Iowa and New Hampshire. Evidence that the race is already in an advanced stage long before voters become directly involved can be seen in the large sums candidates raise a full year before the primaries (see table 4.1).[8]

During the long preprimary phase, the candidates also undertake a certain amount of ideological preparation, attempting to shape a message that will appeal to probable voters in their party primaries. Knowing that most of the voters in Republican primaries are right of center, Vice President Bush,

TABLE 4.1 EARLY MONEY IN THE 2000 ELECTION

Candidate	Money raised 1 January–30 June 1999 (in millions of dollars)
Republicans:	
George W. Bush	37.2
Steve Forbes	9.5
John McCain	6.3
Elizabeth Dole	3.5
Dan Quayle	3.5
Gary Bauer	3.4
Lamar Alexander	2.5
Patrick Buchanan	2.4
Alan Keyes	1.9
Robert Smith	1.6
Democrats:	
Al Gore	19.6
Bill Bradley	11.7

SOURCE: "Money for the Presidential Campaign," *New York Times*, 24 July 1999, A9.

Representative Kemp, and Senator Dole spent a lot of time in 1987 aiming their remarks (and shading their voting records) toward this part of the spectrum. Similarly, the fact that the dominant faction of the Democratic Party is left of center has not been lost among Democratic contenders. As an adviser to a rival candidate described Gary Hart's preprimary activities in 1986, "He saw how liberals and labor dominated things in 1984 and he's determined he's not going to let anyone get to his left."[9] In 1995 Senate Majority Leader Dole, the most visible of the Republican hopefuls, struggled in public with the challenge of finding the correct "conservative" stand on new issues such as the conflict in Bosnia.[10]

Part of the preprimary task of the candidate is to achieve the status of being "taken seriously" by the news media. Being taken seriously ordinarily requires that a candidate should have won some major election for public office. In addition, the news media pay attention to signs that candidates are hiring competent campaign staff—fund-raisers, lawyers, accountants, poll takers, media buyers, advance staff, speechwriters, issue analysts, spotters of political talent in the early states—and are establishing a beachhead in early battlegrounds, visiting Iowa and New Hampshire, doing respectably in straw polls conducted at various party meetings around the country, polls that everyone says "don't count." All this activity is highly visible to the increasingly watchful news media, who in turn pronounce candidates to be "serious" or "not serious," with attendant consequences for the candidate's public visibility and credibility with donors of campaign funds.

The lessons of the preprimary period in the emerging nomination system have become clear: before the delegate-selection season begins, candidates must organize to achieve personal visibility. Visibility is important because in order to win it is necessary to appeal to voters in primary elections and caucuses. Organization is important because that is what it takes to turn out voters. Because a great many candidates begin the election season with presidential hopes, the course of selection is a winnowing process in which the successive hurdles of the weeks in which primaries and caucuses are held knock off more and more hopefuls until only one survivor is left. In advance of these events, the candidate's tasks are to raise money, increase personal visibility, and give personal attention to states that will select delegates early in the process.

Preprimary activities thus take up more and more time and absorb more and more resources in preparation for delegate-selection caucuses and especially the primary elections, which in 2000 will select delegates in as many as forty-four states.

Iowa and New Hampshire: The First Hurdles

The party rules that provide for all delegate selection to take place in the year of the election also prescribe that the selection processes—state caucuses and primaries—take place within a limited period of time. Two exceptions, based on accidents of history, have thus far always been granted by the Democratic Party, and the Republicans have always gone along. Iowa, which selects its delegates through a series of broadly participatory local, regional, and state conventions, has a license to be first in the nation. New Hampshire, the nation's first primary, comes next—in recent years, within a week.[11]

These Iowa precinct caucuses are only the first stage of a delegate-selection process that actually occurs somewhat later, at state party conventions. Although it is the caucuses, the early events, that get the publicity, frequently candidates who do not win in the caucuses may end up with Iowa delegates to the national convention, as George Bush did in 1988.[12]

Given the complications in ascertaining what the outcomes of the precinct caucuses will yield in eventual delegates, it is a wonder that there is so much news coverage of the Iowa caucuses. In 1984, according to an actual count of news coverage appearing on all three television networks plus in the *New York Times*, Iowa, with 2.5 percent of the U.S. population, received 12.8 percent of the total news coverage accorded the presidential race from January to June.[13]

The coverage is there because the Iowa caucuses are, in effect, the gateway to a long and complex nomination process, and all players and all observers very much want whatever information they can glean from the Iowa precinct caucuses, if only to position themselves for the next round. The media need to know to whom to give special attention. Financial supporters of various candidates want to know whether it is worthwhile to continue to give, or to steer, money to their first choices or whether it is time to jump to other alternatives. Voters want to know which candidacies are viable, which futile.[14] Thus the grounds for paying special attention to the Iowa caucuses are that the system as a whole is conspicuously front-loaded, and Iowa is farthest to the front. What does it mean to have a front-loaded nomination process?

The temptation to ignore history is ever present. Each quadrennial nomination sequence has plenty of elements of uniqueness, and our entire historical experience of presidential elections yields very few instances at best. Even further constraining a historical view is the fact that whatever happened before the drastic changes of the post-1968 reforms should probably be ignored on the grounds that the system overall was fundamentally altered by these reforms. It is the reforms that front-loaded the presidential nominating process.[15] Consequently, considering evidence from 1968 and before is bound to be drastically misleading as a guide to the structural constraints and strategic opportunities that shape the choices of contemporary actors. So we are left, in effect, with exactly fourteen historical data points, seven Democratic, seven Republican, representing the elections of 1972, 1976, 1980, 1984, 1988, 1992, and 1996. Owing to the effects of incumbency, these can be reduced even further.

1972

In 1972 the Iowa caucuses were for the first time set early in the year, on 24 January. This date was arrived at because the Democratic state convention was to be held on 20 May, owing to the availability on that date of a suitable hall. Working backward from 20 May, adequate time had to be provided to prepare for each of the earlier stages of the process, and the entire sequence had to be completed within the same calendar year as the national convention. Thus the January date.[16]

In 1972 the Republican incumbent, Richard Nixon, had only token opposition in Iowa from two representatives in Congress, Paul (Pete) McCloskey of California, ideologically on his left, and John Ashbrook of Ohio on his right.

The Democratic caucuses, in contrast, were quite important. The presumed front-runner, Senator Edmund S. Muskie of Maine, operating under obsolete strategic premises, had failed to announce his candidacy until 4 January 1972. Neither Muskie nor Senator George McGovern invested much effort in Iowa. The day after the first-round caucuses, the newspapers reported unofficially, with incomplete returns, that Muskie beat McGovern in the precinct caucuses in Iowa 35.5 percent to 22.6 percent with 35.8 percent uncommitted. The unexpected closeness of this margin pushed Muskie into overwork and an unaccustomed public display of emotional behavior in front of the building housing the offices of the *Manchester Union Leader* in New Hampshire.[17] When the news media analysts were finished with the New Hampshire results, prior "expectations" that the U.S. senator from a neighboring state should win an overwhelming victory, over 50 percent, completely obscured the fact that Muskie had in fact won once again (46 percent to 37 percent). Because his win was 4 or 5 points less impressive than "expected," Muskie's support, especially financial support, began to dry up, and he withdrew from the race altogether by 27 April.

The front-running Muskie presidential campaign was nibbled to death by ducks before it began. This extraordinary spectacle gave unmistakable evidence that changing the rules had changed the game. Preconvention skirmishes were no longer simply important evidence to be taken into account by party leaders in making nominations; they were the contest itself.

Iowa did not administer the coup de grace to Muskie; that happened in New Hampshire. At most, what happened in Iowa energized the participants in the New Hampshire primary and structured the alternatives for New Hampshire voters.

1976

Once again, an incumbent was running on the Republican side. This time, however, Gerald Ford was the incumbent. Ford, who succeeded to the presidency when Richard Nixon resigned, had never been a Republican presidential nominee, and he was not an eloquent defender of his presidency. He was faced by a serious challenge from Ronald Reagan. Iowa came out a dead heat between the two; both ended up with eighteen delegates to the national convention. Ford won the official straw poll the night of the precinct caucuses, but by only a small margin. R. W. Apple of the *New York Times* characterized the Republican effort in Iowa by both candidates as "all but invisible, with only marginal organizational efforts by the supporters of Mr. Ford and Mr. Reagan."[18] Ford's victory in New Hampshire made him the front-runner for renomination, although Reagan rallied later in the year.[19]

On the Democratic side, the candidate who focused hardest on Iowa was Jimmy Carter. Hamilton Jordan, Carter's campaign manager, put together a strategy that was exactly three events deep, requiring strong showings in Iowa and New Hampshire, and a careful positioning as the anti-Wallace southerner in the Florida primary.[20] The Carter strategy dovetailed nicely with those of his main competitors. Henry Jackson's campaign was designed to start late: a token effort in Iowa (19 January) and New Hampshire (24 February) followed by an unequivocal win in Massachusetts (2 March), only a week later. After all, Massachusetts's 104 delegates greatly exceeded the Iowa–New Hampshire combination of 64. Thus Jackson's decision to play from "strength."[21]

Morris Udall's campaign was strategically incoherent. First Udall made an effort in Iowa, then, in an attempt to stretch his resources to cover as many primaries as possible (there were thirty Democratic primaries in 1976), Udall's campaign slackened its Iowa effort. As news coverage focused ever more strongly on Iowa, however, Udall at the last minute recommitted resources to the race.[22] He was too late. Although he finished as high as second in seven primaries in 1976, in Iowa Udall came in fifth with 5.9 percent of the vote, behind uncommitted with 37 percent of the caucus vote and Jimmy Carter with 28 percent.

The next day, *New York Times* reporter Apple minimized the strong uncommitted sentiment and created the first major instance in which the Iowa caucuses combined importantly with mass-media spin to launch a presidential candidacy. His story on the front page read:

> Former Governor Jimmy Carter of Georgia scored an impressive victory in yesterday's Iowa Democratic precinct caucuses, demonstrating strength among rural, blue-collar, black, and suburban voters.
>
> Mr. Carter defeated his closest rival, Senator Birch Bayh of Indiana, by a margin of more than 2–1, and left his other four challengers far behind. The uncommitted vote, which many Iowa politicians had forecast at more than 50 percent, amounted to only about a third of the total, slightly more than that of Mr. Carter.[23]

This article, with its strong and coherent story line, cast a long shadow. It contained many elements that in later years would worry journalists, notably the use of such a word as "impressive" (to whom?) in the lead of what ostensibly was a news story and the belittling of the uncommitted vote because of the disappointed "forecasts" or expectations of anonymous politicians. *New Yorker* political writer Elizabeth Drew's diary for the day after the Iowa caucuses said:

> This morning, Carter, who managed to get to New York on time, was interviewed on the *CBS Morning News*. The *Today* show and ABC's *Good Morning America* also ran segments on Carter. On the *CBS Evening News,* Walter Cronkite said that the Iowa voters have spoken "and for the Democrats what they said was 'Jimmy Carter.' "[24]

This coverage set the stage for New Hampshire, where Carter alone ran as a centrist Democrat and received 28.4 percent of the vote. Although he filed a slate of delegates, Jackson sat the primary out, and no fewer than four candidates, Udall (at 22.7 percent), Sargent Shriver (at 8.2 percent), Fred Harris (at 10.8 percent), and Birch Bayh (at 15.2 percent) divided the liberal Democratic vote.

1980

By 1980 it was beginning to be understood that there was no such thing as a successful presidential strategy that ignored early delegate-selection events. President Carter's managers worked hard to structure the order in which states selected delegates so as to maximize the impact of favorable publicity, seeking to move southern primaries where they expected to be strong up to the head of the line.[25] Carter, aided by a rally round the flag at the start of the Iranian hostage crisis, beat Edward Kennedy in Iowa 59.1 percent to 31.2 percent. Iowa momentum helped Carter amass a majority of delegates far more quickly in 1980 than he had done in 1976.[26]

On the Republican side, Iowa nearly did in the front-runner, Ronald Reagan. Saving his energy, Reagan campaigned only eight days in the state and passed up the major all-candidate Republican debate. Caucus turnout on the Republican side jumped to 110,000 participants from a mere 22,000 in 1976. Howard Baker, an interested party, remarked that the Iowa caucuses had become "the functional equivalent of a primary." George Bush edged Reagan 31.5 percent to 29.4 percent in the caucus vote—actually a straw poll reported early to the news media—and as political commentators Jack Germond and Jules Witcover observed, the Iowa caucuses served in 1980 to clear "the underbrush of candidates with little future ... establishing a definite pecking order among those who remained."[27]

Only a drastic change of strategy (including the replacement of John Sears, the strategist) and, as we have seen, some extraordinarily vigorous propagandizing by the *Manchester Union Leader* saved Ronald Reagan's bacon by aiding his comeback in New Hampshire.[28] Reagan campaigned energetically and ambushed Bush at a key New Hampshire debate by "spontaneously" agreeing to let also-rans onto the platform. It also helped Reagan enormously that the gap between Iowa and New Hampshire was a full month (21 January to 26 February), thus permitting *Union Leader* publicity to counteract Iowa momentum. In 1976 that gap had helped Carter, a "winner" in Iowa; in 1980 it helped Reagan, an Iowa "loser."

By the 1980 election, the strong interdependence between early delegate selection and media publicity could easily be observed. The "pecking order" of which Germond and Witcover wrote was, after all, a fabrication chiefly valuable in the construction of coherent news stories. The success of Jimmy Carter in 1976, and even more striking, the failure of Henry Jackson, suggested that it would be hard, perhaps impossible, to ascertain the preferences of primary electorates unmediated by the news—and news media evaluations—of how the various candidates were doing. These characterizations could easily take on the coloration of self-fulfilling prophecies.

1984

Nothing doing on the Republican side; Reagan's incumbency meant no contest in Iowa. Democratic rules were rewritten, ostensibly to counteract media influence: states were required to select delegates within a three-month "window" so that many states would act on any given Tuesday, thus (it was hoped) confounding media attempts to start a single unified bandwagon. The effort was a failure, in part because both Iowa and New Hampshire received exemptions from the window and continued to act first. In Iowa, on the Democratic side, Walter Mondale overwhelmed everybody, collecting 44.5 percent of the vote in a large field of contenders. Gary Hart came in second with a dismal 14.8 percent of the vote.

This was enough to identify Hart, rather than John Glenn, who finished in sixth place with 5.3 percent of the vote, as the strongest non-Mondale candidate. The news media constructed a horse race out of the unpromising material of the Hart candidacy, gave him extraordinary news coverage for the ensuing week, and boosted him into a win in the New Hampshire primary.[29]

It seems clear enough why the news media need a horse race, given their extraordinary investment in delegate-selection coverage and the logic of their competition for business. Iowa caucuses help the news media sort out the story: it was the Iowa caucuses in 1984 that decreed that Gary Hart and not John Glenn should be the "unexpected" horse to make the race against Mondale, and it was the media that made the horse race.

1988

In 1988, with only one week separating Iowa and New Hampshire, the two events might have been expected to interact strongly. Massachusetts Governor Michael Dukakis entered Iowa as the Democratic candidate with the most money and the best organization in the most states—but not in Iowa—and with extremely high and favorable name recognition in New Hampshire, whose Democratic voters are mostly located on the fringes of the Boston metropolitan area. This meant that the only chance the other candidates had to neutralize the favorable impact that the New Hampshire primary was bound to have on the fortunes of the governor of Massachusetts was in Iowa.[30]

In the event, the Iowa Democratic result did not help the Iowa winner in New Hampshire, mainly because what happened on the Republican side in Iowa had such a strong impact on the Democratic race. The big story of Iowa 1988—and there always has to be one big story—was that Pat Robertson came in second and George Bush came in third in the Republican straw poll. That is how the story played in the news media for the week between Iowa and New Hampshire. Obviously, that was bound to have some impact on the Republican race, but not as much as on the race on the Democratic side. Because the Robertson blip absorbed so much attention, it spoiled the chances of the Democratic winner, Richard Gephardt, to capitalize on his Iowa win to become the focal alternative to Michael Dukakis in New Hampshire.

In 1984 Gary Hart was able to parlay a 15 percent second-place showing into a media spin that made him the winner in New Hampshire, as figures on late-deciding Democrats showed.[31] In 1976 Jimmy Carter was able to pull out in front of the pack with 29 percent of the vote in the Iowa caucuses. In 1988 a 31 percent win was not enough for Gephardt to turn the same trick. Indeed, the *Wall Street Journal* reported that in the week between the Iowa caucuses and the New Hampshire primary, the coverage Gephardt got on the network evening news programs actually diminished from the week before, from 6:05 minutes to 4:55 minutes.[32] Thus it is not farfetched to argue that although the winner in Iowa did not win the nomination of either party, Iowa did in fact play an influential role in determining the 1988 outcome.

1992

A Senator from Iowa, Tom Harkin, ran for president, and the other Democratic candidates quickly declared the Iowa caucuses irrelevant—a judgment reporters accepted. As Harkin's press secretary said later, "You can't force people to cover what they perceive as a non-event."[33] The focus of press coverage leading up to the New Hampshire primary, then, was not the events in Iowa, but instead the foibles of the Democratic front-runner, Bill Clinton. Governor and Mrs. Clinton had appeared on the CBS news program *60 Minutes* immediately following the Super Bowl in January to respond to questions of marital infidelity, and in early February questions regarding the governor's military service were in the headlines around the nation. Clinton, who had been the front-runner in early New Hampshire polls, eventually finished second to former Massachusetts Senator Paul Tsongas, and the national press corps interpreted the result as the beginning of a two-way race between Tsongas and Clinton.[34]

On the Republican side, early expectations of a noncontest were jarred when former White House aide Pat Buchanan received 37 percent of the New Hampshire vote against incumbent President George Bush, who was held to 53 percent.[35] Just as Eugene McCarthy's surprisingly close loss to incumbent President Lyndon Johnson persuaded the press that Johnson was unpopular in 1968, Buchanan's loss to Bush focused the attention of the press on the nation's economic recession, rather than Bush's successes in foreign policy. In 1992 Bush's ability to win renomination was never in doubt; he won every primary and took the bulk of delegates from each caucus state.

1996

Bill Clinton was only the second president, along with Ronald Reagan in 1984, to be renominated without challenge under the reformed nomination system in place since 1972. Two incumbents, Nixon and Bush, faced relatively minor protest candidates; two others, Ford and Carter, had to win nomination by beating back serious challenges.

The Republican race was a classic example of the media's bias in favor of creating a horse race. The front-runner, Senate Majority Leader Bob Dole of Kansas, won the Iowa caucuses. Not only that, but the candidates widely considered to be his most serious rivals did poorly. Publisher Steve Forbes finished fourth despite spending freely from his personal fortune. Texas Senator Phil Gramm, the only candidate to rival Dole in fund-raising, finished far behind, effectively ending his candidacy. However, instead of reporting a victory for Dole, reporters focused on the (in their view) disappointingly narrow margin separating him from the rest of the candidates. Words used by pundits that night and the next day about the Dole victory included "weak," "narrow," "shaky," "vulnerable," "wobbly," and "disappointing." Dole was the "quasi-loser" according to one, while another called it an "unimpressive showing." Fred Barnes, of the conservative weekly *The Standard,* opined on *CBS This Morning* that "another victory like this for Bob Dole and he'll join the pantheon of political losers like Edmund Muskie." The following day David Yepsen of the *Des Moines Register* said of Dole: "He didn't win anything."[36]

The media interpretation of Dole's weakness had consequences, at least in the short run. Eight days later, the candidate who finished second in Iowa, Pat Buchanan, was the immediate beneficiary of Dole's perceived failure. In tracking polls taken just before the Iowa results were known, Buchanan trailed Dole in New Hampshire by about six percentage points. Within two days, he had pulled even, and he eventually beat Dole to win the New Hampshire primary by about 2,100 votes, which worked out to one percentage point.[37]

This left the national media with a rather tricky challenge in interpreting the results. Unlike Gary Hart's in 1984, Buchanan's views were well-known; he had a well-defined public image and little plausible chance of winning the nomination. Indeed, Buchanan won a smaller percentage of the New Hampshire vote in 1996 than in his best showing of 37 percent of the Republican vote in the 1992 New Hampshire primary. So why did Buchanan receive a media puff? Primarily because the news media could not accept that Dole was so far ahead—in name recognition, organization, and finances—that on the Republican side there was in truth no horse race to report. Because the media needed a horse race, for the next few weeks it was anybody but Dole in the headlines.[38]

What Do These Historical Vignettes Teach?

1. Candidates ignore Iowa and New Hampshire at their peril. This does not mean that doing badly in Iowa and New Hampshire is sufficient to lose everything or that doing well is sufficient to win everything. It does mean that they can be a tremendous help or a tremendous hindrance to each and every candidacy.

2. This is so not because of their size but because of their temporal primacy: Iowa results, plus media spin, structure the alternatives for the New Hampshire primary. These two events together plus media spin structure alternatives for everything that follows. In 1992, when Iowa was ignored, the results of New Hampshire alone provided a structure for the nomination contest.

3. While winning Iowa or New Hampshire does not insure nomination, losing badly quickly ends a candidacy. No eventual nominee since the modern nomination process was put in place in 1972 has ever finished below third place in either Iowa or New Hampshire. Iowa and New Hampshire effectively winnow out anyone who cannot draw at least that level of support.[39] With few exceptions, candidates have learned these lessons and responded, in the months preceeding the voting, by focusing on Iowa and New Hampshire to the exclusion of almost every other state (see table 4.2).

Doing well in Iowa and New Hampshire takes organization as well as good publicity because organizations get people to attend caucuses and sustain their loyalty as the public shufflings and reshufflings take place, especially at the Democratic caucuses. Doing well as the result of Iowa and New Hampshire, however, chiefly requires good publicity: spin control at least to hold down adverse expectations, but also, if possible, to attract the good luck to be the story on which the national news media converge coming out of Iowa and as the first primary approaches. The closer the next event in time, the narrower the temporal gap between Iowa and New Hampshire, the greater the potential that both events can be interpreted together, and thus the more influential the news media response to Iowa and New Hampshire overall in the election year.

Primaries

After long months of campaigning without any votes cast, and after Iowa and New Hampshire, the parties finally get around to the main events of the nomination process, a series of state primary elections and caucuses that choose delegates pledged to successful candidates.

As we have seen, the national parties, especially on the Democratic side, impose rules on how things proceed, but much is left up to the choices of the individual states. About four-fifths of the states, selecting the bulk of the del-

TABLE 4.2   **EARLY CAMPAIGNING FOR THE 2000 NOMINATION**

	Days Campaigning in State, 15 March through 2 August 1999			
Candidate	Iowa	New Hampshire	Home State	All Others
Alexander	31	8	26	23
Bauer	20	11	—	44
Buchanan	20	6	—	55
Bush	6	4	18	26
Dole	19	10	—	39
Forbes	23	11	—	38
Hatch	5	1	4	0
Kasich	13	22	11	25
Keyes	2	4	—	8
McCain	1	14	3	31
Quayle	14	7	1	34
Smith	8	8	—	18
Bradley	18	11	2	42
Gore	14	7	7	50
Totals	194	124	72	502

SOURCE: "White House 2000 Candidate State Visit Tallies," *The Hotline*, August 2, 1999.

NOTES: Candidates' home states are Tennessee (Alexander), Texas (Bush), Utah (Hatch), Ohio (Kasich), Arizona (McCain), Indiana (Quayle), New Jersey (Bradley), and Tennessee (Gore). For Senator Bob Smith of New Hampshire (and for those residing in Washington, D.C.), home state is left blank.

egates, hold primary elections. A more critical choice than the choice between primary or caucus, however, is when the primary or first-round caucuses occur. The design of the nomination process itself has its own independent influence on outcomes. State parties and state legislatures know this, and have moved their procedures to entice candidate and press attention to their states. The most successful of these strategies has been to go first; the early Iowa caucuses and the first-in-the-nation New Hampshire primary have exceptional impact. Whatever choices the states make create new incentives and opportunities for the candidates, who adapt their campaign plans to exploit the calendar of primaries and caucuses.

The most common change states have made in their primaries is to move them earlier and earlier in the process. In 1976 Democratic presidential primaries were spread out over a relatively long period: after New Hampshire on 24 February, only five states held primaries in March, and only two held primaries in April. Twelve primaries were held more than three months after the New Hampshire primary, including 8 June contests in California, New Jersey, and Ohio.[40] This schedule certainly emphasized the importance of early primaries because winning in March helped candidates receive attention and raise money for the later events. This meant that early and vigorous participation in primaries was already the only strategy available to serious presidential aspirants. Nevertheless, many of the actual delegates were selected late in the process.

As people began to understand the influence of the early states, more and more states moved earlier and earlier. In mid-March of the presidential election year of 1984, both major parties had chosen around a quarter of their delegates. By 1988 this proportion had increased to one-third; twenty states held primaries within a month of the New Hampshire primary.[41] While little changed in 1992, the process accelerated again for 1996 and for 2000 (see table 4.3, pp.112-15). In 1996 the big difference was the size of the states with early primaries. New York moved its primary from the mid-point of the process to 7 March; California, which traditionally had held its primary in June, moved to late March.[42] For 2000 California has moved up again to share an early March date with New York, New Jersey, Massachusetts, Maryland, and several smaller states. Thus, in 2000, winning the early primaries will be important not to signal the viability of a candidate or to raise money for future contests but because most of the delegates will be chosen early in the process. It remains to be seen what strategies candidates will adopt as a reaction to the new schedule. As recently as 1984, candidates without substantial financial resources for their campaigns had counted on strong showings in early primaries to give them the momentum they needed to raise more money and then carry on into the rest of the primaries. This strategy, like the stalking horses and favorite sons of a previous era, is part of the history of the nomination process, not the present.[43] Longshot candidates of the future will be even more dependent on the free publicity provided by the mass media than were candi-

TABLE 4.3   DELEGATE-SELECTION SCHEDULES, 1992, 1996, AND 2000

		1992	1996	2000
24	Jan.			Alaska (R, straw poll)
27–29			Alaska (R, straw poll)	
31				Iowa
Before 1 Feb.				Louisiana*
				Hawaii*
1	Feb.			New Hampshire
5				Delaware (D)
8				Delaware (R)
10		Iowa		
12			Iowa	
18		New Hampshire		
19				S. Carolina (R)
20			New Hampshire	
22				Michigan
				Arizona (R)
23		Maine		
24			Delaware	
25		S. Dakota		
27			Arizona (R)	
			N. Dakota (R)	
			S. Dakota	
29				Virginia
				N. Dakota
				Washington
2	March		S. Carolina (R)	
3		Colorado		
		Georgia		
		Idaho (D)		
		Maryland		
		Minnesota (D)		
		Utah (D)		
		Washington (D)		
		A. Samoa (D)		
4				Delaware
5		N. Dakota (D)	Colorado	
			Connecticut	
			Georgia	
			Idaho (D)	
			Maryland	
			Minnesota	
			Vermont (R)	
			Washington (D)	
			A. Samoa (D)	

TABLE 4.3 CONTINUED

		1992	1996	2000
7	March	Arizona	Montana (D)	California
		S. Carolina	New York	Connecticut
		Wyoming	N. Dakota (D)	Delaware
				Georgia
				Maine
				Massachusetts
				Maryland
				Minnesota
				Missouri
				New York
				Rhode Island
				Vermont
8		Nevada		
9			Missouri (R)	
10		Delaware	Nevada (D)	Colorado
		Florida		S. Carolina (D)
		Hawaii		Utah
		Louisiana (R)		Wyoming
		Massachusetts		
		Mississippi		
		Missouri		
		Oklahoma		
		Rhode Island		
		Tennessee		
		Texas		
11				Arizona (D)
12			Florida	Nevada (D)
12			Hawaii (D)	
			Louisiana	
			Maine (D)	
			Mississippi	
			Oklahoma	
			Rhode Island	
			Tennessee	
			Texas	
14				Florida
				Louisiana
				Mississippi
				Oklahoma
				Tennessee
				Texas
15		P. Rico		

(continued)

TABLE 4.3 CONTINUED

		1992	1996	2000
17	March	Illinois Michigan	P. Rico (R)	
19			Michigan Ohio Wisconsin Illinois Michigan Ohio Wisconsin	
21		Kansas (D)		Illinois Ohio
23			Wyoming (D)	
24		Connecticut		
25			Utah (D)	Alaska (D)
26		Louisiana (D)	California Vermont (D) Nevada (R)	
28		V. Islands (D)		
30			V. Islands (D)	
31		Vermont		
2	April	Alaska (D)	Kansas	
4			Alaska (D)	Wisconsin Kansas
7		Kansas (R) Minnesota (R) New York Wisconsin	P. Rico (D)	
11		Virginia		
13			Virginia (D)	
23			Pennsylvania	
25				Pennsylvania
26			Alaska (R)	
27		Utah (R)		
28		Pennsylvania		
2	May		Nevada (R)	D.C. Indiana N. Carolina
3		Guam (D)	Maine (R)	
4			Wyoming (R)	
5		D.C. Indiana N. Carolina Ohio	Guam (D)	

TABLE 4.3 CONTINUED

		1992	1996	2000
7	May		D.C. Indiana N. Carolina	
9				Nebraska West Virginia
12		Nebraska W. Virginia		
14			Nebraska W. Virginia	
16				Oregon
19		Oregon Washington (R)		
21			Arkansas (R) Oregon	
23				Arkansas Idaho Kentucky
25				Nevada (R)
26		Idaho (R) Arkansas Kentucky		
28			Arkansas (D) Idaho (R) Kentucky Washington (R)	
2	June	Alabama Montana California New Jersey New Mexico		
4			Alabama Montana New Jersey New Mexico	
6				Alabama Montana New Jersey New Mexico S. Dakota
N.A.				Guam (R) Utah caucus V. Islands (R)

dates such as Jimmy Carter in 1976 or Gary Hart in 1984, should they manage to succeed in doing well in Iowa or New Hampshire.

One strategy front-runners have followed in reaction to front-loading is simply to raise more early money, hoping that the campaigns they purchase can compensate for any stumbles along the way. This tactic was successful for Bob Dole in 1996. As we have seen, he "lost" in Iowa by failing to meet expectations, then lost outright in New Hampshire. Within the next week, he finished second two more times, to Steve Forbes in Delaware on 24 February and to Pat Buchanan in Arizona on 27 February. Dole, however, had the money (and broad support) to contest several primaries at a time. In the first week of March, nine primaries were scheduled, and he won them all. At least part of the reason for that success was that Dole had the money to organize and advertise in those states, while his opponents were concentrating all their efforts on Iowa, New Hampshire, Delaware, and Arizona. Money trumped momentum in 1988 on the Democratic side. In that year, Albert Gore and Michael Dukakis outspent Richard Gephardt, the winner of the Iowa caucuses, by a two-to-one margin in southern and border Super Tuesday states. No candidate had the resources, in time or money, to campaign seriously in each state. But those with the money to do so were able to offer competition in more areas and may have reaped more delegates as a result.[44] This may be the reason that several Republican candidates dropped out of the 1996 race in early 1995; the more extreme the front-loading of the system, the more money is needed to contest primaries in states the candidates themselves will have no time to visit.

As front-loading increases, the "exhibition season," when candidates display their policies and capabilities to party activists, donors, and the media will be pushed forward even earlier and squeezed into a shorter period of time. The first delegate-selection rounds in Iowa and New Hampshire may, in the words of Republican consultant John Sears, be "more the end of the process than the beginning,"[45] and may serve to eliminate all but the most well-prepared candidates.

Is this elimination round more or less important if the bulk of the delegates are selected hard on the heels of New Hampshire? Because Iowa and New Hampshire are so close to these primaries, whatever momentum candidates gain in those two states—and not local interests—might provide the major influence on the voting in front-loaded states.

In short, Iowa and New Hampshire might give some candidate "momentum" going into the early primary states. Momentum is stimulated from overwhelming victories and crushing defeats, and also by how well candidates have been able to influence expectations and how thoroughly the media converge on an interpretation of who is ahead and behind. Small, separate primaries maximize the ability of candidates to make their own statements to voters. The larger the number of primaries on any given day, the greater the number of voters, and the larger the geographical spread, the less impression management candidates are able to do and the more the media take over this activity. In this respect, front-loading of the process can increase media influence.

We conclude that the continued trend in front-loading has at least two possible effects. First, it gives a larger advantage to those candidates who "win" the preprimary period, securing endorsements (where those endorsements are useful), and most of all money. Second, for candidates able to generate momentum from Iowa and New Hampshire, it magnifies the effect of such media effects.

A variation of the front-loading strategy occasionally used by states is an attempt to be "first" also in some way, thereby sharing some of the attention normally reserved for Iowa and New Hampshire. In 1996 Delaware Republicans positioned their primary just four days after the New Hampshire primary, and Louisiana Republicans went even further, holding their first-round caucuses a few days before Iowa. This strategy was not particularly successful. New Hampshire and Iowa, eager to retain their status as first in the nation, asked candidates to boycott Delaware and Louisiana. Most agreed. Only Steve Forbes risked the anger of New Hampshire voters by actively campaigning in Delaware. He did win there—but he finished fourth in New Hampshire, and his candidacy never recovered. Both states intended to continue this challenge in 2000, and Iowa and New Hampshire have responded again by urging candidates to ignore them.[46]

A more common strategy states have used to attract candidate and press attention is to hold regional primaries. Perhaps if several states with (presumably) similar interests coordinate their delegate selection, candidates will be forced to show interest in whatever issues are peculiar to that region. The most famous of these attempted regional primaries was made by southern states in 1988, when eleven southern or border states held a "Super Tuesday" on 8 March. In 1996 North and South Dakota held primaries on the same day; a week later, five of the six New England states held their primaries, and four midwestern states (Illinois, Michigan, Ohio, and Wisconsin) coordinated their primaries later in the process.

Such primaries have not, for the most part, been particularly successful. For one thing, states are unable to monopolize a date. Should other states share the day, then candidates may choose to only campaign in the largest states within the region (say, Massachusetts in a New England regional primary) and ignore the smaller states. Even worse, some candidates might skip the region altogether and concentrate on the other states.

The case of Super Tuesday in 1988 is instructive. The idea behind the creation of the Super Tuesday primaries was twofold: (1) to give the South a larger voice in presidential nominating politics, and (2) by switching from caucuses to primaries and by holding primaries relatively early in the campaign (that is, before it was all decided), they hoped some more moderate or conservative Democratic politicians would be in the race, thereby attracting voters into the primaries. But it was not to be. Turnout in Super Tuesday primaries in 1988 was only 25.5 percent as compared to 33.8 percent for the other primaries.[47]

The results of the southern Super Tuesday of 1988 did not achieve its creators' goal of helping moderate or conservative candidates in the race for the Democratic nomination. Instead, it helped Jesse Jackson, who received support across the South from black voters and some liberal white voters.[48] It ended the candidacy of Richard Gephardt. It kept the southern moderate candidate, Senator Albert Gore, in the race. This harmed the front-runner, Governor Dukakis, and thus helped Jackson, who with his small but devoted following and his thirst for publicity was determined to persist until he could appear on television at the national convention. But Dukakis was probably the biggest winner. He won the two largest southern states, Florida and Texas. Meanwhile, he also won primaries that day in Maryland, Rhode Island, and his home state of Massachusetts.

Possibly in reaction to the questionable success of regional primaries, some states have opted for the alternative strategy of separating themselves from others in their region. In 1988 South Carolina Republicans held a primary the Saturday before the southern Super Tuesday; in 1992 the Georgia primary was a week before six southern states. In each case, a southern candidate (George Bush in 1988, Bill Clinton in 1992) won the early state and then swept the rest of the region. The result was the same in 1996. Bob Dole's solid victory on 2 March in South Carolina foreshadowed his sweep in eight mostly southern states on 5 March. By separating themselves from their region, these states gambled that candidates would spend more time on them than on any other individual state in a regional primary.

At least one other strategy is common. States that are home to a prospective candidate may manipulate the delegate selection process in order to help the "favorite son." If the candidate is expected to win the state, that means following one of the avenues to extra publicity. If the candidate is worried about losing the state, however, the opposite strategy is called for. Even hinting at this may generate negative publicity. This happened to Arizona Senator John McCain in 1999. Arizona Republicans had moved their primary to mid-February in 1996, following New Hampshire by only a week. McCain was reported to be in favor of moving the primary back in the schedule, after the delegate-rich California and New York primaries, presumably in order to avoid the possibility of an embarrassing loss in his home state affecting his successs elsewhere. In this case, however, Arizona Republicans failed to support McCain and left the date of the primary early.[49]

Selecting a date is not the only way states can affect what candidates do. The varying rules of the major parties for counting primary votes make a difference to candidate strategies. Under Republican rules, state primaries and caucuses may (and most do) follow plurality "winner-take-all" procedures. This gives a strategic opportunity not available to Democrats. A Republican late bloomer, by winning later "mop-up" primaries, conceivably could hope to overcome a front-runner's early lead. Ronald Reagan in 1976, for instance, though he won no primaries until late March, almost took the nomination from Gerald Ford by getting all the delegates from such large states as California and Texas. In contrast, Democratic rules requiring proportional representation make it difficult for lagging Democratic candidates to catch up. Even if front-runners falter, proportional representation slows their momentum only a little in the later primaries.

What helps a candidate overcome an early poor showing? "One of the problems of being a dark horse," notes Hart's 1984 poll taker, Dotty Lynch, "is that you need some true believers with you. Without an issue like George McGovern had in 1972 or a [devoted, ethnically based] constituency like Jesse Jackson has, a lot of people give up on you and you may give up on yourself."[50] Raising enough money up front to outlast disappointing showings obviously is also important. The two factors—a loyal activist following and the capacity to raise money early—may be but do not have to be connected.

The existence of candidates with narrow but intense followings leads us to ask how such candidates might be affected by a Super Tuesday or a similar regional primary. If moderate or more broadly based candidates are more numerous and divide the great middle among themselves, it is quite possible for such a marginal candidate to do extremely well. Under Republican "winner-take-all" rules, candidates with small but intense followings are less likely to prevail because a substantial majority of party identifiers oppose them. The Reverend Pat Robertson in 1988 was a good test of this proposition. Following proportional representation, Democrats presumably would be more likely to reward with delegates candidates who have narrowly focused but intense followings. The Reverend Jesse Jackson was a good test of this deduction. In 1988 Jackson lasted longer than Robertson did.

Thus the design of the presidential primary process continues to be an ongoing saga of trial and error. A good summary of the way in which the various forces are aligned is Rhodes Cook's: "Regardless of the different nominating rules, ... there is a dynamic affecting both parties that makes early defeats devastating. No candidate in either party in recent years has mounted a successful comeback during the mop-up period."[51]

Since primaries are the battlegrounds of the nomination process, the role of the news media is central to how nominees are chosen. By reporting as they do, the electronic media alter the character of presidential nominations. Since primary voters lack the guidance that the endorsement of political parties provides during general elections, and since primary events are often full of uncertainty, media reporting about who is ahead or behind or how seriously candidates should be taken assumes considerable importance. Were officials of political parties able to select their own candidates, the media would matter much less. But with primaries replacing caucuses and conventions, candidates have to care much more about how they do on television than whether they please leaders of their party.

Therefore, a significant part of the nomination process includes trying to manipulate what the mass media say about primary elections before and after they take place, to engage in "spin control."[52] The contestant who loses but does better than expected may reap greater advantage from a primary than the one who wins but falls below expectations. It is therefore manifestly to the advantage of a candidate to hold his preelection claims down to a minimum. John Kennedy tried in 1960 to follow this strategy in Wisconsin, but the press, radio, and television took note of his extensive organization and of favorable polls and in advance pinned the winner-by-a-landslide label on the senator from Massachusetts.[53] Early predictions in the 1968 New Hampshire primary were that Eugene McCarthy would receive somewhere around 10 percent of the vote. When he eventually polled 42 percent—against Lyndon Johnson's 48 percent write-in vote—it was widely interpreted as a victory, in part because it was so unexpected.[54] George McGovern benefited from a similar process in 1972.

A good example of spin control was the effort of Bill Clinton's campaign to declare a victory in New Hampshire in 1992. Clinton had run behind Tsongas in the polls preceding the primary and in fact finished behind him in the voting. Yet the decision was made for the candidate to appear in front of his supporters just before the television network coverage of the primary ended, and for him to declare a sort of victory: Clinton claimed to be the "comeback kid."[55] The press accepted the idea of a resurgent Clinton challenged by Tsongas, ignoring the other candidates, and giving Tsongas little of the coverage a front-runner might ordinarily receive.[56] In contrast, Bob Kerrey's decisive victory (with 40 percent of the vote) in South Dakota one week later netted him much less favorable publicity than Clinton's second-place showing in New Hampshire. Kerrey succeeded with the voters, but failed in the crucial job of spin control.

Is the selection of presidential candidates best carried out by party leaders bargaining in conventions (old system) or by the mass electorate voting in primaries (new system)? In order to discuss this question we need to know something about the information possessed by those who do the selecting. Do primaries convey enough information to those who vote about a candidate's character, competence, issue positions, electability, and capacity to govern? What the media do best is to provide information on the viability of candidates, their standing in the nomination race. Primary voters soak up this information. Substantial evidence exists that voters absorb opinion poll results and gather other impressions of viability, and these exert considerable influence over voting decisions. But information on policies, character, and leadership ability is comparatively scarce and is assimilated slowly.[57] "It appears safe to conclude," John G. Geer writes, "that most primary voters do not compare the issue positions of candidates when voting."[58] One reason is that primary voters do not perceive much issue distance between the candidates, perhaps because, being members of the same party, there is in fact not that much difference. Another reason may be that candidates are purposely unclear. Since it may well be advantageous for candidates to appeal differently to various audiences, they may, like Bill Clinton or George Bush, appear moderate to some people, liberal to others, and conservative to still others.

There are bandwagon effects in primaries. Gary Hart rose from 2 percent of national support early in February 1984 to 33 percent in three weeks. Jimmy Carter went from near obscurity, 0.7 percent in January 1976, to 29.3 percent by mid-March. As Collat, Kelley, and Rogowski define the term, "a bandwagon effect may be said to exist if a given decision-maker supports, from among some set of contenders, not the contender he most prefers, but the contender who seems most likely to win."[59]

Issue preferences or assessments of leadership ability must be very low if voters can be swept along by the sheer momentum of events. On what basis, then, do citizens choose? As the nominating campaign moves along, voters do develop feelings about the personalities of the candidates. In a study of primary voters in Los Angeles, California, and Erie, Pennsylvania, John Geer demonstrates that comments centered on the candidates' personalities predominate in the reasons given for voting in primaries (see table 4.4, p.122).[60]

Since much of the debate in the primary is about who among members of the same party can provide the best leadership, Geer thinks voter concentration on candidates is reasonable. Others disagree. Henry E. Brady and Michael C. Hagen argue that "primaries seem to be seriously flawed by forcing voters to commit to candidates before they can learn about … policy positions, electability and leadership ability of those standing for the nomination.… American primaries force people to choose before they are ready."[61]

The political parties have written their rules in a way that makes it impossible to avoid primaries. Now that the national party conventions ratify rather than choose candidates, the function of reducing uncertainty about which candidates are ahead and behind is transferred from successive convention ballots to the sequence of primary elections.

It could be said that primaries are more important than general elections because primaries do more to limit the choices available to voters. Since the effects of primaries are cumulative, it is especially important to study how earlier events affect later ones. Larry Bartels argues that the nomination victories of Republican Gerald Ford and Democrat Jimmy Carter in 1976 were the result of the accumulation of momentum, with over half of Carter's support in

TABLE 4.4   REASONS FOR SUPPORTING A CANDIDATE FOR NOMINATION: THE DENSITY OF
THE OPEN-ENDED COMMENT (IN PERCENTAGES)

	N	Personality	Issues	Ideology	Group	Campaign	Other	Don't know
Erie Dems	264	70.1	10.2	.8	9.5	8.7	.4	.4
Erie Reps	101	79.2	15.8	2.0	0	2.0	1.0	0
L.A. Dems	270	68.9	15.9	5.2	1.9	7.8	.4	0
L.A. Reps	161	73.9	19.9	3.1	0	1.2	1.9	0

SOURCE: John G. Geer, *Nominating Presidents: An Assessment of Voters in Presidential Primaries* (New York: Greenwood, 1989), 77.

primaries coming from his early successes.[62] Perhaps the most interesting preliminary finding comes from a study by Richard Brody and Larry Rothenberg showing that voter turnout declines toward the end of the primary season.[63] This makes sense; if the early primaries dominate the process, and sharply constrain alternatives available later on, then it would follow that people would see less purpose in turning out for later ones.

Since primaries have become so important—indeed, indispensable—for presidential nominations, it increases our interest in such questions as: Which candidates, and which interests represented by them are advantaged or disadvantaged by primaries? Will radicals, conservatives, or moderates do better or worse with more extensive use of primaries? Are citizens' preferences more or less likely to be reflected in the results? If not citizens', then whose preferences will be expressed? How do the rules for counting votes affect the results? We begin with this last important question because it turns out that the way votes are counted in large measure determines whose preferences count the most.

No one pretends that primaries are perfect representations of the electorate that either identifies with a particular political party or is likely to vote for the party's leading vote-getter. For one thing, voters are not allowed to rank their preferences, so a candidate's popularity with voters who gave their first-choice votes to others is unknown. It is quite possible for a candidate to be the first choice of the largest clump of voters but to be only the fourth or fifth choice of all voters taken together. In 1972, for example, the candidates of the Democratic Party's right and left—George Wallace and George McGovern, respectively—won pluralities in more states than any other candidates, yet they also attracted widespread opposition. This opposition was ineffectively expressed in the primary process. Voter turnout in primaries is usually much lower than in the general election and is likely to contain a larger proportion of dyed-in-the-wool party supporters than would be true in a general election. Austin Ranney has shown that average turnout in primaries is approximately 27 percent of all people of voting age, compared with roughly double that in the presidential election.[64] It is not so much low turnout, however, as the combination of low turnout with plurality elections that biases the results. In 1972

Senator McGovern had a plurality in six states. In those states his total primary vote compared with the total vote cast in the general election ranged from 4 to 22 percent. Clearly, his primary voters could not have been a representative sample of those who actually voted in November.[65]

Nevertheless, it may appear that McGovern was entitled to most of the primary delegates because he won more often than any other candidate. This would depend, however, on how the votes were counted. There are three basic ways of counting votes. One is winner take all: whichever candidate gets a plurality of votes in the entire state gets all the delegates. Another is proportional: all candidates who pass a certain threshold, say, 15 percent, divide the delegates among themselves in accordance with their percentage of the vote. A third is congressionally districted: after delegates are allotted (by population or past party vote or both) to districts, the candidate who wins a plurality in each area gains all of its delegates.

Rumination about the three rules reveals the kinds of constituencies (and hence interests) they are likely to favor. Winner take all gives more power to populous and competitive states, which have a large number of delegates. These are, Texas and Florida excepted, the states of the Northeast and California, known for their large concentration of urban voters, ethnic minorities, and union laborers. The proportional rule favors noncompetitive areas because in these places a high degree of support for a single candidate pays off. That is why George Wallace did so well wherever the proportional rule was in force. The congressional district rule would fragment the large states, where many candidates could get some support, but not the smaller, less competitive states that have a few homogeneous districts. It should be evident, as James Lengle and Byron Shafer conclude, that

> the widespread adoption of Districted primaries after 1968, or the prohibition of Winner-Take-All primaries after 1972 [by Democrats], were not, then, just inconsequential decisions to hand out delegates via a certain mechanism. They were far-reaching, if almost accidental, choices about the type of candidates who would bear the party's standard, the type of voters who would have the power to choose those standard bearers, and the type of issues with which both groups would try to shape history. They were, in short, a decision on how to (re)construct the Democratic Party.[66]

The purpose of the McGovern-Fraser Commission, which rewrote Democratic delegation selection rules between the 1968 and 1972 elections, was to take control of the presidential nomination away from state and local party officials, as well as from national officeholders, and give it over to party activists attached to candidates and elected through primaries with safeguards to assure representation of those deemed insufficiently represented: women, youth, racial minorities. After each of the elections from 1972 through 1984, the Democrats sought to refine the version of representativeness enacted by the McGovern-Fraser Commission. Should proportional representation always be the rule, or was winner take all an acceptable system in some form? What was the proper threshold for representation in a proportional system? Should special rules ensure a place for party leaders and elected officials at the convention, even if they chose not to endorse any candidate early in the process?

The compromise system established by the Hunt Commission in the wake of the crushing defeat of the Democrats in 1980 was to insist on strict proportional representation and to add about 15 percent of the slots for delegates to be reserved for uncommitted party and public officials. In each state, positions were reserved for the party chair and vice-chair, and up to three-fifths of the members of Senate and House caucuses could serve as delegates. The remainder of the unpledged delegates were turned over to state parties with the suggestion they be given to governors and mayors of large cities. Finally, 305 delegates were allotted to pledged elected and party officials.[67]

So far, we have the results of the 1984, 1988, 1992, and 1996 Democratic nominating processes to gauge the effects of these rules changes. In 1988, 1992, and 1996, close nomination battles did not develop, so "superdelegate" behavior was not important. In 1984 the uncommitted delegates overwhelmingly supported Walter Mondale, and did so not late in the convention but relatively early in the primary season. Whether Mondale could have won without them, or, as is more likely, they helped sustain his strength during his bid, the unpledged delegates did matter.

How did the rules for counting votes in primaries affect the outcome in 1984? Where Jesse Jackson's highly concentrated 18 percent of the vote got him just 10 percent of the delegates, and Hart came out even with 36 percent of the vote and the delegates, Mondale won 49 percent of the delegates with 39 percent of the vote. Jackson was hurt by the concentration of his support in largely black areas. Hart's results were proportional because he happened to win mostly in states following proportional rules. Mondale was helped because he won in big states with bonus "winner-take-more" systems, which the Democrats outlawed again after the 1988 contest.[68]

Did the Hunt Commission reforms enacted before the 1984 election enhance the prospects of moderates with close ties to party officials, as they were intended to do? Walter Mondale fit this description, and as we have seen, the rules in 1984 worked to his advantage. Still, reserving 15 percent of convention seats for party officials is unlikely to be enough to reverse the trends we discussed earlier. The declining role of state parties, the greater emphasis on primaries, and the logic of primary election choice all favor candidates with intense factional followings over moderate insiders.

In any event, for party officials to play a moderating role, they must be moderate. Recent trends toward party polarization make this somewhat less likely. As conservatives, mostly southerners, have left the Democratic and moved into the Republican Party, conflict between the parties might substitute for conflict within them. Certainly, the prospects of a conservative Democratic or a liberal Republican presidential candidate have diminished. To the extent this is so, party officeholders may no longer be the bastions of moderation they once were. To test this hypothesis, we would like to know whether the views of politician delegates are closer to or further from those of voters of their party than are activist delegates chosen through primaries or caucuses. We do know that politician delegates are more loyal to their party, 85 percent saying they support its candidates every year compared to two-thirds of the other delegates. Tom Mann argues that some politicians at the 1984 convention tried to push the Democratic Party platform farther to the left. Similarly, some Republican delegates from the House of Representatives pushed hard to the right.[69] In 1988 the House Republicans put public pressure on George Bush to select a vice-presidential candidate from the right wing of the party.[70]

Where once it was useful to be the second choice of 90 percent of all delegates, today first choices, even of as few as 30 percent, are far preferable. This is a good measure of the change over the past three decades in the nomination process. Whether the country will do better with presidents who are the strong preference of party minorities rather than the weak preference of party majorities remains to be seen. One key test for presidents selected by modern processes will be what happens when they attempt to gather the support they need to govern or, even more significantly, what happens to them and to their governments if they neglect to make the attempt. The warning words of a British observer, Anthony Teasdale, merit careful consideration:

> One irony of the primaries may ... be that in the name of greater democratic participation, nominations more often go to those less representative of party opinion. A second irony seems to be that in pursuit of more authoritative and legitimate government, primaries often favour candidates with less governmental experience, reduce the usefulness of party, increase popular expectations of politicians, and generally make America more difficult to govern....
>
> Above all, by establishing direct personal contact between candidates and the mass electorate, primaries erode the importance of party as an intermediary between the elected and the elector in the United States. Candidates establish their own national organization, with their own mobile campaigners now imported into States as necessary. In government, this weakens the attachment of party loyalty

which might give the President additional leverage to secure action on his proposals in Congress and the States.[71]

State and District Conventions/Caucuses

As we have mentioned, the vast majority of convention delegates are selected through the primary process. In 1996, for example, approximately 70 percent of the delegates at the Democratic convention were chosen in primaries, 15 percent were unelected superdelegates, and state and district conventions chose the other 15 percent. How do candidates go about securing delegates through the convention/caucus system?

In the past, attempts by candidates to influence delegates chosen outside of primaries were usually made after these delegates were selected by state parties. The first strategic requirement for the candidate seeking to influence these delegates was an intelligence service, a network of informants who could report on which delegates were firmly committed, which were wavering, and which might be persuaded to provide second- or third-choice support. Advance reports on the opportunities offered by internal division in the state parties, the type of appeal likely to be effective in each state, and the kinds of bargains to which leaders were most susceptible were also helpful. The costs of this information were high in terms of time, money, and effort, but it was worthwhile to the serious candidate, who needed to know how to move to increase support and block opponents.

These days, no one wants to wait for delegates to be chosen before trying to influence them. The idea is for candidates to get their supporters selected as delegates. By the time they are selected, delegates are likely to be committed to a particular candidate or point of view. In any event, they cannot be selected before the year of the election. The same forces that persuade candidates to begin their drive for the nomination ever earlier impel them to begin the hunt for delegates ahead of time. Since fund-raising must go on in at least twenty states to attract federal matching money, it can be combined with the identification of local allies, who eventually will be designated delegates if the candidate does well in the state selection process.

The major change between past and present stems from the rules adopted by the Democrats after 1968. Delegates, even where there is no primary, are almost always pledged from the moment they are chosen. In the past, delegates were chosen to represent the state parties, and the choice of delegates could not easily be influenced by the candidates. Now, delegates are chosen to reflect the presidential preferences of some set of voters, whether those voters are a primary electorate, party activists, or party officials. Therefore, even in strong party states, the delegates are representatives not of the party but of the candidates who attracted support within the party. The only role remaining for party leaders is influencing the electorate; even if the party should choose this role, it is one of advocacy rather than the traditional party role of intermediation.

When and where there were strong state party organizations in the past, aspiring candidates had to deal with them. Decisions on whether to enter a primary or influence delegate selection were mediated through party leaders. If party leaders thought a contest in a state would be divisive, candidates would have to worry about incurring their enmity. The decline of state parties in the nomination process has lowered these obstacles. Relatively small numbers of activists without a continuing connection to the party may mobilize around a candidate and, by appealing to caucus attenders and primary electorates, overwhelm the party regulars. If the test is numbers of followers who will come to a particular meeting, rather than present party position or past service, an activist surge can carry the day, as McGovern and Goldwater demonstrated so well.

Aspirants for nomination vary greatly in the degree to which they know other politicians throughout the country. Men like Bob Dole, Richard Nixon, Hubert Humphrey, and Barry Goldwater, who traveled extensively and gave assistance to members of their parties, simply needed to keep their files up to date in order to have a nationwide list of contacts. When the time came, they knew from whom they could request assistance in gathering information, persuading delegates, and generally furthering their cause. Candidates who lacked this advantage had to take special steps in order to build up their political apparatus.

Nowadays every candidate seeks to sway voters, not party leaders, and contacts of a different sort are more valuable. The sort of organization that candidates need today includes poll takers, fund-raisers, and media experts—consultants who aim their message at voters. Indeed, it may not be too much to say that a key question for candidates today is which poll taker or manager to attract to the campaign, rather than which party leaders.[72] Now everybody believes, and with good reason, that the early aspirant gets the nomination. Candidates will need more publicity than they used to have, and they will need it earlier than they used to have it, to compete in the future.

This could be seen in the way George Bush in 1988 and Bill Clinton in 1992 sought their nominations. Bush and Clinton had extensive contacts with party leaders across the nation, cultivated over many years of preparation for eventual White House bids. Bush, of course, was also the sitting vice president. Yet each of them campaigned for the nomination in exactly the same way political unknown Jimmy Carter had in 1976, appealing directly to voters through small events in Iowa and New Hampshire and television ads and large public rallies in the larger states. Political networks nowadays may help candidates raise money or survive scandal (if their allies are willing to go on television to support them), but the nomination is fought and won in mass electorates.

At the Convention: Housekeeping

While the selection of a site for the convention has often been interpreted as one of the preballot indicators of various candidates' strength, in the past it usually was the rather routine outcome of the weighing of one major and several very minor factors. The major factor was the size of the convention city's proffered contribution to the national party committee. This contribution, in cash or in services, came partly from the city government but mostly from various business groups—hotels, restaurants—that stood to profit from a week-long visit of 6,500 delegates and alternates, their families and friends, and thousands of media representatives, dignitaries, and convention personnel. The cloud over the offer of several hundred thousand dollars by the Sheraton hotel chain as part of San Diego's bid to host the 1972 Republican convention, as well as the reaction to Watergate, has inspired some changes. The federal government now makes available a sum of over $12 million to each of the national parties to finance their nominating conventions, thereby lessening the pressure to acquire cash contributions or contributions in kind.[73] But while the pressure has lifted, the temptation has not; in 1992 the Republicans selected Houston over front-runner San Diego in part because the Texas city donated $10.6 million in cash to the party coffers, as well as donating security and bus services.[74]

A variety of other factors may tip the balance between cities. Political considerations are often important. San Francisco was chosen by Democrats in 1984 partly because the party was having trouble in the West and partly because the city had a popular female Democratic mayor.[75] In 1988 both parties wanted to bolster their strength in the South, Republicans because they were gaining and Democrats because they were declining, and so the Democrats selected Atlanta and the Republicans New Orleans.[76] Cities in large states, especially those expected to be competitive in the fall, are logical choices. Thus the Democrats selected Los Angeles and the Republicans Philadelphia for their conventions in 2000.

Other factors include the quality of facilities, the suitability of the convention hall to the television networks, hotel and entertainment accommodations, and the caliber of the local police force. For example, Philadelphia's James Tate headed as large and as loyal a Democratic organization in 1968 as Chicago's Richard Daley, and his city was closer geographically to Lyndon Johnson in Washington, but Philadelphia simply could not provide 20,000 first-class hotel rooms.[77] San Diego's proposal in 1992 to split the Republican proceedings between the convention center and an outdoor stadium was considered too complicated and inconvenient. All things being equal, incumbent presidents are likely to prefer a city near enough to Washington to allow them to keep close tabs on convention business and travel easily back and forth to the convention, and at the same time play their role away from it as "president of all the people." Naturally, the president's wishes will not be furthest from the minds of the members of the site-selection committee of the national committee, which does the choosing.

The parties prefer to bring their publicity and their business to cities and states where the mayor and the governor are friendly members of the party, since this may give added access to (and control of) public facilities. The aloof attitude of California's Governor Jerry Brown toward the site-selection committee of his party evidently tipped the decision of the Democrats toward New York City in 1976 and away from Los Angeles.[78] In 1984 the fact that the party chair, Charles Manatt, was a Californian may have tipped the balance back to San Francisco for the Democrats. The desire to maintain the autonomy of the convention from demonstrators, who were involved in the Democratic debacle in Chicago in 1968, led to a choice in 1972 of Miami Beach, where a causeway facilitated crowd control. In 1992 Democratic National Committee Chair (and native New Yorker) Ron Brown's close relationship with New York City Mayor David Dinkins was considered a significant factor in that city's selection for the Democratic convention.

The time of a convention varies between mid-July and late August. The "out" party will normally hold its convention before the "in" party, on the theory that its candidate will need a publicity boost earlier. In 1976, 1984, 1988, and 1992, this put Democrats before Republicans; in 1964, 1968, 1980, and 1996 it was the other way around. In 2000, there will be no incumbent candidate, but there will be an incumbent party. We therefore expect Republicans to meet first. An incumbent president will schedule the convention to fit his or her timetable. At its most momentous, the convention may coincide with an international peace offensive; in 1968 the date of the Democratic convention seems to have been set with nothing more in mind than President Johnson's birthday.

Once assembled, the national convention is a mass meeting in which the participants necessarily play widely varying and unequal roles. The candidates and their chief supporters are busily, perhaps frantically, perfecting their organizations and trying to maintain communication with as many of their delegates as they can. In the old days, "pledged" delegations actively supported their candidate, while "bossed" delegates negotiated for the disposal of their votes. The leaders of these delegations were the people who conducted negotiations among the delegations when an impasse developed. There were also factional leaders and independent delegates within state delegations who played an important part in determining what their delegation or a part of their delegation would do. They bargained within their delegation, rather than among the various state delegations. Now the roles of both these relatively autonomous types of politicians have sharply diminished, since most delegates come to the convention pledged to one or another presidential candidate. This means that candidate organizations, not state party leaders, have to do the bargaining. But it will be difficult for the candidates' representatives to bargain if they cannot transfer the votes of their supporters; it will be even harder if the nomination has already been decided as it normally is in caucuses and primaries.

Candidates and Their Organizations

At the national convention, before the balloting for the presidential nomination starts, one or more days are consumed in a variety of party rituals: making speeches, seating delegates, presenting the platform, and so on. During that time, delegates and their leaders mill about, exchanging greetings and gossip. This set of circumstances challenges even the most efficient candidate organization.

There is a wide divergence among candidate organizations. They range from the comprehensive, integrated, and superbly effective to the fragmented, uncoordinated, and virtually nonexistent. We can only suggest the range of organizational alternatives through some general comments and a few examples.

The first modern candidate organization at a national convention, tied together with sophisticated communication equipment, was the expensively mounted organization of Senator John F. Kennedy in 1960. His communication network provided him with a continuing and accurate stream of vital information.[79] He wanted detailed personal knowledge about as many delegates as possible in order to know how they were likely to vote and how they might best be persuaded to stay in line or change their minds. This was all quite necessary in the days, now gone by, when conventions made significant decisions rather than ratifying the results of decisions made elsewhere. More than a year before the convention, the Kennedy-for-President organization—still in the precomputer age—started a card file containing information on people throughout the nation who might be delegates and who might influence delegates. Included on each card were the prospective delegate's name, occupation, religion, party position, relation (if any) to the Kennedy family or its leading supporters, ambitions, policy preferences if strongly held, and likely vote. This was brought up to date before convention time, and entries were made in a central register as new information developed. Thus, when it appeared that a delegate needed to be reinforced or might not vote for Kennedy, his card was pulled and the information was used in order to determine the best way to convince him.

In order to keep an up-to-date and, when necessary, an hour-by-hour watch on developments within the state delegations, the Kennedy organization assigned an individual coordinator to each state. This person might have been a delegate or an observer, such as a senator or a member of the candidate's staff. When it was deemed inadvisable to choose a delegate for fear that any choice would alienate one faction or another, a person outside the state was chosen. These coordinators kept tabs on individual delegates and maintained a running record of the likely distribution of votes. When necessary, the coordinators sent messages to the candidate's headquarters, and reinforcements were sent to bolster the situation. At the Kennedy headquarters the seriousness of the report would be judged and a decision made on how to deal with it. Senator Kennedy himself might call the wavering delegate, one of his brothers might be dispatched, a state party leader might intervene, or some other such remedy might be applied.

In the hurly-burly, crush, and confusion of convention activity, it cannot be assumed that messages sent are received or that decisions are communicated to those who must carry them out. The Kennedy organization took great care to establish a communication center that would receive messages and locate the intended recipients and that could send out instructions and receive feedback on the results. In this prebeeper era, key staff were required to phone their whereabouts periodically to a central switchboard. This made it possible for the Kennedy forces at the convention to deploy and reassign their people on a minute-by-minute basis as developments required.

A system set up only to deal with emergencies would have limited usefulness to a candidate who wanted regular reports that could be appraised in a consistent way. Every morning, the coordinators assigned to the Kennedy headquarters attended a staff meeting at which they deposited with the secretary a report on their activities for the previous day. These reports were sent to what was called the "secret room," and the information was transferred to state briefing files. From these files, a daily secret report on delegate strength was written and given to the candidate and his top advisers.

At the morning staff meetings, Robert Kennedy, who acted as campaign manager for his brother, would ask each coordinator for an estimate of the number of Kennedy votes. Keenly aware of the dangers of seeming to want high estimates, Robert Kennedy challenged the coordinators if he felt that their estimates were too high, but not if they appeared too low. On occasion he would reprimand a coordinator for including a delegate as a certain Kennedy supporter when other information indicated that this was not true. The success of this procedure was indicated by the fact that when the alphabetical balloting reached Wyoming on the first (and last) ballot, the Kennedy organization's estimate of its delegate strength was proved correct within a one-vote margin.[80]

The danger of confusion and mishap is multiplied during the balloting because the convention floor is filled, and it is difficult to move about freely. To deal with this, the Kennedy organization arranged for telephones on the convention floor. Six were set up beneath the seats of chairmen of friendly delegations around the gigantic convention hall. These phones were connected to the Kennedy headquarters outside the hall. Inside the headquarters, staff members sat near the telephone and simultaneously scanned several television sets to look for possible defections. Had the pretested telephones failed to work, walkie-talkie radios were available to take their place.[81]

By comparison with the Kennedy efforts, most of the organizations that have successfully nominated presidential candidates in American history have been uncoordinated, diffuse affairs. For example, in 1952 none of the various factions in the Democratic Party that favored the nomination of Adlai Stevenson had the wholehearted cooperation of their candidate; information gathering was casual and tactical maneuvers were in some cases hit upon accidentally or as afterthoughts. The factions working for the Stevenson nomination did not cooperate to a significant degree and squabbled on occasion. Yet Stevenson was nominated; his success came about because he was the second choice of an overwhelming number of delegates who could not agree on any of their first choices and the first choice of a significant number of leaders in spite of his disinclination to pursue the nomination in an organized fashion.[82]

We have devoted so much space to the Kennedy organization because, unlike the Stevenson example, it became a harbinger of the future. Candidate organizations since then are like Kennedy's, only more so—more telephones, more communication apparatus, and computer networks have replaced the old-fashioned file cards. No nomination since 1976 has been in real doubt when the convention opened, but the possibility of floor fights on the platform or rules requires candidates to prepare for the worst.

An interesting test of the importance of convention organizations took place in 1976 at the closely contested Republican convention. Following recent practice, the President Ford Committee installed an effective communication apparatus. Rather than rely entirely on the geographic leaders of their earlier delegate monitoring operation, the President Ford Committee divided the convention floor into zones, whose floor leaders wore red hats. They were tied by telephone to the Ford trailer and to subleaders responsible for each state. By contrast, Ronald Reagan, in his unsuccessful first bid for the nomination, relied on style and ideology rather than hierarchy and division of labor. As a convention leader said, "Our conservatives don't like to be told what to do, and they don't need to be. The Ford people need all that hardware because they can't count on their delegates to vote with them consistently." F. Christopher Arterton, who observed the convention, believes that at crucial moments, as when the Mississippi delegation caucused on the floor before a crucial vote, Reagan "was handicapped by key coordinators having to fight their way through jammed aisles."[83]

The closest thing to a contested convention since then was the 1984 Democratic convention, when Walter Mondale had the nomination sewed up in advance but both Gary Hart and Jesse Jackson won large numbers of delegates. The Mondale nerve center composed of 14 delegate trackers in a trailer, 35 cluster organizers (clusters were groups of states) covering 300 to 350 delegates each, 60 state whips, and 390 line whips, all responsible for seeing to it that delegates fulfilled their pledges. Thus, by the 1980s, all serious candidates brought to the convention as part of their normal equipment a full complement of electronic communication gear. All had trailers parked near the convention hall in which they could monitor trends on the floor and entertain friends and allies. What was extraordinary about the Kennedy effort in 1960 has, with the passage of time and the progress of technology, become commonplace.

Delegates and Caucuses

Through improved use of technology, modern strategy, and teamwork, candidate organizations have clearly increased their control over delegates. It is still important, however, to know something of the delegates themselves. Who are they? What do they believe? How loyal to their parties are they? Excellent studies of convention delegates allow us a perspective on the changing nature of party activists. In recent conventions, delegates, pledged in state primaries and caucuses, have had little flexibility in the choice of the party's nominee. Still they play a role in platform debates and establishing the image the party projects on television. If we should ever have a deadlocked convention, in which delegates are released from their pledges, delegate attitudes and behavior will take on importance.

Each of the major parties has its own distinctive style and norms. "Republicans," Jo Freeman observes, "perceive themselves as insiders even when they are out of power, and Democrats perceive themselves as outsiders even when they are in power."[84] This difference can be elaborated: Republicans in convention are relatively unified, while Democrats think of themselves as members of subgroups. As the more hierarchical party, Republicans stress loyalty to the chosen leader and the organization. The more varied and egalitarian Democratic Party, in Freeman's words, "has multiple power centers that compete for membership support in order to make demands on, as well as determine, the leaders."[85] For Democratic delegates, therefore, subgroup caucuses are significant reference groups. The component parts of the Republican Party, states and geographic regions and ideological factions, do not maintain robust lives outside the party structure, as do the Democratic caucuses of African Americans, gays, or Asians, and so on, nor on the Republican side do they make decisions and proposals as much as serve as conduits of information to delegates. At national conventions Democrats go to caucuses, as Freeman says, while Republicans go to receptions. Republicans "network" with the candidate organizations, while Democrats make demands. Democrats expect their nominee to pay attention to their problems, while Republicans are more likely to think that the winner ought to get his way until the next time.[86]

Both parties run one risk. At times, the delegates may move to the ideological extremes, while the bulk of the voters out in the country remain firmly in or near the center. The classic examples were the 1964 Republicans and the 1972 Democrats. The former selected the very conservative Senator Barry Goldwater of Arizona, while the latter chose the very liberal Senator George McGovern of South Dakota. In each case, studies found that convention delegates held issue positions not shared by the party rank-and-file. In each case, the nominee lost badly in November partially because of defections from his own party. In the McGovern convention, his supporters shared the same political attitudes whether they were male or female, white or black, young or old. Perhaps what happened is that activists in both parties, enjoying high social and economic status but without professional commitment to party unity or party organization, grew at once farther apart from one another and from the voters. The participant sectors of the parties were far more polarized in 1972 than they had been in the 1940s and 1950s in two directions—one party from the other at the elite level, and elites in both parties from their followers.[87]

The Democratic rules governing delegate selection have succeeded in increasing the proportion of African Americans and women at the past seven Democratic conventions. But even if delegates differ somewhat by income and education, political activists are still a rather elite group. Table 4.5 gives income figures for 1996 for both parties.

Educational differences between delegates and party rank and file were even more striking. About seven in ten delegates from both parties had college degrees, compared to one in five among rank-and-file Democrats and one in three of rank-and-file Republican identifiers. Little had changed from 1975, when Jeane Kirkpatrick concluded, "the delegates to both conventions were an overwhelmingly middle to upper class group."[88] Table 4.6 (pp.136-37), prepared by Barbara G. Farah, on the composition of delegates from 1944 to 1984 reveals that the big change over that time is the four-and-a-half-fold increase in the participation of women. Much smaller changes involve decreases in delegates with little formal education, lawyers, and public officials. The categories of executive and teacher, where there have been considerable changes, deserve further examination.[89]

From 1972 to 1976, half of female Democratic delegates were employed in the public sector, either in government itself or in public education. This was also true of a little over a third of Democratic male delegates. Among Republicans, somewhat more than a third of female and just under a fifth of male delegates were government employees. Over a quarter of all delegates were union members, most of them from teachers' and other public-sector unions. For women in particular, then, Kent Jennings concludes, "public employment is a key route to the avenues of party power."[90]

TABLE 4.5   INCOMES OF DELEGATES AND PARTY IDENTIFIERS (IN PERCENTAGES)

Democrats' Income

Identifiers, 1996		Delegates, 1996	
Less than $50,000	78	Less than $50,000	29
$50,000 to $75,000	10	$50,000 to $75,000	22
Over $75,000	8	Over $75,000	46

Republicans' Income

Identifiers, 1996		Delegates, 1996	
Less than $50,000	60	Less than $50,000	23
$50,000 to $75,000	19	$50,000 to $75,000	18
Over $50,000	17	Over $75,000	47

SOURCE: "Convention Delegates: Who They Are...," *New York Times*, 26 August 1996.

As the traditional party favoring government, it is to be expected that Democratic delegates would come more frequently from the public sector. This may also explain why they seek higher spending on domestic programs. But there is nothing inherent in public-sector employment that would necessarily lead to a preference for lower spending on defense or against military intervention in Central America or for liberal positions on social issues. For that we must look to an ideological explanation. Jo Freeman conjectures that

> the 1984 conventions solidified the direction in which both parties had been moving for the previous ten years. The Democrats adopted the feminist perspective on all public issues directly affecting women and made it clear that women, under feminist leadership, were an important part of the Democratic coalition. The Republican Party adopted antifeminist positions on almost every issue. Its public script was written by Phyllis Schlafly. But it didn't repudiate women; instead it affirmed their importance by showcasing them extensively and devoting more real resources to help women, as individuals, get elected, than the Democratic Party has done.[91]

What happens when party and ideology conflict? A "requirement of participating in the mainstream of the party," Freeman says, "is that one not become an electoral liability. NOW (National Organization for Women) demonstrated its awareness of this rule by endorsing Democratic men running against Republican feminist women, arguing that anyone who supports [President Ronald] Reagan's economic program, and ... doesn't support pro-choice [on the abortion issue], is not really a feminist."[92]

Evidence from representative governments throughout the world demonstrates that voters have more moderate views than elected officials, who in turn

TABLE 4.6 DELEGATE SURVEYS FORTY YEARS APART (1944–1984) (IN PERCENTAGES)

	1944 Dem.	1944 Rep.	1968 Dem.	1968 Rep.	1976 Dem.	1976 Rep.	1984 Dem.	1984 Rep.
By sex								
Men	89	91	87	83	67	69	49	54
Women	11	9	13	17	33	31	51	46
By education								
High school or less	24	23	N.A.	N.A.	N.A.	N.A.	11	12
Some college	18	18	N.A.	N.A.	N.A.	N.A.	18	25
College graduate	12	16	10	—	21	27	20	28
More than college degree	46	41	44	34	43	38	51	35
By age								
Average age (in years)	52	54	49	49	43	48	44	51
By occupation								
Lawyer	38	37	28	22	16	15	17	14
Union leader	2	—	4	—	6	—	6	—
Executive	9	10	27	40	17	30	14	26
Other profession/teacher	24	35	8	2	26	12	36	27
Public official	11	6	13	13	12	9	9	6
Housewife	6	5	*	*	7	15	4	13

Convention attendance							
Never attended convention before	63	63	67	66	80	78	74	69
By ideology								
Liberal	*	*	*	*	40	3	50	1
Moderate	*	*	*	*	47	45	42	35
Conservative	*	*	*	*	8	48	5	60

SOURCE: Barbara G. Farah, "Delegate Polls: 1944 to 1984," *Public Opinion* (August/September 1984): 44. Reprinted with permission of American Enterprise Institute for Public Policy Research.

NOTES: 1984 figures are a combination of the CBS News poll, the *New York Times* poll, and the *Los Angeles Times* poll; the 1968 and 1976 figures come from the CBS News poll. The occupation categories are not exactly the same for the 1944 study and the later polls. That will explain the disparity between values for "executive" in the early year and the later ones.

*Questions not asked in these years.

are more moderate than party activists.[93] In 1984 poll evidence sustained this view, showing Democratic voters to be slightly and delegates vastly more liberal than the average of the general population (see table 4.7), except on national health care. Moreover, Democratic delegates grew more liberal from 1980 to 1984 (see table 4.8).[94] While the general public prefers smaller government and lower taxes far more than do Democratic elites, the public also likes welfare and health spending a lot more than Republican elites do. We conclude that when party elites talk about the great issues that separate them, they are not talking about the public, which is much more moderate, but about themselves. With the increase of ideological consistency among activists in the major parties has come a decline in their party loyalty. While Republican delegates have consistently seen themselves as stronger party supporters than have Democrats, delegates from both parties (with the exception of the Democratic convention when there were moderate Carter delegates) show a steady decline in strong party support.[95]

TABLE 4.7 DEMOCRATIC DELEGATES TO THE LEFT OF RANK-AND-FILE PARTY MEMBERS AND PUBLIC, 1984 (PERCENTAGES IN AGREEMENT WITH STATEMENTS)

Here's how the delegates measured up against the Democratic rank and file and the public at large on some of these issues.

	Public	Democrats	Delegates
Ratify ERA	60	64	91
Blacks are a long way from having the same chance as whites	55	63	85
CIA should help friendly governments and undermine hostile governments	40	36	14
Reinstitute the draft	49	51	26
U.S. should take all steps including force to stop communism	63	59	22
Government should raise taxes to deal with deficit	23	22	53
U.S. can meet security obligations with smaller military budget	49	59	85

However, polling showed some issues on which the delegates, their fellow Democrats and the general public agree.

	Public	Democrats	Delegates
Government should stop building nuclear power plants for safety reasons	56	64	65
Government should institute a national health care program	71	81	70

SOURCE: Peter Begans, "The ABC News/*Washington Post* Poll," survey nos. 0122–25, 4.

Asked to say who they represented at the convention—the party organizations, a candidate support group, an interest group, or voters—Democrats from 1972 to 1984 overwhelmingly went with their favorite candidates. Their support for party never went above 25 percent. Their adherence to special groups has grown in recent years to 22 percent, double that of Republicans.[96]

In summary, trends in the ideological dispositions of party activists in the two parties seem to reflect changes in the composition of the two delegate populations. Notably, Republican delegates include more women and more ex-Dixiecrats; Democratic delegates include more women and fewer conservative southerners. Thus Democratic delegates are becoming somewhat more liberal, and Republicans more mixed and less cohesive. Similar trends can be observed in the Democratic caucus of the House of Representatives, where the subtraction of a large number of Dixiecrat seats over the past twenty years has led to the emergence of liberal mainstream sentiment strongly expressed through caucus action.

Now we can guess why in the midst of a considerable change in policy preferences, wholesale party realignment fails to appear: the major parties have realigned themselves internally. This is most evident in the South as newcomers and young white voters have become increasingly Republican.[97] The older view that the major parties were essentially alike, which was never true, is even less true today.

The consequences of ideological polarization, which is what we have been describing, are well known: heightened conflict and perhaps political instability. According to the theory of crosscutting cleavages, when people agree on some issues and disagree on others, the need to call on each other for support sometimes moderates the severity of conflict at other times. Polarization, by putting the same people in opposition on issue after issue, increases antagonism.

TABLE 4.8 **POSITIONS TAKEN BY 1984 DEMOCRATIC DELEGATES COMPARED TO PREDECESSORS IN 1980 (PERCENTAGES IN AGREEMENT WITH STATEMENTS)**

	1984	1980
Ratify ERA	91	86
Blacks are a long way from having the same chance as whites	85	79
CIA should help friendly governments and undermine hostile governments	14	30
Reinstitute the draft	26	39
Government should stop building nuclear power plants for safety reasons	65	48
Government should institute a national health care program	70	65

SOURCE: Peter Begans, "The ABC News/*Washington Post* Poll," survey nos. 0122–25, 4.

The Convention as Advertising

Party conventions were probably always seen, in part, as a means of advertisement; at the least, listening to convention speeches and talking to peers might furnish delegates with rhetoric to use in local campaigns. But until the age of television, conventions were primarily concerned with nominating candidates and conducting other party business.

Television arrived at the conventions in 1952 and changed all that, with the help of party reforms that ended the old business of conventions. Now, conventions are for campaign launching.[98] Conventions are planned in order to sell the ticket and the party to a national audience. The actual business of conventions, such as putting the names of candidates before the convention and approving the platform, is scheduled for afternoon or early evening sessions before the broadcast networks' news teams go on the air. Prime time is filled with speeches meant to appeal to voters, along with films prepared beforehand to keep the audience interested.[99] Indeed, conventions are judged by pundits on how well they are organized as advertisements. Any intrusion of party business (such as platform disagreements) into the convention is considered a breach of unity and therefore a sign of weakness in the party. More serious still is poor entertainment: woe to any convention such as Jimmy Carter's renomination convention in 1980 in which the mechanism for releasing the brightly colored balloons malfunctioned, thus providing commentators with a metaphor for his stalled reelection bid.[100]

The advertising content of the conventions is influenced by the decisions of network news teams; the parties try to provide programs they believe the networks will allow people to see, now that the parties cannot count on "gavel-to-gavel" coverage. Currently, the networks cover the conventions through their nightly news broadcasts, their morning shows, and one- or two-hour live wrap-up shows from the conventions during prime time.[101] Examples of the old gavel-to-gavel coverage can be found only on cable; in 1992 ABC, for example, "did not go live to the podium even once" on the second day of the Democratic convention.[102]

By using the convention as advertising, the parties hope to receive a "bounce" in the approval candidates get from the polls. From 1964 to 1984, only Lyndon Johnson in 1964 (who was high in voter approval to begin with) and George McGovern in 1972 (who had a disastrous convention) failed to improve in voter surveys taken immediately after their conventions. One might think that this effect would dissipate as broadcast networks reduced the amount of convention coverage and as viewers had more options than network television. But the public appeared as ready to be influenced by the conventions in 1992 as ever; Bill Clinton's bounce in the polls after his convention, which was everywhere reported to be a success, was as large as any on record.[103] In 1996 both Clinton and Bob Dole had healthy bounces of several percentage points in the polls.[104]

How do the parties turn what once was a business meeting into advertising?

1. The layout of the convention hall itself is designed with television, not the comfort of the delegates, as the first priority. As Democratic media consultant Robert D. Squier says, "To be blunt, the room is designed to be a television set." Another high-profile Democratic media expert, Frank Greer, said in praise of the 1988 convention: "It has become clear that, as it should be, this is a convention designed and presented for TV viewers more so than for delegates on the floor. It's a chance to talk to people in their living rooms and not the delegates on the floor."[105]

2. Not just the appearance of the hall is designed for television. The delegates, far from having an important role in deciding party business, have been reduced to serving primarily as extras. "Homemade" signs are actually constructed by the party; in 1992 neither party allowed delegates to bring in their own banners. Even crowd noises are not left to chance: the GOP in Houston in 1992 "arranged that, at key moments, troops of rehearsed young people flooded onto the floor and filled the first fifty feet in front of the podium and in the aisles. They knew what to chant when, and they were standing in front of most of the delegates so they couldn't be missed by the cameras."[106]

3. Both parties try to script all the words spoken at the convention, whether that means carefully orchestrating the words and images delivered from the podium or faxing suggested responses to likely interview targets. The Republicans in 1992 required each of the more than 100 podium speakers to submit their speeches to a small team of speechwriters charged with keeping the talk from the podium tuned to the "theme of the day." The speechwriters' job ranged from fine-tuning some speeches to drafting others from scratch.[107] Speeches are eventually fed into teleprompters and timed so that signs and chants from the floor can be properly coordinated with them.

Very little is left to chance: the parties coordinate their schedules with network broadcast plans. As Tom Rosenstiel reports:

> The parties and the networks worked together for months planning and organizing these affairs in tandem, setting camera angles for mutual benefit, coordinating logistics, all of it off the record.
> The coordination was sometimes secret, sometimes not. And sometimes the network news was even temporarily allied with the party to gain leverage inside their own network. Once the Republicans

decided they would have Patrick Buchanan speak on the Monday of their Houston convention in prime time and sent ABC a schedule with Buchanan going on shortly after 10 P.M., ABC vice-president Jeff Gralnick would quietly call Republican convention chairman Craig Fuller.

Put Buchanan on at 9:50, Gralnick would tell the party official, not 10:05. Then I can convince my network to let me go on at 9:30, not 10:00 and we can both get thirty minutes more airtime....

Lane Vernardos, Gralnick's counterpart at CBS, would put in a similar call to Republican organizers.

Fuller would quickly agree.[108]

The parties, then, treat their conventions as four-day-long commercials for the presidential ticket and for the party as a whole.[109] This is not necessarily a bad thing: many pundits have urged the networks to make available free airtime for the parties to present their messages directly to the voters during the fall campaign, not realizing that the conventions already serve that purpose. The presidential campaign is limited to the extent that some of the delegates may belong to losing candidates; thus Clinton and Bush were required in 1992 to negotiate with losing candidates Buchanan, Brown, and Tsongas to ensure that their delegates would act like fully cooperating extras for the cameras, and each losing candidate received what he wanted—an opportunity to address the convention. Better still were the positions of the 1996 nominees. Clinton was unopposed for nomination and therefore could select all the delegates, and Bob Dole had dominated the Republican primaries enough that almost all the delegates were loyal to him.

First and foremost, the candidate wants a united party.[110] Party leaders who are in a position to disrupt unity may extort small advantages from the nominee, a significant strategic resource in recent years for Jesse Jackson's candidacy. As Jackson approached the Democratic convention of 1988, he made speeches demanding a greater role in the party, threatening to stage a floor fight over the party platform, "and renewed his threat to challenge [Lloyd] Bentsen's [vice-presidential] nomination."[111] Dukakis's backers voted down Jackson's platform proposals. These would have raised taxes to much higher levels, frozen military spending, tilted to the Palestinian side in their Middle East conflict with Israel, and pledged the United States not to be the first to use nuclear weapons. In return, Jackson temporarily won changes in Democratic Party rules, cutting the number of superdelegates nearly in half and requiring that all delegates be awarded to candidates on a proportional rather than a winner-take-all basis. All along, Jackson's complaint had been that it was undemocratic for him to have fewer delegates as a proportion of the whole convention than votes in the primary election.[112] In order to preserve the peace, Dukakis gave in on the procedural issues, just as Humphrey gave in to McCarthy delegates in 1968 and granted them the formation of what became the McGovern-Fraser Commission.[113]

The Vice-Presidential Nominee

When the convention finally selects its presidential candidate, it turns to the anticlimactic task of finding a running mate. The vice-presidential nominee is chosen to help the party achieve the presidency. Party nominees for president and vice president always appear on the ballot together and are elected together. Since 1804 a vote for one has always been a vote for the other.

The vice president's post in the legislative branch of the government is mostly honorific, and his or her powers and activities in the executive branch are determined by the president.[114] The electoral interdependence of the two offices gives politicians opportunities to gather votes for the presidency. Therefore, the prescription for the "ideal" vice-presidential nominee is the same as for the presidential nominees, with two additions: the vice-presidential nominee must possess some desirable qualities the presidential nominee lacks and must be acceptable to the presidential nominee.

The vice presidency is the position from which presidents of the United States are most frequently drawn. A third of our forty-two presidents were once vice presidents. Five were later elected to the presidency in their own right; eight first took office on the death of a president; and of course Gerald Ford succeeded because of President Nixon's resignation. American history has given us fourteen good reasons—one for each man who succeeded to the presidency—for inquiring into the qualifications of vice presidents and for examining the criteria by which they are chosen.

The presidential candidate who has firm control over his nomination is in a position to use the vice-presidential slot to help win the election. This is what Abraham Lincoln did in 1864 when he chose a "War Democrat," Andrew Johnson, who he hoped would add strength to the ticket. In the same way, John F. Kennedy chose Lyndon Johnson to help gather southern votes, especially in Texas, and Richard Nixon chose Henry Cabot Lodge of Massachusetts in 1960 to help offset the Democratic Party advantage in the Northeast. In 1964 President Johnson chose an outstanding liberal, Senator Hubert Humphrey of Minnesota. Johnson's own credentials as a liberal Democrat down through the years were not strong; when Kennedy picked him as vice president, he had been opposed on these grounds by many labor leaders and by leaders from several of the most important urban Democratic strongholds.

Recent vice-presidential candidates sometimes have been distinguished politicians who had a great deal to recommend them. But the help they could offer their parties was undoubtedly an important consideration. In choosing Senator Humphrey, President Johnson adhered to the familiar strategy of ticket balancing, as Kennedy had done in choosing him. President Ford, with his midwestern and congressional background, may have had the same thing in mind when he chose a more liberal, eastern establishment figure, Nelson Rockefeller, to be his vice president on his elevation to the presidency. Later, threats from the right wing of the Republican Party to his own nomination chances caused him to dump Rockefeller and replace him for the 1976 convention with Senator Bob Dole of Kansas. Reagan, more securely tied to the Republican right wing than Ford, leaned toward the moderate side of his own party in picking George Bush. Bush, in turn, looked to the right when selecting a running mate, settling on Senator Dan Quayle of Indiana, who not only offered solid conservative credentials but also promised to appeal to youth and women, two groups of voters the Republicans were targeting.[115] One measure of how the Republican Party had changed in twenty years was that Bob Dole, once chosen to please party conservatives, turned to Jack Kemp in 1996 in part to placate those in the party not convinced of Dole's tax-cutting zeal.[116]

Another way of balancing the ticket is to focus on experience. Jimmy Carter chose a popular senator, Walter Mondale, in part to make up for his own lack of "insider" qualifications. Similar considerations drove two other governors to choose prominent Washingtonians as their running mates— Michael Dukakis's selection of Texas Senator Lloyd Bentsen and Bill Clinton's choice of Tennessee Senator Al Gore fit this model.

Walter Mondale's choice of Representative Geraldine Ferraro in 1984 did not fit either of these patterns of ticket balancing; her views were quite similar to his own. Instead, it was hoped that the historic choice of a woman on a major-party ticket could help exploit the "gender gap" that had emerged in 1980. Far behind in the polls, Mondale may also have been hoping that a bold move would invigorate his campaign. Richard Brookhiser argues that "the best justification for Mondale's audacity, though, was that it was audacious.... Prudent losers remain losers. The first woman on a major party ticket might shake things up."[117]

Sometimes a presidential candidate will try to help heal a breach in the party by offering the vice-presidential nomination to a leader of a defeated party faction. Or the presidential candidate may try to improve relationships with Congress by finding a running mate who has friends there. Humphrey balanced his ticket in 1968 by choosing Senator Edmund Muskie, a quietly eloquent moderate man, and a member of an ethnic group (Polish Americans) concentrated in the cities of the eastern seaboard, to balance his own midwestern populist background and fast-talking style.

A Republican presidential candidate from the East will try to pick a vice president from the Midwest or Far West. It has been thought desirable, as in the case of Reagan (California) and Bush (Texas), for both to reside in large, two-party "swing" states. Bob Dole, from Kansas, managed to find a running mate, Jack Kemp, who claimed both New York and California as home states.

With the mode of delegate selection among Democrats biased in favor of one-party states (owing to the abolition of the unit rule and the winner-take-all primary), however, this tendency may no longer prevail. None of the Democratic presidential nominees since the post-1968 rules changes has been from a large state. But a liberal Democrat running for president will frequently try to find a more conservative running mate. If it is impossible to find one person who combines within his or her heritage, personality, and experience all the virtues allegedly cherished by American voters, the parties console themselves by attempting to confect out of two running mates a composite image of forward-looking conservative, rural-urban, energetic-wise leadership that evokes hometown, ethnic, and party loyalties among a maximum number of voters. That, at least, is the theory behind the balanced ticket.

When especially able politicians have appeared in the vice-presidential office from time to time, this may have been more because of the blessings of Providence than because of wise actions on anyone's part. If good results require noble intentions, then the criteria for choosing vice presidents leave much to be desired. Why should the great parties, we might ask, not set out deliberately to choose the candidate best able to act as president in case of need? Should ticket balancing and similar considerations be condemned as political chicanery? Former Vice President Henry A. Wallace once declared: "The greatest danger is that the man just nominated for President will try desperately to heal the wounds and placate the dissidents in his party....My battle cry would be—no more deals—no more balancing of the ticket." In 1964 the Republican Party evidently also endorsed this view. The selection of the 1964 Republican vice-presidential nominee, Representative William Miller of upstate New York, was intended to violate criteria used in the past for balancing the ticket. Although he came from a region different from Barry Goldwater and, unlike Goldwater, was a Catholic, Miller was chosen primarily because of his ideological affinity with the presidential candidate. The special style of Goldwater and his supporters required that consistency of views, opposition to the other party on as many issues as possible, and refusal to bargain prevail over the traditional political demands for compromise, flexibility, and popularity.[118] This was also apparently the sentiment of many Republicans in 1976. Yet the candidate of the conservatives that year, Ronald Reagan, said he would choose as his running mate a liberal easterner, Senator Richard Schweiker of Pennsylvania. This was his last-ditch attempt to win the nomination, and it was a gamble he lost. But it was consistent with Reagan's view four years later, when he said: "There are some people who think that you should, on principle, jump off the cliff with the flag flying if you can't have everything you want....If I found when I was governor that I could not get 100 percent of what I asked for, I took 80 percent."[119]

From the standpoint of the electoral success of candidates, balancing the ticket seems only prudent. But there are other reasons for ordinary citizens to prefer that candidates make an effort in this direction. One of the chief assets of the American party system in the past has been its ability, with the exception of the Civil War period, to reduce conflict by enforcing compromise within the major factions of each party. A refusal to heal the wounds and placate dissidents is easily interpreted as a declaration of internal war. It can only lead to increased conflict within the party. Willingness to bargain and make concessions to opponents is part of the price for maintaining unity in a party sufficiently large and varied to be able to appeal successfully to a nationwide population divided on economic, sectional, racial, religious, ethnic, and perhaps also ideological grounds. To refuse entirely to balance the ticket would be to risk changing our large, heterogeneous parties into a multiplicity of small sects of true believers who care more about maintaining their internal purity than about winning public office by pleasing the people.

There is obvious good sense in providing for a basic continuity in policy in case a president should die or be disabled. But this need not mean that the president and vice president should be identical in every respect, even if that were possible. Within the broad outlines of agreement on the basic principles of the nation's foreign policy and of the government's role in the economy, for example, a president would have no great difficulty in finding a variety of running mates who appealed to somewhat different groups or who differed in other salient ways. To go this far to promote party unity, factional conciliation, and popular preference should not discomfort anyone who understands the costs of failing to balance the ticket.

Actually there is little evidence to suggest that vice presidents add greatly to or detract severely from the popularity of presidential candidates with the voters. By helping unite the party, however, and by giving diverse party leaders another focus of identification with the ticket, a vice-presidential nominee with the right characteristics can help assure greater effort by party workers, and this may bring results at election time. Even if balancing the ticket does not help the party at the polls, it may indirectly help the people. It may aid our political parties to maintain unity within diversity and thereby to perform their historic function of bringing our varied population closer together.

One of the destructive effects of the newer norms of media coverage of politicians might be to make such balancing somewhat less likely in the future. Candidates, of course, have access to sophisticated polling, and are aware that they are unlikely to win election by finding the perfect candidate. However, intense negative publicity can turn the advertising potential of the convention into a highly publicized embarrassment. No presidential candidate has the resources fully to research every aspect of a potential vice president's background. Instead, nominees have increasingly in recent years turned to the one pool of people who not only have been fully investigated but also have extensive experience dealing with the national media: former presidential candidates. Jack Kemp in 1996, Al Gore in 1992, Lloyd Bentsen in 1988, and George Bush in 1980 had all been tested in presidential primaries. None of them encountered scandal or significant bad press during the fall campaigns. The two vice-presidential nominees over that period who had not been previously exposed to the national media, Geraldine Ferraro in 1984 and Dan Quayle in 1988, had far more than their share of turmoil during their campaigns. We suspect that future presidential nominees will be tempted to play it safe by limiting their selections to this small group of prescreened possibilities.

The Future of National Conventions

If conventions are really only for advertisement, why are the delegates still important? A comparison with the Electoral College is instructive. Ever since the early days of the republic, electors virtually always vote as they have been instructed by their states. The majority wins. Should no candidate receive a majority, electors still have no say in the outcome, because under the Constitution the selection is made by Congress.

Delegates to nominating conventions, even under the current rules, are in a somewhat different position. While their votes on the nomination are (in normal years) simply a matter of registering the choices of the voters who chose them, even then they have votes to make on platforms and rules. These votes may be important, and the delegates can in principle make their own decisions. Even hand-picked delegates have the option of opposing their candidate, should they so choose.

Far more important, however, is that in the event of deadlock delegates would have the responsibility of selecting the nominee. If the contest is merely close, we would expect few delegate defections, since they have been in most cases selected by candidates mainly on grounds of their personal loyalty. A good illustration of that was the Democratic Convention in 1980, when Senator Edward Kennedy hoped to use favorable preconvention publicity to sway the convention. The hope turned out to be unrealistic. In the key test vote, Carter delegates stayed loyal.

However, should no candidate enter the convention with a majority, loyalty to the candidate might no longer matter. These scenerios are mainstays of pundit thinking every four years early on in the primaries, when no candidate has yet built a sizable majority in the delegate count. As we have seen, an "open" convention is not particularly likely. Such a result would almost certainly require not two, but at least three candidates to reach the convention with large numbers of delegates; if only two candidates have delegates, one or the other will have a majority, no matter how slender. Since the normal operations of primaries and caucuses, along with the media interpretations of victory and defeat, quickly winnow out most candidates in a typcial year, a deadlocked convention with three or more candidates is an improbable result (see table 4.9, p.149) This is particularly true on the Republican side, where numerous winner-take-all primaries reduce the potential of spoiler candidates to accumulate delegates. Still, deadlock is possible, and if it happens, it will be the delegates who will have to choose.

How would a reformed convention handle such a decision? The same rules that have made conventions rubber stamps for voters in primaries also would make bargaining difficult once there. In order to reach the convention, candidates would need intense factional support; delegates selected for those traits would, presumably, be ill-equipped to negotiate away their vote for the candidate to whom they were loyal. The candidates themselves, then, might be the only ones able to negotiate—and candidates fresh off the campaign trail, having endured negative ads and other attacks from each other, might not be eager to cut a deal, or even able to bring along their supporters if they did make a deal.

If the candidates did not resolve their differences, how else would the delegates reach a decision? Some, no doubt, would turn to factional leaders. State delegations might work together, even across candidate lines. Still others might remain unconnected, waiting until someone found a resolution. Given the enormous size of modern conventions (the Democrats in 1996 sent almost two thousand delegates, compared to the eleven hundred delegates who nominated Franklin Delano Roosevelt in 1932), it would be impossible for serious, one-on-one deliberation to take place without some sort of organization emerging. If not, we might expect the media to dominate the proceedings, with delegates swayed by the latest reported rumors and speculations.

We remain convinced that a mixed system, including both primaries and deliberative conventions, is a good method for parties to select their nominees. We doubt that conventions as presently populated are properly equipped to handle that job. Chief among the needs of a deliberative convention would be a manageable size and delegates who represent someone other than the candidates. In part this problem may have been mitigated by the 1982 decision of the Democrats to admit public officeholders to the convention as unpledged delegates. Over 15 percent of the 1996 convention was constituted in this fashion. So far, it has made no difference.

A healthy political party requires activists as well as voters. As long as the policy preferences and group identifications of these two populations are reasonably compatible, their differing interests can be reconciled by bargaining. Once they grow far apart, however, the tension between them may become unbearable until one another leaves their ancestral party. In Europe this tension frequently takes the form of a clash between militant party activists and more moderate parliamentarians interested in winning elections. Where parliamentarians elect party leaders in Parliament, including the prime minister, they have real resources with which to combat militants. The separate elections of senators and representatives and the federal system in the United States, however, take the presidential nomination outside of normal politics. Congressional and gubernatorial candidates, who want to win elections, rarely run on as radical or conservative a basis as the rhetoric of their activist supporters might suggest, and they participate less than they used to in picking the presi-

TABLE 4.9   NUMBER OF PRESIDENTIAL BALLOTS IN NATIONAL PARTY CONVENTIONS,
1928–1996 (NOMINATIONS WON BY INCUMBENTS ARE IN PARENTHESES)

Year	Democrats	Republicans
1928	1	1
1932	4	(1)
1936	(1)	1
1940	(1)	8
1944	(1)	1
1948	(1)	3
1952	3	1
1956	1	(1)
1960	1	1
1964	(1)	1
1968	1	1
1972	1	(1)
1976	1	(1)
1980	(1)	1
1984	1	(1)
1988	1	1
1992	1	(1)
1996	(1)	1
First Ballot Total	16/18	16/18
	(7 incumbents)	(6 incumbents)

Combined (Democratic and Republicans) first-ballot nominations:
Nonincumbents   19/23
Incumbents   13/13

dential nominee. Thus these elected officials have much less of a stake in the presidency. On the Democratic side, the party leaders who used to guard that stake were so weak or absent during the conventions after 1968 that the Democratic Hunt Commission of 1982 provided that a large number of members of Congress should be welcomed as unpledged delegates.

What is remarkable, when one thinks of it, is that special arrangements should have to be made to bring party officeholders back into the conventions or to allow the people who probably know most about the candidates to support whomever they think best. Leaving politicians—who have to appeal to electorates—out of the process, we think, is a poor way to choose candidates for the greatest national office.

Bringing into the convention a bloc of uncommitted "superdelegates" composed of officeholders and public officials might appear on the surface to reflect a desire to give the convention greater discretion and more options in choosing a candidate. It has not worked out that way. Evidently for the first couple of conventions where superdelegates have been present, the chair of the Democratic National Committee and others have wanted to assure a consensus behind a candidate well before the convention meets. The chair's concern was that the nominating decision not "be taken away from the millions who do participate in our primaries and caucuses and be given to a few in the 'back rooms' of a brokered convention."[120]

In 1984 the superdelegates went early and massively for Mondale. Jesse Jackson and Gary Hart supporters, as part of their price for uniting behind Mondale, got agreement that the Democratic National Committee would appoint superdelegates later in the 1988 process, after the caucuses and primaries were over.[121] Would placing politicians at the national conventions in this fashion lead to different convention choices? There would have to be differences in candidate preference between these politicians and the other delegates. And the other delegates, pledged to various aspiring candidates, would themselves have to be split because, if they were united, they would have more than enough for a majority.

Just as the news media have interacted with political forces to produce the ratifying rather than the deciding convention, so the two have combined to give the conventions their electoral meaning. Deprived of their decision-making role, the conventions become the first opportunity for campaign publicity with the party united behind a single candidate. Not having to worry about winning the nomination at the convention, candidates can more carefully consider how they want to manage the presentation of their party for advertising purposes. Thus national conventions have changed from being the big guns of the nominating process to the first shots of the election campaign.

The candidates may want their delegates to look presentable to television viewers, but they are not in a position to do much about it. They can, as we have seen, assure the presence of delegates pledged to them, making sure the delegates do their duty by voting for them. So far, from the candidate's point of view, so good. While the delegates have mostly pledged their votes, however, they have not hocked their souls. As Jimmy Carter discovered in 1980, platform issues were all the more important to delegates by virtue of the fact that they had no other decisions to make. What is more, delegates who have come to the convention to express support for their varied lifestyles can do that simply by being who they are and showing up on television. Black or white, male or female, straight or gay, liberated or conventional, delegates can make a statement about what they stand for simply by being there.

To appear before the public, of course, delegates must get on television. What gets across to the voter is what television journalists choose to show. Aside from the few obligatory famous names, the usual principles apply: controversy and deviance make better copy than uncomplicated gestures of support. Whatever the delegates appear to be, television accentuates that pattern at its edges, stressing differences rather than similarities with the past. Should voters look in and say to themselves and friends and neighbors that these delegates are not "my kind of people," candidates may find that their ability to project a certain image is overwhelmed by contrary notions that voters have gathered for themselves.

CHAPTER 5
The Campaign

Once the conventions are over, it is a tradition, now increasingly ignored, for the two presidential candidates to relax for a few weeks until Labor Day, when they ordinarily begin their official campaigning. From that day onward they confront the voters directly, each carrying the banner of a major political party. How do the candidates behave? Why do they act the way they do? What kind of impact do their activities have on the electorate?

For the small minority of people who are party workers, campaigns serve as a signal to get to work. How hard they work depends in part on whether the candidates' political opinions, slogans, personalities, and visits spark their enthusiasm. The workers may sit on their hands, or they may pursue their generally unrewarding jobs—checking voting lists, mailing campaign flyers, ringing doorbells—with something approaching fervor.

For the majority of the population, most of whom keep their distance from politics, campaigns call attention to the advent of an election. Some excitement may be generated and some diversion (as well as annoyance) provided for those who turn on the television to find that their favorite program has been preempted by political talk. The campaign is a great spectacle. Conversation about politics increases, and some citizens may even become intensely involved as they get caught up in campaign advertising.

For the vast majority of citizens in America, campaigns do not function so much to change minds as to activate or reinforce previous convictions. As the campaign wears on, the underlying party identification of most people rises ever more powerfully to the surface. Republican and Democratic identifiers are split further apart—polarized—as their increased awareness of party competition emphasizes the things that divide them.[1]

The contents of election campaigns appear to be largely opportunistic. The swiftly changing nature of events makes it unwise for candidates to lay down all-embracing rules for campaigning that cannot meet special situations as they arise. Candidates may prepare for battle on one front and discover that the movement of events forces them to fight on another. Yet on closer examination it is evident that the political strategist has to rely on some sort of theory about the probable behavior of large groups of voters under a few likely conditions. For there are too many millions of voters and too many thousands of possible events to deal with each as a separate category. The candidates must simplify their pictures of the political world or its full complexity will paralyze them; the only question is whether or not their theories, both explicit and implicit, will prove helpful to them.

What kind of organization should they use or construct? Where should they campaign? How much time should they allocate to the various regions and states? What kinds of appeals should they make to what voting groups? How specific should they be in their policy proposals? What kind of personal impression should they seek to create or reinforce? How far should they go in attacking the opposition? These are the kinds of strategic questions for which presidential candidates need answers—answers that necessarily vary depending on their party affiliations, their personal attributes, whether they are in or out of office, and on targets of opportunity that come up in the course of current events.

What Do They Do?

The candidate's primary responsibilities are to get the campaign's message out to the voters and to energize activists. This requires showing up at events all over the country and talking to the crowds assembled there, thus making "news."

There was a time when presidential nominees faced the serious choice of whether to conduct a "front porch" campaign or to get out and meet the people. The first president to make a campaign speech, William Henry Harrison at Columbus, Ohio, in June 1840, was scolded for his pains: "When," the *Cleveland Adviser* asked, "was there ever before such a spectacle as a candidate for the Presidency, traversing the country advocating his own claims for that high and responsible station?" Those days are long gone. Now, each candidate hires an airplane and speechwriters, maps out an itinerary, and flies off in all directions. Patrick Anderson, who wrote speeches for Jimmy Carter in 1976, describes how it feels:

> We were so isolated on the plane. Our world extended from Peanut
> One [the name of the plane] to the motorcade to the rally to the
> hotel, and was populated by the candidate, four or five staff people,
> and a dozen or so reporters. Everything beyond that was a blur.
> There are few experiences more exhilarating than to see tens of thou-
> sands of people cheering your candidate, to feel the tide running
> your way, to think your man will win and you helped this miracle
> come to pass. The cities flew by: Erie, Cleveland, Gary, Toledo.[4]

There is method in this. In deciding where to campaign, the candidates are aided by distinctive features of the national political structure that go a long way toward giving them guidance. They know that it is not votes as such that matter but electoral votes, which are counted on a state-by-state basis. The candidate who wins by a small plurality in a state gains all of that state's electoral votes. The candidates realize that a huge margin of victory in a state with a handful of electoral votes will not do them nearly as much good as a bare plurality in such states as New York and California, with large numbers of electoral votes. So the first guideline is evident: campaign in states with large numbers of electoral votes. There is not much point, however, in campaigning in states where they know they are bound to win or to lose. Thus, states that almost always go for a particular party receive less attention. The original guideline may be modified to read: campaign in states with large numbers of electoral votes that are doubtful. In practice, a "doubtful" state is one where there is a decent chance for either party to capture the state. Politicians usually gauge this chance by the extent to which the state has delivered victories to both parties within recent memory. Candidates of both parties thus spend more time in New York, Ohio, Illinois, Pennsylvania, Texas, Florida, and California than they do elsewhere. Thus the states that candidates will not visit are likely to be those that are small and uncontested. In September 1996, the states neither campaign visited included Alabama, Alaska, Hawaii, Idaho, Indiana, Kansas, Maine, Maryland, Minnesota, Mississippi, Montana, New Hampshire, North Carolina, Oklahoma, South Carolina, Vermont, and Wyoming.[5] The closer the election contest overall, of course, the more close races. As the campaign wears on, the candidates take soundings from the opinion polls and are likely to redouble their efforts in states where they believe a personal visit might turn the tide. In 1976 Hamilton Jordan had these matters worked out to a mathematical formula—awarding points to states based on size and winnability and then allocating campaign days to each of them for his candidate, Jimmy Carter, the vice-presidential candidate Walter Mondale, and members of the Carter family.[6]

The itinerary is made by a campaign scheduling team—a phalanx of up to 250 employees, approximately thirty to forty to plot the schedule and the rest to handle the press and advance work. Schedulers start the process rolling as they determine where the candidate will appear. They adopt two rules for this task: "Go where the polls say an appearance by the candidate can make a difference. Make it look good on television."[7] Peter Hart, a Democratic pollster, breaks the scheduler's job down into units: a presidential campaign is made up of approximately eighty working days with an average of four events a day, which gives the scheduler a total of 320 "units" to work with.[8] The scheduler's task is to manage these units so the candidate gets the most value from his or her appearances. Thus schedulers arrange more candidate appearances in big competitive states such as Illinois or California than in smaller, more secure states. The payoffs from these units are expected to be higher.

Schedulers generally work with thirty-day schedules, but arrangements constantly change as the poll numbers suggest increasing margins of safety in a given state or reveal new states in need of targeting. In 1976 scheduler Eliot Cutler was convinced that Jimmy Carter would win or lose the race in Ohio.

He suggested that the campaign bombard the state and schedule 65 percent of Walter Mondale's time there during the last two weeks. Overcoming resistance by threatening to quit, Cutler had Mondale skipping across Ohio, sometimes visiting the same city twice in one week. Carter and Mondale eventually won Ohio by 8,000 votes, a critical victory in a very close election.[9]

Schedulers also decide on the type of event to put into the candidate's itinerary. Early on in a campaign, a candidate will attend many fund-raisers, some large dinners, some intimate gatherings of significant contributors. As the campaign gains momentum, fund-raising is increasingly transferred to a full-time staff and the candidate's time is geared to large rallies, usually with a theme to attract media attention and television news coverage. For example, in 1992 Bush visited a Waffle House restaurant in South Carolina to make a symbolic reference to his criticism of Bill Clinton for waffling on his draft record. That same day, Bush spoke to a rally of Republican supporters in Thomasville, North Carolina, home of The Largest Chair in the World, rode a train through southern towns, waving at crowds from the back of the caboose, spoke again in Burlington, North Carolina, and joined Senator Jesse Helms and stockcar racing hero Richard Petty for a rally in Raleigh—all potential media events.

Once the schedulers have booked an appearance for the candidate, the press and advance team move in. Their responsibility is to ensure that the event happens without a hitch and that the candidate's message is presented to an adequately prepared press corps, ready to include the day's sound bite in their story or on the evening news. The advance team's responsibilities include ensuring security for the candidates, arranging transportation (candidates can change vehicles a dozen times or more in one day) and housing, overseeing site setup, and providing campaign placards, buttons, and banners for the crowd. They must make sure that the press has audio and visual access to the candidate, that equipment feeds are working, and that the promotional materials in evidence evoke the campaign's theme. Late in the 1992 campaign, the Bush advance team provided local events with banners stating that the community "Trusts George Bush." Trust was the principal theme in the later Bush campaign.[10]

It is beside the point that no one knows whether all this does any good. Richard Nixon learned from his enervating experience in 1960, when he pledged to visit each and every state and then had to follow through despite a severe illness. In 1968 he ran a different kind of campaign, taking account of the fact that radio and television made it possible to reach millions without leaving the big metropolitan areas. Nixon did a small amount of traditional campaigning, which was faithfully chronicled by the press corps that followed him around the country. But more basic to his strategy was the technique of fixing upon regional centers and making major appearances and speeches in these places, followed by elaborate, regionally oriented television commercials that reached the voters directly—"over the heads," so to speak, of the news media that were covering and interpreting only the part of the campaign they could see, which did not include Nixon's television programs.[11] Nowadays most candidates follow a regional strategy geared to television markets, but they benefit from the existence of a national market as well. No matter where the candidates are, the network news shows are likely to report on their activities, extending the reach of a candidate's message beyond his immediate audience.[12]

It is the candidate's job, in this environment, to stay "on message"—that is, if the campaign theme is trust, to emphasize words such as "honesty" or "reliable" in prepared speeches and to work themes of trust into impromptu remarks to audiences and to the press. It is also the candidate's job to deliver a speech with great enthusiasm, no matter how many times he or she has had to reuse the same lines; to avoid anything that could be considered embarrassing; and, generally, to be "on" at all times. Presidential candidates must expect to be before audiences live and on television throughout the campaign, knowing that a small mistake can have devastating consequences.

Sheer physical endurance is required. Bob Dole, in the final stages of the 1996 contest, embarked on a "96 Hours to Victory Tour," the idea being that he would not stop campaigning (except for quick naps) until Election Day:

> Dole caught a cold, and by Monday he could barely speak. But he was buoyant and cheerful, drinking a tea called Throat Coat and gaining strength from surprisingly large and lively crowds that showed up at diners and bowling alleys, high-school gyms and airport hangars, in small towns across the country...Dole's plane got a flat tire on Monday afternoon, so Dole moved into [the press plane],where he dozed up front while his aides tried to hush the serenades by reporters.

The press, not the public, is the immediate audience for much of what candidates do while running for the presidency. John Buckley, press secretary to Jack Kemp in 1988, estimated that "if you discount travel time, I'd say that the media take a third of a candidate's entire day. It's not just the news conferences, but one-on-one interviews, hotel room press briefings, radio and TV shows, editorial board discussions, back-of-the-car interviews and conversations."[14] "In a sense," media consultant Robert Squier says, "presidential candidates are their own spot-makers as they get their messages across on the stump before the television cameras."[15] Indeed, the nationalization of media markets and improvements in technology may actually reduce the necessity for campaign travel in the future. Instead of traveling to meetings, candidates can interact "live" with crowds via satellite. The 1992 candidacy of Ross Perot might be a model for this type of campaign. Perot traveled infrequently and did not meet with groups. He preferred to spend time in the television studio, taping his infomercials.[16]

The effect of all this planning and the demands on the candidates' time mean that candidates can seem to be puppets with the schedulers and advance

---

Box 5.1   A Day in the Life of the Candidate

**The Schedule of Bill Clinton on 3 October 1992
in St. Louis, Missouri, and Washington, D.C.**

9A.M.   Departs Adams Mark Downtown Hotel en route to Soulard Farmer's Market, St. Louis, Mo.

9:15A.M.   Arrives Soulard Farmer's Market, 730 Carroll Street.

9:20A.M.   Tours Soulard Farmer's Market.

9:40A.M.   Addresses the people of St. Louis, Soulard Farmer's Market.

10:30A.M.   Departs Soulard Farmer's Market en route to airport.

10:55A.M.   Arrives Lambert–St. Louis International Airport and proceeds to private time.

NOON   Departs St. Louis, Mo., en route to Washington, D.C.

---

team pulling the strings, ushering the candidates from performance to performance. Indeed, candidates often complain of stress, fatigue, and sometimes confusion as they are whirled from place to place. But this view underestimates the importance of the candidate, who is ultimately responsible for communicating his or her vision to the voters and, if victorious, is responsible for implementing it.

The Professionalization of the Campaign

Presidential candidates have never lacked for willing accomplices in their quest for office. In the first partisan election battle in American history, the election of 1800, the crucial New York campaign was led by Alexander Hamilton (for the Federalists) and Aaron Burr (for the Democratic-Republicans). With the resumption of party competition in the 1830s, campaign managers assumed primary responsibility for the conduct of the battle, a pattern that has continued to the present.

Contemporary campaigns—since, let us say, 1952—have evolved into something qualitatively different from the pattern of the previous century. It

2:40P.M.   Arrives Washington National Airport, Washington, D.C.

3:15P.M.   Departs airport en route to Washington Hilton Hotel.

3:30P.M.   Arrives Washington Hilton Hotel, 1919 Connecticut
Avenue, NW.

4:00P.M.   Announces formation of Italian American Leadership
Council, Washington Hilton Hotel. Press coverage
arrangements TBA.

9:00P.M.   Attends National Italian-American Foundation's Jeno
Paolucci Dinner, International Ballroom, Washington
Hilton Hotel.

Remains overnight in Washington, D.C.

SOURCE: *The Reuters Daybook of Presidential Campaigns*, Reuters Washington
Report, 3 October 1992.

Continued

is not the professionalization of the campaign that is new, for the old-time
party managers were extremely interested in monetary rewards for their services, but the fact that modern consultants are business professionals, not
party professionals. The individuals who directed the first century and a half
of presidential elections were closely tied to one or another of the political
parties and were often part of the party structure. Moreover, the technologies
and strategies at the disposal of modern consultants that can help them sell
their candidates have transformed the entire process of running for the
nation's highest office.

In the nineteenth century, campaigns were often carried out by the party
organizations. Nowadays, candidates must form their own campaign organizations. These are typically composed of: paid staff, usually including a campaign manager; paid consultants; volunteers; close advisers, often known as a
"kitchen cabinet"; and a formal organization, typically consisting of a campaign committee and a finance committee. The first two categories, paid staff
and consultants, are campaign professionals.[17]

What is the nature of this new campaign animal, the campaign professional? In some ways, they are very different from the party professionals of

Box 5.1   A Day in the Life of the Candidate

**The Schedule of George Bush on 3 October 1992
in Clearwater, Homestead, Fort Lauderdale, Orlando, Florida, and
Washington, D.C.**

8:25A.M.   Boards motorcade and departs Holiday Inn, Clearwater, Fla., en route to On Top of the World Retirement Community.

8:42A.M.   Arrives On Top of the World Retirement Community.

9:05-9:50A.M.   Gives remarks at retirement community. Open press coverage.

9:55A.M.   Boards motorcade and departs On Top of the World Retirement Community en route to St. Petersburg/ Clearwater International Airport.

10:15A.M.   Arrives St. Petersburg/Clearwater International Airport and boards Air Force One.

10:20A.M.   Departs Clearwater, Fla., en route to Homestead, Fla.

11.15A.M.   Arrives Homestead Air Force Base, Homestead, Fla., to view hurricane relief efforts. Pool coverage.

1:45P.M.   Departs Homestead, Fla., en route to Fort Lauderdale, Fla.

2:10P.M.   Arrives Hollywood International Airport, Fort Lauderdale, Fla., for Fort Lauderdale welcome.

2:15P.M.   Gives remarks. Open press.

2:50P.M.   Boards motorcade and departs AMR COMBS Hangar en route to Naval Warfare Center Detachment.

2:55P.M.   Arrives Naval Warfare Center Detachment for Historical Association Ceremony. Travel pool coverage.

3:25P.M.   Boards motorcade and departs Naval Warfare Center
Detachment en route to AMR COMBS Hangar.

3:30P.M.   Arrives at AMR COMBS Hangar for private time.

4:10P.M.   Departs Fort Lauderdale, Fla., en route to Orlando, Fla.

5:15P.M.   Arrives Orlando International Airport, Orlando, Fla.

5:20P.M.   Boards motorcade and departs Orlando International
Airport en route to Church Street Market.

5:50P.M.   Arrives Church Street Market for Church Street
Market Rally.

6:00P.M.   Gives remarks at rally. Open press coverage.

6:35P.M.   Attends private reception. Closed press.

7:05P.M.   Boards Motorcade and departs Church Street Market
en route to Orlando International Airport.

7:35P.M.   Arrives Orlando International Airport and boards
Air Force One.

7:40P.M.   Departs Orlando, Fla., en route to Andrews Air Force Base.

9:25P.M.   Arrives Andrews Air Force Base.

9:35P.M.   Boards Marine One and departs Andrews Air Force
Base en route to the White House.

9:45P.M.   Arrives White House.

SOURCE: *The Reuters Daybook of Presidential Campaigns*, Reuters Washington
Report, 3 October 1992.

earlier eras. The people who ran campaigns through the first half of the twentieth century generally were compensated by the spoils system: winning candidates hired or appointed their supporters to a variety of government jobs. Those who run campaigns now are mostly compensated in salaries and fees for services. Earlier generations of party professionals were mainly generalists. Now, the business of electioneering requires specialization and therefore diversity.[18] There are still old-style generalists who coordinate campaigns from top to bottom, but increasingly the business of the campaign is subcontracted to firms that specialize in a particular aspect of the process. *Campaigns and Elections*, the trade magazine of political consultancy, lists the following categories of consultants (among forty-five subcategories) in its "Annual Directory of Political Consultants, Products and Services": attorneys, database/file management, direct mail (strategy and creative), fax services, field operations and organization, fund-raising consultants, media buying, media and speech training, online information services, printing and promotional groups, political web sites on the internet, research (opposition), research (issues, voters, and legislative), satellite services, targeting, video duplication.[19]

Professionalization of the political campaign is a process that has advanced, by all accounts, considerably further in the United States with its long drawn-out nomination processes than anywhere else among the world's democracies. What is the cumulative effect of the introduction of modern polls, media campaigns, fund-raising efforts, and the people who run these operations on the conduct of the presidential campaign? Does the new agenda-setting mechanism of the opinion poll change the character and conduct of presidential campaigns? Have the campaign professionals altered the substantive content of politics? Are they in it for the money, or do they have their own ideological axes to grind?

Some of the murkiness in the relationship between candidates and paid professionals clears away if one looks closely at the initial phases of the relationship. Although candidates are more typically to be found in the role of the suitor, it is not at all unusual for consultants to go prospecting for a candidate if they are short on contracts in a particular election cycle.[20] Once the initial contact has been made, the two sides begin a bargaining process over a contract that, if signed, will formalize responsibility, set payment agreements, and establish general ground rules that will guide their interactions over the course of the campaign. Whether this courtship is consummated or not depends on the resources each side brings to the bargaining table. The key resources, for both parties, are money and a winning reputation. Candidates are looking for the most successful consultant their money can buy, which generally means the firm with the best recent win-loss record on their side of the ideological spectrum. Consultants likewise prefer winners over probable losers (so they can protect their record) and fat cats over lean. Neither side wants to end up with a partner who is ideologically or personally incompatible.[21]

Not surprisingly, top-flight consulting firms are besieged with offers from candidates and would-be candidates. Direct-mail wizard Richard Viguerie claimed (with possible exaggeration) to have turned down 98 percent of the campaigns in 1978 that requested his help.[22] Big-name presidential hopefuls are similarly able to pick and choose, while no-name candidates must often wait patiently until relatively late in the game and settle for whoever is left. Sometimes a prominent consultant will take on a long-shot candidate to advance a political agenda or because of a personal friendship. Even if the campaign is not generously bankrolled, the publicity attached to running a presidential campaign may lead to future business opportunities for the firm.

Has the increasingly sophisticated technological component of presidential campaigns altered the essential character of the enterprise of seeking office? No longer limited to the analysis of poll data, computers have colonized every level of the campaign process. In 1988, according to one survey, computers and electronic machines were used, "for tracking convention delegates, writing fund-raising letters and thank-you notes, processing donations, drafting news releases, maintaining electronic news libraries,... communicating between field and headquarters," and automatic telephoning. "Asking a political professional in 1988 how he uses a computer is a little bit like asking a reporter how he uses his telephone," declared Pamela Lowry, a director of computer operations for Dukakis.[23]

The results of this electronic revolution are a higher rate of computer literacy among campaign managers, a small reduction in envelope stuffing and stamp licking on the part of campaign volunteers, the greatly enhanced ability of the campaign to raise small amounts of money and get its message across to specially targeted segments of the electorate. But unless there exists a "computer gap" among competing candidates, the political effect of the new technologies is marginal.

How powerful are the campaign professionals within the campaign organization? The candidate-client relationship varies considerably from case to case, depending on the experience and stature of each party and the terms of the original contract. It is the candidate, all agree, who draws the "bottom line," who approves the general strategy of the campaign.[24] Having done this, however, many candidates apparently prefer to absent themselves from the nitty-gritty choices of the campaign. One survey found that 44 percent of a population of consultants agreed that candidates generally backed off from making decisions on the priority of different issues on the campaign. Most "were neither very involved nor influential in the day-to-day tactical operation of the campaign."[25]

Consultants (not a shy and self-effacing group of people) will gladly tell you all about the power they enjoy—and should enjoy—as campaign managers. Robert Squier, for instance, who works for Democrats, says: "It is very possible to go through an entire campaign with a candidate, and when it is all over, they have no idea what went on. It is not to our advantage to explain to them. It is to our advantage to get them to do what we want—what's best for them—with the least amount of fuss."[26]

Explanations for the rise of consultants can be found in several related developments. The increasingly advanced technology involved in the campaign process means a candidate must hire technocrats to do most of the work.

Volunteers, family and friends, and party leaders will tend to be sidelined to one degree or another because of their lack of technical experience in law, accounting, media production, advertising, and the like. The significance and sophistication of modern polls places their proprietors in the role of oracles. Similar developments in media marketing produce parallel results for these manufacturers of public opinion.

Moreover, the average campaign organization has a brief and tenuous life. Even in the age of the seemingly permanent campaign, a campaign organization lasts only a year or so. This means that the candidate needs in addition to expertise a base of organizational capacity and institutional experience to draw on. Instead of having to build a national organization from scratch, it is now possible—and often desirable—to buy one ready-made. "All-service" consultants will cover all contingencies, from general strategy to licking stamps.[27]

Have consultants made presidential campaigns more ideological? Probably not. With the exception of a few ideologically motivated firms, consultants tend to be party loyalists but not advocates. There are exceptions. Fund-raising and direct-mail firms (an overlapping set of categories) can afford to be more purist than other sorts of consultants because they are holding the purse strings and they generally target a narrow range of like-minded, politically motivated donors.[28] Possessed of precious lists of the names of cobelievers, they are more likely to administer an ideological litmus test before entering into a relationship with a candidate, and more likely to call the candidate on the carpet afterward if his or her behavior is not exemplary.

Nevertheless, as Larry Sabato says, "for most consultants ideology is a surprisingly minor criterion in the selection of clients."[29] The business logic of consultancy militates against an approach that would limit a firm's clientele, and the game-playing logic of the campaign itself demands the use of any strategy that will win, regardless of its ideological consequences.

Do campaign professionals help candidates obfuscate and blur the issues? With candidates from both parties being coached to court the swing vote in the middle, perhaps consultants contribute to the "Tweedledum-Tweedledee" effect in presidential elections. Mitchell E. Daniels Jr., former White House staff member, sums up the consultant effect this way: "You tend not to make major gaffes, because somebody will spot them. On the other hand, you may not take very many bold actions, because someone will be very nervous."[30]

Has the professionalization of campaigns lowered standards of conduct in presidential elections? Even though the candidate is ultimately responsible for all campaign decisions, the use of paid staff and consultants may change the range of campaign options available and the types of strategies ultimately chosen. Consider the issue of negative campaigning. "I love to do negatives," declares media consultant Bob Squier. "It is one of those opportunities in a campaign where you can take the truth and use it just like a knife to slice right through the opponent. I hate the kind of commercials that are just music and pretty pictures."[31] This bit of refreshing candor raises the possibility that the average campaign professional may in fact be different from the average politician. One study found that "most media consultants admitted often having considerable difficulty in convincing their clients to go negative."[32]

Candidates are aware, of course, of most of what goes on in their name, but it is in any case easier to sign on the dotted line and have someone else take care of your dirty business for you than to have to haul the bodies away yourself.[33] Other commentators point out that there are limits to what campaigns can say on television, limits that did not apply to old-fashioned campaigns run by thousands of semi-independent and localized party bosses, newspapers, and partisans.

Do campaign professionals undermine partisanship? There is no doubt that they have replaced party leaders as major actors in the campaign process. But the decline of traditional party leaders was not caused by consultants; it was caused by changes in the party nomination and election system, which demand that candidates form their own organizations so that they can appeal to large primary electorates in order to win nomination. Those who are hired by those organizations, with rare exceptions, have strong partisan affiliations and do not work both sides of the street. In fact, many have worked for party organizations, and parties provide training in electioneering skills in order to have reliably partisan professionals."[34] Party affiliation," according to one study, "is by far the most important factor considered by consultants in selecting their clients, outweighing a candidate's electability, ideology, or financial standing."[35] A good example of the way this works can be seen in looking at Bob Dole's campaign manager from 1996, Scott Reed. Reed was a deputy regional campaign director for the Reagan campaign in 1984. In 1988 he was the Iowa coordinator for the presidential campaign of then Congressman Jack Kemp. When Kemp became Secretary of Housing and Urban Development, Reed was his chief of staff. In 1993 Reed became executive director of the Republican National Committee. Only then, in 1995, did he first meet Bob Dole when he was hired to run the campaign.[36]

Issues

ADVISING THE CANDIDATE

Everyone has advice for the would-be president. In the old days most of the policy advice came after the general election as the victor prepared to assume office. Nowadays the advising process has been incorporated into the process of campaigning. The function of the policy adviser is no longer simply to help the future president govern but to help the candidate define and publicize the campaign's position on the issues. There is still some reluctance on the part of candidates to publish lists, but all campaigns develop extensive contacts with academics and policy analysts who draw up position papers on specialized issues of foreign and domestic policy and help set the general ideological tone of the campaign.[37] The experts do this at least in part so as to position themselves to have influence if their candidate wins.

The lengthy duration of presidential campaigns means that candidates have to develop their issues at least two years in advance of the election. It is at this initial period, long before a candidacy is officially announced, that decisions on national policy issues will be made. "If you're ... in the policy-advising business," explains Pat Choate, an analyst for TRW Inc., "you must move on that time schedule." Introducing a novel idea later on, during the heat of the campaign, is risky, first because the candidate may gain a reputation as an opportunist or a waffler, and second because there will be no opportunity to test the new idea for technical or political feasibility, to get its "rough edges smoothed out."

Since in the course of the campaign the candidate is expected to offer judgments on world events as they break into the news, every campaign will typically rely on a "little black book" with the telephone numbers of advisers in different policy areas who can be contacted during emergencies. News of a crisis in international finance surfaced as the Reagan campaign was in flight, remembers Martin Anderson, Reagan's policy research coordinator in 1980. By the time the plane had touched down at the next location, the campaign had contacted famous economists Milton Friedman and Arthur Burns, formulated a response, and issued a press release.[39]

Campaign policy experts come in three flavors, according to Janne E. Nolan, Gary Hart's foreign policy and defense adviser in the 1984 campaign: those who believe in the issues they are pushing, those adrenaline junkies attracted by the chance to participate in the events of a presidential campaign, and those who have attached their ambitions to a particular candidate in the hopes of achieving a position in a new administration.[40]

Policy advisers, even of the third type, are a very different breed from poll takers and media consultants. With the exception of the candidate's most senior policy coordinators, they are usually not paid. Their ties to the day-to-day campaign may be tenuous, and they all have nonpolitical careers to return to. Well-known academics may offer advice in an informal capacity to several campaigns in the same election.

Not surprisingly, there is a certain degree of tension between the "flack masters and [the] idea mongers," as Richard Allen (of the latter camp) puts it. "People in flackery don't know ideas and wouldn't know if one hit them at a great rate of speed," continues Allen, who headed the foreign policy issues team on the Republican side for the Reagan elections.[41]

There may, however, be some justification for this, in view of the demands of the presidential campaign. "There's a big difference," explains William A. Galston, Mondale's issues director in 1984, "between having a position paper and having a politically salable commodity."[42] "If an idea can't be communicated to the public, then it won't be part of the campaign," concludes John Holum, Gary Hart's issues man in 1984 and 1988. Someone, in other words, must administer the "test of political marketability."[43]

DOMESTIC ISSUES, FOREIGN ISSUES

On the broad range of domestic affairs and "pocketbook" issues, the Democrats, since the New Deal, have been highly favored as the party most voters believe will best meet their needs. Statements like "The Democrats are best for the working man" and "We have better times under the Democrats" abounded when people were asked to state their feelings about the Democratic Party. The Republicans, in contrast, were viewed as the party of depression under whose administration jobs were scarce and times were bad.

These attitudes have had considerable staying power through the years. In 1987 and again in 1990 the *Times Mirror* asked samples of American adults, "What does it mean to be a Democrat? What does it mean to be a Republican?" and got the spontaneous replies shown in table 5.1. A campaign in which the salient issues are economic, therefore, is more likely to aid the Democrats than the Republicans (see table 5.2, p.166).[44] Of course, if the incumbent president is Democratic and the economy is faltering, emphasizing economic issues may not do him much good. After the advent of "stagflation" under the Democrats in the late 1970s, the Republican Party was for some time deemed the party of prosperity. Recession during the Bush presidency reversed those gains. The party that is in office when the economy is suffering does badly.

The Democratic Party's modern task has been to be "liberal" in several senses of that word. It promises something for everyone. There are extensions of social welfare programs financed by the federal government, an increased minimum wage for the underpaid, medical insurance for new groups of people,

TABLE 5.1 WHAT DOES IT MEAN TO BE A REPUBLICAN? (UNPROMPTED REPLIES, IN PERCENTAGES)

Top mentions	1987	1990
Conservative	21	22
Rich, powerful, monied interests	18	21
Business oriented	13	10
Not for the people	5	4
Against government spending	5	6

WHAT DOES IT MEAN TO BE A DEMOCRAT? (UNPROMPTED REPLIES, IN PERCENTAGES)

Top mentions	1987	1990
For working people	21	18
Liberal	18	18
Too much government spending	7	3
Cares for poor, disadvantaged	7	7
For social programs	7	9

SOURCES: *The Polling Report* (1 October 1990), and Times Mirror Center for the People and the Press press release (undated).

TABLE 5.2   **WHICH PARTY IS BETTER FOR PROSPERITY (IN PERCENTAGES)**

	Republican	Democratic	No opinion
1952 January	31	35	34
1956 October	39	39	22
1960 October	31	46	23
1964 October	21	53	26
1968 October	34	37	29
1972 September	38	35	27
1976 August	23	47	30
1980 September	35	36	29
1984 August	48	36	24
1988 September*	52	34	14
1990 October	37	35	28
1992 October*	36	45	19
1996 July	41	42	17

SOURCE: Data from *Gallup Poll Monthly,* August 1996, 5.
*Based on registered voters.

better prices for the farmer, irrigation for arid areas, flood protection for river basins, and so on. No one is left out, not even business people, who are promised prosperity and given tax benefits. Although voters say they are in favor of these programs, they do not like the spending totals that emerge from them—hence Democratic vulnerability to being tagged as run by the "special interests," especially labor unions. This hurt Mondale especially in 1984. Should the issue become "excessive spending" as leading to inflation or huge deficits or decreasing investment, Democrats are at a disadvantage.

Republicans were once clearly on the defensive in the realm of domestic policy, a situation stemming from the fact that they were in office when the Great Depression of 1929 started, and during three sizable but shorter depressions more recently (1970–1971, 1982–1983, 1991–1992). They try to play down economic issues when their president is in office during a depression and play them up when the Democrats are in office or their party is in power during good times. The "misery index," a combination of inflation and unemployment, taken together with which party is in office, is a nearly infallible guide to how economic policy is used, and by whom, in the campaign. Republicans attack the Democrats as the party that likes to tax and spend, tax and spend. The Republican candidate is thus well placed to benefit if the issue becomes one of excessive spending. As most spending programs are quite popular, however, the candidate is well advised to be vague concerning the exact items of excessive spending he or she opposes. Ronald Reagan in 1980, for example, directed his attacks mainly against "inefficiency" and "waste" and ran on a platform that promised tax cuts that would actually raise tax revenues.

**TABLE 5.3   DEMOCRATS VERSUS REPUBLICANS ON FOREIGN POLICY
(IN PERCENTAGES)**

	Republican	Democratic	No opinion
1952 January	36	15	49
1956 October	46	16	38
1960 October	40	25	35
1964 October	22	45	33
1968 October	37	24	39
1972 September	32	28	40
1976 August	29	32	39
1980 September	25	42	33
1984 August	30	42	28
1988 September*	43	33	24
1990 October	34	36	30
1992 February*	39	39	22

SOURCE: Party Best for Peace," *Gallup Poll Monthly,* February 1992.
*Based on registered voters.
**1992 question: "Which party is the best for peace?" Prior to 1992: "Which party will
keep the country out of WWIII?"

On the other hand, the Republican candidate is understandably upset at
Democratic insinuations that he and his party have not become fully reconciled to Social Security. Indeed, when Walter Mondale challenged him during
a 1984 debate, President Reagan promised not to cut Social Security then or
the next year or ever.

In the realm of foreign affairs, the Republicans may be losing their traditional advantage (see table 5.3 and table 5.4). The fact that the Democrats occupied the presidency during World Wars I and II, the Korean war, and the initial
stages of heavy American involvement in Vietnam once convinced most voters
that Democrats tend to lead the country to war. Republicans were then known
as the party of peace, a position underscored by Senator Dole in the 1976 vice-
presidential debate when he said: "I figured up the other day, if we added up
the killed and wounded in Democrat wars in this century, it would be about
1.6 million Americans, enough to fill the city of Detroit."[45] This image
changed in 1964 when Senator Goldwater had people believing he would inter-

**TABLE 5.4   PARTY IMAGES AFTER IMPEACHMENT (PERCENTAGE BELIEVING
THE FOLLOWING APPLY TO THE REPUBLICAN PARTY/DEMOCRATIC PARTY)**

	Republican Party	Democratic Party
Out of touch with the American people	60	41
Too extreme	55	39
Has a good program for the country	53	64

SOURCE: CNN/Gallup Poll, 4–8 February 1999, report in *Polling Report,* 1 March 1999, 2.

vene in a great many places, and so the Democrats became the party of peace, a feeling reinforced during Jimmy Carter's presidency, by President Reagan's belligerent rhetoric, and by President Bush's leadership in the Persian Gulf conflict, Desert Storm. Thus, in recent years, the Democrats have enjoyed the advantage of being considered the peaceful party.

The distinction between domestic and foreign policy has always been a bit artificial. It has been maintained because of the ability of the United States to insulate its domestic economy from international forces. Today that ability is diminishing. The Clinton, Bush, and Reagan administrations wanted to reduce trade barriers to serve their foreign policy, but each had a hard time beating back protectionist forces worried about domestic unemployment. Policies such as the North American Free Trade Agreement, a Republican presidential initiative adopted by Clinton once he took office, were supported or attacked for their effects on international relations and on the domestic economy. During the cold war, it was occassionally possible to see American relationships with European or Asian nations only in the context of containing the Soviet Union; since then, it is increasingly clear that American workers and consumers have foreign policy interests.

Whereas the major parties once enjoyed long-term advantages in foreign or domestic policy, these have lately become more sensitive to evaluations of performance. For example, the fact that Jimmy Carter was in office when national income declined during an election year gave the Democrats a turn at being blamed for a depression. Nor can we say with any certainty that foreign and domestic economic policy are the only issue areas that over the long run will matter to voters.

SOCIAL ISSUES

What about the third great cluster of problems, the "social issues"—variously labeled (and understood) as law and order, domestic violence, race relations, abortion, the environment, school prayer, and gun control—that involve lifestyles as well as distributions of benefits?[46] As Richard Scammon and Ben Wattenberg point out, the first three have grown enormously in saliency to voters over the past three decades: "Suddenly, some time in the 1960's, 'crime' and 'race' and 'lawlessness' and 'civil rights' became the most important domestic issues in America."[47] The environment has been politicized mostly in a Democratic direction, while being against abortion has become mostly a Republican issue. It is difficult to tell whether this entire cluster of issues works consistently for or against a particular political party.

Social issues are affecting the parties in different ways. The Republican Party may be thought of as a coalition of social conservatives and free-market libertarians. As long as it concentrates on economic issues, both factions can usually agree on limited government. But on social issues the libertarians favor individual choice and are against government intervention even to protect traditional values. Social conservatives, however, oppose abortion and support school prayer.

Democratic activists, as we have seen, despite their social heterogeneity, are more united than previously on some issues. As the larger of the two major parties, spanning the entire country, the Democrats have in the past experienced difficulty in uniting on any programmatic principles. One consequence of the migration of conservative southerners into the Republican Party has been to facilitate the emergence of a more ideologically coherent Democratic mainstream, but as recently as the *Times Mirror* survey of political attitudes in 1987 (reported in *The People, Press, and Politics*), the Democrats at the grassroots level divided into four separate and distinct blocs of voters, whereas the Republicans were split into two groups on issues.[48]

In the National Election Studies, respondents have been asked to indicate their positions on policy issues by placing themselves on a series of seven-point scales; and to indicate how favorably they view a variety of politically active groups by rating each group on a 100-point "feeling thermometer." In table 5.5, we have tried to assess how united or divided each party is by calculating the standard deviation—a measure of central tendency, hence of agreement—among party identifiers' responses to these questions. As the table clearly shows, the Democratic rank and file are more divided on the vast majority of issues and in their feelings toward important political groups. Similar results are found for all the years in which results are reported. On some issues, the difference between the two parties is not large; in other cases, however, the spread of Democratic opinion shows the Democrats' standard deviation more than 50 percent larger than the Republicans'.[49]

Getting a Good Press

Although we have seen that it is highly questionable whether press reports, on television or in newspapers, markedly influence voter opinion when the strong cue of party is present, it is still important for a candidate to get the most favorable coverage possible. At least, the candidates and their organizations behave as though it is important; they can and do assiduously court the newspaper, periodical, and television journalists assigned to them.[50] Not only do candidates coddle the press people who travel with them, but they follow their coverage and complain about it.[51]

The space candidates get in the paper, their time on television, and the slant of a story may depend to some extent on how the reporters regard them. If they find it difficult to get material, if they find a candidate suspicious and uncommunicative, this may affect how much and what gets on the air or published. ABC's then White House correspondent Brit Hume speculated that this was part of George Bush's press problems in 1992. He told White House

TABLE 5.5 PARTY UNITY

	Democrats' standard deviation	Republicans' standard deviation	Difference (Democrats – Republicans)
1994 Seven-Point Scale			
Aid to blacks	1.78	1.44	0.34
Ideology	1.30	1.10	0.20
Defense spending	1.51	1.31	0.20
Guaranteed jobs	1.76	1.61	0.15
Health insurance	1.89	1.82	0.07
Role of women	1.76	1.71	0.05
Services vs. spending	1.50	1.51	−0.01
1988 Feeling Thermometers			
Gays and lesbians	30.80	26.35	4.45
Big business	22.80	18.61	4.19
Christian fundamentalists	28.70	24.87	3.83
Wealthy people	21.21	18.12	3.09
Illegal immigrants	26.95	23.94	3.01
People on welfare	23.46	22.32	1.14
Conservatives	20.24	19.41	0.83
Labor unions	22.23	23.49	−1.26
Liberals	19.44	22.16	−2.72
Environmentalists	20.59	23.60	−3.01
Women's movement	21.04	25.48	−4.44

SOURCE: Nelson W. Polsby and William Mayer, "Ideological Cohesion in the American Two-Party System," in *On Parties: Essays Honoring Austin Ranney*, ed. Nelson W. Polsby and Raymond Wolfinger (Berkeley: Institute of Governmental Studies Press, 1999), 232.

spokesperson Marlin Fitzwater that reporters were uncomfortable with the president's responses to challenges—he appeared uncertain, rather than confident, and reporters didn't like it.[52]

Getting good press, like the rest of the campaign, has become professionalized, with press and communication assistants who know how to make candidates look good on television and in the newspapers. Little things, such as phasing news to meet the requirements of both morning newspapers and the evening network news shows, or supplying reporters with human-interest material, can be helpful to candidates. The personality of the candidates, their ability to command the respect of the occasionally cynical men and women assigned to cover them, may count heavily. Democratic candidates probably have to work a little harder at cultivating good relations in order to help counteract the editorial slant of most papers. But Republicans have to work harder to win the sympathies of reporters of liberal tendency who dominate the national press corps.[53] Candidates also must make the most of their opportunities in public appearances or radio and television speeches. If what they say and do "makes news," and their press sec-retaries are effective in promoting the stories, they may get space through the desire of the media to attract customers.

Thus far, we have spoken of the news media as if they were a monolithic entity. But there are all sorts of news outlets with differing biases, needs, and audiences. A great deal of a candidate's attention is devoted to stories destined for the racial, religious, and ethnic interest-group press. The circu-lations of these publications may not be huge, but it is assumed that they have readers who are concerned with topics of special interest to smaller and more attentive constituencies. A story on religion in politics in a religious journal may do more to convince people than much greater coverage in the daily press. Web-published journalists may have different audiences than print or television reporters, as well as different news cycles and norms, as Matt Drudge demonstrated when he broke news of scandal during the Clin-ton administration.[54]

Finally, there is the overwhelming importance of staging the daily bit of news for the nightly television programs of the networks. Candidates know they will be on these programs every night; but doing and saying what? In order to seize control of the situation, they stage little dramas: an announcement in front of the Statue of Liberty or in the midst of a picturesque slum; visits to a series of ethnic shops, delicatessens, farms, factories, and shopping centers. If the back-drop is right, the candidate thinks, the coverage may be too. Sometimes it is.

In the 1988 campaign, there was a great contrast between the two cam-paigns' abilities to control the news agenda. George Bush's media advisers planned the vice president's appearances in camera-ready settings that pro-vided excellent videotape for the newscasts. In front of a defense plant in St. Louis, he talked up America's need to remain strong. Michael Dukakis made speech after speech in front of the backdrop of a drab blue curtain, behind a wooden podium.

Another Bush success was the ability to deliver manufactured "sound bites"—one-liners that he knew would be broadcast on television. "Dukakis gives me the impression that he is opposed to every new weapon since the slingshot," said Bush. NBC used the line immediately, and the other networks followed suit when he repeated the line a few days later. "I wouldn't be sur-prised," Bush said in another sound bite, "if [Dukakis] thought that a naval exercise was something you find in Jane Fonda's workout book."[55]

A new use of television emerged during the 1992 campaign: the appearance of a candidate on television talk shows such as *Larry King Live* and *Good Morning America*. The Clinton campaign was the first to make use of this tac-tic during the New Hampshire primary campaign. They staged several "Ask Bill" television shows where candidate Bill Clinton took questions from the audience. Clinton did extremely well in this format, and from early on in the campaign, media consultant Mandy Grunwald was pushing him to do more such appearances. In a 27 April memorandum entitled "Free Media Scheduling," Grunwald told the candidate:

> We have spoken generally about the need to do pop-culture shows
> like Johnny Carson, but we have yet to lay out a plan to do this sort
> of thing, or to incorporate local radio talk shows into our schedule in
> any concerted way. What are we waiting for? We know from research
> that Bill Clinton's life story has a big impact on people. We know that
> learning about the fights he's taken on (education reform, welfare
> reform, dead-beat dads, etc.) tells people a lot about his personal con-
> victions. We know that moments of passion, personal reflection and
> humor do more for us than any six-second sound bite on the network
> news or for that matter any thirty-second television spot.[56]

Eventually, Clinton's campaign took this advice and placed the candidate on a number of talk shows. On Phil Donahue's daytime talk show, Clinton stood up for his right not to have the privacy of his marriage dissected by the press, and the audience applauded him.[57] On the late-night *Arsenio Hall Show*, Clinton played the saxophone and talked about welfare reform. He took questions on *Larry King Live* several times, as well as on *Good Morning America* and *Today*, and he even did a question-and-answer format aimed at young voters through MTV's *Rock the Vote* programming.

Clinton did consistently well in this format; his handlers felt that it brought out the personal side in him and allowed voters to get to know and connect with the candidate. Another candidate who succeeded on this circuit, albeit with some significantly bad moments, was Ross Perot. Perot actually announced his willingness to run for president on a talk show: Larry King on *Larry King Live* was, with persistent prodding, able to get a "reluctant" Perot to agree to run if volunteers placed his name on all fifty ballots before the deadline.[58] With that single interview, King launched a candidate and achieved the status of the premier political interviewer of the 1992 campaign season.

Perot appeared on King several more times and made a number of appearances on other talk shows. In the beginning, the talk shows, like all the media, were easy on him and generally gave him a forum for promoting his easy slogans and folksy ideas. After a while, however, the media became more probing and Perot became less folksy. In one famous confrontation, Katie Couric of the *Today* show persisted in asking Perot to provide the details of his plans. Perot, unwilling to discuss specifics in this appearance as in others, resisted and finally blew up at Couric. He later criticized Couric in front of reporters as trying too hard to "prove her manhood."[59]

Perot was perhaps more effective at the talk shows he produced himself—the "infomercials" that consisted of Perot wielding a pointer and a large number of graphs, numbers, and, his favorite, pie charts. The Perot shows, where he explained the problems of the economy and detailed the deficit, were actually very popular with American television viewers. An estimated 16 million viewers tuned in to his first program.[60]

The overall value of these candidate appearances is unclear. Some political commentators have criticized the strategy, arguing that the hosts of these shows are easy on the candidates and do not ask tough questions or follow up on answers. Instead, these commentators argue, candidates should spend more time on the Sunday morning political shows such as *This Week* and *Meet the Press*, where tough interviewers will make sure the candidates meet a certain standard. On the other side are those who argue that pop-culture shows are good for the system because they get people involved and even empower voters by allowing them to get direct answers to their questions. Whatever the contribution these shows make to American political life, positive or negative, there is no doubt that candidates will continue to make appearances as long as show hosts will invite them. The free media and direct access to voters are valuable properties, especially for candidates like Bill Clinton, who shine in such situations.[61]

POLLING

Multimillion-dollar polling is the norm in today's presidential elections. Polls have been used, in varying ways, since the 1930s,[62] but they have not always been so important in shaping campaigns. As recently as the 1950s, most candidates still viewed polls with considerable skepticism. Some, like Harry Truman, were downright hostile. "I wonder," he said, "how far Moses would have gone if he'd taken a poll in Egypt? What would Jesus Christ have preached if he'd taken a poll in Israel? Where would the reformation have gone if Martin Luther had taken a poll? It isn't polls or public opinion of the moment that counts. It is right and wrong leadership—men with fortitude, honesty and a belief in the right—that makes epochs in the history of the world."[63] Winston Churchill, inhabiting the same political universe, said: "Nothing is more dangerous than a Gallup poll, always taking one's pulse and taking one's political temperature. Like all long-lived politicians in democracies, these exemplary figures undoubtedly paid attention to their intuitions about public opinion. But intuition has now largely been replaced by more accurate methods, and it is hard to ignore or disparage this more thorough sounding of the popular will.

The first significant use of polls within a campaign organization occurred in 1960, when surveys taken by Louis Harris helped guide John Kennedy's campaign in key primary states. Pioneers such as Harris and George Gallup were followed in succeeding decades by hundreds of polling firms throughout the country that now make up the polling industry.[65] General nationwide public opinion polls not owned or paid for by particular candidates are now regularly taken by Gallup, Harris, Roper, Yankelovich, and several national media groups: *Wall Street Journal*/NBC, *Washington Post*/ABC, *Los Angeles Times*, and *New York Times*/CBS.

Other poll takers work for political campaigns, and among these, a few are involved in all phases of presidential campaigning.[66] The modern pollster's role goes far beyond gathering data and analyzing trends. "There's no question that our role has changed from collector of facts to interpreter and strategist," Richard Wirthlin says.[67] They ask: What should be the major campaign themes, or at least, which would be most attractive to the electorate? Should the candidate attack an opponent's record? If so, how? Which regions and states should be emphasized? What is the proper role of the vice-presidential candidate? The campaign pollster helps make these and a variety of other crucial campaign decisions, such as which states to visit and which groups within the electorate to court, all subject to the candidate's approval.

The first nationwide polls in behalf of candidates typically begin many months before the first caucuses or primaries. These initial polls, called "benchmark polls," are based on twenty- to thirty-minute interviews with large samples (600–1,000 people in a state, and up to 4,000 nationally) of potential voters.[68] The object of this poll is to determine what proportion of the population is committed to various candidates, how many are still undecided, and why people are disposed to vote (or not vote) as they indicate. A second poll of benchmark length is often done several months before the general election. There can also be "trend" polls of shorter length. Sometimes, pollsters conduct callback interviews to see if respondents' opinions have changed.[69] All such polls are used to test the political climate and try out possible campaign themes.

In June 1979, Richard Wirthlin conducted a national study in behalf of Ronald Reagan of "six scenarios for the future." Given a choice of options ranging from "less is better" to "America can do," the majority chose the "can do" theme. This theme pervaded Reagan's campaign. "Don't let anyone tell you that inflation can't be controlled," Reagan declared in a thirty-second television spot. "It can be, by making some tough decisions to cut federal spending."[70]

Campaigns monitor any number of "target voters"—blocs of the electorate considered key swing votes—to determine which themes should be stressed. The Dukakis campaign targeted two major groups: white Reagan Democrats (about 10 percent of the voters) and white independents (about 20 percent of the voters), but the campaign failed to win these voters back from the Republicans.[71] In 1992 Clinton's team adopted a similar strategy; they hoped to target white suburban voters: the Reagan Democrats, political independents who supported "change" in politics, and women disaffected with the Republican Party. The first blow to this strategy came during the New Hampshire primary when allegations of womanizing hit Clinton, damaging his standing with some female voters. The second blow came shortly thereafter: Ross Perot's entrance into the race took Clinton's message of change away and bestowed it on the folksy billionaire who spoke strongly about sweeping out the barn.

That left the suburban white vote as the primary target for Clinton and, as it turned out, for Bush. Although they aimed their messages at the same voters, the two campaigns adopted strikingly different strategies. Clinton focused on the economy, describing the past twelve years as a failed experiment that had enriched the wealthy at the expense of the "forgotten middle class." He advocated such proposals as health-care reform and family medical leave to help the struggling middle class and attacked Bush for being out of touch with the needs of the American people. In his acceptance speech at the Democratic convention, he showcased this message: "In the name of all those who do the work, pay the taxes, raise the kids and play by the rules, in the name of the hardworking Americans who make up our forgotten middle class, I proudly accept your nomination for president of the United States. I am a product of the middle class. And when I am president, you will be forgotten no more."[72]

Bush polls showed that voters did not trust Clinton. They either thought that he "lied" about incidents in his past or that he stretched and molded the truth so much that he could not be trusted.[73] Bush played on these results, calling Clinton "Slick Willie" and continually calling on Clinton to "tell the truth" and "set the record straight." Bush attacked Clinton for his changing stories about his draft experience. During one *Larry King Live* appearance, Bush challenged Clinton's patriotism, alleging that he had "demonstrated against the United States on foreign soil" (referring to antiwar demonstrations during Clinton's time at Oxford) and hinted that a Clinton trip to Moscow during that time was for more than a vacation.[74]

Polling within particular states allows campaigns to decide which states to contest fiercely and which to downplay. In 1984, when Wirthlin's polls showed Reagan's strength in the South, the campaign decided to invest its scarce resources in the less secure Northeast. They reasoned that it was a waste of time, energy, and money to campaign in states they were already assured of winning.[75]

In the 1988 campaign, pollsters realized that with the exceptions of Texas, Colorado, and possibly Montana, the Republicans were solidly ahead in the entire South and Mountain West regions. As Republican pollster Vincent Breglio noted, "approximately 125 to 135 electoral votes in eighteen or nineteen states were going to end up in the Republican column unless a major mistake was made."[76] With these 130 electoral votes out of reach, Dukakis had to win his 270 votes from the remaining 408. But Bush needed only 140 of those 408 to win entrance to the White House. That is why talk among Democrats of a "fifty-state strategy," a strategy emphasized at their convention in Atlanta, quickly subsided. For Dukakis to win, he would have to sweep the Northeast, the industrial belt, and the Pacific states. Both candidates spent little time in states where Dukakis was far behind; there was no point since the outcome was not likely to change. They emphasized states with many electoral votes over those with few votes.[77] Thus, over the final six weeks of the campaign, Dukakis spent nearly three-fourths of his time in only eight states—California, Illinois, Michigan, Texas, New York, Ohio, Pennsylvania, and Missouri. Bush spent more than half his time in only six—California, Illinois, Michigan, Missouri, Ohio, and New Jersey.[78]

In 1992 the situation was almost exactly reversed. Early on in the campaign, Democratic National Committee strategist Paul Tully had decided that the Democrats could not afford to concede the South and the West to the Republicans. He devoted himself to designing a more sophisticated targeting strategy than the Democrats had used in the past. His first step was to analyze the 1988 campaign and identify the mistakes made by the Dukakis campaign. Most significantly, Tully found that Dukakis had spent most of his money on national media buys, a waste of money because they were more expensive and less targeted than Republican advertising. Next, to identify the places where the Democrats should make media buys in 1992, Tully looked at individual media markets and analyzed their election returns. Markets that showed some tendency to vote Democratic Tully identified as "persuadable," and these markets, even if they were in the South or West, were targeted for media buys by the Clinton campaign.

Clinton's 1992 team adopted Tully's map and created a sophisticated media targeting plan from his findings. The results were positive. By the beginning of September, Clinton was beating Bush in virtually every state, giving the Democrats the luxury of specifically targeting very close states while forcing the Republicans to spread themselves out more and thus spend more. In the last few weeks of the campaign, the Clinton team was confident of winning California, New York, Hawaii, Rhode Island, and Massachusetts, and they were 10 to 15 points ahead in Pennsylvania, New Jersey, and Illinois. They considered ten states closely contested—those where they led by only 1 to 10 percentage points—and these states were targeted for the most attention, both personally by the candidates and through media buys. Of these ten states—Colorado, Michigan, Ohio, Georgia, Louisiana, North Carolina, Connecticut, New Mexico, Kentucky, and Tennessee—Clinton lost only one, North Carolina.[79]

Benchmark polls are only the first and most basic tool of the pollster. Focus groups have been a tool of communication and advertising research for forty years, including earlier presidential campaigns. But it was not until the 1980s that they became an integral part of campaign strategy. The ideal group is about a dozen to fifteen people, citizens or voters chosen from the general population to discuss the election and the candidates. A much smaller number is likely to place too much of a burden on each individual, while more than fifteen or so tends to reduce each member's participation. A moderator guides the discussion, focusing on matters of interest to the campaign. Discussions are lengthy—anywhere from one and a half to three hours—so that respondents have a chance to express their feelings. The Bush campaign picked Paramus, New Jersey, for their main focus group because to them it represented a typical American city. They conducted similar sessions in other middle-America settings across the country.

Unlike opinion polls, which depend for their validity on randomly selecting a representative cross-section of voters, focus groups are usually structured to be socially homogeneous "so that the numerous interacting demographic variables do not confuse the issues; to be most productive, all the participants must be on the same wavelength."[80] For example, Young and Rubicam Enterprises, which conducts hundreds of focus-group discussions every year, almost never puts married, full-time housewives with children at home in the same group as unmarried, working women because they regard their lifestyles and goals as too different.[81] "The key to focus groups is homogeneity," Bill Clinton's sometime pollster Stanley Greenberg says. "The more homogeneity, the more revealing."[82]

The composition of the various groups depends on the needs of the campaign. In 1988 the Bush team interviewed white Catholic Reagan Democrats because they were considered a critical swing group. The idea was for Bush to pursue groups that voted for Reagan but were in danger of drifting back toward the Democrats. In 1992 both Bush and Clinton were pursuing these white middle-class voters, and both campaigns featured them in their focus groups.

Focus-group interviewing violates most of the accepted canons of survey research. As William D. Wells of the University of Chicago Graduate School of Business says:

> Samples are invariably small and never selected by probability methods. Questions are not asked the same way each time. Responses are not independent. Some respondents inflict their opinions on others; some contribute little or nothing at all. Results are difficult or impossible to quantify and so are not grist for the statistical mill. Conclusions depend on the analyst's interpretive skill. The investigator can easily influence the results.[83]

With so many defects, why have focus groups come to be so widely used in political campaigns? Part of the reason is that they are fast and relatively cheap—a few thousand dollars as opposed to $20,000 to $25,000 or more for sample surveys. Another reason to use focus groups is to test ideas or ads not yet released to the general public. Regular opinion polls have long been used to test campaign themes and specific ideas that campaigns may use. Typically, respondents are asked questions about a candidate, then read some new information about that candidate, and then are asked again for views of that candidate. In this way, a pollster can check whether a candidate's potential weakness would actually affect voters if it received publicity. Focus groups allow campaigns to go further. Instead of merely describing a piece of information about a candidate, the moderator can show the group an actual ad and ask them for a reaction. Like Hollywood movies, which are changed if preview audiences object to something, political ads can be altered or eliminated if focus groups don't like what they see.

The most important reason focus groups are employed is that they give the campaign an opportunity to probe respondents to a greater depth than in regular polls. Deeper feelings and half-formed thoughts of ordinary voters emerge, and in their own words. It is true that the group's responses cannot easily be quantified, but in the hands of a sensitive analyst, focus groups may reveal important insights. "Focus groups allow you to put flesh on the bones," Democratic pollster Mark Mellman says; they provide "a sense of texture you can't get from a poll."[84]

Using focus groups in 1988, Bob Teeter discovered that when Bush spoke of "a thousand points of light," nobody knew what he was talking about. Bush fared best, Teeter found, when he sounded strongest, as when he depicted Dukakis as overly liberal on every issue from the death penalty to taxes to prison furloughs to saluting the flag.[85]

The Dukakis campaign also used focus groups extensively and, interestingly, found many of the same sentiments in the population that the Bush people were discovering.[86] "We polled. We had extensive focus groups," said Susan Estrich, Dukakis's campaign manager. "You know, you can go wrong, but you don't go wrong for lack of trying—at least in the general election we were polling constantly. We were focus grouping their ads probably as much as they were."[87] The polls and focus groups enabled the Democrats to identify their weaknesses. "They told us that we were vulnerable on the liberal-conservative issues and on crime," said Irwin "Tubby" Harrison. "We looked at Dukakis's involvement in the prison furlough program in Massachusetts early and knew we had a problem. There was a possible vulnerability on defense, on taxes, and on capital punishment, too."[88]

But recognizing a problem and remedying it are two different things. Pollsters reign supreme at the former task, but there may be little they can do about the latter. Dukakis's closest aide, Nicholas Mitropoulos, suggested that the governor was uncomfortable responding to Bush's attacks. "Dukakis deep down inside is just a good guy and felt that ... the American people were going to see that these issues were not real issues," Mitropoulos said. "He wanted to take the campaign on the high road... he wanted to stay positive."[89] A Bush pollster, Vincent Breglio, took a different view. "Dukakis tried to explain away the furlough program, Boston harbor, his Pledge position," Breglio said. "It just didn't work."[90]

In 1992 Clinton was heading into the general campaign in a weak and vulnerable position after enduring a brutal primary season. Besieged by questions of character brought on by allegations of womanizing, draft-dodging, and noninhaling drug use, Clinton's popularity ratings before the Democratic convention were low. Clinton's team used focus groups to pull its campaign out of the hole it had fallen into.

Clinton's consultants began a search for a revival strategy, a search they privately called the "Manhattan Project." The first step they took was to convene focus groups consisting of the targeted white middle-class voters. They found that the focus-group participants viewed Clinton's difficulties as part of a larger problem: that Clinton was just another "typical politician." The memorandum to Clinton summarizing the findings read as follows:

> For the most part, people were reluctant to write [Clinton] off as corrupt, dishonest or immoral, but the highly publicized "shading of the truth" has reinforced an impression that he will do what is necessary to "look good." The questions about personal morality certainly matter, but their larger impact is contained in the general impression that he will say what is necessary and that he does not "talk straight."[91]

By providing the focus groups with additional information, Clinton's political consultants found that this negative perception could be turned around. Specifically, participants responded positively to information about Clinton's life, to stories about how Clinton had stood up to "special interests" in the past, and to proposals that avoided political talk and showed empathy and concern for people. Ultimately, the findings from these focus groups helped convince Clinton that he needed to tell voters about his past—his childhood as the oldest son of a widowed mother, his adolescent showdown with his abusive stepfather, his success at putting himself through both college and law school—and helped shape his communication with voters during the rest of the campaign. This meant more direct contact through such media as popular talk shows and the bus tours, less traditionally political events and speeches.

Clinton's polling team in 1996, Mark Penn and Doug Schoen, were less impressed with the quality of focus-group research. They believed that the setting of focus groups—people sitting around having a conversation dedicated to talking politics—was too far from the circumstances in which ordinary Americans thought about politics. Instead, they preferred polling in shopping malls. For Penn and Schoen, this gave them answers that matched, as they saw it, the way most people thought of politics, as a "momentary distraction in their lives."[92]

Instead of asking focus groups to discuss ads, some pollsters prefer a more direct response. Using hand-held, dial-equipped electronic boxes, participants watching an ad or a candidate's performance are asked to twist a knob on a scale of zero to one hundred. Two reporters who witnessed a demonstration of this technology in 1988 reported that their colleagues in the press "sat transfixed as computer-generated graphics, showing the audience's second-by-second reactions, were superimposed above the television image of each candidate."[93]

Jimmy Carter's analysts used a similar instant-reaction technique to measure responses to the debate with Reagan in 1980 and determined that Carter was most liked when he promised to keep Social Security sound. Reagan peaked with his call for a strong military and with his recitation of the "misery index" (the continuation of unemployment and inflation, which, as the challenger, Reagan could blame on the incumbent).[94] Richard Wirthlin used the "pulse dials" in 1984 to study the Reagan-Mondale debates. Bob Teeter used the tool in several of his focus groups and included EKG-like etchings in his memorandum to the other members of the Bush campaign. Many of Teeter's core findings found their way into the advertising campaign, and public feelings about Dukakis's negatives began their steady uphill climb.[95]

Dial groups were also used by Clinton's consultants in the Manhattan Project campaign-revival effort. While trying to figure a way out of Clinton's problems, pollster Stanley Greenberg convened a group of middle-aged white women at a hotel in Dayton, Ohio, and asked them to "dial" their reactions to prepared presentations of the candidate and the campaign. Greenberg found that Clinton scored poorly when he looked and sounded like a politician but did well when he answered questions directly and addressed certain popular issues, such as welfare reform. When presenting the results to the campaign, Greenberg superimposed a tracing of the dial readings on the video the subjects had watched, giving Clinton a blow-by-blow report on the "grades" the dial group had given his various responses.[96]

Both campaigns convened dial groups for the 1992 presidential debates, hoping to identify the sound bites and ideas that pleased voters and thus deserved repeating in the general campaign. During the first presidential debate, however, any information the campaigns were able to glean was greatly overshadowed by the dial groups' response to Ross Perot's performance. Everything he said—from a joke about the size of his ears to a complaint about "America's crazy aunt locked up in the basement" (Perot's depiction of the deficit)—won an immediate and strongly positive response from the observers. Both campaigns' private conclusion after the debate was that Perot had won hands down.[97]

Still, the campaigns gained some information from their dial groups. After the first debate, Bush's team told him that he did better when he explained why he opposed a policy, such as committing troops to Bosnia or legalizing drugs. "You were more convincing in this context than when you were explaining what you were for," his pollsters wrote. "Keep counter-punching—you do it well. However, you need to improve your presentations of what you are proposing for your second term." The memorandum also recommended that Bush back off on his criticism of Clinton for "demonstrating on foreign soil," that he not object to others' descriptions of the country being in trouble (it made people think he was out of touch), and that he immediately attack Clinton any time he used the word "change," because that was a powerful word for his opponents.[98]

The benchmark poll gives general strategic guidelines to the campaign, but day-to-day tactical decisions are driven by another polling technique, overnight tracking, especially in the last weeks of an election. Rarely used until the late 1970s, tracking polls have "become de rigueur in the business," says Democratic pollster Paul Maslin.[99] Shifts in sentiment among voters are "tracked" by calling approximately 100 voters each night, asking a half dozen very specific questions, usually about perceptions of the latest ads, issues, or the candidates. With each increment of new respondents, the responses from six-day-old interviews are dropped. Thus, rolling averages can be calculated. The overnight figures facilitate fine-tuning of a campaign in the crucial last days.

In late October 1988, Dukakis made a last-minute surge, narrowing the gap between himself and Bush, who was so distressed by Dukakis's improvement that aides tried to keep the tracking numbers from him. "Bush would start each morning agreeing that they [the numbers] were bad for him," Peter Goldman and his colleagues report, "but his resolve not to ask would typically break down by, say, 8A.M. 'What did Teeter tell you?' he would ask urgently. 'Have you heard from Teeter?'" Teeter's disconcerting tracking results kept the entire Bush team in suspense right up to election day.[100]

Bush's concern in 1988 might have been forestalled, however, if he had known just how imprecise tracking polls can be. Four years later, just days before Bush was defeated by Clinton, several tracking polls were reporting Bush ahead or trailing by only an insignificant two points. The general consensus among pollsters was that these results were wrong. Both Bush's polling team and the Clinton pollsters were reporting gaps of six to eight points in Clinton's favor, and there was no evidence to suggest a major shift in support during the last few days. The pollsters agreed: there was no way that Bush could be ahead. This was believed even though the small sample size of the tracking polls meant that the results were unreliable from day-to-day and the "snapshot" results some tracking polls were reporting were surely mistakes. To address this concern, pollsters generally average tracking results over several days to increase reliability, and they still consider tracking results good only for spotting "trends," not predicting outcomes.[101]

Why are polls and pollsters so important in the campaign? Why have they replaced party bosses, cronies of the candidate (these are still in evidence, but at the top levels the campaign staff is, increasingly, a meritocracy), and the candidates themselves as the key decision makers? Plenty of attention has been focused on the mistaken or misleading results of polling. Nevertheless, taken together, polls are reasonably accurate indicators of public sentiment. Thus they are a better tool for shaping campaign strategy and content than anything else now available, and this, in the uncertain universe of the presidential campaign, is all that is really necessary to make polls indispensable to the candidate.

One need only consider the information sources that used to govern campaign strategy to appreciate the significance of the advent of modern polling techniques. Nineteenth- and early-twentieth-century campaign indicators consisted of reports from precinct captains and state party leaders, crowd sizes and responses, newspaper editorials and letters to the editor, the candidate's mail, man-in-the-street interviews, and pure hunches. Most of these indicators were unreliable. Editorials may signify the views of only a few newspaper owners; letters to the editor represent a lot of writing by a rather small number of activists; crowd responses can be manipulated, or variously interpreted; party leaders may let the candidate know only what they think the candidate wishes to hear.

While polls themselves may be indispensable, their interpreters are more and more playing larger roles in presidential politics than would seem warranted for mere keepers of statistics. Bush, for example, was persuaded by Teeter (with the aid of his managers Roger Ailes and Lee Atwater) to adopt the get-tough strategy of his 1988 campaign.[102] The modern-day poll taker, in the words of one practitioner, plays an instrumental role in deciding "which states to hit, where people should go, how much money should be spent where, which groups [to] target, and the kinds of money and messages [to] use."[103]

The explanation for this abdication of authority on the part of the candidates and their personal advisers lies partly in the changing nature of polling. With computer-assisted sample selection processes and polling techniques, it has been possible to increase the number of polls taken in the course of a campaign to as many as the 133 surveys from separate states that Pat Caddell took between late August and election eve for Jimmy Carter in 1980—which works out to about one every other day.[104] In addition to conducting their own polls, polling experts are responsible for gathering and interpreting whatever other public or private polls are available. Whereas the polling consultant after 1960 might have reported to the campaign on a monthly basis during the spring and fall of an election year, the present-day pollster is always present, with daily, and sometimes hourly, updates to report.

Moreover, the information obtained from polls has expanded greatly. Originally, polls were merely a device to measure candidate support; good pollsters would try to isolate which groups within the electorate were more and less likely to vote for the candidate. Nowadays, polls are constructed to address not just how social groups will vote—and the categories here have become progressively more precise—but why they will do so and what might change their behavior. Pollsters, in other words, are now being asked to do more than simply report on the state of public opinion; they are now routinely expected to aid in influencing it.

Advertising

TELEVISION

Campaigns expend considerable resources on political television commercials. Commercials serve a variety of purposes. They can be used to establish name identification or to improve a candidate's personal image. They can focus on campaign issues, targeting key subgroups in the population. They can be used to capture the attention of the press. Or they can be used to attack the candidate's opponent. This practice has come to be called negative advertising.

In 1948 fewer than 3 percent of the population owned a television set.[105] That year marked the debut of television advertising in presidential campaigns. President Truman taped just a single speech encouraging citizens to vote.[106] Since that modest beginning, campaigning via television has taken on a life of its own.

The landmark presidential election year, by all accounts, was 1952. By then, 45 percent of the nation's households owned a set,[107] and presidential campaign teams felt they could ill afford to ignore the medium. Dwight Eisenhower's campaign utilized the services of Ted Bates and Company advertising agency in New York. The three central themes of the commercials—corruption, high prices, and the Korean war (all the fault of the Democrats, of course)—were chosen after consultation with pollster George Gallup.[108] Spot ads developed with Gallup's advice managed to overcome Ike's abrupt speaking style and to create the confident, avuncular figure now associated with Eisenhower.

There is no standard formula for a political ad, but there are standard time slots. When introduced in the 1950s, television advertising was generally produced to fill five-minute slots. One-minute spots predominated in the 1960s and 1970s, to be eclipsed in the late 1970s by the thirty-second ad. Finally, around 1982, the now-popular ten-second spot was introduced.[109]

After the advertisement is filmed, edited, and approved by the candidate, a schedule is prepared that is supposed to help the ad reach the right people. Every ad campaign is somewhat different and must be crafted to take account of the unique assets and deficits of the candidate. But amid the varying styles of each campaign, a relatively small number of tried-and-true themes have established themselves over the past several decades. These constitute the advertising consultant's tool kit, from which virtually every television campaign is built. There is the "man-in-the-street" ad, sometimes scripted and sometimes culled from actual interview footage, showing the average voter (or the average member of a targeted constituency group) endorsing the candidate's accomplishments or general integrity. The "sainthood spot" is "devoted to celebrating the candidate's life story and accomplishments." The "news-look" spot ad attempts to use the legitimacy of experts and legitimacy of television newscasters who relate facts about the candidate's record. The "apology" ad is used, usually out of desperation, when a liability develops that is considered so serious to the candidate's chances of election that he or she must personally apologize to the electorate. "Cinema verité" spots offer the audience a view into the life of the candidate as he is working, walking, or addressing another audience, while the other "talking head" approach (still a staple of the spot ads) places the candidate directly in front of the camera so that he can talk personally and directly to the audience. The "issue-position" spot defines the candidate's record on an issue of high salience to the electorate or to a swing group of voters.[110]

One measure of the centrality of television advertising in the current campaign process can be found in the "back-and-forth" ad. This innovative format begins with an excerpt from an opponent's spot ad, which is then "answered" in the second sequence, an ad within an ad. This is possible because technological developments have enabled campaigns to produce television ads more quickly, cheaply, and easily. Campaigns can respond to the opposition's latest round of advertising in a matter of days. Evidence shows that technology may be closing this time lag even more. In one exceptional case, the Clinton 1992 campaign team was able to respond to a Bush ad within forty-eight hours of its first broadcast.

The key to this quick turnaround was satellite technology. The Clinton team had hired a satellite tracking company to monitor Bush's activity and alert them whenever a new Bush commercial was broadcast in hard-fought locations. When the Bush campaign broadcast a commercial criticizing Clinton's tax record in Arkansas and claiming that Clinton's campaign proposals would require $220 billion in taxes, the Clinton campaign knew about it within five minutes. Within an hour, the campaign team members had consulted with Clinton, reviewed the ad that the satellite company had beamed to campaign headquarters, and devised a plan for response. That night, Clinton's economists analyzed the Bush ad, trying to determine how the opposition had come up with its numbers. The next morning, campaign staff called reporters at major newspapers and encouraged them to write critiques of the new Bush ad. These commentaries on political advertising had become common in major newspapers and news magazines. Next, the media team headed by Mandy Grunwald put together a response ad on the "back-and-forth" model: they included some of the copy from the Bush ad and added a stamped "UNTRUE" across a frozen frame. By six in the evening after the Bush ad's first airing, Grunwald was showing the ad and the Clinton response to a focus group in Pennsylvania. She determined that the ad needed more authority, so the campaign gathered quotes from the newspaper critiques they had set in motion that morning. By the next day—less than forty-eight hours after the Bush ad's debut—the Clinton campaign had distributed its response ad to reporters and television stations across the country.[111]

It is important to note that ad makers are not always guided by the pollster's revelations. In the 1980 general election, ads showed Carter working long hours at the White House. "The responsibility never ends," said the voice-over. "Even at the end of a long working day, there is usually another cable addressed to the Chief of State from the other side of the world where the sun is shining and something is happening." But polls said that voters never doubted that Carter

worked hard. They doubted whether all the hard work was paying off. This crucial point—Carter's effectiveness—was not addressed in the ad.[112]

TARGETING

Media professionals attempt to place political commercials so as to reach a targeted viewing audience. "Dissimilar kinds of people," Larry Sabato notes,
"watch and listen to different sorts of programs at various times of the day.
The better educated, information-oriented, undecided voters have been found
to cluster around late news shows." A media manager might go after such a
group with information-packed ads or spots discussing issues. Middle-aged
housewives, Sabato believes, are partial to family-oriented or charismatic
image spots during afternoon soap operas.[113]

The latest frontier in targeting promises to extend this strategy by exploiting the rapidly expanding media market of cable television. Well over half the
households in the country now subscribe to one or more cable systems.[114] The
audiences watching cable channels are often more socially and culturally
homogeneous than even the smallest local television station, so messages can be
tailored accordingly. Also, according to one researcher, cable audiences tend to
be more politically active than regular television viewers, raising the prospect
of media advertising aimed at recruiting not just voters but also volunteer campaign workers.[115] The late Richard N. Neustadt, a communications law attorney, predicted: "When we watch the narrowcasting [approach of cable]
networks, we may see campaign ads and news programs showing candidates
advocating bilingual education on Spanish channels, defending Social Security
on channels aimed at the elderly, or playing football on sports channels."[116]

RADIO AND NEWSPAPERS

Like television talk shows, radio talk shows were used by the 1992 candidates
to deliver their messages directly to the people. When Clinton was in trouble
in the New York primary, for example, he appeared on the Don Imus morning show. On the advice of his media consultant Mandy Grunwald, other radio
guest spots were booked for Clinton across the country.[117]

Eventually the Clinton campaign went further in pursuing radio publicity.
Over the summer, campaign aides set up a computerized voice-mail system
that allowed radio producers to call a 1-800 number, select from the digital
menu, and download recorded sound bites and campaign information. The
system was individualized for different markets: Latino radio stations could
hear a message in Spanish, African American stations had a message aimed at
their audience, and there were further choices of sound bites from Clinton,
vice-presidential candidate Al Gore, or prominent Clinton supporters. The
campaign also set up local substations of the system so that endorsements from

local personalities could be added to the menu and made available to area radio shows. This effort was enormous. One author estimated that the system allowed the campaign to deliver its message to 2,200 stations every day, 30 percent of the national radio market.[118]

Perot, too, benefited greatly from the national growth in talk radio; indeed, his candidacy might have died at birth had it not been for talk radio. In the two weeks after his appearance on *Larry King Live*, the major newspapers ignored Perot's candidacy; only the *Los Angeles Times* ran a small story, burying it on page eighteen of the paper. But the day after the King appearance, talk-radio stations across the country were deluged with callers wanting to talk about the billionaire and his candidacy. Talk-show hosts were apparently taken by surprise by this show of interest, but they caught on quickly; the traditional media were not as quick. By the time the major media outlets started paying attention to Perot, he was winning 20 percent support in the polls.[119]

Radio also remains a staple in the advertising diet of presidential campaigns. The main advantage over television, of course, is cost. With audiences that are frequently more demographically focused than even cable television, radio outlets also offer a campaign the opportunity to pitch to narrow slices of the electorate. The McGovern campaign, for example, was the first to take aim at the rock n' roll audience, which contained many of the 18–21 year olds just enfranchised by the Twenty-sixth Amendment.[120]

Newspapers have clearly lost out in the bid for campaign advertising dollars in the contemporary period. Consultants, according to one survey, consider the effect of a print ad to be "almost negligible." Several factors account for this revolutionary change in campaign strategy. First, people tend to view newspapers as less credible than other media as sources of information. Second, a newspaper ad can be more easily ignored than a television or radio spot. Third, the portion of the electorate that reads newspapers is more highly educated and more politically committed than the portion that attends to electronic media and therefore is less likely to be swayed by advertising of any sort. If you want to communicate to the politicians, take out a newspaper ad. If you want to communicate with the voters, use radio and television. Such is the orthodoxy among the consultants.

One continuing attraction of newspapers for the presidential campaign has nothing to do with advertising. "Some candidates," according to Democratic pollster Bill Hamilton, "particularly on the Democratic side, are forced to buy newspaper ads if they want to get the paper's endorsement."[121]

OTHER MEDIA

Two-thirds of the electorate now own videocassette recorders, and the fact has not been lost on political consultants. Walter Mondale became the first presidential candidate to produce a videocassette for mass circulation during the 1984 campaign. The purpose in this case was fund-raising, but the trend is clearly to use the new medium to replace personal campaigning. Eleven of the thirteen major-party candidates in 1988 distributed videos of themselves. "Video parties" were held by the thousands in New Hampshire before that state's primary elections.

Why the sudden popularity? Frank Luntz explains:

> At a cost of from $10,000 to $40,000…, home videos are relatively inexpensive to prepare, and can also save the campaign money by using video footage for their television advertising, or vice versa. These cassettes allow the candidate to appear "in person" at five or even fifty places at once, and are designed to give voters a personal sense of the candidate, not just a recitation of proposals or issues.

As John Buckley, Jack Kemp's press secretary, put it, "It's the political equivalent of cloning."[122]

In 1992 the Clinton campaign put together a video that included "The Man from Hope," the Hollywood-produced story of Clinton's life that was screened at the Democratic Convention, and a tailored message from Bill Clinton. The video was distributed to loyal Democrats for use at "Clinton House Party" fund-raisers and was a successful part of the campaign's money plan.[123]

The first use of satellite broadcasting in a presidential campaign is described by Richard Armstrong:

> During one … impossible week in 1984, when both Florida and Georgia were preparing for their primaries, Walter Mondale took an hour out of his campaign schedule in Georgia to go to an Atlanta television studio. [Frank] Greer [the first consultant to use the new satellite technology] had arranged for an "uplink" to a satellite and had made appointments with the news anchormen of Miami's three biggest television stations. As Mondale stared into the camera, each Florida newsman took turns asking him questions over long-distance phone lines. Mondale's replies were shot in Atlanta, relayed by microwave to an uplink dish outside the city, beamed 22,300 miles through space to a satellite over the equator, reflected back to the downlink dishes in three Miami television stations, and recorded for use on the evening news later that day.[118]

The result? Mondale captured the lead spot on all three network-affiliated stations' news shows that day in Miami. As his face appeared on the screen behind the anchormen, each repeated the questions asked earlier in the taped satellite interview. "To the viewers it appeared to be a live interview in the studio, a real coup for the local news team. But as virtually everyone in southern Florida watched Mondale live on local television, Mondale himself was busy meeting his commitments in Georgia."[125] Mondale, one technological step ahead of his opponent John Glenn, managed to appear in three places while actually being in none, and scooped up the nightly news programs in the process.

In addition to conducting press conferences in situations where the candidate and the press audience he or she is trying to reach are on different parts of the earth, satellite communications can be used to disseminate stories to local media across the country, to bring the candidate into direct contact with potential donors at several locations, and to bring many local groups of campaign workers together for one, big television conference.

An innovation of the 1992 election was the use of 1-800 numbers. Virtually every candidate in the 1992 primary and general election campaigns at one point set up a 1-800 number for supporters to call. Ross Perot's candidacy was built on a 1-800 number that supporters called to volunteer for the campaign and get in touch with the individual state Perot organizations. The surprising strength of Jerry Brown's primary campaign was attributable in part to his refusal to accept campaign donations larger than $100 and in part to his constant promotion of his 1-800 number. Calls flooded in with offers of support and money, and his insubstantial campaign was sustained for a while.[126] Clinton, Bush, and Perot all promoted 1-800 numbers during the general campaign; in many cases, a call to the 1-800 number would get the caller a copy of the candidate's "plan."

Strategies and Tactics

Historically, the outstanding strategic problem for Democratic politicians who wish to capitalize on long-standing party habits is to get their adherents to turn out to vote for Democratic candidates. Democrats therefore stress appeals to the faithful. One of the major problems, as we saw in chapter 1, is that most citizens who identify with them are found at the lower end of the socioeconomic scale and are less likely to turn out to vote than those with Republican leanings. So the Democrats put on mobilization drives and seek in every way to get as large a turnout as possible. If they are well organized, they scour the lower-income areas for voters, they provide babysitters, they arrange for cars to get the elderly and infirm to the polls, or make sure they have absentee ballots.[127] Whether the neutral campaigns put on by radio, television, and newspapers stressing the civic obligation to vote help the Democrats more than the Republicans depends on whether in any given locality there are more Democrats who are unregistered because they are poor and uneducated than Republicans who are unregistered because they have recently moved. Raymond Wolfinger and his colleagues, who have studied the matter closely, conclude that nationwide the partisan advantage is about a wash.[128]

For Republicans involved in presidential elections, the most important fact of life is that their party has been the long-term minority party in the United States. In presidential elections in which considerations of party are foremost, and allowing for the greater propensity of Republicans to turn out to vote, it was plausibly argued in 1960 that the Democrats could expect to win around 53 or 54 percent of the vote.[129] Nowadays it appears that the Republicans have better presidential prospects. The party's share of citizens who actually vote (40 percent in 1980) is considerably greater than their proportion of voters in the eligible general population (34 percent in 1980). The gap the Republicans have had to overcome has diminished since the 1960s, from 20 percent (54 percent Democratic versus 34 percent Republican) to 12 percent (52 percent Democratic to 40 percent Republican) in the 1980s. Additionally, Democratic voters have been much more likely to defect to a Republican candidate than Republicans to defect to Democrats.[130]

Further factors in calculating party advantage are the various biases built into the electoral college. On the one hand, Republicans have an advantage because they tend to do better in the sparsely populated states, and therefore benefit from the extra weight those states receive from the electoral college formula. On the other hand, Democrats receive an advantage because their votes are better distributed among the states, leading to fewer "wasted" votes. That is, Republican candidates, even in close elections, will generally win several states by lopsided margins, while very few states will return Democratic landslides. Overall, any consistent partisan advantage is small.[131]

We conclude that while Republicans have to come from behind, the predisposing factors are sufficiently close so that Republicans have a good chance of winning, and either major party can win a presidential election.

When one party is considered more likely to win, either because it has more party identifiers (as the Democrats have had since the Great Depression) or because it holds the presidency (as the Republicans have in most elections since 1972), the strategic alternatives available to the underdog party can hardly be regarded as secret. We consider these possibilities from the perspective of the Republicans, the out party in 2000. First, Republicans can attempt to deemphasize the impact of party habit as a component of electoral choice by promoting a more compelling cue to action. The nomination of General Eisenhower, the most popular hero of World War II, overrode party considerations and is a clear example of the efficacy of this strategy.[132] Efforts to play on popular dissatisfaction in a variety of issue areas, such as "stagflation" in 1980, also exemplify this strategy, but these dissatisfactions must already exist in the population and must be widespread and intense before they will produce the desired effect. When issues do come to the fore in a compelling way, the payoff to the advantaged party is sometimes enormous because these are the circumstances under which new party loyalties can be created. Or the Republican candidate can do as Ronald Reagan did in 1980 and emphasize popular themes of patriotism and national renewal, while hoping his or her opponent's personal unpopularity will keep enough Democratic voters at home to make a Republican victory possible. The Republican candidate also can stress the issue differences between the parties, as Goldwater did in 1964 and Reagan, less stridently, in 1984. When Democratic policies are popular, as they were in 1964, this tactic is suicidal. But when they are unpopular, as was the case for "liberalism" and "crime" in 1988, stressing differences works very well.

Goldwater thought that conservative elements of the population were alienated from politics and were sitting in the wings, frustrated, immobilized, and without party loyalties, until someone gave them the "choice" they were looking for. In 1964 he called this a "hidden vote" theory. But it was nonsense. What evidence we have points to the probability that the dedicated conservatives sufficiently interested in politics to hold strong opinions about public policy do in fact belong to political parties and participate actively in them. These people are almost all Republicans. This is now true even in the South, where many of these people used to vote Democratic.[133]

Another assumption underlying the hidden-vote theory is that in 1964 it would have been possible to attract this mythical vote in substantial numbers without losing the allegiance of large numbers of more moderate people. Not so. Goldwater aroused great antipathy among the general population. Louis Harris surveys found that sizable majorities in the general population defined themselves as opposed to positions they believed Senator Goldwater held.[134] They let him know at the polls.

Negative Campaigning

In the closing days of what appears to be a close race, there may be a temptation for the parties, now thoroughly engrossed in the heat of battle, to let loose a stream of negative advertising at the other side. How much of this they do and how often they do it is partially determined by the kind of people they are. In the long run, however, the standards of the voting population determine the standards of the candidates. Should it happen that vituperation is rewarded, we can expect to see it occur again. Should it prove to be the case, however, as in the Scandinavian countries, that departures from proper deportment are severely punished at the polls, candidates can be expected to take the hint. Alas, such elevated levels of morality have not yet been reached in the United States. In that case, whether campaigns "go negative" depends on a calculation of whether or not it will help win the election. As the *New Republic* explained in response to an outbreak of negative ads in 1986:

> the proliferation of negative ads is simply a result of the consultants' discovery that attacks make a more lasting impression on voters than positive commercials. More candidates are making the attacks personally, rather than working through stand-ins, because research shows that the ads work better that way. The surge in negative advertising has even given rise to the countertactic known as "inoculation": ads designed to answer potential negative ads even before the attacks air.[135]

Negative campaigning is hardly new to American politics, or even new to television advertising. In 1964 Tony Schwartz produced the most famous political advertisement of its era, the "Daisy spot" for the Lyndon Johnson campaign. It shows a little girl standing in an open field, plucking petals from a daisy as she miscounts "four, five, seven, six, six..." When she reaches "nine," an ominous voice-over begins a countdown of its own: "ten, nine, eight,..." At zero, an explosion is heard and a mushroom cloud appears. President Johnson's voice is heard saying, "These are the stakes. To make a world in which all of God's children can live, or to go into the dark. We must love each other or we must die." Like many effective attack ads, the Daisy spot capitalized on a fear that already existed. Voters saw Barry Goldwater, Johnson's Republican opponent, as a man who might start a nuclear war, and the Daisy spot, although it aired only once and never mentioned Goldwater, gained sufficient notoriety to reinforce this perception.[131]

Johnson's negative campaign also attacked Goldwater for his views on the United Nations, the Social Security Administration, and Medicare. Goldwater responded with his own negative ads, linking the Johnson administration to the "moral decay" of America as the screen filled with pictures of race riots, dope peddling, alcoholism, and crime. Another spot accused Johnson of corruption and voting fraud.[137]

In the commercial world, this is known as "comparative advertising." The campaign consultants' trade journal *Campaigns and Elections* regularly counsels candidates, in the words of one article title, to "Nail the Opposition."[138] This is a risky strategy. Research has shown that voters prefer positive, informational advertising that appears to be fair.[139] Negative advertising is not, therefore, the consultants' panacea, but it is a tool to achieve several common campaign objectives: to stigmatize or "characterize" a relatively unknown opponent, to focus the agenda of the campaign on weaknesses of an opponent, to call attention to an embarrassing blunder on the part of the opposition.[140]

Media consultants pay especially close attention to polling results when devising negative ads because they are risky. In the 1980 primaries, for example, Patrick Caddell's polls revealed that voters disillusioned with President Carter nevertheless liked and trusted him personally. Edward Kennedy, however, was perceived as untrustworthy. Thus Gerald Rafshoon, Carter's ad maker, invited a comparison between Carter's and Kennedy's integrity. Concluded one ad: "You may not always agree with President Carter. But you'll never wonder whether he's telling the truth. It's hard to think of a more useful quality in a president than telling the simple truth. President Carter—for the truth." In the general election, the Republicans noted the voters' respect for Carter as a person and so decided to attack his performance and not the man.[141]

In the 1988 campaign, the results of focus groups and polls were instrumental in devising the ad campaign. The result was a series of harsh negative ads. Why did the Bush campaign attack? As his political adviser Roger Ailes explains it, Bush's campaign sought to capitalize on the fact that Michael Dukakis was known to very few voters at the beginning of the campaign:

We always knew we would have to define Dukakis ... and whichever of us defined the other and ourselves most effetively would win...

You've got to understand that the media has [sic] no interest in substance. Print has a little more interest because they have to fill a lot of lines. But electronic media has no interest in substance.

There are three ways to get on the air: pictures, attacks, and mistakes, so what you do is spend your time avoiding mistakes, staying on the attack and giving them pictures.[142]

One of the results of the Watergate scandals of the early 1970s is said to have been the advent in the populace at large of a "post-Watergate morality" in which failure to abide by rules of common decency was expected to be strongly disfavored. This does not necessarily provide much guidance to candidates, however. It may, in fact, be a gross violation of common decency, as elites understand such matters, to hurl an accusation at an opponent that forces him or her into a complex explanation that few people will understand. Yet it may be winning politics to indulge in such tactics under the incentives set up by post-Watergate morality. For example, there are frequently adequate and legitimate reasons of public policy for members of Congress to travel abroad on public funds, even if they have a good time doing it. But woe betide the member of Congress who for one reason or another is forced to defend this practice before an aroused electorate.

Many observers claim that Senator Edmund Muskie fatally injured his campaign for the 1972 Democratic nomination by showing too much emotion in response to a Republican smear that falsely branded his wife a bigot. Muskie, it is true, had in many prior campaigns managed with enormous success to show indignation at the moral lapses of opponents who attacked him,[143] but this time something went wrong, and he was widely criticized for showing the wrong demeanor. Perhaps on this one occasion he should have taken a leaf from the book of Franklin Delano Roosevelt, who paid no attention to most accusations about him but seized on an attack involving his dog, Fala, to rib his opponents unmercifully for impugning an animal that could not reply.[144]

Both Carter and Ford in 1976 eschewed opportunities for mudslinging. When it looked like his fortunes were in decline, Carter was urged to link Ford explicitly to Watergate through his pardon of Nixon. Carter refused, saying, "It will rip our country apart."[145] Presented with an opportunity to accuse Carter of corruption in regard to the family peanut business, Ford squelched the matter.[146]

It is ironic that President Nixon and his campaign managers should have sought, in 1972, to adapt to their own uses the tactics they attributed to the far-out left. The contempt of insiders for a political system that nurtures them is a far more serious phenomenon than the antics of dissidents. Yet the Nixon campaign hired people to fake evidence tending to discredit former Democratic presidents and to harass Democratic presidential candidates by playing "dirty tricks" on them (such as ordering the delivery of huge numbers of pizzas in their name). Presumably the passage of laws prohibiting such behavior in the future will be of some help, but the fact that the reelection campaign of a president of the United States sheltered such disgusting behavior is a shameful blot on our history.[147]

Campaign professionals maintain that there is a clear line between legitimate attacks on the record, or even the personal background, of opposing candidates, and illegitimate dirty tricks. They even argue that "comparative" ads are beneficial, because they give voters important information they otherwise might not learn. There is some justification for this view. The line between fair and unfair is easily blurred. The newest wrinkle in dirty tricks is called "push polling." As we have seen, legitimate polls sometimes test specific pieces of information by telling respondents the story and gauging reactions. In Iowa in 1996, Bob Dole's campaign called potential caucus-goers and under the guise of polling (and without identifying which campaign was making the calls), spread negative information about his Republican opponents.[148]

In the United States we seem to be in a middle position in regard to mudslinging. It is not everyday practice, but neither is it a rarity. It works best, as one might guess, when it is not answered; when it is answered, it can backfire. A glance at the history of presidential campaigns suggests that vituperation is usually irrelevant to the outcomes of campaigns and that its benefits are problematical. Nevertheless, we expect candidates in the future to turn to negative campaigning and mudslinging when they believe the potential benefits outweigh the risks to their own reputations for fair play and serious attention to the issues of the day.

Presentation of Self

Another set of strategic problems concerns the personal impression made by the candidates. A candidate is helped by being thought of as trustworthy, reliable, mature, kind but firm, devoted to family, and in every way normal and presentable. No amount of expostulation about the irrelevance of all this ordinariness as qualification for an extraordinary office wipes out the fact that candidates must try to conform to the public stereotype of goodness, a standard that is typically far more demanding of politicians than of ordinary mortals. Gary Hart's precipitous withdrawal from the 1988 race for the Democratic nomination following charges of adultery tells a part of the story. Bill Clinton faced similar charges in 1992 but was able to overcome them, in part, we assume, because the experience of Hart had removed some of the shock factor from the revelations. Clinton also had to face attacks on his avoidance of service in Vietnam—charges Dan Quayle had faced in 1988—as well as investigations into his financial dealings and his well-reported noninhaling drug use. Because the media now feel obliged to report on such matters, their importance is bound to grow. Back in John F. Kennedy's time, reporters knew of his philandering but would have thought it wrong to say so in public.

194 PRESIDENTIAL ELECTIONS

It would be a painful process for a candidate to remodel his entire personality along the indicated lines. To be fair, most of the people who end up as candidates are not so far from the mark as to make this drastic expedient necessary, or they would not have been nominated in the first place. What the candidates actually try to do is to smooth off the rough edges, to counter what they believe are the most unfavorable impressions of specific aspects of their public image. John F. Kennedy, who was accused of being young and immature, hardly cracked a smile in his debates with Nixon, whereas the latter, who was said to be stiff and frightening, beamed with friendliness. Michael Dukakis, suspected of excessively pacific leanings, allowed himself to be driven around in an army tank.[149] George Bush was told to lower his voice so as to subdue the impression that he was a "wimp."[150] Clinton was told to "talk straight" and avoid smiling too much, for his previous persona had come across as too slick and insincere.[151] Kennedy restyled his youthful shock of hair, and Nixon thinned his eyebrows to look less threatening. Jimmy Carter made intimate revelations to show he was not cold and calculating but serious and introspective. Gerald Ford was photographed a lot around the White House to show he was in command. Ronald Reagan smiled and ducked when Jimmy Carter tried to portray him as dangerous. Just as Kennedy made it possible for Roman Catholics to be considered for the presidency, Reagan broke the taboo on divorce.

The little things that some people do not like may be interpreted favorably by other people. Hubert Humphrey was alleged to be a man who could not stop talking. His garrulousness, however, was just another side of his encyclopedic and detailed knowledge of the widest variety of public policies. He might have talked too much to suit some, but the fact that he knew a lot pleased others. Was Bill Clinton thoughtful and deliberate, or just evasive? Was Ronald Reagan amiable and charming, or was that a vacuous expression on his face?

The political folklore of previous campaigns provides candidates with helpful homilies about how to conduct themselves. Typical bits of advice include the following: always carry the attack to your opponent; the best defense is offense; separate the other candidate from his or her party; when in doubt as to the course that will produce the most votes, do what you believe is right; guard against acts that can hurt you because they are more significant than acts that can help you; avoid making personal attacks that may gain sympathy for the opposition. Unfortunately for the politicians in search of a guide, these bits of folk wisdom do not contain detailed instructions about the conditions under which they should and should not be applied.

The experience of Adlai Stevenson suggests a familiar dilemma for candidates. Shall they write (or cause to have written for them) new speeches for most occasions, or shall they rest content to hammer home a few themes, embroidering just a little here and there? No one really knows which is better. Stevenson is famous for the care he took with his speeches and the originality he sought to impart to his efforts. Had he won office, he might have established a trend. Clinton too is known for addressing large numbers of issues in his speeches. On the one hand, this tendency has contributed to Clinton's image as a highly intelligent man who understands complex issues. On the other hand, he has been criticized for being unfocused, scattered, and windy.

Most candidates are likely to follow Kennedy and Nixon, Johnson and Goldwater, and Carter and Ford in using just a few set speeches. Ronald Reagan's virtuoso shuffling of his well-worn index cards, with their anecdotes of questionable accuracy, seems to have served him well enough. In view of the pervasive inattention to public affairs and political talk in our society, this approach may have the advantage of driving points home (as well as driving mad the news correspondents who must listen to the same thing all the time).[152] Newspaper people and television journalists who cover the campaigns complain quite a lot about the repetitiousness of presidential candidates, as though the campaign should be designed mostly to amuse them. In 1996 Bob Dole frustrated his campaign staff by constantly departing from his prepared text in stump speeches. Dole, an easily bored man, was more concerned that he was boring the reporters in the back of the room by repeating the same lines night after night than he was with making sure that the partisans in the rest of the room would hear his prepared remarks. It did not work. Rather than being pleased with the variety, reporters wrote that Dole's campaign wasn't properly disciplined and organized.[153] This dilemma ranks high on the list of unsolved (and no doubt unsolvable) problems of American democracy: how to get through to the relatively inattentive American people without totally alienating the superattentive mandarins of the news media through whom a candidate ordinarily reaches the rank-and-file voter.

More important, perhaps, is the desirability of appearing comfortable in delivery. Televised speeches are the major opportunities for a candidate to be seen and evaluated by large numbers of people. Eisenhower's ability to project a radiant appearance helped him; Stevenson's obvious discomfort before the camera hurt him. On this point we have evidence that those who listened to Stevenson's delivery over radio were more favorably impressed with him than those who watched him on television.[154] Jimmy Carter's paste-on smile and rigid bearing contrasted poorly with Ronald Reagan's easy grin and relaxed manner, though these surface indicators, like Gerald Ford's alleged clumsiness, may have nothing to do with performance in office.

The major difficulty with the tactical principles we have been discussing is not that they are too theoretical but that they do not really tell the candidates what to do when they are mutually incompatible. Like proverbs, one can often find principles to justify opposing courses of action: "Look before you leap," but "He who hesitates is lost." Nixon in 1960 could not take full advantage of international affairs without hitting so hard as to reinforce the unfavorable impression of himself as being harsh and unprincipled. Kennedy could hardly capitalize on the Rooseveltian image of the vigorous leader without attacking the foreign policy of a popular president. The result is that the candidates must take calculated risks when existing knowledge about the consequences of alternative courses of action is inadequate. Hunch, intuition, and temperament necessarily play important roles in choosing among competing alternatives.

Debates

The famous television debates of 1960 between Vice President Richard Nixon and Senator John F. Kennedy provide an excellent illustration of the difficulty of choosing between competing considerations in the absence of knowledge of the most likely results. With the benefit of hindsight, many observers now suggest that Nixon was foolish to engage in the debates. Let us try to look at the situation from the perspective of each of the presidential aspirants at the time.

Kennedy issued a challenge to debate on television. The possible advantages from his point of view were many. He could use a refusal to debate to accuse Nixon of running away and depriving the people of a unique opportunity to judge the candidates. Among Kennedy's greatest handicaps in the campaign were his youth and the inevitable charges of inexperience. Television debates could help to overcome these difficulties by showing the audience not so much that Kennedy was superior in knowledge but that there was not that much difference in the information, age, and general stature of the two men. Whatever administrative skills or inside information Nixon might have had would not show up on the screen as the candidates necessarily confined themselves to broad discussions of issues known to all politically literate people. Kennedy could only guess but he could not know that Nixon would not stump him in an embarrassing way in front of millions of viewers. But Kennedy understood that despite the reams of publicity he had received, he was unknown to many voters, much less known than the vice president. Here was a golden opportunity to increase his visibility in a sudden and dramatic way. Moreover, his good looks would not hurt him with those who like to judge the appearance of a man.[155]

Nixon was in a more difficult position. To say no would not have been a neutral decision; it would have subjected him to being called a man who was afraid to face his opposition. Saying yes had a number of possible advantages. One stemmed from the numerical disadvantage of the Republican Party. Normally, most people do not pay very much attention to the opposition candidate, making it difficult to win them over. Televised debates would provide a unique instance in which huge numbers of people attracted to both parties could be expected to tune in attentively. Nixon had good reason for believing that if he made a favorable impression, he would be in a position to convince more of the people he needed to convince (weak Democratic identifiers) than would Kennedy. The risk that Kennedy might use the opportunity to solidify the support of those attracted to a Democrat simply had to be taken. Another potential advantage that might have occurred to Nixon arose from his previous political life. He had been labeled by some people as "Tricky Dick," an untruthful and vindictive man. This picture could be supplanted on television by the new Nixon of smiling visage and magnanimous gesture who had it all over his opponent in knowledge of public affairs. Nixon had to judge whether his handicap was serious or whether it was confined to confirmed liberals whose numbers were insignificant and who would never vote for him in any event.[156] Perhaps a record of success in debate situations going back to high school was not irrelevant in guiding Nixon to his eventual decision to go on television with his opponent.[157]

Surveys taken after the event suggest that Nixon miscalculated.[158] But if he had won the election instead of losing it by a wafer-thin margin, he would hardly have been reminded of any error on his part, and there would probably have been discussions of what a brilliant move it was for him to go on television.

The election of 1964 presented an entirely different set of circumstances. President Johnson, an incumbent enjoying enormous personal popularity at the head of the majority party, had nothing to gain and everything to lose by debating his rival. Thus, despite strenuous efforts by Senator Goldwater and his allies to involve the president in debates, none were held. By 1968 observers were beginning to question whether candidates would ever again seek an epic confrontation with one another on the 1960 model. What seems to be required before the occurrence of such a debate is two major candidates equally eager for such a battle. If one is an incumbent, or feels securely in the lead, there is little incentive to debate. Hubert Humphrey pursued Richard Nixon fiercely on this point in 1968, but Nixon prudently refrained from a debate that would needlessly have risked his chances of victory. His excuse in 1972 was that a president in office could not tell all he knew.

Because inertia had begun to work against the idea of debates, the fact that they occurred again in 1976 was somewhat surprising. Neither candidate had been elected to the presidency, but Gerald Ford, the less articulate of the two, was the incumbent president. Although the Democrats did not do especially well in the debates, Ford's side, the Republicans, which had the most to lose by debating, undoubtedly lost ground twice. One time was when Ford left the impression that in his opinion Poland and Eastern Europe were not under Soviet domination, an occasion for a subsequent week's worth of "clarifications." The other was when Senator Robert Dole, his vice-presidential running mate, misjudged the nationwide audience entirely and bounced partisan one-liners ineffectually off the beatific brow of Senator Walter Mondale, thus spoiling one of the few chances the Republicans had to woo Democratic voters.[159]

The strategy of participation in presidential debates was well illustrated in the 1980 Democratic Party primaries. In the fall of 1979 President Carter's public popularity was exceedingly low, Senator Kennedy's was exceedingly high, and Governor Brown of California was struggling for recognition as a serious candidate. Thus, each of the three candidates had an interest in participation: the president needed it because he was way behind; Senator Kennedy needed it because he was still a challenger; and Governor Brown needed it most of all because he considered himself a good debater and hoped to show that he could hold his own with the front-runners. Then the Iranian seizure of American hostages served almost instantly to raise the president's popularity. Senator Kennedy's popularity plummeted after he gave an embarrassingly bad television interview to Roger Mudd and had difficulty explaining the Chappaquiddick incident. Thus, the situation changed. President Carter no longer stood to gain a lead but to lose one, so he bowed out of the debates on the grounds that it would be inappropriate to campaign while the hostages were being held, a circumstance that might continue almost indefinitely. The senator and the governor protested in vain. Hurt worst of all, Brown lost the chance to share the limelight with the president, which at that stage might have given him the public prominence he needed.

In 1980 there were problems in deciding what to do about including the major independent candidate, John Anderson, in debates after the major parties picked their nominees. President Carter refused to publicize Anderson, and so in the end only one debate took place instead of a series, and it was held very late in the campaign only between Carter and his Republican challenger, Ronald Reagan. On balance it seems to have helped Reagan, who may have lost on high-school debate rules but projected a benignity that was helpfully at odds with the picture of a dangerously radical opponent that Jimmy Carter was trying to paint.[160] So Carter became another incumbent who lost ground by submitting to a staged debate.

There were two presidential debates in 1984; after the first, it looked as if the incumbent had lost ground. President Reagan's performance was followed by a series of negative news and television stories telling the public how badly the president had performed. A *Wall Street Journal* article suggested that perhaps Reagan's age was catching up with him.[161] Challenger Walter Mondale moved up slightly in the polls. Perhaps, it was thought, Mondale could come from behind to win. In the second debate, President Reagan put in a stronger showing, and the age issue was put to rest. "I will not make age an issue of this campaign," the president joked. "I am not going to exploit, for political purposes, my opponent's youth and inexperience."[162] Reagan regained the large lead he had held throughout the campaign and went on to a landslide victory.[163]

Unlike John Anderson in 1980, Ross Perot was allowed to participate in the three 1992 presidential debates. The decision to invite him appears to have been a major strategic error. Apparently, the thinking in the Bush camp was that since Perot was disproportionately hurting their candidate, Bush needed to take him on and show, as one author put it, that he was "too small and too shifty to be president."[164] The tactic failed. During the first debate, the overwhelming consensus was that Perot had in fact won the contest. His folksy, quick one-liners were popular with viewers. Both major candidate's dial groups recorded more positive ratings when Perot spoke than anyone had ever seen before.[165] Bush, in contrast, did poorly. He needed to come off as strong and capable while depicting his opponents as weak in character. Instead, he seemed confused, mangled the one-liners he had practiced, and generally gave a weak performance.[166] Clinton did better, but his performance was still second to Perot's.

The second debate used a new format—questions from a specially selected studio audience rather than from news media personalities, as was traditional. This format favored Bill Clinton, and he was indeed the victor in the debate. Perot, being short, refused to sit on the stools provided, as his two opponents did, because his feet would not touch the floor. Instead, he stood awkwardly and his discomfort permeated his performance. Overall, Bush did fairly well, but one major gaffe marred his performance and that was all the press would discuss for days afterward. A woman from the audience asked him what effect the "deficit" had had on him personally. She may have meant to say the "recession" but misspoke, and Bush did not understand her meaning. "I'm not sure I get it," Bush said, essentially confirming the message the Clinton campaign had been putting forward throughout the season: Bush was out of touch with voters, he didn't even acknowledge there was a recession, much less suffer from it.[167] There was a third debate, but it had no major impact.[168]

In 1996 Bill Clinton and Bob Dole debated twice. Dole wanted four debates, but the incumbent—with a large lead in the polls—agreed to only two. Perot, far behind in the polls and without the benefit of Bush's mistaken strategy, was not invited this time. The innovation from 1992, the "town hall" format, was retained for the second debate. However, this time the debates produced little in the way of memorable moments, and appeared to change little in the race.[169]

The strategic imperatives surrounding debates seem to be emerging with some clarity. Debates can hurt incumbents. Challengers have far less to lose and may gain simply by keeping their countenance and appearing on the same stage with the holder of high public office. Opinion makers and the custodians of the flame of disinterested public spiritedness seem agreed that debates are wonderful exercises in public enlightenment. This scarcely seems credible to minimally intelligent viewers of the actual debates we have had, but this sentiment nevertheless exists and may tempt candidates to engage in public debates against their better strategic judgment.[170]

Indeed, there is growing sentiment to institutionalize debates so that whether or not to participate in them will no longer be a matter for the candidates to decide for themselves. In the beginning, presidential debates were run as a public service by the League of Women Voters, who represented a nonpartisan perspective in working out the arrangements. This meant that the candidates could protect their own interests in deciding whether to debate and under what conditions. Much haggling took place over ground rules, as anxieties in the camps of candidates ran high over such matters as use of the presidential seal on the podium, or bad camera angles, or what journalists would appear as moderators or to ask questions. In 1987 the Democratic and Republican national committees formed a bipartisan commission to determine the format (number, location, ground rules) and run the debates. This was designed to reduce the power of candidates to influence the conditions under which they would appear. In a joint statement explaining why they thought they should control the debates, Paul G. Kirk Jr., chairman of the Democratic National Committee, and Frank J. Fahrenkopf Jr., chairman of the Republican National Committee, stated that "we will better fulfill our party responsibilities; to inform and educate the electorate, strengthen the role of political parties in the electoral process and most important of all, we can institutionalize the debates, making them an integral and permanent part of the presidential process."[171]

Once a candidate is nominated, however, the leverage of the national committee to compel participation largely disappears. Candidates find most of the alternative formats that have been suggested to them too risky. So it is doubtful that the Presidential Debate Commission will have any more power over these events than the League of Women Voters used to have. The commission certainly had no such power in 1992 when debates were held under its auspices. For months, the Bush campaign delayed agreement on the debates because it disagreed with the format and because the candidate was not enthusiastic about participating. The Clinton team seized on the situation, playing up their willingness to participate and Bush's reluctance to debate their candidate. The Democrats took to sending a staffer dressed up like a chicken to Bush's campaign appearances.

Eventually the criticism and the drop in Bush's ratings made debating essential to the president's campaign. Having reached this conclusion, Bush's people tried to win back some momentum by challenging Clinton to a series of six debates, one every Sunday until election day. The Clinton campaign demurred, saying they preferred to stick with the format originally devised by the commission—three presidential debates and one for vice-presidential candidates. After a meeting between the campaign representatives, the Clinton team got essentially what they wanted—three debates crammed into little more than a week with two weeks to spare before the election—time to recover, they hoped, if anything went wrong.[172] This confirms the conventional wisdom that debates are more about accidents and mistakes than about enlightenment or the capacities of candidates to govern.

Blunders

One hears much about campaign blunders, as if there really were objective assurance that another course of action would have turned out better for the unfortunate candidate. An example was Thomas E. Dewey's decision in 1948 to mute the issues, which was said to have snatched defeat from the jaws of victory.[173] A vigorous campaign on his part, it was said, would have taken the steam out of Harry Truman's charges and would thus have brought victory to Dewey. Perhaps. What we know of the 1948 election suggests that it provoked a higher degree of voting on the basis of economic class than any of the elections that have succeeded it.[174] A slashing attack by Dewey, therefore, might have polarized the voters even further. This would have increased Truman's margin, since there are many more people with low than with high incomes. Had the election gone the other way— and a handful of votes in a few states would have done it—we would have heard much less about Dewey's blunder and much more about how unpopular Truman was supposed to have been in 1948.

A whole series of mistakes have been attributed to Richard Nixon in 1960, the year he lost the election by such a small margin. Here are two, culled from Theodore H. White's best-selling book on the 1960 campaign. On the civil rights plank of the Republican platform:

> The original draft plank prepared by the Platform Committee was a moderate one....This plank, as written, would almost certainly have carried the Southern states for Nixon and, it seems in retrospect, might have given him victory....On Monday, July 25th, it is almost certain, it lay in Nixon's power to reorient the Republican Party toward an axis of Northern-Southern conservatives. His alone was the choice....Nixon insisted that the Platform Committee substitute for the moderate position in civil rights (which probably would have won him the election) the advanced Rockefeller position on civil rights....[175]

On Nixon's failure to protest the imprisonment of Martin Luther King Jr., during the campaign:

> He had made the political decision at Chicago to court the Negro vote in the North, only now, apparently, he felt it quite possible that Texas, South Carolina, and Louisiana might all be won by him by the white vote and he did not wish to offend that vote. So he did not act—there was no whole philosophy of politics to instruct him.[176]

Hindsight is capable of converting every act of a losing candidate into a blunder. Victory can have the same effect in reverse. Consider the situation of Richard Nixon, 1968 version, as he dealt with the same southern-white/northern-black dilemma, in the same way. Theodore White reports:

> Nixon had laid it down, at the Mission Bay gathering, that none of his people, North or South, were to out-Wallace Wallace. He insisted, as he was to insist to the end of the campaign, that he would not divide the country; he wanted a campaign that would unify a nation so he could govern it. To compete with Wallace in the South on any civilized level was impossible.... Instead, Nixon would challenge Wallace in the peripheral states—Florida, North Carolina, Virginia, Tennessee, South Carolina....It was only later that the trap within this strategy became evident—for, to enlarge his base in the

Northern industrial states, Nixon would have to reach across the rock-solid Republican base there, across center, to the independents, the disenchanted Democrats, to the ghettos. But to do that would be to shake the peripheral strategy limited his call to the North.[177]

Nixon's strategy was aimed, in both years, at chipping off the "peripheral" southern states while not taking such a strong anti-civil rights position as to bring northern black voters to the polls in great numbers and to turn northern suburban whites against him.

In 1968, of course, he won; his margin over 1960 consisted of North Carolina, South Carolina, Illinois, and New Jersey. Would it have been a gain for him to "out-Wallace Wallace"? Not likely, in view of the heavy margins Wallace piled up in the states he did carry and his inability to do very well elsewhere. Would it have been a gain for Nixon to repudiate all possible anti-civil rights voters? Not likely, in view of the near unanimity against him of the black vote and probably of most strongly pro-civil rights white liberals. In short, did his strategy of equivocation almost win or almost lose the presidency for Richard M. Nixon in 1960 and 1968? Absent the opportunity to rerun these elections with different strategies, no one can say.

More recently, Michael Dukakis in 1988 declared that the campaign would be about "competence, not ideology." But he did not campaign competently, failing to answer the barrage of charges made by the campaign of Vice President Bush in its attempt to introduce Dukakis, unfavorably, to the mass of American voters who had never heard of him. The list of Dukakis's campaign errors, real and alleged, was a long one. The should-haves and should-not-haves were legion. When asked what he would do if his wife were raped, a question, one must admit, candidates have not usually been asked, he took it not as a request to pour out his emotions, an act he viewed with distaste, but as a request for the kind of governmental policies that might cut down on rapes and murders. This presumably showed he lacked emotion and was heartless.

Dukakis's critics spoke of a "candidate possessed of little understanding of the voters or the election and, more important, of a candidate offering no compelling message or rationale for his campaign."[178] The first part of the criticism is merely a restatement of the fact that he lost, for had he won he would obviously have possessed the correct understanding. As for the second, he did offer a message, which was that he was the more competent of the two and that his party had better answers to questions of modern life. This was not, to be sure, the answer his critics wanted to hear, but it was his genuine answer, and it might have served him well if the electorate had felt they were in bad straits and needed a competent president.

As the *Times Mirror* National Survey reported in late September 1988, more voters were satisfied with the way things were than were dissatisfied, and this represented a change in the final few months.[179] Dukakis's detractors wanted him to portray himself as a populist (i.e., more liberal), claiming this would have rescued his campaign from the beginning. Not according to anything we know. The *Times Mirror* poll, in its own words, "shows that Bush has succeeded in portraying the Massachusetts governor as a liberal by focusing on such issues as Dukakis's prison furlough program, his veto of 'pledge of allegiance' legislation, and his opposition to major weapons systems." Whereas 31 percent thought Dukakis was a liberal in June, when he had a huge lead over Bush, 46 percent considered him a liberal in September, when his support had dropped precipitously. We therefore may suspect that being perceived as liberal was not the best thing that could happen to a candidate. Indeed, the proportion of people in the electorate who considered themselves to be more conservative than Dukakis increased from 22 percent in June to 35 percent three months later.[180]

Over and over again, Dukakis told his campaign managers that he would not engage in mudslinging no matter what the provocation. Presumably this eminently desirable position was seen as a source of weakness.[181] "How many times do I have to tell you?" an aide heard him say, "That's not me."

Candidate Dukakis was also governor of Massachusetts and felt he should abide by a pledge to the citizens of that state to spend several days a week doing the job. He might have done better had he put full time into the campaign.[182] There were other faults. Dukakis failed to answer questions about national defense, which is, after all, a major presidential responsibility. He did not intervene to decide how to halt damaging internal squabbles in his campaign team. Almost from the beginning, the organization of the campaign was poor in that phones were not answered, supplies were not provided, activities were not coordinated.[183] By September 1989, Dukakis had learned how to blame himself. "I have reluctantly come to the conclusion," he told students at the University of California, "that if they throw mud at you, you've got to throw it back."[184]

The problem, in our opinion, was not the candidate but the party. By the beginning of October, according to the Gallup poll, Republicans led the Democrats by wide margins on the two big issues of peace and prosperity. Another large-scale national poll, taken early in May when Dukakis was supposed to have lost his edge, shows that except for items where Bush's long experience in national government gave him an edge, Dukakis came out very well.[185] What happened as a result of cumulative developments, including the fading of the Iran-*contra* incident and the warming of relations between the United States and the Soviet Union, was that voter optimism began to rise. President Reagan's popularity went way up; confidence in the economy was rising. "Simply put," John Dillon wrote for the *Christian Science Monitor*, "Americans are feeling better about things."[186] The highest level of support for Dukakis naturally came from those citizens who felt that times were getting worse. Sixty-two percent of them voted for him. "Unfortunately for Dukakis," as Dillon commented, "there just aren't enough of those people."[187]

No election campaign is without its faults. What are we to make of Vice President Bush's explanation—that his supporters were at country clubs helping their daughters come out in society—for his relatively poor showing in Iowa in 1988?

His Freudian slips might have become legendary. But he won. In 1992 he was not so lucky, and the many mistakes Bush made caught up with him. Perhaps the first crucial mistake was to deny the existence of the recession and to refuse to put together a legislative proposal to address the situation. From record high approval ratings after the Gulf War, Bush's popularity plummeted as he was increasingly seen as "out of touch" with the country. A second mistake compounded the first—Bush dragged his feet in starting his campaign. Many close associates suggested that Bush himself was uncertain that he even wanted to run again until late in 1991.[188]

Although Bush did declare his candidacy for reelection and did indeed end up campaigning, his uncertainty remained and seemed to permeate his campaign. His staff tried to get Bush to "get a plan" and stick to it, but his proposals seemed to change almost daily. When the campaign finally came up with a domestic and economic agenda for a second Bush term, its presentation was mishandled. Bush's unveiling of the new plan was scheduled for a rally in Detroit, but the expected press coverage failed to materialize owing to advance team oversights.[189] The campaign was not able even to use video footage of the speech—one of Bush's best during the campaign—because the video platforms had not been properly reinforced and the resulting film footage was shaky and unfocused.[190]

Bob Dole's campaign in 1996 certainly had its share of blunders. Like Dukakis in 1988, Dole hesitated in responding to attack ads. Like Bush in 1992, Dole had difficulty settling on campaign themes and strategies. All three suffered from internal dissension in their campaigns. Decisions never seemed to be made. For example, Dole was given two drafts for his convention speech, one nostalgic and the other future oriented. Rather than choose one, he patched them together, delivering a two-headed speech that was reviewed as inconsistent and confused.

Dole had other difficulties. A good example was the fate of an ingenious plan his campaign hit on for the first debate. To remind voters of scandals associated with Bill Clinton, and especially to throw the incumbent off his stride, the Dole campaign arranged for Billy Dale, the former head of the White House Travel Office (and the victim, or so Republicans argued, of Clinton corruption), to have a prominent seat in the audience. With any luck, Clinton would be distracted, or possibly even lose his cool. Alas, Bill Clinton had no idea what Billy Dale looked like; the incident wound up as nothing more than another chance for the press to remark on the Dole camp's inadequacies.[191]

Clinton was reelected easily, so it is easy to dwell on Dole's campaign weaknesses. Again, this can be taken too far. A list of Clinton campaign blunders and problems would be almost as long. Right before the Democratic convention, the campaign lost its chief strategist, Dick Morris, to a scandal. Gleeful reaction by many in the White House proved that the Dole campaign had no monopoly on internal dissension. Whether to classify various White House scandals as campaign blunders is a judgment call, but scandals involving how money was raised during the campaign certainly would qualify. When Bob Dole became personally involved in campaign strategy, he was seen as incapable of delegating; when Bill Clinton did the same thing, he was praised for his political instincts.[192] None of this means that campaigns are irrelevent, only that blunders in losing campaigns are the ones that are remembered. No campaign is perfect; winning campaigns only seem so in retrospect.

Should the candidate arrive at a coherent strategy that fits reasonably well with what is known of the political world, he or she still will find that the party organization has an inertia in favor of its accustomed ways of doing things. The party workers, on whom candidates are dependent to some extent, have their own ways of interpreting the world, and a candidate disregards this point of view at some risk. Should the candidate fail to appear in a particular locality as others have done, the party workers may feel slighted. More important, they may interpret this as a sign that the candidate has written off that area and they may slacken their own efforts.

Suppose the candidate decides to divert funds from campaign buttons and stickers to polls and television or transportation, as during the years before soft money they were more or less required to do, given expenditure limitations under the federal subsidy? The candidate may be right in believing that the campaign methods he or she prefers will bring more return from the funds that are spent. But let the party faithful interpret this as a sign that the candidate is losing—where, oh where, are those familiar indications of popularity?—and their low morale may encourage a result that bears out this dire prophecy. An innovation in policy may shock the loyal followers of the party. It may seem to go against time-honored precepts that are not easily unlearned. Could a Republican convince the party that a balanced budget is not sacred? Or a Democrat that it is? Both parties adopted these views, innovative for them, in 1984. But it left each of them unhappy. The Democrats were left without the rationale for deficit spending in behalf of good causes that had kept them going since the 1930s. The Republicans, who were in office when Reagan built up deficits of unprecedented size in peacetime, had more to worry about. Any adverse economic results—a too-high or too-low dollar on world markets, inflation, lack of industrial competitiveness, unemployment, a cloud of dust keeping food from growing—would surely be attributed to the deficit.

Anthropologists tell us that everyone in the tribe knows what comes next when a taboo is violated: bad things happen. If Republicans are not more frugal than Democrats, what are they good for? A selling job may have to be done on the rank and file; otherwise they may sit on their hands during the campaign. It may make better political sense (if less intellectual sense) to phrase the new in old terms and make the departure seem less extreme than it might actually be. The value of the issue in the campaign may thus be blunted. The forces of inertia and tradition may be overcome by strong and persuasive candidates; the parties are greatly dependent on their candidates and have little choice but to follow them, even if haltingly. But in the absence of a special effort, in the presence of enormous uncertainties and the inevitable insecurities, the forces of tradition may do as much to shape a campaign as the overt decisions of the candidates.

Box 5.2   Forecasting the Outcome

AS THE TIME for voting draws closer, more and more interest focuses on attempts to forecast the outcome. This process of forecasting elections is not at all mysterious; it depends on well-settled findings about the behavior of American electorates, many of which have already been discussed. But it may be useful for citizens to understand how the "experts" go about picking the winner.

There are several ways to do it. One way, popularized forty years ago by journalists Joseph Alsop and Samuel Lubell, is to interview the residents of neighborhoods which in the past have voted with great stability in one pattern or another. There are neighborhoods, for example, that always vote for the Republicans by a margin of 90 percent or better. Let us say that the interviewer finds that only 50 percent of the people he talks to tell him they are going to vote for the Republicans this time, but when he visits areas voting heavily Democratic, respondents continue to support the Democratic nominee heavily. A finding such as this permits the reporter to make a forecast, even though it is based on only a very small number of interviews that may represent not at all the opinions of most voters.

Reporters who use this technique very rarely make firm predictions about election outcomes. Instead, they concentrate on telling about the clues they have picked up: what they learned in heavily black areas, what the people in Catholic areas said, what midwestern farmers said, what people from localities that always vote with the winner report, and so on.[1] This technique is impressive because it digs into some of the dynamic properties of what goes into voting decisions. Like a focus group out on the doorstep, it reports which issues seem to be on people's minds. It examines the different ways in which members of different subgroups see the candidates and the campaign. It is also a technique that can be executed at relatively low cost. But it is unsystematic, in that people are not polled in proportions reflecting the distributions of their characteristics in the population (so many men, so many women, so many white, so many black, and so forth). Thus the results of this technique would be regarded as unreliable in a scientific sense, even though they may enhance an observer's intuitive grasp of what is going on. The results are also unreliable in the sense that two different journalists using this method may come to drastically different conclusions, and there is no certain way of resolving the disagreement; nor is there any prescribed method for choosing between their conflicting interpretations.

The strength of forecasting from historical voting statistics arose out of the marvelous stability of American voting habits. But the weakness of such a technique is also manifest. Sometimes gross changes in population through immigration or changes in the appeals of the parties to different voting groups will throw the historical two-party vote ratios in the sample area out of joint. Since the 1940s, voting habits, particularly at the presidential level, have become much less stable. When a forecast made with this technique is wrong, it is usually quite difficult to tell whether transitory or lasting causes are at the root of it. This limits the usefulness of the forecast greatly because, in the end, it rests on assumptions that have only partial validity in any one election, and nobody can say precisely how or where or to what extent they may be valid.

A second technique is a variation of the foregoing type of analysis and at one time was used by television networks on election night. The network computers were fed information about the past voting history of various locales. As these locales reported their returns on election night, the machines compared current results with information about previous years and arrived at predictions of how the current election would turn out when all the votes were counted. The system is exactly the same as that already described for Alsop and Lubell, but because the computer can be loaded with historical information about many localities—precincts, wards, and so on—it is able to compare this historical information, not with voting intentions as expressed by a few interviewees, but with voting results as expressed by the whole voting population of the area. Networks now supplement this information with the results of exit polls, statements about voting behavior collected as voters leave the polling place. These findings can be fed into the computer very rapidly—well before votes are officially counted—and give the networks an early feel for what is going on. They do not tell us why nonvoters failed to vote, of course, or the disposition of absentee ballots, an increasing fraction of the vote. These may be important in the end in understanding a given election.

Television network projections have proven controversial in recent years. As the networks' techniques have improved, their predictions have been coming in earlier. In 1980 NBC proclaimed a landslide Reagan victory nearly three hours before West Coast polls closed. Many believed that this depressed turnout and affected the outcome of state and local races. This led to calls for legal prohibition of early projections. Thus far, legislation of this type has not been successful. The controversy however, has caused the networks to be more cautious.[2]

Continued

The final method for predicting elections is the most controversial and by all odds the most well known: polls. These are based on a few simple assumptions that have been found to be quite serviceable over the years. One is that people generally will tell you the truth if you ask them how they are going to vote. Another is that it is not necessary to ask everyone's intentions in order to get as accurate a forecast as if you had asked nearly everyone.

The polls are commercial operations, and these days they are big businesses. In addition to the publicly available polls, such as the Gallup and *New York Times*/CBS newspaper reports, politicians commission private polls. These are expensive. They entail writing up a list of questions and asking them all, and all in the same way, to several thousand people spread all over the country; collecting the answers; and figuring out what it all means. Each of these phases of the operation—writing questions, selecting the sample of the total population to be interviewed, interviewing, organizing the answers, and interpreting the results—requires skill and training. This expertise is what commercial polling organizations provide.

In the past, regrettably, some of these organizations have treated the technical aspects of their operation as trade secrets (which they are not) and have left the impression that their forecasts are the result of a particularly efficacious kind of magic. Since the fiasco of 1948, when pollsters were so sure of the result that they became professionally careless, there has been less ballyhoo. But the general reader will do well to keep a sharp eye on the following points as the polls begin reporting early in the campaign.[3]

1. How big is the population that is reported to be "undecided"? In some elections, members of this group cast the crucial ballots that determine the outcome. In reporting their results, poll takers have a rule that says: "If the undecided people were to cast their ballots in the same proportion as those who have made up their minds,…" But wait. If those people were like the decided, they too would have made up their minds. Sometimes they do vote like early deciders, but sometimes they don't. Unfortunately, not enough is known about when they do and when they don't; the best advice we can give is to pay close attention to what the poll takers say they are doing about them, and if they are more than 10 to 15 percent of the population sampled, then place little confidence in the reliabil-

ity of the reported outcome. Until these people make up their minds, it is too early to tell about the result.

2. How stable is general sentiment in the population? Very often the polls will report wide swings from week to week. In 1960 the Gallup organization began averaging one week's totals with the previous week's partway through the campaign—without telling its readers.[4] This tended to depress the extent of an apparent shift of sympathy from Nixon to Kennedy, and it also tended to make the figures appear a great deal more stable and settled than they actually were. In general, wide swings of sentiment from week to week mean that opinions have not crystallized sufficiently for a reliable prediction to be made. The rush to Reagan in the last week of the 1980 election, for example, led to a much stronger showing for him than any of the major polling organizations predicted.

3. Remember that the polls are based on a gross, overall, nationwide sample but that presidential elections are decided by the distribution of votes in the electoral college. Thus a really reliable prediction would have to include a state-by-state breakdown. This is prohibitively expensive, and so it is not done. If it were done, it would be possible to detect situations like the following: Candidate A has 49 percent of the popular vote in polls taken in all the populous states and 75 percent of the popular vote in sparsely settled states. He loses badly to Candidate B in the electoral college, although it appeared to be going the other way. Poll takers generally caution that they are trying only to forecast the percentage distributions in the popular vote. Here again, if the result is closely divided at around 50 percent, then the poll may be quite close to being perfectly accurate but still forecast the wrong winner. Regional polls and statewide polls in such places as Minnesota and California, when professionally conducted, can help a great deal to mitigate this problem.

4. Some people never show up to vote on election day; these tend to be undecideds and Democrats (in that order) more

Continued

often than Republicans, but in any event some sort of grain of salt has to be taken with poll results in order to account for the phenomenon of differential turnout. Most experienced polling organizations build some sort of correction into their results based on assumptions about how many people in their sample will actually vote. It is important to know precisely what this assumption is and what the resulting corrections are.

5. Many people think that the samples used by poll takers—of 1,200 to 5,000 people—are inadequate to represent the feelings of the millions of Americans whose voting they are supposed to represent. This, by and large, is a false issue. Experience has shown that very few of the errors one makes with a sample of 3,000 are correctable with a sample of 15,000 or 20,000, although the expense of polling such a population rises steeply.[5]

Generally it is not a sampling error that is at fault when poll takers' predictions go awry, but illicit "cooking" of the data or incompetent interpretations of findings. One famous instance of a sampling error occurred when polling was in its most rudimentary stages. In 1936 the *Literary Digest* predicted a landslide for the Republican Alfred Landon.[6] When Franklin D. Roosevelt won overwhelmingly, the *Digest* became a laughingstock and soon thereafter went out of business. What had happened was simple enough. The magazine had sent out millions of postcards to people who had telephones asking them how they intended to vote. The returns showed a huge Republican triumph. Surely, the *Digest* must have thought, we cannot possibly be wrong when our total response is so large and so one-sided. But, of course, something was terribly wrong. Only 2.3 million people responded out of 10 million recipients of the cards, and these were all voluntary respondents. So the *Digest* got its returns from a group in the population more likely to vote Republican and completely ignored the larger number of poorer people who were going to vote Democratic. There is a much greater tendency for people of wealth and education to return mail questionnaires, so there was a bias in favor of people likely to vote Republican.[7] As Peverill Squire says: "The 1936 *Literary Digest* poll failed not because of its initial sample, but because of the non-random response rate. Those who received straw vote ballots were strongly supportive of the president. But a slight majority of those who returned their ballot favored Landon."[8]

In 1948 a whole series of errors were made, but none of them were connected with the size of the sample. In that year, the Gallup, Roper, and Crossley polls all predicted that Governor Dewey would unseat President Truman. Among the problems with the polls that year, the following were uncovered by a committee of social scientists after the event.[9]

1. The poll takers were so sure of the outcome that they stopped taking polls too early in the campaign, assuming that the large population of undecideds would vote, if they voted, in the same way as those who had already made up their minds.

2. The undecideds voted in just the reverse proportions.

3. Many instances were revealed where polling organization analysts, disbelieving pro-Truman results, arbitrarily "corrected" them in favor of Dewey. The methods of analysis employed were not traced in any systematic way, however, because they could not systematically be reconstructed from records of the polling organizations.

4. Sampling error occurred not because of the size of the samples, but because respondents were selected by methods that gave interviewers too much leeway to introduce biases into the sample. The so-called quota-control method (which instructs interviewers, for example, out of twenty interviews to pick ten men, ten women; fifteen Protestants, four Catholics, one Jew; seventeen whites and three blacks; and so on) has since been replaced with "stratified random samples," in which geographic areas are picked randomly, and neighborhoods and houses within neighborhoods are selected randomly with controls so that areas representing a variety of economic levels are sure to be selected. This gives the people in charge of the poll greater control over who is going to be in their sample and prevents interviewers from asking only people who live near them or who are conveniently accessible in some other way and are likely to be similar to them in social standing and political outlook. Today, when virtually all American households have telephones (far more than in 1936), telephone surveys using sophisticated methods of randomization

Continued

have been developed. Because they are cheaper than door-to-door sampling, larger numbers of respondents can be contacted.[10]

Predicting presidential elections is largely a matter of satisfying curiosity. It is a great game to guess who will win, and we look to the polls for indications of the signs of the times. But the importance of this kind of prediction is not great. After all, we get to know who has won very soon after the polls close with much greater detail and accuracy than surveys can supply. The bare prediction of the outcome, even if it is reasonably correct, tells us little about how the result came to occur. More may be learned if it is possible to break down the figures to see what kinds of groups—ethnic, racial, economic, regional—voted to what degree for which candidates. Yet our enlightenment at this point is still not great. Suppose we know that in one election 60 percent of Catholics voted Democratic and in another election this percentage was reduced to 53. Surely this is interesting, but unless we have some good idea about why Catholics have switched their allegiance, our knowledge has hardly advanced. The polls often tell us "what" but seldom "why." There is, however, no reason polling techniques in the future cannot be used to answer "why" questions.[11]

The usual polling technique consists of talking to samples of the population at various points in time. The samples may be perfectly adequate, but different people constitute each successive sample as the interviewers seek out people who meet their specifications. It is difficult to discover with any reliability why particular individuals or classes of people are changing their minds because interviewers ordinarily do not go back to the same people who gave their original preferences. A panel survey is used to overcome this difficulty.[12] In a panel survey, a sample of the voting population is obtained and the very same people are interviewed at various intervals before election day and perhaps afterward. This technique makes it possible to isolate the people who make up their minds early and those who decide late. These groups can be reinterviewed and examined for other distinguishing characteristics. More important, perhaps, voters who change their minds during the campaign can be identified and studied. If a panel of respondents can be reinterviewed over a number of years and a series of elections, it may become possible to discover directly why some people change their voting habits from election to election. Or focus groups can be used to frame survey questions more sensitively.

The attentive reader may have observed that reports of party identification vary somewhat according to the observer. Poll data during the 1984 election campaign suggested that the gap between the parties had narrowed to zero or that it was as large as 19 percentage points. Why don't all reports agree? One reason for the discrepancy involves the time the poll was taken; the nearer to election day, the more likely that voters will bring their party preferences into line with their chosen candidates. A second reason is that different polls often sample somewhat different populations. Exit polls, for instance, sample only those who actually go to polling stations to vote. Other polls report results only for registered voters or those who say they are likely to vote, which is different from sampling a cross-section of the population. The closer the population polled is to the actual electorate (which is, remember, far smaller than the total population eligible to vote), the more likely it is to reflect electoral influences. Thus in 1984 exit polls, in view of President Reagan's popularity, showed a greater gain in identification with the Republican party than polls of all those of voting age.

A third reason concerns wording. A question that includes a phrase such as "as of today" is more likely to tap current feelings than one that specifically asks the respondent to answer "usually" or "generally" or "regardless of how you may vote." A test of these factors by Borrelli, Lockerbie, and Niemi reveals that they explain most of the discrepancies among polls reporting different figures in partisan allegiance. As they say,

> all else equal, 1980 and 1984 polls that worded the partisanship question in a general way reported a Democratic-Republican gap roughly five percentage points larger than reported by polls that asked "as of today"; nonexit polls in those years reported gaps, on average, five points larger than did exit polls; polls taken more than 10 days before or after the election in 1984 reported gaps three point larger than did polls taken within 10 days of the election.[13]

Understanding what is being measured, when, and how, is indispensable in interpreting the results of polls.

NOTES

1. See, for example, Samuel Lubell, *The Future of American Politics* (New York: Harper, 1951); his "Personalities and Issues," in *The Great Debates*, ed. Sidney

Continued

Kraus (Bloomington: Indiana University Press, 1977), 151–62; and Joseph Alsop, "The Negro Vote and New York," *New York Herald-Tribune* (and elsewhere), 8 August 1960. Reporting of this sort has become a feature of the election-year coverage of the *Washington Post*. See, for example, Rowland Evans and Robert Novak, "Stronghold Lost," *Washington Post*, 4 August 1980.

2. On the import of early projections, see Philip L. Dubois, "Election Night Projection and Voter Turnout in the West," *American Politics Quarterly* 11 (July 1983): 349–64. Dubois argues (against a number of other studies) that the early projections did have a significant impact on turnout. For a sophisticated analysis of the policy problems involved, see Percy Tannenbaum and Leslie J. Kostrich, *Turned-On TV/Turned-Off Voters: Policy Options for Election Projections* (Beverly Hills, Calif.: Sage, 1983).

3. These suggestions are drawn in part from a reading of the Report of a Committee of the Social Science Research Council, Frederick Mosteller et al., *The Pre-Election Polls of 1948*, Social Science Research Council Bulletin 60 (New York, 1949).

4. Joseph Alsop, "The Wayward Press: Dissection of a Poll," *New Yorker*, 24 September 1960, 170–84.

5. There are several sources about the technology and tactics of polling. Many years ago George Gallup published *A Guide to Public Opinion Polls* (Princeton: Prineton University Press, 1948). See also *Opinion Polls, Interviews by Donald McDonald with Elmo Roper and George Gallup* (Santa Barbara: Center for the study of Democratic Institutions, 1962); and Charles W. Roll Jr. and Albert H. Cantril, *Polls* (New York: Basic Books, 1972). In 1972 Representative Lucien Nedzi of Michigan held congressional hearings on the possible effects of information about polls on subsequent voting. See *Public Opinion Polls, Hearings Before the Subcommittee on Library and Memorial*, Committee on House Administration, House of Representatives, 93d Cong., 1st sess., H.R. 5503, 19, 20, 21 September and 5 October 1972. A further flap occurred in 1980, as the result of Jimmy Carter's concession of defeat and the television network predictions of a Reagan victory before voting was completed on the West Coast. See Raymond Wolfinger and Peter Linquiti, "Tuning In and Turning Out," *Public Opinion* 4 (February/March 1981), 56–60; John E. Jackson, "Election Night Reporting and Voter Turnout," *American Journal of Political Science* 27 (November 1983); *Election Day Practices and Election Projections, Hearings*

Before the Task Force on Elections of the Committee on House Administration and the Subcommittee on Telecommunications, Consumer Protection, and Finance of the Committee on Energy and Commerce, U.S. House of Representatives, 97th Cong., 1st and 2d sess., 15 December 1981 and 21 September 1982; and Tannenbaum and Kostrich, *Turned-On TV/Turned-Off Voters*.

6. Robert Sherwood, *Roosevelt and Hopkins* (New York: Harper, 1948), 86. See also Archibald M. Crossley, "Straw Polls in 1936," *Public Opinion Quarterly* 1 (January 1937): 24–36; and a survey of the literature existing at that time, Hadley Cantril, "Technical Research," *Public Opinion Quarterly* 1 (January 1937): 97–110.

7. Maurice C. Bryson, "The Literary Digest Poll: Making of a Statistical Myth," *The American Statistician* 30 (November 1976): 184–85. As a matter of fact, this method produced a correct prediction in 1932, when the *Literary Digest* said that Roosevelt would win. Sampling error is tricky; an atypical sample may still give the correct prediction by luck; but sooner or later, the law of averages is bound to catch up with it.

8. Peverill Squire, "The 1936 Literary Digest Poll," *Public Opinion Quarterly* 52 (Spring 1988): 125–34.

9. Mosteller et al., *The Pre-Election Polls of 1948*.

10. For an even more detailed discussion of the problems of election forecasting, see Gary King and Andrew Gelman, "Why Do Presidential Election Campaign Polls Vary So Much When We Can Forecast Votes So Accurately?" Center for American Political Studies at Harvard University, Occasional Paper, 91–96, October 1991.

11. Election day exit polls often come close to offering answers to the "why" questions. For an analysis of four different 1980 exit polls, see Mark R. Levy, "The Methodology and Performance of Election Day Polls," *Public Opinion Quarterly* 47 (Spring 1983): 54–67. In many states the increasing use of absentee ballots may in the future diminish the usefulness of exit polls, since a steeply rising proportion of the voters will never enter—or exit—a polling place.

12. See Paul F. Lazarsfeld, "The Use of Panels in Social Research," *Proceedings of the American Philosophical Society* 92 (November 1948): 405–10.

13. Stephen Boarelli, Brad Lockerbie, and Richard G. Niemi, "Why the Democrat-Republican Partisanship Gap Varies from Poll to Poll," *Public Opinion Quarterly* 51 (1987): 115–19; quote on 117–18.

Part III

ISSUES

In the concluding chapters we discuss issues of public policy raised by the way in which Americans conduct their presidential elections. There are always great complaints about election processes, as there are about nearly every aspect of American politics. Our discussion attempts to deal with some of the more long-lasting and widely held criticisms. We attempt also to put presidential elections into the broader context of the American political system, asking whether these elections serve the purposes of democracy.

CHAPTER 6
Appraisals

In 1968 the Democratic Party endured a season of turmoil: its incumbent president, Lyndon Johnson, withdrew his candidacy to succeed himself; a leading candidate to succeed him, Robert Kennedy, was assassinated; and its national convention was conducted amid extraordinary uproar. In that convention, party leaders chose Vice President Hubert Humphrey, who had not entered a single primary, to be the party's candidate for the presidency. In the aftermath of that convention, a party commission on reform of the nomination process—the McGovern-Fraser Commission, as it was called—was constituted and a year later brought in some proposals for changing presidential nominations. These were adopted by the Democratic Party.

After every national nominating convention from 1968 through 1984, the Democrats formed such a commission. Table 6.1 (p.220) gives pertinent facts about their leadership and their main effects. Even Republicans were affected by the changes sparked by those commissions, since in some cases new state laws have had to be enacted to comply with changes in Democratic Party regulations. Since 1984 the Democrats have not made major changes in their national party rules, although their national committee retains the power to tinker, a reminder that within the Democratic Party centralized reform efforts are never entirely off the agenda. After 1988 the DNC used that authority to require strict proportional representation for allocating delegates in states using primary elections. Even without significant changes in the national rules, changes adopted by the states such as organizing regional primaries among themselves and moving primaries to earlier time slots have made important differences in the way nominees are chosen, and have sparked calls for further attention to the process. It is fair to say that for much of the past thirty years, reform has been in the air.

Previous chapters have incorporated the results of these reforms into the description we have given so far, concentrating on features of the presidential nomination process as it exists at present and on the political consequences that flow from the system as it is now organized. Some of these features have been part of the landscape of American politics for a generation or more; others are

TABLE 6.1 REFORM COMMISSIONS OF THE DEMOCRATIC PARTY, 1969–1990

Name	Duration	Leadership	Main Effects
McGovern–Fraser	1969–1972	Senator George McGovern (S.D.); Representative Donald M. Fraser (Minn.)	Established guidelines for the selection of delegates; outlawed two systems of delegate selection.
Mikulski	1972–1973	Barbara A. Mikulski, Baltimore city councilwoman	Banned open crossover primaries; replaced stringent quotas on blacks, women, and youths with nonmandatory affirmative action programs.
Winograd	1975–1980	Morley Winograd former chairman of Michigan Democratic Party	Eliminated loophole primary; shortened delegate selection season; increased size of delegations to accommodate state party and elected officials; required states to set filing deadlines for candidates 30 to 90 days before the voting.
Hunt	1980–1982	Governor James B. Hunt Jr. (N.C.)	Provided uncommitted delegate spots for major party and elected officials; relaxed proportional representation; ended ban on loophole primary; shortened primary and caucus season to a 3-month window; weakened delegate binding rule.
Fowler, or "Fairness"	1985	Donald L. Fowler, former chairman of South Carolina Democratic Party	Slightly expanded super-delegate spots; allowed certain states to return to open crossover primaries; lowered from 20 percent to 15 percent the threshold of primary voters candidates must surpass to receive delegates.
DNC Rules and Bylaws Committee	1989–1990	Fowler and Anne D. Campbell (N.J.)	Slightly expanded super-delegate spots; rebanned loophole primaries.

SOURCE: Adapted from William Crotty, *Party Reform* (New York: Longman, 1983), 40–43. Additional sources: Adam Clymer, "Democrats Adopt Nominating Rules for '80 Campaign," *New York Times*, 10 June 1978; Clymer, "Democrats Alter Delegate Rules, Giving Top Officials More Power," *New York Times*, 27 March 1982; Rhodes Cook, "Democrats' Rules Weaken Representation," *Congressional Quarterly Weekly Report*, 3 April 1982, 750; Austin Ranney, "Farewell to Reform—Almost," in *Elections in America*, ed. Kay Schlozman, (Boston: Allan and Unwin, 1987), 106; Rhodes Cook, "Democratic Party Rules Changes Readied for '92 Campaign," *Congressional Quarterly Weekly Report*, 17 March 1990, 847; "Democrats Alter Nominating Rules," *Congressional Quarterly Weekly Report*, 14 April 1990, 148.

NOTE: Loophole primaries include direct district election of delegates and therefore do not necessarily yield proportional allocation of delegates.

new, and the changes they may bring about lie mostly in the future. Nevertheless, if there is one certainty about presidential elections, it is that this process is subject to continuous pressure for change.

In this chapter we appraise some of these changes and proposals for future change of the American party system and its nomination and election processes. Because of the rapid reforms of the past few years, some of the impetus behind certain suggestions for further reform has slackened, while other ideas seem likely to be pursued with renewed vigor. Few observers are satisfied with the nomination process as it now is. As past solutions lead to future problems, new proposals enter the agenda and old ones depart. As times change, moreover, old concerns become outdated and new ones take their place. Under the party system of the 1950s and 1960s, for instance, with conservative Democrats and liberal Republicans reducing policy agreement within their parties, the cry went out for greater party cohesion. Too little ideology was widely blamed for the lack of consistent party policy positions across a wide range of issues. How, it was then argued, could voters make a sensible choice if the parties did not offer internally consistent and externally clashing policy views? This is not so great a problem today, as evidence of ideological consistency within each party grows. Instead, one can confidently expect concern about the negative consequences of polarization between the parties. In the same way, reforms stressing participation have in due course been succeeded by measures emphasizing experience, such as the creation of superdelegates. Thus the preoccupations of one era give way to those of its successors.

New proposals for change stem on the whole from two camps, which for purposes of discussion we wish to treat as distinct entities. The first movement we call *policy government;* the second we refer to as *participatory democracy.* Advocates of policy government urge strengthened parties, not as the focus of organizational loyalties so much as vehicles for the promulgation of policy. Participatory democrats urge "openness" and "participation" in the political process and advocate weakening party organizations and strengthening candidates, factions, and their ideological concerns. While the two sets of reformers appear to disagree about whether they want parties to be strong or weak, this comes down to a difference in predictions about the outcome of the application of the same remedy, for both in the end prescribe the same thing: more ideology as the tie that binds voters to elected officials and less organizational loyalty.

The Political Theory of Policy Government

Policy government reform had its antecedents at the turn of the century in the writings of Woodrow Wilson, James Bryce, and other passionate constitutional tinkerers who founded and breathed life into the academic study of political science. The descendants of these thinkers have through the years elaborated a series of proposals that are embodied in a coherent general political theory. This theory contains a conception of the proper function of the political party, evaluates the legitimacy and the roles of Congress and the president, and enshrines a particular definition of the public interest. Different advocates of this reform have stated the theory with greater or less elaboration; some reformers leave out certain features of it, and some are disinclined to face squarely the implications of the measures they espouse. We try here to reproduce correctly a style of argument that, though it ignores the slight differences separating these party reformers one from another, gives a coherent statement of their party reform theory and contrasts it with the political theory that critics of their position advance.[1] Since in time we may achieve much of the kind of party cohesion that these reformers of yesteryear wanted, it is worthwhile to attend to the pros and cons of the debate their proposals brought about.

This group of party reformers suggested that democratic government requires political parties that (1) make policy commitments to the electorate, (2) are willing and able to carry them out when in office, (3) develop alternatives to government policies when out of office, and (4) differ sufficiently to "provide the electorate with a proper range of choice between alternatives of action."[2] They thus come to define a political party as "an association of broadly like-minded voters seeking to carry out common objectives through their elected representatives."[3] In a word, party should be grounded in policy.

Virtually all significant party relationships are, for these reformers, mediated by policy considerations. The electorate is assumed to be policy motivated and officeholders conscious of mandates. Policy discussion among party members is expected to create widespread agreements upon which party discipline will then be based. Pressure groups are to be resisted and accommodated only as the overall policy commitments of party permit. The weaknesses of parties and the disabilities of governments are seen as stemming from failure to develop and support satisfactory programs of public policy. Hence we refer to this theory of party reform as a theory of policy government. This theory suggests "that the choices provided by the two-party system are valuable to the American people in proportion to their definition in terms of public policy."[4] It differs from the participatory brand of party reform (which we address later) in that policy reformers believe they are revitalizing party organizations, whereas participatory democrats are likely to be indifferent to party organization.

Opponents of policy reform believe that democratic government in the United States requires that parties first and foremost undertake the minimization of conflict between contending interests and social forces.[5] We call them supporters of consensus government. For consensus government advocates, the ideal political party is a mechanism for accomplishing and reinforcing adjustment and compromise among the various interests in society to prevent severe social conflict. Where policy government reformers desire parties that operate "not as mere brokers between different groups and interests but as agencies of the electorate," supporters of consensus government see the party as an "agency for compromise." Opponents of party reform and policy government hold that "the general welfare is achieved by harmonizing and adjusting group interest."[6] In fact, they sometimes go so far as to suggest that "the contribution that parties make to policy is inconsequential so long as they maintain conditions for adjustment."[7] Thus, the theory of the political party upheld by critics of the policy reform position is rooted in a notion of consensus government. Advocates of policy government behave as if problems of consensus, of gaining sufficient agreement to govern, have already been solved. Believing that there is no problem of stability, therefore, they concentrate on change. Their critics downplay policy not because they think it unimportant but because they think maintaining a capacity to govern is more important than any particular policy. Fearing instability, they are less concerned with enhancing the system's capacity to change.

A basic cleavage between advocates of policy government and advocates of consensus government may be observed in their radically opposed conceptions of the public interest. For advocates of consensus government, the public interest is defined as whatever combination of measures emerges from the negotiations, adjustments, and compromises made in fair fights or bargains among conflicting interest groups. They feel the need for no external criteria by which policies can be measured in order to determine whether or not they are in the public interest. As long as the process by which decisions are made consists of intergroup bargaining, within certain specified democratic, constitutional "rules of the game," they regard the outcomes as being in the public interest.

For advocates of policy government, the public interest is a discoverable set of policies that represents "something more than the mathematical result of the claims of all the pressure groups."[8] Some overarching notion of the public interest, they argue, is necessary if we are to resist the unwarranted claims of "special interest" groups. While this suggests that there are in principle criteria for judging whether a policy is in the public interest, apart from the procedural test applied by supporters of consensus government, these criteria are never clearly identified. This would not present great difficulties if policy government advocates did not demand that an authoritative determination of party policy be made and that party members be held to it. But information about the policy preferences of members is supposed to flow upward, and orders establishing and enforcing final policy decisions are supposed to flow downward in a greatly strengthened pyramid of party authority. Without criteria of the public interest established in advance, however, party leaders or commentators can define the public interest in any terms they find convenient.

If we were to have parties that resembled the ideal of this first set of party reformers, what would they be like? They would be coherent in their policies, reliable in carrying them out, accountable to the people, disciplined and hierarchical internally, sharply differentiated from and in conflict with partisan opponents. What would it take to create a party system organized by the principles of policy government?

For the parties to carry out the promises they make, the people responsible for making promises would have to be the same as or in control of the people responsible for carrying them out. This means, logically, one of two alternatives. Either the people who controlled party performance all year round would have to write the party platforms every four years at the national conventions, or the people who wrote the platforms would have to be put in charge of party performance. In the first case, the party platforms would have to be written by leaders such as the members of Congress who at present refrain from enacting laws favored by both national conventions. State and local political leaders would write their respective platforms. Under such an arrangement, which reflects the procedural complications introduced by the separation of powers and the federal structure embedded in the U.S. Constitution, very little formal, overall coordination or policy coherence seems likely to emerge. Since the main point of policy government is to create logically coherent, unified policy that makes possible rational choices by voters, we must reject this first alternative as a way to fulfill the demands of party reformers.

In fact, an alternative most often recommended by advocates of policy government is that national party conventions should be in charge. They must make policy that will be enforced on national, state, and local levels by means of party discipline, that is, getting rid of party officeholders who disagree. This arrangement also has a fatal defect: it ignores the power of the people who do not write the convention platforms. How are independently elected members of Congress to be bypassed? Will present-day local and state party leaders acquiesce in this rearrangement of power and subject themselves to discipline from a newly constituted outside source? It is hard to see what the enforcement mechanism would be. Party reform has already gone some distance toward reducing the influence of elected officials in the presidential nomination process. Will they give up their independent capacity as public officials to make policy in their own arenas—Congress, the state legislatures—as well? Generally, we assume they will not.

One reformer says: "As for the clash of personal political ambitions in the United States, they are being completely submerged by the international and domestic concerns of the American public. War and peace, inflation and depression are both personal and universal issues; tariff, taxes, foreign aid, military spending, federal reserve policies, and hosts of other national policies affect local economic activities across the land. Politicians who wish to become statesmen must be able to talk intelligently about issues that concern people in all constituencies."[9]

But the increasing importance of national issues will not necessarily lead to placing greater power in the hands of party leaders with national (that is to say, presidential) constituencies. There is no necessary connection between political power in the national arena and the national scope of issues. Politicians who exercise national political power such as Congressional committee chairs frequently themselves come to be influential because of their local control of nomination, alliances with local interest groups, and many other bases. National issues may become more important, especially among the ideologically more cohesive Republicans, who are capable of coordinating a promise of a "contract with America," although not necessarily delivering. But delivery on national promises is frequently thwarted by the power of local interests able to influence national institutions, for example, as mentioned, the people in the congressional districts that elect influential members of the House of Representatives. So far, the increasing nationalization of policy has been most conspicuously accompanied by increases in the strength of single-issue groups.

The people who have the most to lose from policy government are the leaders of Congress. The major electoral risks facing national legislators are local. This does not mean that legislators will necessarily be parochial in their attitudes and policy commitments. But it does mean that they are not bound to support the president or national party leader on issues of high local saliency. In order to impose discipline successfully, the national parties must be able either to control sanctions at present important to legislators, such as nomination to office, or to impose still more severe ones upon them. At the moment our system provides for control of congressional, state, and local nominations and elections by geographically localized candidates, electorates, and (to a lesser extent) party leaders. Presidents are not totally helpless in affecting the outcomes of these local decisions, but their influence, especially considering the power of incumbent members of Congress to maintain themselves in office, is in most cases quite marginal.[10]

In the light of this, one obvious electoral precondition of disciplined parties is that local voters must be so strongly tied to national party issues that they will reward their local representatives for supporting national policy pronouncements, even at the expense of local advantage. To a certain extent, by virtue of the influence of national news media and the rising educational level of the electorate, as well as some increase in the general propensity of the most active citizens to think ideologically, this condition can be met. The issues on which the national party makes its appeal must either unify a large number of constituencies in favor of the party or appeal at least to some substantial segment of opinion everywhere. But even if this could be accomplished with regularity, it would be strategically unwise for parties to attempt to discipline members who lived in areas that are strongly against national party policy. This would mean reading the offending area out of the party. Therefore, reformers must show how they intend to contribute to the national character of political parties by enforcing national policies on members of Congress in those areas where local constituencies are drastically opposed to national party policy or whose constituents do not pay attention to issues but care more for the personality or the constituent services of their congressional representative.[11] Insofar as leeway exists, let us say, for liberal northeastern Republicans, a diminishing breed, to support liberal programs and for conservative southern Democrats, who are also more scarce than they once were, to oppose them, the parties in fact will have retained their old, "undisciplined," "irresponsible" shapes. Insofar as this leeway does not exist, splinter groups of various kinds are encouraged to split off from the established parties. This is a consequence regarded as undesirable by most party reformers.

Another way of achieving disciplined parties may be more promising. We have seen that party activists and, to a lesser but meaningful extent, legislators have become ideologically more coherent. This has not occurred by command but by evolution: northern liberal Republicans have moved into the Democratic Party and conservative southern Democrats into the Republican Party. As the parties have become more ideologically distinctive across a wider range of issues—social, environmental, and defense, as well as economic—those who feel most uncomfortable have been changing allegiances. For proponents of party cohesion, this is the good news. The bad news is that a strong party line breeds splits. Among Republicans, this means the prospect of future conflict between free-market libertarians and social conservatives. Among Democrats, factionalism has become so severe that it may be preventing them from mobilizing their historic edge in party identification for presidential elections. Party leaders increasingly seek to activate "wedge issues" that divide their opponents. Democrats raise the abortion issue, which splits Republicans; Republicans raise affirmative action, which divides Democrats.

Conflict within and between parties may be good for them and for the nation. Conflict can invigorate discussion and enlighten the public about the bases of party differences. Much depends on the extent to which discussion quickly polarizes groups that have strong interests in definitions of the situation that are already so well formed and structured as to inhibit the search for creative solutions.

A second method for reducing the independent power over policy of independently elected congressional leaders has begun to have an effect in national politics. This method addresses not the prospects for nomination and election of congressional leaders but rather their capacity to lead in Congress. Adherence to the conservatism of the majority of Republicans in Congress has in general been a prerequisite of leadership within the Republican Party. What internal conflict there has been among Republicans has been based not on ideology but style. The emergence of Newt Gingrich as Republican leader meant not a shift to the right but the adoption of a confrontational approach to House business by Republicans. Gingrich's successors have, like him, been mainstream conservatives, as are the leaders of the Senate Republicans.

Among congressional Democrats, in the past more leeway existed for congressional leaders—at any rate for committee chairs, who were selected by seniority—to take whatever policy positions they pleased. Since the late 1950s, sentiment grew in Congress that conservative Democratic committee chairs should be more responsive to the policy preferences of the majority of the majority party, and the Democratic caucus of the House of Representatives has acted to remove committee chairs they have regarded as unresponsive. This did not, however, proceed strictly along ideological lines. One of the first chairmen to be removed, Wright Patman of Texas, was as liberal as any Democrat in the House, including his replacement, Henry Reuss of Wisconsin. Another chairman, Edward Hebert of the Armed Services Committee, was replaced by a leader ideologically indistinguishable from him on matters coming before the committee.[12] So, despite the unlimbering of a new weapon that could encourage party cohesion in Congress, it was not used consistently quite in this way, and concerns related to the management of Congress itself were more significant than the shaping or enforcement of party policy in the activities of the reactivated Democratic caucus when they were in the majority. The Republicans, during the Gingrich speakership, violated seniority as part of an effort to centralize control of policy. The revolt against Gingrich was at least in part an effort to return greater powers to the committees.

Reform by Means of Participatory Democracy

The second type of reform movement we identify as participatory democracy. The efforts of those who advocate participatory democracy and who have attempted to make the Democratic Party the vehicle of this approach to government have met with considerable success over the past twenty years. Here we wish to contemplate the theory of politics that underlies this position. Ordinarily, participatory democrats criticize the American political system in two respects. First, they argue that elections have insufficient impact on policy outcomes of the government. These critics see too weak a link between public policy and the desires of electoral majorities. Second, there is the critique of the electoral process itself, which argues that policy does not represent what majorities want because undemocratic influences determine election results. These criticisms are simple-minded in one sense and cogent in another. They are simple-minded in that they ignore the immense problems that would have to be overcome if we were truly serious about transforming America or any large, diverse population into a participatory democracy. They are cogent in that responsiveness to majorities on questions of policy is a fundamental value that gives legitimacy to democratic government. The connection between such criticism and the legitimacy of government makes it important to deal at least briefly with some of the issues and problems that should be raised (and usually are not) by judgments of this fundamental nature.

The first and obvious question to ask is whether the criticisms are based on fact. Is the American system unresponsive to the policy desires of a majority of its citizens? Unfortunately, there is no unambiguous way to answer this question. If we focus our attention, for example, on the mechanics of the policy process, we find what appears to be government by minorities. In some policy areas a great number of people and interests, organized and unorganized, may have both a say in the open and some influence on the final product. But fewer individuals may be involved in areas dealing with other problems and policies, some of which will be of a specialized nature, of limited interest, and so on. Certainly it is true that even members of Congress do not have equally great influence over every decision: committee jurisdictions, seniority, special knowledge, party, individual reputation, all combine to weigh the influence of each member on a different scale for each issue.

So we must conclude that if we adopt direct participation in and equal influence over the policy decisions of our government (the decisions that "affect our lives") as the single criterion of democracy, then our system surely fails the test. So, we might note, does every contemporary government of any size known to us, possibly excepting two or three rural Swiss cantons.

Another approach might focus on public opinion as an index of majority desires. Using this standard, a quite different picture emerges. Policy decisions made by the government mostly have the support of popular majorities. Where this is not true, the apparent lack of "responsiveness" may have several causes, not all of them curable: (1) conflicts between majority desires and intractable situations in the world (for example, a hypothetical desire for peace in the Middle East); or (2) public attitudes favoring certain sets of policies that may be mutually incompatible (such as the desire for low taxes, high benefits, and balanced budgets); or (3) clear, consistent, and feasible majority desires that are ignored by the government because the desires are unconstitutional or antithetical to enduring values of the political system, to which leaders are more sensitive than popular majorities. Surveys, for example, have from time to time revealed majorities in favor of constitutionally questionable repressive measures against dissenters and the press.

Criticisms of the popular responsiveness of presidential elections are more difficult to assess. American electoral politics does respond to the application of resources such as money that are arguably nondemocratic and that cause the influence of different actors to be weighed unequally. In a truly democratic system, it could be argued, the system would respond to numbers and only numbers. All other methods of achieving political outcomes beyond the registering of preference by voting would be deemed illegitimate. As we have indicated, however, money, incumbency, energy and enthusiasm, popularity, name recognition, ability, and experience are all valuable assets within the structure of American politics. Is this avoidable? Should we attempt to eradicate the influence of these resources?

Political resources and the people who possess them are important primarily because campaigns are important. Campaigns are important because the general public needs to be alerted to the fact that an election is near. Partisans must be mobilized, the uncommitted convinced, perhaps even a few minds changed. Resources other than votes are important because—and only because—numerical majorities must be mobilized.

American politics responds to diverse resources because many citizens abstain from voting and are hard to reach by campaigners. Sometimes this is described as political apathy. Why is political apathy widespread? There are several alternative explanations. Perhaps it is because the system presents the citizenry with no real alternatives from which to choose. In the election of 1964, however, there was at least a partial test of this "hidden vote" theory, and the evidence was negative. In 1972, another year when there was an unambiguous choice, nonvoting hit a high for elections up to then. Voting participation in presidential elections seems to rise and fall without much regard for the ideological distance between candidates of the major parties.

Perhaps there is apathy because the public has been imbued with a "false consciousness" that blinds them to their "real" desires and interests. They would participate if they knew better. This explanation is traditionally seized on by the enlightened few to deny value to the preferences of the ignorant many. The people, we are told, are easily fooled; this testifies to their credulity. They do not know what is good for them; this makes them childlike. But when the people cannot trust their own feelings, when their desires are alleged to be unworthy, when their policy preferences should be ignored because they are not "genuine" or "authentic," they are being deprived of their humanity as well. What is left for the people if they are held to have no judgment, wisdom, feeling, desire, and preference? Such an argument would offer little hope for democracy of any sort, for it introduces the most blatant form of inequality as a political "given": a structured, ascribed difference between those who know what is "good" for themselves and those who must be "told." No doubt it is true that much of the time we do not know (without the advantage of perfect foresight) what is best for us. But that is not to say that others know better, that our consciousness is false but theirs is true. Persons who make the "false consciousness" argument do not believe in democracy.

A more hopeful and less self-contradictory explanation of political apathy might note that throughout American history a substantial number of citizens have not wished to concern themselves continually with the problems and actions of government. Many citizens prefer to participate on their own terms, involving themselves when they feel like it with a particular issue area or problem. These citizens' participation is necessarily sporadic and narrower than that of the voter interested in all public problems and actively involved in general political life. Many other citizens (surely a majority) are more interested in their own personal problems than in any issue of public policy.[13] These citizens meet their public obligations by going to the polls at fairly regular intervals, making their selections on the basis of their own criteria, and then supporting the actions and policies of the winners, whether they were their choices or not. In the intervals, unless they themselves are personally affected by some policy proposal, most of these citizens may wish to be let alone. Given the complexity of issues and the uncertainty surrounding the claims of candidates, citizens may arrive at their voting decisions by asking themselves a simple, summary question: Are things (the domestic economy, world affairs) better or worse than they were? This is a reasonable way to decide, but it does not offer much future policy guidance to political leaders.

The literature on apathy may say more about the values of the students of the subject than about the ostensible objects of their studies. Those observers who approve of existing institutions are likely to view apathy as relatively benign; they believe people do not participate because they are satisfied and they trust institutions to do well by them. Those who disapprove of existing institutions naturally find the defect in the institutions themselves; they believe people do not participate because they are denied the opportunity or because they rightly feel ineffectual. Observers who view individuals as capable of regulating their own affairs see these individuals as deciding case by case whether it is worth the time and effort to participate. Projecting the investigator's preferences onto citizens does not seem to us a useful way of learning why this or that person chooses to participate in political life. As political scientists and citizens, we think self-government an ideal so valuable that we would not impose our own views on those who decide they have better things to do.

Studies have from time to time shown unfavorable citizen attitudes toward the political system, a phenomenon sometimes called "alienation," which has been on the upswing in recent years. As we have argued earlier in this book, these attitudes do not explain low rates of voting participation; persons who score high in these unfavorable attitudes evidently participate at about the same rate as the nonalienated.[14] So we surmise that a great many citizens who do not vote abstain because they are concerned with other things important to them, like earning a living or painting a picture or cultivating a garden, and not because they feel it is so difficult to influence outcomes. In short, for them, politics is peripheral. Given the peripheral importance of politics in many people's lives, making it easier to vote does make a difference in turnout. But because politics is peripheral, even making voting easier does not reduce abstention from voting to zero or anything like zero.

Consider a society in which all citizens were as concerned about public matters as the most active. Such a society would not require mobilization: all who were able to would vote. The hoopla and gimmickry associated with political campaigns would have little effect: this citizenry would know the record of the parties and the candidates and, presumably, would make reasoned choices on this basis. Should such an active society be the goal of those whose political philosophy is democratic? This question should not and cannot be answered without first addressing the problem of how such a society could be achieved.

Without attempting to be comprehensive, a few difficulties merit some specific comment. First and foremost, political participation, as Aristotle made clear several thousand years ago, takes a great deal of time. For this reason (among others) a large population of slaves was felt necessary to assist participatory government: it freed Athenian citizens from the cares of maintaining life and thus provided them the leisure time that made their political activity possible. But having rejected some hundred years ago this ingenious solution to the problems related to relatively large-scale participation, we must deal with the fact that most American citizens work for a living. They lack the disposable time that permits professionals and college students and other privileged people to choose their working hours. Most citizens lack the time, even if they had the temperament and training, to engage continually in politics. To the degree that representative institutions—political parties, legislatures, elected executives—are disregarded in favor of more direct modes of activity, the majority of the people will be without the means through which they can most effectively make their will felt. In short, to impose requirements of direct participation on those desiring a voice in decisions would be to ensure that the incessant few rather than the sporadic many would rule: thus the 1960s' slogan "power to the people" really proposed to replace a representative few, who were elected, with an unrepresentative few, who were self-activated.

In well-known work, the philosopher Jürgen Habermas has argued that the only way to make a democracy legitimate, for it to be considered a true democracy worthy of support, is for it to approximate the conditions of what he calls "an ideal speech situation." Every person would be equally interested and active. Each would have equal rights, money, information, and all other resources necessary for effective participation.[15] What could be wrong with such an ideal? Nothing at all, we think. If it were to be realized in practice in a very diverse society, however, it might lead to surprising results. For a diverse society may lead to the expression of diverse values. Individualists, for example, adhere to the ideal of equality of opportunity so that people can be different, and some may consequently end up with more resources than others. This expresses a different equality from that postulated by Habermas. Other people, for example, Christian fundamentalists, may prefer a more patriarchal or hierarchical set of values in which different people occupy different statuses. Thus it is helpful to consider whether democracy is only about equality or whether it may be about enabling people who hold different values to live together peaceably.

Thus there are practical difficulties with a theory that requires high levels of political participation. We raise this issue not because we are opposed in principle to the idea of an active, participatory, democratic society. By persuasion and political education the majority of our citizens might indeed be convinced that the quality of our shared existence could be improved through more continuous devotion to public activity. This is quite different from arguing that the rules of the game should be changed to reduce the influence of those who at present lack the opportunity or desire to be active. Efforts to implement ideal goals when the preconditions and the means of achieving these goals do not exist are self-defeating. Actions that in the name of participatory democracy restrict the ability of most of the people to have their political say are not as democratic as advertised.

Some Specific Reforms

Comprehensive reform of the party system rides in on tides of strong feeling. Until such feelings exist among party activists, rational advocacy looking toward reform is wasted; once such feeling exists, rational advocacy is superfluous. So the type of analysis we undertake here is bound to be uninfluential. We attempt it only because thoughtful citizens may find it instructive to consider the consequences of the best-laid plans. Once these consequences have had an opportunity to manifest themselves, however, a new generation of reform may be in order. After all, practically everything that reformers object to now was once somebody's favorite reform.

We suspect that the achievement of many—not all—of the specific objectives of party reformers would be detrimental to their aims and to those of most thoughtful citizens. Let us consider, for example, specific reforms of governmental machinery that are commonly advocated to make the parties more responsive to popular will and more democratic. Party reformers often advocate a variety of changes in the nomination process, including changes in party convention procedures and modification or abolition of the electoral college.

THE NOMINATION PROCESS

In order to evaluate the nominating process, it would be helpful to suggest a set of goals that most Americans might accept as desirable and important.[16] The following seven standards appear to meet this test: any method for nominating presidents should (1) aid in preserving the two-party system, (2) help secure vigorous competition between the parties, (3) maintain some degree of cohesion and agreement within the parties, (4) produce candidates who are likely to win voter support, (5) lead to the choice of candidates who are reasonably well qualified, (6) lead to the acceptance of candidates as legitimate, and (7) result in officeholders who are capable of generating support for public policies they intend to pursue. We first look at some suggested alternatives to the current nominating system.

A national direct primary to select party candidates for the presidency has often been suggested. Many people took heart in 1968 from the way in which the piecemeal primaries around the country facilitated the expression of antiwar sentiment, and they noted that nonprimary states were on the whole less responsive to persons whose participation in party activities was largely precipitated by strong feelings about the war. Their conclusion was that primaries were rather a good thing and that, therefore, a national primary was in order.

We believe this would have serious disadvantages. First, it would have been self-defeating as far as the professed goals of many antiwar people who advocated it were concerned. By entering primaries one at a time in 1968, Senator Eugene McCarthy, and later Senator Robert Kennedy, were able to construct "test cases." We doubt that McCarthy, given the limitations of his resources before New Hampshire, could have even entered a national primary.

Charles O. Jones has said that in some respects we already do have a national primary, and that it is held in New Hampshire. He is entirely correct to call attention to the enormous influence that early delegate-selection processes have on the fortunes of candidates later on. But the Iowa caucuses and New Hampshire primary do differ from a national primary in one major respect: they are small, and as Everett Carll Ladd says,

> By leading off, manageable little Iowa and New Hampshire enable
> less well-known and well-heeled candidates to gain attention
> through presenting their wares to real people in real election settings.
> If a candidate with moderate resources, and previously lacking a
> national reputation, manages to impress a fair number of voters in
> these small states, isn't this laboratory experience of some consider-
> able interest to the country?[17]

This merely points to a more general problem of financing national primary elections. It is quite probable that many candidates—perhaps as many as ten of them—might obtain enough signatures on nominating petitions or qualify by some other device to get on the ballot for a true, fifty-state, national primary. In a year when there is no incumbent president in the race, it is not hard to imagine a crowd of challengers in both parties hustling all over the United States campaigning in such a primary. It would take, of course, enormous amounts of money. The parties could hardly be expected to show favoritism and so could not finance these candidates. Although government financing would no doubt be made available, this would have to depend on demonstrated ability to raise money previously in order to discourage frivolous candidates. The preprimary campaign, therefore, would assume enormous importance and would be exceedingly expensive. Nationwide challengers would have to have access to very large amounts of money. It would help if they were already well known. They would also have to be quite sturdy physically.

Ordinarily, nobody would win a clear majority in a primary with a large number of contenders. Since all contenders would be wearing the same party label, it is hard to see how voters could differentiate among candidates except by already knowing one or two of their names in favorable or unfavorable contexts, by liking or not liking their looks, by identifying or not identifying with their ethnic or racial characteristics, by attending to their treatment in the press and in television news reports, or by some other means of differentiation having nothing whatever to do with ability or inclination to do the job, or even with their policy positions. Since patents on policy positions are not available, it is reasonable to suppose that more than one candidate would adopt roughly the same set of positions. Or they might, for the purpose of the primary, falsely portray themselves as disagreeing. Thus, voters would be fortunate if the intellectual content of the campaign consisted of quibbling about who proposed what first and, more relevantly, who could deliver better.

Suppose, then, that the primary vote was divided among several candidates. Suppose, as is the case for gubernatorial elections in some southern states, that ten or twelve aspirants divided the votes. One possibility is that the party nominee would be the candidate with the highest number of votes, say, 19 percent of those cast, a much less democratic outcome than we now have, since who knows how the other 81 percent might have distributed themselves if they had known what the rank order of the candidates was going to be? Another possibility would be for the two highest candidates to contest a fifty-state runoff after the first primary and before the general election in a campaign that would begin to remind observers who can remember that far back of a marathon jitterbug contest. The party might end up with a good candidate, of course, if there was anything left of that candidate to give to the party in the real election campaign, which would follow. Then the poor candidate, if elected, would have to find the energy to govern. By following this procedure, the United States might have to restrict its presidential candidates to wealthy athletes.

We are not ready to give up at least some of the state primaries we now have, although it is now widely believed—and we agree—that we have too many. It is eminently desirable that it be possible in a number of states, separated geographically and in time, for test cases to be put to voters and for trial heats to be run among aspirants for high office. But a national primary would be like a steady diet consisting exclusively of dessert.

National primaries would lead not only to the weakening of political parties but also to the weakening of the party system. It is not unusual for a party to remain in office for a long period of time. If state experience with primaries is any guide, a prolonged period of victory for one party would result in a movement of interested voters into the primary of the winning party, where their votes would count for more.[18] As voters deserted the losing party, it would be largely the diehards who were left. They would nominate candidates who pleased them but who could not win the election because they were unappealing to a majority in the nation. Eventually, the losing party would atrophy, seriously weakening the two-party system and the prospects of competition among the parties. The winning party would soon show signs of internal weakness as a consequence of the lack of opposition necessary to keep it unified.

A national primary might also lead to the appearance of extremist candidates and demagogues who, unrestrained by allegiance to any permanent party organization, would have little to lose by stirring up mass hatreds or making absurd promises. On the whole, the convention system of the past discouraged these extremists by placing responsibility in the hands of party leaders who had a permanent stake in maintaining the good name and integrity of their organization. This is one of the costs of the eclipse of national party conventions as serious decision-making bodies. Some insight into this problem may be had by looking at the historic situation in state elections in several southern states, where most voters voted only in the Democratic primary and where victory in that primary, even with only a small percentage of the vote, was tantamount to election. The result was a chaotic factional politics in which there were few or no permanent party leaders; the distinctions between the "ins" and "outs" became blurred; it was difficult to hold anyone responsible; and demagogues sometimes arose who made use of this situation by strident appeals.[19] The fact that under some primary systems an extreme personality can take the place of party in giving a kind of minimal structure to state politics should give pause to the advocates of a national primary.

We believe that very widespread use of direct primaries weakens the party system. It encourages prospective candidates to bypass regular party organizations in favor of campaigns stressing personal publicity, and it provides for no peer review, that is, consideration of those aspects of fitness of candidates to hold office that can best be observed by politicians who actually know the candidates, who have themselves a heavy investment of time and energy in making the government work, and who know that they may have to live at close quarters with the results of their deliberations.

It is difficult to persuade activists who participate only casually in politics, and those who tend to do so only when moved by a great issue of the day, that the intensity of their feelings does not confer a sweeping mandate. These feelings, no matter how worthy, do not make occasional participants more worthy than steady participants. They do not confer a special moral status on latecomers to politics as compared with people who are already active. Party regulars or even party leaders cannot be excluded on grounds of their moral inferiority from decision making in the presidential nomination process.

The great virtue of state-by-state piecemeal primaries is, of course, that they provide a means—increasingly supplemented by polls—of gauging the popularity of various candidates and their effectiveness in public speaking under adverse circumstances. The virtue of conventions has been that by living at closer quarters than ordinary citizens with the results of the collective choice, party leaders can bring to the selection greater knowledge and even, sometimes, a higher sense of responsibility.

It is generally conceded that Adlai Stevenson would have made a better president than Estes Kefauver, who ran and won in most of the primaries in 1952. Stevenson, for his entire career in elective office, was the product of selection by party leaders—in some cases even by "bosses"—who were knowledgeable and continuously involved in the political process, acquainted with what governing demanded and with the personal capabilities of the politicians among whom they chose. Walter Mondale, who withdrew from the 1976 preprimary sweepstakes because of a reluctance to spend a year in various motels around the country, was not a conspicuously worse—indeed, by some standards he was a better—public servant than some of those who leaped joyfully into the fray. Mondale first served in the Senate by appointment and was picked by Jimmy Carter to be his running mate without the sanctification of an election. Yet nobody supposes Mondale was picked without regard for democratic constraints. When in 1984 either Mondale decided that motels had improved or he had become more ambitious, he certainly represented the views of the mainstream of his party. While it is doubtful that any Democrat could have beaten Ronald Reagan that year, few doubted that Mondale was well qualified to be president.

Giving politicians some rights to influence political choices is not per se an evil system. Unchecked by the ultimate necessity to appeal for votes, it would no doubt degenerate. Political leaders would not dominate a system that responded easily to short-run opinions of high intensity in the electorate. Sometimes this sort of system will pick a popular candidate over a candidate in whose personal capacities the delegates have more faith. This, we think, is what delegates to the Republican convention of 1952 did when they nominated Dwight Eisenhower over Robert A. Taft. Even when they decide to make a popular choice rather than go with their personal favorite, party leaders can invoke criteria of judgment unavailable to mass electorates.

In short, we believe that as long as we demand many things of a president—intelligence as well as popularity, integrity as well as speaking ability, private virtue as well as public presentability—we ought to foster a selection process that provides a mixture of devices for screening according to different criteria. The mixed system we advocate is not perfect, of course, but it is greatly superior to the unmixed nonblessing of the national primary.

The use of primaries at the state level has produced a variety of anomalous experiences: totally unqualified candidates whose names have resembled those of famous politicians have been nominated by innocent voters; ethnic minorities concentrated in one party have defeated attempts by party leaders to offer "balanced tickets," thus dooming to defeat their entire ticket in the general election; and palpable demagogues have defeated responsible candidates. All these consequences may not persuade reformers that the increased use of direct primaries is not a good idea, but they must be faced. If we value political parties, which reformers often profess to do, then we must hesitate to cut them off from the process of selecting candidates for public office, to deprive them of incentives to organize, and to set them prematurely at the mercy of masses of people whose information at the primary stage is especially poor.

Responsible political analysts and advocates must face the fact that party identification for most people provides the safe cognitive anchorage around which political preferences are organized. Set adrift from this anchorage, as they are when faced with an intraparty primary election, most voters have little or nothing to guide their choices. Chance familiarity with a famous name or stray feelings of ethnic kinship under these circumstances seem to provide many voters with the only clues to choice.[20] Given the conditions of popular interest and participation that prevail, we question throwing the future of the party system entirely into the hands of primary electorates.

What is more, a nomination process dominated by primaries gives the media great—possibly too much—influence. Their extensive influence was illustrated in a dramatic way in the spring of 1987, when the front-running candidate for the Democratic nomination, Gary Hart, suddenly fell victim to publicity calling attention to a close personal relationship that he evidently had with a young woman who was not his wife. This episode of intensive negative commentary caused many thoughtful journalists to express concern about the extraordinary influence of the news media in the nomination process. Some journalists felt that they and their colleagues were unable to do justice to the special circumstances of the private lives of public figures, and that even public figures have rights to privacy in those areas of life that have little to do with the performance of public duties. Others argued that the way people behave in private is bound to affect the way they do their public chores.

Not long ago, when there was something like peer review in the nomination process, other politicians who were influential in the process and who knew the candidates could make assessments about the suitability of presidential hopefuls for office. Perhaps they would be forgiving in cases of alcoholism, chronic pettiness, bad temper, manic-depressive behavior, marital infidelity, laziness, bigotry, slowness of wit, vindictiveness, duplicity, stubbornness, or any of the other infirmities and imperfections that afflict human beings. Or perhaps not. At least, it was possible for reasonably well-informed judgments to be made about the qualities of candidates by people who knew something about what these qualities were.

Today, when presidential nominations are made almost entirely by primary electorates, we must ask: What do these electorates know of the human qualities of the candidates? Typically, very little. But virtually all of what they do know comes via the news media. So journalists, through no fault of their own, have had thrust on them far greater responsibilities to tell what they know and to find out whether what they suspect is true or not.

Not all candidates receive the same treatment, however. In 1972 the history of emotional depression of Thomas F. Eagleton, briefly the Democrats' vice-presidential candidate, weighed more heavily in the scale than did the history of receiving bribes of Spiro T. Agnew, his Republican opponent. Journalists found out about one but not the other in time to influence an election.

So we must wonder whether attention to any candidate's possible flaws of character ought not to be compared more conscientiously against flaws that some of the others may have. Surely, if these are qualities of candidates, they will also be qualities of the presidents these candidates might become. But it is hard to predict just how these qualities will work in any given presidency. There is no foolproof method for making sensible inferences from private behavior about the conduct of public office. Can we suppose that a lazy candidate will be a lazy president? Possibly. Still, some candidates hate campaigning but love governing and may be mediocre in a stump speech but superb negotiating a legislative compromise.

What is worse, the opposite may be true, and a great campaigner may turn out to be an incompetent president. Equally serious difficulties may be in store for those who attempt to make inferences about the conduct of the presidency from knowledge of candidates' sexual irregularities (or regularities), drinking habits, relations with their children and grandchildren, and so on.

What are ordinary citizens to do? Ignore information that might be relevant to our primary vote if we knew about it? Attend to information about candidates even though it may be irrelevant to their conduct of the presidency? If we could tell in advance the difference between relevant and irrelevant information, it would help. But mostly we cannot, nor can the journalists who must decide what to report and what not to report. As long as primary elections and, therefore, the votes of citizens matter as much as they currently do, the only hope of achieving informed choices is by means of publicly available information. Thus, it may be regrettable but it is understandable that journalists are leaning toward disclosure and away from the protection of candidates' private lives.[21]

Regional primaries, of which 1988's Super Tuesday was a harbinger, have apparent appeal as a halfway house between a single national primary and a multitude of state primaries. There are basically three "degrees" of regional primary that have been proposed thus far. The mildest form merely requires that all states holding presidential primaries schedule them for one of four sanctioned dates, spaced a month apart, and that all candidates on a list prepared by the Federal Election Commission appear on the ballot. A second proposal would group states into geographic regions. All states within a given region that choose to have a primary would be required to hold it on the same day, on the second Tuesday of a month between March and July. Further down the slippery slope is a plan to make primaries mandatory for all states.[22]

Under the regional primary system candidates would not have to campaign in as many distant places at nearly the same time; this would save them money and effort. Since each election would encompass a larger geographic area, however, the need to campaign earlier, to be better known at the start, and to have more money with which to begin would be even greater than it is now. It also seems likely that regional primaries would, in effect, push all states to hold primaries, thereby increasing the total territory a candidate must cover and the consequent cost of campaigning. The major advantage of regional primaries, assuming they were spaced about one month apart, as in one plan, would be that both politicians and people could reconsider their earlier choices in the light of the latest information. Yet if delegates were pledged to candidates, their flexibility as bargainers—in the event they were needed at the national conventions—would still be diminished. In addition, the predilection of the media to simplify complex phenomena would mean that voters in states given later dates would have their choices severely constrained because of the results of earlier primaries. It is possible that conflicts among states may doom the entire enterprise. If not, we suspect that regional primaries, which create an opportunity to reconsider the rules of voting, will become stalking horses for a national primary. Thus all the difficulties of a national primary should be weighed as these partial alternatives are proposed. As long as the relevant choice is between a mixed system of delegate selection and a national primary, our choice lies with the mix.

THE DECLINE OF THE NATIONAL CONVENTION

High on the list of practices that in the past were regarded as objectionable was the secret gathering of party leaders in the smoke-filled room. Some likened this to a political opium den where a few irresponsible men, hidden from public view, stealthily determined the destiny of the nation.[23] Yet it is difficult to see who, other than the party's leaders, should have been entrusted with the delicate task of finding a candidate to meet the majority preference. If head-on clashes of strength on the convention floor could not resolve the question, the only alternatives were continued deadlock, anarchy among scores of leaderless delegates splitting the party into rival factions, or some process of accommodation.

National conventions no longer pick presidential nominees; they merely ratify the work of primaries and caucuses. But let us suppose that some national convention in the future has authentic work to do, and because no single candidate has the nomination sewed up, it must pick a nominee. Would we require that a smoke-free successor to the smoke-filled room be abolished and with it all behind-the-scenes negotiations? All parleys would then be held in public, before the delegates and millions of television viewers. Could the participants resist spending their time scoring points against each other in order to impress the folks back home? Bargaining would not be taking place because the participants would not really be communicating with one another. No compromises would be possible; if they were attempted, leaders would be accused by their followers of selling out to the other side. Once a stalemate existed, breaking it would be practically impossible, and the party would probably disintegrate into warring factions.

An extensive system of state primaries in which delegates are more or less compelled to vote for the candidate who wins in the state has led to the eclipse of negotiation processes without any formal action of a convention. Since delegates cannot change their positions except by direction of the candidate to whom they are pledged, there is little point in bringing party leaders together for private conferences. Sharply increasing the number of pledged delegates introduces great rigidity into the convention because under conditions of stalemate no one is in a position to switch his or her support.

This more or less resembles the situation of the two parties today. Recent rule changes have led to the following contradiction: by fragmenting delegations, they have increased the chances of a contested convention, and by giving preference to pledged delegates they have decreased the likelihood that delegates will be able to bargain with one another. These conditions have been masked by the overriding influence of primaries and television, which, by forcing earlier and earlier decisions, have spared the parties so far the consequences of a meaningful convention under conditions of extreme fragmentation. Failure to arrive at a decision to nominate a candidate acceptable to all could conceivably lead to withdrawal of the defeated factions from the party. Since the national party is unified, if at all, only by the choice of a presidential candidate, inability to bargain out an agreement invites serious party fragmentation. Therefore, if as is now unlikely, primaries do not produce a nominee who is certain to be ratified, what happens at a national convention will matter.

Even though the nominee has actually already been chosen, each party has a stake in the presentation it makes of itself to the public. Much criticism over the years has been leveled at the raucousness of demonstrations that take place on the convention floor while candidates are being nominated.[24] Criticism of demonstrations on the grounds that they are unseemly and vulgar seems to us to be trivial. There is no evidence to substantiate a claim that the final decision would be better in some way if demonstrations were banned. Undoubtedly, the demonstrations have in the past been overdone, but not in recent years owing to the requirements of television. Briefer demonstrations retain the attention of the vast television audience that both parties would like very much to influence in their favor. The dominance of primaries has actually made demonstrations into what their critics always said they were—purely stage-managed affairs with no relation to the final outcome.

The television coverage of the 1968 national conventions raised a number of questions concerning their management. We wonder if all the things that went wrong at the Democratic convention of that year were the result of willful mismanagement by Lyndon Johnson and Chicago mayor Richard J. Daley or whether at least some of the difficulty can be attributed to the increasing unwieldiness of the convention. Delegates complained of an inability to attract the attention of the chair. The microphones allocated to each delegation on the floor were turned on and off at the rostrum, so it was impossible to use them to get the chair's attention. Attempts to telephone the chair from the floor were often ignored. Attempts to approach the rostrum were repulsed by security guards. Attempts to signal the chair were defeated by the noise and movement in the hall.

It is hard to see how such a huge and chaotic organization can conduct itself as anything like a parliamentary body. In fact, plenary sessions of the convention have two functions: ceremonial and business. We think it is time to consider a separation of these functions. Ceremonial activities can take place in an amphitheater or a stadium. The general public can be invited. On such occasions there are two classes of people: performers and spectators.

When the convention is conducting its business, however, a different division of labor is involved, and a different decorum should prevail. If it is not possible for a convention to conduct itself as a parliamentary body when all 2,000 or 4,000 members are present, perhaps some democratic and equitable means could be found to restrict the number of official delegates so as to make communication among them feasible. In fact, one effect of reforms designed to increase the representativeness of delegations has been to increase the size of each state delegation. According to this perspective, quotas, whether implicit or explicit, have not only increased the numbers of delegates but also decreased the probability that they could deliberate as a body. If, let us say, 1,000 delegates met at business meetings, much of the paraphernalia needed for meetings of 10,000 could be dispensed with. The number of guards and security officers could be cut. The business of keeping order could be placed where it belongs—in the hands of the chair, who directs sergeants-at-arms publicly, rather than in the hands of an anonymous functionary, who in 1968 at Chicago apparently felt free to dispatch security officers to harass delegates on the floor.

A smaller number of people on the floor, the possibility of spontaneous communication with the chair and with other members, and parliamentary decorum would unquestionably facilitate and properly dignify the business of the convention. It would also provide a warrant for the reexamination of the role of television cameras at national conventions.

We believe television and other news media should cover national party conventions thoroughly. Though the networks have lost their enthusiasm for it as the serious decision-making functions of the conventions have disappeared, we would like to see full gavel-to-gavel coverage by all the major networks. But we question the propriety of wandering television and newspaper reporters on the floor of a convention. To be sure, as long as conventions continue in their present overblown form, reporters may as well be on the floor, since everyone else is. But if conventions were reduced in size and, for business purposes, maintained parliamentary decorum, perhaps it would be possible to consider the problems created by news media representatives at national conventions. Neither Democrats nor Republicans alone will take the lead in grappling with this problem because both fear the wrath of the media. Thus, academic observers are ideally situated to open this discussion.

We want to increase respect for presidential nominations by having them conducted in a serious atmosphere conducive to mature deliberation. But the very presence of numerous reporters, with their microphones and television cameras, creates a carnival atmosphere. No one would ordinarily make an important decision surrounded by people hurriedly throwing questions. No one would take seriously a decision made by people constantly distracted from the main proceedings by side conversations.

A superabundance of television cameras on the convention floor plays up to the worst instincts of the delegates, alternates, and hangers-on gathered there. It is hard for ordinary mortals to resist publicity; it is asking too much of convention attendees to forego an opportunity for national exposure. Yet the purpose of the convention (if it were again to become a decision-making body) is not only to make the delegates look good at home but for them to make a wise choice where they are.

The mass media not only report events; they create news. They are always after bizarre and unusual sights and sensational stories. If conflict and controversy are not inherent in a situation, they will seek to create it. A momentary misunderstanding on the floor might be cleared up later on, but reporters will jump in immediately to widen the breach. In 1980, for example, we could see television reporters leaving the floor of Madison Square Garden in hot pursuit of a small rump group of Alaskans; these few delegates wanted to distract television coverage with their boycott of the Democratic keynote address of Morris Udall, who as chair of a House of Representatives Interior Committee subcommittee had in some way offended them.

Imagine what football games would be like if they were reported as national conventions currently are. A quarterback is getting clobbered in the Super Bowl. His line is weak and defenders are pouring all over him. After the fifth interception, he receives a fearful blow. Before he can pick up his shattered bones, a dozen television reporters stick their microphones and cameras in his face, shouting questions at him. "Are you getting good protection today?" "Anybody let you down, hey?" A few answers on the spot, and the team might never be able to work together again.

Is it asking too much for nominations of future presidents to be conducted with at least the same dignity as at present obtains at football games? The press, radio, and television can broadcast the proceedings and report events from booths above the convention floor. No one but delegates and frail, elderly, nonthreatening sergeants-at-arms should be allowed on the floor while the convention is at work. Ample interview facilities should be provided just off the floor. When delegates are wanted for an interview, a page should be sent to fetch them, just as is done in Congress. "Ms. Delegate," the page might say, "a network wants to hector you in room nine," and if Ms. Delegate wants to be hectored, she can walk off the floor to attend to that mission.[25] The American people deserve full reporting of the national conventions; no one wants to limit the media in any legitimate coverage. But improving the conduct of national conventions and increasing public respect for their decisions are reasons enough to ask the media to pay a small cost for a large public benefit.

These proposals assume, of course, that the conventions have a good deal to deliberate about. If the nominee is a foregone conclusion, as is now normally the case, then it may make sense to organize the convention entirely as a ceremonial exercise. Even then, the parties might still want to regulate coverage to maximize the effectiveness of the ceremony.

The convention, as we have said, normally aids party unity in a variety of ways. It provides a forum in which initially disunited fragments of the national party can come together and find common ground as well as a common nominee. The platform helps in performing this function. In order to gain a majority of electoral votes, a party must appeal in some way to most major population groups. Since these interests do not always want the same thing, it is necessary to compromise and, sometimes, to evade issues that would lead to drastic losses of support.

Reformers' concerns with party platforms stem primarily from two assumptions: first, that there is a significant demand in the electorate for more clear-cut differences on policy; second, that elections are likely to be a significant source of guidance on individual issues to policy makers. Yet both these assumptions are either false or highly dubious. As we have seen, on a wide range of issues leaders in both parties are much farther apart than are ordinary citizens, who have been separated by rather small differences.[26] When party platforms spell out clear and important differences between the parties on policy, it usually reflects a desire of party leaders to please themselves rather than demands from the electorate.

Some critics objected to the traditional convention's stress on picking a winner, rather than the "best candidate," regardless of popularity. This objection is not compatible with the democratic notion that voters should decide who is best for them and communicate this decision in an election. Only in dictatorial countries does a set of leaders arrogate unto themselves the right to determine who is best regardless of popular preferences. An unpopular candidate can hardly win a free election. An unpopular president can hardly secure the support needed to accomplish his or her goals. Popularity can be regarded as a necessary element for obtaining consent in democratic politics.

Although popularity is normally a necessary condition for nomination, it should not be the only condition. The guideline for purposes of nomination should be to nominate the best of the popular candidates. But "best" is a slippery word. A great deal of what we mean by "best" in politics is "best for us" or "best represents our policy preferences," and this can hardly be held up as an objective criterion. What is meant by "best" in this context are such personal qualities as experience, intelligence, and decisiveness. Nevertheless, it is not at all clear that an extreme conservative would prefer a highly intelligent liberal to a moderately intelligent candidate who shared his conservative policy preferences. Personal qualities clearly are subject to discount based on the compatibility of interests between voter and candidate.

For some critics, the defect of conventions lies not only in their poor performance in nominating candidates but also in their failure to become a sort of "superlegislature," enforcing the policy views of the platform on party members in the executive branch and Congress. We have previously indicated that such enforcement is most unlikely to be achieved. Let us suppose for the purposes of argument that the conventions could somehow become much more influential on matters of national policy. How could either party retain a semblance of unity if the stakes of convention deliberations were vastly increased by converting the platform into an unbreakable promise of national policy? If one believes that an increase in heated discussion necessarily improves the chances of agreement, then the problem solves itself. Experience warns us, however, that airing sharp differences, particularly when the stakes are high, is likely to decrease agreement. At the 1964 Republican convention, for example, African American delegates, bitter about the defeat of Governor Scranton's proposed amendment on civil rights to the GOP education plank, held a protest march around the Cow Palace and, when Barry Goldwater was nominated, announced that they would sit out the campaign.[27] This did not help Goldwater's chances of election. The fact that platforms are not binding permits a degree of unity necessary for the delegates to stay put long enough to agree on a nominee. By vastly increasing the number of delegates who would bitterly oppose platform decisions and possibly leave the convention, the binding platform would jeopardize the legitimacy of the convention's nominating function. Paradoxically, in such circumstances it would be difficult to resist the temptation to make the platform utterly innocuous in order to give offense to no one. GOP candidate Robert Dole went so far in 1996 to say that he hadn't read the platform he was presumably running on.

Even so, platforms do have a far from negligible impact on public opinion. Platform planks are enacted as governmental policy slightly more than half the time.[28] Programs favored by the public, according to opinion polls, are twice as likely to be enacted if they also appear in party platforms.[29] When large majorities favor programs, both parties are likely to put them in their platforms; when the public is somewhat more divided and important constituencies object, the parties are capable of going against popular majorities. Thus Republican platform planks on welfare and economic issues and Democratic provisions on labor unions and affirmative action tend to run counter to majority opinion.[30] The question of whom the parties are for, special or general constituencies, is resolved by going for the majority when it is substantial and modifying that position when it conflicts with special party concerns.

Now that they no longer have a role beyond advertising, the superiority of the traditional, decision-making national conventions to presidential selection by alternative means is clear. Only the convention permits us to realize in large measure all of the seven goals—maintenance of the two-party system, party competition, some degree of internal cohesion, candidates attractive to voters, qualified candidates, acceptance of nominees as legitimate, and a connection between winning the nomination and governing later on—that we postulated earlier would commonly be accepted as desirable.

THE ELECTORAL COLLEGE

Close presidential elections, those in which the new president has only a narrow margin in the total popular vote, always lead to renewed public discussion of the merits of the electoral college, since close elections remind people of the mathematical possibility that the candidate with a plurality of all the votes will not necessarily become president. Reform interest surges even higher when a regionally based third party, such as the party George Wallace led in 1968, or a conspicuous independent candidate, such as Ross Perot, becomes strong enough conceivably to prevent any candidate from having an electoral vote majority. In such a situation the Constitution designates the U.S. House of Representatives as the official arbiter of the decision; under this procedure, each state delegation has one vote.

The number of reform plans generated in the aftermath of the 1968 elections was legion. There were, however, only three basic alternatives to the present system proposed, and the rest were variations. One would abolish the electoral college outright and weigh individual votes equally everywhere. The net effect of such a proposal would be to undermine slightly the current strategic advantage enjoyed by populous, two-party, urbanized states. It might also have some long-run effects on the two-party system itself, but these would depend on other changes in the social situation within the country. The second proposal would retain the apportionment of the electoral college (which gives numerical advantage to the smaller, rural states) but abolish the unit-rule electoral vote (which operates strongly in favor of populous states). This proposal is quite extreme in its import, which would be to confer an additional political bonus on states traditionally overrepresented in positions of congressional power. A third, quite similar, proposal also retains the apportionment of the electoral college but distributes an electoral college vote for the plurality vote winner in each congressional district and two additional electoral votes for the winner in each state. Since this system maximizes the strength of one-party states, it could work to realign the presidential coalition in fundamental ways.[31]

The Constitution provides that each state, regardless of its population, shall be represented in the Senate by an equal number of senators. This means that the eight largest states, with just under 50 percent of the voters in 1996, have 16 percent of the senators. In the course of legislative proceedings, these sixteen senators' votes can be canceled by the sixteen votes of the senators from the eight least populous states, with 2.5 percent of the voters in the 1996 presidential election. At one point in early 1960, an average vote in Nevada was worth eighty-five times as much as an average vote in New York in elections for the Senate. The imbalance roughly corresponds to the advantage that more populous, urbanized, two-party states enjoy in the electoral college, and thus in access to the presidency.

The present electoral college system, with its votes apportioned according to the total of Senate and House seats a state has, awarded on a "winner-take-all" basis state by state, does provide a clear advantage to two groups of states. It yields a secondary advantage to the smallest states, since their overrepresentation in the Senate guarantees them overrepresentation in the electoral college; after the 1990 census, the seven states with three electoral votes each had a ratio of 268,000 or fewer citizens per electoral vote, while every state with thirteen or more electoral votes had a ratio of 475,500 or more citizens per electoral vote.

But it is primarily the larger states, through the unit-rule principle, which benefit from the electoral college. A candidate who can get a narrow majority in California alone can bag almost as many electoral votes (fifty-four) as he could by carrying all of the sixteen smallest states (sixty); he can, mathematically, carry California by one vote and not receive any votes in those sixteen states and do just as well. This fact suggests that presidential candidates should spend their energy in the larger states and tailor their programs to appeal to voters there, provided that energy expended there is likely to yield results.[32] In fact, the larger states are usually quite close in their division of the major-party vote, while a fair number of the smaller states are more nearly "sure" for one party or the other.

The large states are also the home of many organized minorities, especially racial and ethnic minorities, and this has traditionally meant that presidential candidates have had to pitch their appeals to attract these groups, or at least not to drive them off. Some of the critics of the current system have pointed to this advantage for the larger states, and especially their urban minorities, as a drawback of that system, to be reformed out of existence,[33] but most have concentrated their fire on the possibility of the "wrong winner" and the "undemocratic" nature of the unit rule.

Allowing a majority (or plurality) of voters to choose a president has a great deal to commend it. This is the simplest method of all; it would be most easily understood by the greatest number of people; it is the plan favored by the majority of Americans; and it comes closest to reflecting intuitive notions of direct popular sovereignty through majority rule.

Moreover, the outright abolition of the electoral college, and the substitution of the direct election of the president, would reduce the importance of the larger states. It would mean that the popular vote margin that a state could provide, not the number of electoral votes, would determine its importance. For example, under the present system a candidate who carries California by 144,100 votes (as Reagan did in 1980) has garnered one-sixth of the support needed to win, while under the direct-vote system, states such as Massachusetts or Alabama can sometimes generate three and four times that margin. In the two-party states, in which category most of the larger states fall, voters are cross-pressured in many ways, and a candidate can seldom count on defeating an opponent by a very large margin. The reason, then, that the large states lose influence is that this system switches influence from the close states to one-party states; in some states where one party's organization is weak, it is easier for the other party to achieve a large turnout at election time, and special rewards might be forthcoming for interest groups particularly strong within states that could provide a large margin of victory for their candidate. As candidates currently look with favor on those who can bring them support in the large states, because this spells victory, so might they be expected to look with favor on those who can bring them large popular margins in the one-party states, should that become the preferred strategy for winning. The emphasis would not be on which candidate was going to win the state, already a foregone conclusion, but by how many votes he or she was going to win.[34] The small states do not gain, however, because even when they are one-party, they are not large enough to generate big numbers of voters. Direct election thus changes the advantage from the biggest and the smallest two-party states to the medium-sized one-party states, and these, in recent elections, happen most commonly to be located in the South.[35]

This does not, of course, settle the matter, for one of the reasons that direct election is touted is that third parties cannot deadlock the process. In fact, those southern states with the largest 1968 margins—when George Wallace was a sectional candidate—were not powerful but weak, for they did not contribute to a winner but to a third-place loser.

How one feels about direct elections depends on (1) how one feels about the diminution of large-state influence and the gain by sundry other smaller states, (2) how much of a plurality one feels a newly elected president should have, and (3) how this plurality limit will affect others in the system.

Clearly, third-party votes under a direct election system are wasted if the candidate with a plurality is declared the winner, no matter how small that plurality. At best, voters could express only their anger by voting for third-party candidates, and this would be at the cost of foregoing the chance to influence an election. We suspect, however, that most Americans would feel uncomfortable with a president who, even though winning a plurality, was elected by, say, only 35 percent of the voters. One of the virtues of the present electoral vote system is that it magnifies the margin of a presidential victory (as, for instance, in 1996 Clinton's 8 percent victory margin gave him 72 percent of the electoral vote), presumably conferring added legitimacy and with it acceptance of the new president's responsibility to govern in fact as well as in title. Any system of direct election would almost have to eliminate the majority principle in favor of some plurality, or it would clearly lead to much more, not less, deadlock; in four out of our last eleven presidential elections, the winning candidate was without an absolute majority.

Reformers have generally agreed, though, that the winner must win by at least a substantial plurality; consequently, the electoral college reform amendment that passed the House in late 1969 provided for a runoff between the top two candidates if no one secured as much as 40 percent of the popular vote in the initial election.[36] The first effect of this provision would be to hand back influence to splinter parties; if one's candidate is going to have a second chance to win the office anyway, there is an incentive for any sizable organized minority to contest the first election on its own. That the runoff would likely be used if it were provided for is suggested by 1992, when there was a fairly strong third-party candidate in the race. A fourth candidate would have needed only 6 or 7 percent of the national total to keep either major-party candidate from having the required 40 percent (Clinton won with 43 percent, although he had 68.8 percent of the electoral vote).[37] Once this becomes even a plausible expectation, there is an incentive for various intense minorities to put up their own candidates, and visions of a white supremacist party, an African American party, a labor party, a peace party, an environmentalist party, a right-to-life party, a farmers' party, and so on, appear. Whereas one of the strong points of the present system is that it enforces a compromise by penalizing all minorities that will not come to terms, the direct election system could well encourage a continental European situation, in which numerous groups contest the first election and then recombine for the second; at the least, severe changes would be worked on the present system.[38] Should such a result occur in the future, the simplicity, ease of comprehension, and inherent majoritarian rightness of the direct election solution would quickly disappear. One of the hidden effects of the electoral college is to restrict the number of parties contesting for the presidency. This helps focus the electorate on a limited menu of choices. In turn, this increases the chance that winners will have the backing of a sizable number of voters and the legitimacy to lead Congress and the nation.

The direct election plan passed by the House in 1969 received a warmer reception in the Senate than the previous time it appeared there—in 1956 it was voted down 66 to 17—but there were, not surprisingly, two major opposition groups. The first was the bloc of liberal senators from the biggest states, which had most to lose. The second was composed of some of the conservative senators from the smallest states, whom we have named as the group deriving second-greatest benefits from the current system. They argued that direct election would be a complete break with the federalism underlying our Constitution, since it would de facto abolish state boundaries for presidential elections.[39]

Another proposal, embodied in the 1950s in the unsuccessful Lodge-Gossett Resolution, is seen by some reformers as an acceptable "compromise" between outright abolition of the electoral college and its retention.[40] In this scheme, the electoral vote in each state is split between the candidates according to their proportion of the state's popular vote. This may seem to be a procedural compromise, but it is a rather extreme reform in political terms.

Under proportional allocation of electoral votes, campaigning presidential nominees would have to give special attention to those states in which they thought a large difference in electoral votes could be attained. Once again, the proposed reform emphasizes the amount of difference within the state between the winner and the loser. In this case, however, the electoral votes of the states are divided, rather than the popular votes. This effectively cancels out the advantage of the large states entirely. The fact that the electoral college underrepresents the large states in the first place even further reduces their influence. The beneficiaries are again the one-party states, as well as the smaller states, since in any particular election West Virginia and Arizona, for example, may have more to contribute to the difference in electoral votes than Illinois, New Jersey, Ohio, or Texas.

There are two versions of this plan, one that divides electoral votes to the nearest vote and one that divides them to the nearest tenth of a vote. Most proponents favor the plan to divide them to the nearest tenth, since the nearest whole vote in many cases still would understate the closeness of the vote in a large number of states, especially those with few electoral votes to divide, and "representativeness" is the primary theoretical advantage of the plan. Since preventing deadlock is supposed to be one of the goals of electoral college reform, it is interesting to note that, with the majority-vote victory required by proponents of both plans, the tenth-vote system would have thrown all of the close elections beginning in 1960 into the House of Representatives, including the 1992 and 1996 elections (Kennedy and Carter would have won in 1960 and 1976 using whole votes; the 1976 result using tenth-votes would depend on whether 270 electoral votes were needed, as under the current rules, or only 269.1). Under the tenth-vote plan, elections would wind up in the House so frequently (requiring only a very close election, as in 1960, or a moderately strong third candidate, as in 1996, or both, as in 1968) that the presidency would be primarily dependent on Congress, not on the presidential election.

The reduction in influence suffered by the large states under proportional proposals might mean, in effect, that the sparsely populated and one-party states would entirely dominate the national lawmaking process, unchecked by a president obliged to cultivate urban and competitive two-party constituencies. The same problem is present if deadlock is dealt with by letting the plurality candidate win. Even allowing a winner to win with only a plurality, splintering is facilitated under this plan because a party need only attract a fraction of a percentage point of a major state's total vote in order to get some electoral votes. The present system at least cuts off splinter groups without a strong regional base.

A third plan, the district plan, has been proposed as still another "political compromise" between the other two major reform proposals, on the grounds that since thirty-eight states must ratify a constitutional amendment on electoral reform, the thirteen states with three or four electoral votes are not likely to support either of the first two proposals because each dilutes their current strength. The district plan would give a presidential candidate one electoral vote for every congressional district carried, plus two more for every state. This is how electoral votes are now distributed in the states of Maine and Nebraska. It has been pushed largely by conservative senators; it is clearly the most radical of all the reform proposals in its effect on the U.S. political system, and it is least advantageous to the big states. This system would have given Nixon victory in 1968 (289–192–57), but if it had already been in effect, he probably would not have been running, since it would have reversed the results of the election of 1960 (Nixon 278, Kennedy 245).

Since the goals of electoral reform are supposedly to prevent the wrong person from winning, to avoid deadlock, and to do away with winner-take-all arrangements, it is hard to see what is offered by a system that (1) would have given the less popular candidate victory, (2) provides no more guarantee against deadlock than the present system (Wallace in 1968 got forty-five electoral votes under the actual system but would have received fifty-seven under the district plan), (3) uses a winner-take-all principle, and (4) has the incidental feature of ending the activist character of the American presidency and giving policy control to one-party areas for the foreseeable future.[41]

Table 6.2 shows outcomes under the various plans for presidential elections since 1960. The election of 1988 would have come out the same way under all the plans for counting votes we have been considering. Under proportional allocation, the 1992 and 1996 elections would have been thrown into the House of Representatives, but Clinton would still have won under district representation. Plans to abolish the electoral college, by damping down even large landslides, would bring stronger and more splinter parties into the electoral competition, thus changing the climate of electoral competition altogether.

TABLE 6.2 ELECTORAL OUTCOMES UNDER VARIOUS PLANS

	Present plan		Direct plan		Proportional plan		District plan	
1996	*Clinton wins*		*Clinton wins*		*Winner unclear*		*Clinton wins*	
	Clinton	379	Clinton	49.2%	Clinton	262.1	Clinton	345
	Dole	159	Dole	40.7	Dole	222.0	Dole	193
	Perot	0	Perot	8.4	Perot	45.2	Perot	0
1992	*Clinton wins*		*Clinton wins*		*Winner unclear*		*Clinton wins*	
	Clinton	370	Clinton	43.0%	Clinton	231.1	Clinton	324
	Bush	168	Bush	37.4	Bush	202.2	Bush	214
	Perot	0	Perot	18.9	Perot	101.8	Perot	0
1988	*Bush wins*		*Bush wins*		*Bush wins*		*Bush wins*	
	Bush	426	Bush	53.4%	Bush	288.1	Bush	377
	Dukakis	111	Dukakis	45.6	Dukakis	245.1	Dukakis	159
	Others	1	Others	1.0	Others	4.5		
1976	*Carter wins*		*Carter wins*		*Carter wins*		*Winner unclear*	
	Carter	297	Carter	50.1%	Carter	269.5	Carter	269
	Ford	240	Ford	48.0	Ford	258.0	Ford	269
	Others	1	Others	1.9	Others	10.5	Others	0
1968	*Nixon wins*		*Nixon wins*		*Winner unclear*		*Nixon wins*	
	Nixon	301	Nixon	43.4%	Nixon	233.8	Nixon	289
	Humphrey	191	Humphrey	42.7	Humphrey	223.2	Humphrey	192
	Wallace	46	Wallace	13.5	Wallace	78.8	Wallace	57
1960	*Kennedy wins*		*Kennedy wins*		*Winner unclear*		*Nixon wins*	
	Kennedy	303	Kennedy	49.7%	Kennedy	264.8	Kennedy	245
	Nixon	219	Nixon	49.6	Nixon	263.5	Nixon	278
	Others	15	Others	0.7	Others	7.7	Others	15

Under the present electoral college system, at no time since 1876 has any splinter group been able to make good its threat to throw the election into the House. Even in 1948 Harry Truman won an electoral college majority despite sizable threats from both a third (Henry Wallace, Progressive) and a fourth (Strom Thurmond, States Rights) party. In spite of the mathematical possibilities, not once in this century has the loser of the popular vote become president. On the other hand, a direct election plan that required a 40 percent plurality might well have forced a runoff in 1968 and 1992. The proportional plan would have created deadlocks in four recent elections; and the district plan would have thrown the election to the popular vote loser in at least one recent case. In view of this analysis of the effect of electoral reforms, it is curious that many reformers have supported these changes in the electoral college.

Underlying all these arguments, of course, is the premise that most structural reforms "tend" to shift influences in certain ways. There may well be situations of social polarization that electoral system alternatives by themselves cannot paper over. But while we have argued that there is no better system than the current one, from the standpoint of the professed goals of most reformers, there is one minor change that would aid them. Under the present plan the actual electors who make up the electoral college are in fact free to vote for whomever they wish. These electors are usually party faithful who are chosen in each state by party leaders. As an almost invariable rule, they vote for the winner in their state, but abuses are possible, and two within recent memory come to mind:

1. The unpledged electors chosen by citizens in Mississippi and Alabama in 1960 decided for whom they would vote only well after the election, treating the preferences of citizens as advisory, not mandatory. This clearly thwarts popular control.

2. This liberty allowed George Wallace to hope that he could run for president, create an electoral deadlock, and then bargain with one of the other candidates for policy concessions in exchange for his electors.

An amendment making the casting of electoral votes automatic would dispel both these possibilities.

A final gimmick deserves consideration, the creation of a private commission set up by the Twentieth Century Fund (now the Century Foundation) some years ago. It came up with a proposal for a National Bonus Plan, which would award 102 electoral votes en bloc (two for each state plus the District of Columbia) to the plurality winner of the nationwide popular vote. This plan would make it highly probable that no president could be elected who did not get more votes than the nearest rival. An additional feature is that candidates would be encouraged to get as many votes as they could, even in states where they were pretty sure to lose, because these would add on to the candidate's national popular total.[42] The Bonus Plan would guard against a minority president, preserve the form and the spirit of the constitutional structure, and do all this without encouraging splinter parties.

We have argued that there is no serious reason to quarrel with the major features of the present system, since in our form of government "majority rule" does not operate in a vacuum but within a system of "checks and balances." The president, for example, holds a veto power over laws enacted by Congress, which, if exercised, requires a two-thirds vote of each house to be overridden. Treaties must be ratified by two-thirds of the Senate, and amendments to the Constitution must be proposed by two-thirds of Congress or of the state legislatures and ratified by three-fourths of the states. Presidential appointments, in most important cases, must receive senatorial approval. The Supreme Court passes upon the constitutionality of legislative and executive actions. Additionally, there is impeachment, a political check on the Presidency available to Congress. Involved in these political arrangements is the hope that the power of one branch of government will be counterbalanced by certain "checks" from another, the result being an approximate "balance" of forces. In our view, it is not necessarily a loss to have slightly different majorities preponderant in different institutions, but it is definitely a loss to have the same majority preponderant in both political branches while other majorities are frozen out. In the past the electoral college had its place within this system. Originally designed to check popular majorities from choosing presidents unwisely, the electoral college later on provided a check on the overrepresentation of rural states in the legislative branch by giving extra weight to the big-state constituencies of the president.

Party Platforms and Party Differences

Having reviewed some of the major changes proposed by party reformers, let us return to consider their key argument. Parties, reformers claim, are insufficiently ideological. The voters are not being offered clear choices, and the parties, once in office, are not responsibly carrying out the promises made in their platforms. We argue that American parties do indeed differ—more so now than in the recent past—and that, much of the time, they respond to changes in voter sentiment. We believe that the solutions offered by reformers are unnecessary and would lead to consequences that even they might not desire.

Party platforms written by the presidential parties should be understood not only as ends in themselves but as means to obtaining and holding public office. It would be strange indeed if a party understood that policies such as Social Security and unemployment compensation were enormously popular and yet refused to incorporate them into its platform.[43] This would have to be a party of ideologues who cared everything about their own ideas and nothing about winning elections. Nor would it profit them much because they would not get elected and would never be in a position to do something about their ideas. Sooner or later, ideologues have to make the choice between pleasing themselves and winning elections.

Even when the major political parties are in the hands of moderate leaders, there are clear differences between the doctrines espoused by the two parties, and these are reflected in party platforms. Moreover, party platforms change over a period of time in a cyclical movement. The differences between the parties may be great for one or two elections, until innovations made by one party are picked up by the other.

The net change from one decade to the next is substantial. Let us begin when platforms are more or less alike. Their similarity begins to give way as it appears that certain demands in society are not being met. The minority party of the period senses an opportunity to gain votes by articulating and promising to meet these demands. The majority party, reluctant to let go of a winning combination, resists. In one or two elections the minority party makes its bid and makes the appropriate changes in its platforms. Then, in the ensuing elections, if the party that has changed its platform loses, it drops the innovation. If it wins, and wins big, the other party then seeks to take over what seem to be its most popular planks, and the platforms become more alike again.

We can see this cycle clearly in the New Deal period. The 1932 Democratic platform, though hinting at change, was much like the Republican one, especially in its emphasis on balancing the budget. A great difference in platforms could be noted in 1936 as the Democrats attempted to consolidate the New Deal and the Republicans stood pat. The spectacular Democratic triumph signaled the end of widely divergent platforms. By 1940 the Republicans had concluded that they could not continue to oppose the welfare state wholesale if they ever wished to win again. By 1952 the parties had come much closer to each other as the Republicans adopted most of the New Deal. Though the platforms of the major parties were similar to each other in both 1932 and 1952, the differences between 1932 and 1952 for either party were enormous.[44] In keeping with our finding that party leaders are, by historic standards, currently more polarized than usual, it is not surprising to find sharp differences in the party platforms for 1996 (see box 6.1, pp.256-57).

Sometimes reformers deplore what they regard as an excessive amount of mudslinging in campaigns, but they also ask that differences among the major parties be sharply increased in order to give the voters a clear choice. The two ideas are incompatible. It is unreasonable to require that parties disagree more sharply about more and more subjects in an increasingly gentlemanly way. Far more likely would be an increase in vituperation as the stakes of campaigns increased, passions rose, tempers flared, and the consequences of victory for the other side appeared much more threatening than had earlier been the case.

The case for the desirability of party reform used to rest on the assumption that American political parties were identical, that this was confusing and frustrating to American voters, and that it was undesirable to have a political system where parties do not disagree sharply. Now we have a chance to find out what happens during a period of relative party polarization.

Imagine for a moment that the two parties were in total and extreme disagreement on every major point of public policy, more so than they are in the United States. One party would limit American military power to our borders, the other would intervene in every tense situation across the globe. One group would go all-out to improve productivity; the other would put environmental values first. One group would stop Social Security; the other would expand it drastically. One group would raise tariffs; the other would abolish them. Obviously one consequence of having clear-cut parties with strong policy positions would be that the costs of losing an election would skyrocket. If parties were forced to formulate coherent, full-dress programs and were forced to carry them out "responsibly," and in full, then people who did not favor these programs would have little recourse (until the next election). Clearly their confidence in a government whose policies were so little to their liking would suffer, and, indeed, they might feel strongly enough about preventing these policies from being enacted to do something drastic, like leaving the country or not complying with governmental regulations or, in an extreme case, seeking to change the political system by impeachment or by force.

The presidency of Republican Ronald Reagan may give pause to liberal reformers. Though Reagan's campaign rhetoric was too general to alarm voters, in many respects he played the part of the responsible party president who proposed and attempted to carry out a wide-ranging program designed to modify, if not to undo completely, the efforts of his Democratic predecessors. There was no mistaking his thrust—less domestic government and more money for defense. Indeed, if any president has performed according to the "responsible government" model, it is Ronald Reagan, who tried and to some extent succeeded, at least early in his administration, to carry out his campaign promises. If the results did not meet with universal approval, citizens cannot say they were not forewarned as to the direction the candidate would take in the event that he was elected. If some citizens prefer more moderation and compromise, they should then consider whether they really want parties and candidates to carry out their pledges. Is the argument for party reform that the nation needs more Reagans, whether of the right or left? Evidently, given favorable political conditions such as existed in Lyndon Johnson's first term and Ronald Reagan's first year, or the extraordinary skill exercised by the promoters of the 1986 tax reform, coherent presidential programs enacted en masse by Congress are possible without constitutional reform or further changes, such as we have been discussing, in electoral machinery. It is necessary to have enthusiastic party activists, determined and skillful leaders, and public consent. These are not always available, but they sometimes are. When they are not, perhaps it is wise to make the achievement of large changes not too easy.[45]

Box 6.1   Selections from the Democratic and Republican Platforms, 1996

Republican Platform

Economic Policy

"Americans families are suffering from the twin burdens of stagnant incomes and near-record taxes.... They should be allowed to keep more of their hard-earned money so they can spend on their priorities, as opposed to sending ever-increasing amounts to Washington.... In response to this unprecedented burden confronting America, we support an across-the-board, 15 percent tax cut to marginal tax rates.... To remove impediments to job creation and economic growth, we support reducing the top tax rate on capital gains by 50 percent."

Health Care

"Crack down on Medicare and Medicaid fraud.... Reform malpractice laws.... Let individuals set up tax-free Medical Savings Accounts so they can plan for their own medical needs instead of relying on government or insurance companies.... Promote a private market for long-term insurance."

Welfare

"Bill Clinton will sign into law a Republican reform of welfare.... The key to welfare reform is restoring personal responsibility and encouraging two-parent households.... All able-bodied adults must be required to work, either in private sector jobs or in community work projects. Illegal aliens must be ineligible for all but emergency benefits. And a firm time limit for receipt of welfare must be enforced. Because illegitimacy is the most serious cause of child poverty, we will encourage states to stop cash payments to unmarried teens and set a family cap on payments to additional children."

Housing

"We affirm our commitment to open housing, without quotas or controls.... We support transforming public housing into private housing, converting low-income families into proud homeowners. Resident management of public housing is a first step toward that goal, which includes eliminating the Department of Housing and Urban Development."

Democratic Platform

Economic Policy

"Since Bill Clinton became President, America has seen an explosion of job growth, economic renewal, and opportunity.... President Clinton and Democrats in Congress expanded the Earned Income Tax Credit, cutting taxes to help 40 million Americans in 15 million working families.... We believe the minimum wage should be a wage you can live on.... We want a G.I. Bill for Workers to transform the confusing tangle of federal training programs into a simple job-training skill grant that will go directly to unemployed workers."

Health Care

"We held the line against the Republicans' mean-spirited Medicare and Medicaid cuts that would risk the health care of millions of Americans.... We have expanded the Women, Infants, and Children program.... We established a comprehensive effort to immunize children."

Welfare

"Now, because of the President's leadership and with the support of a majority of the Democrats in Congress, national welfare reform is going to make work and responsibility the law of the land.... The new welfare bill includes the health care and child care people need.... We pledge to make sure that legal immigrant families with children who fall on hard times through no fault of their own can get help when they need it.... We challenge states to exempt battered women from time limits.... In addition to health care and nutritional assistance, states should provide in-kind vouchers to children whose parents have reached the time limit."

Housing

"Safe, secure housing is an essential part of strong communities and strong families.... Bill Clinton took executive action to make it easier and cheaper for working and middle-class homebuyers to get a loan.... In the last four years, Democrats demolished more units of unlivable public housing than Republicans did in the previous twelve years, replacing them with lower-density developments that can serve as anchors for neighborhood renewal."

Continued

Crime

"We will establish no-frills prisons where prisoners are required to work productively and make the threat of jail a real deterrent to crime. Prisons should not be places of rest and relaxation. We will reform the Supreme Court's fanciful exclusionary rule.... We will work with local authorities to prevent prison inmates from receiving disability or other government entitlements.... We call for special penalties against thugs who assault or batter pregnant women and harm them or their unborn children."

Civil Rights

"We call on all Republicans and all Americans to reject the forces of hatred and bigotry.... We condemn attempts by the... government to regulate or ban religious symbols from the workplace.... We support the official recognition of English as the nation's most common language. ... We endorse the Defense of Marriage Act to prevent states from being forced to recognize same-sex unions.... We will attain our nation's goal of equal rights without quotas or other forms of preferential treatment.... The unborn child has a fundamental right to life which cannot be infringed."

Crime

"Nothing is more effective in the fight against crime than police officers on the beat, engaged in community policing.... We made the Brady Bill law of the land.... President Clinton lead the fight to ban 19 deadly assault weapons.... We must do everything we can to stand behind our police officers, and the first thing we should do is pass a ban on cop-killer bullets."

Civil Rights

"Today's Democratic Party knows we must renew our efforts to stamp out discrimination and hatred of every kind.... We strongly oppose divisive efforts like English-only legislation.... We support... the Employment Non-Discrimination Act, to end discrimination against gay men and lesbians.... President Clinton is leading the way to reform affirmative action so that it works, it is improved.... The Democratic Party stands behind the right of every woman to choose, consistent with *Roe* v. *Wade*, and regardless of ability to pay."

CHAPTER 7

American Parties and Democracy

Over a relatively short period of time, a new sort of American political system has come into being. Among its features are high degrees of mass participation in formerly elite processes, the replacement of political parties with the news and publicity media as primary organizers of citizen action and legitimizers of public decisions, the rise in the influence of media-approved and media-sustained interest groups, and the decline of interest groups linked to party organizations. Certain sorts of decision making are easy in a system structured in this way: simple voting, for example, in which alternatives are few and clear-cut. However, complex, deliberative decision making, in which various alternatives are compared one after the other, contingencies are weighed and tested tentatively, second and third choices are probed for hidden consensuses, or special weight is given to intensity of likes and dislikes, is extremely difficult in such a system. Therefore, much influence flows into the hands of those who structure alternatives in the first place—self-starting candidates and the news media.

But the need for organizations to do the job of the parties continues even as the party organizations decline in influence. For presidential elections, we have observed the replacement of the convention with primary elections as the most significant part of the process and the rise of party activists who are more ideological and sometimes more extreme than the rest of the population.

Because the American political system is moving toward a role for political parties that stresses their activities as policy advocates, it seems to us important to give some attention to the implications of this trend for democratic government. Our argument makes two main points. The first is that it is necessary for parties of advocacy in a democracy to receive mandates on public policy from popular majorities of convinced believers in their programs, but that this condition is not met in America because of the ways in which electorates actually participate in elections and conceive of public policy.

Our second point is that in view of the actual disposition of attitudes toward public policy in the electorate as compared with party elites, the fact that we are moving toward, or have actually entered into, an era of parties of advocacy poses some significant and largely unmet problems for American democracy. This is because it is not the policy preferences of the bulk of the electorate that are being advocated. Moreover, the implementation of policy through government requires the sort of institutional support that parties can orchestrate only if they have some permanency and are not required to give birth to themselves anew every four years, nominate a candidate, and then wither away.

Elections and Public Policy

Uncoerced and competitive elections aid in making the political system open and responsive to a great variety of people and groups in the population. But elections do not transmit unerringly the policy preferences of electorates to leaders or confer mandates on leaders with regard to specific policies. Consider the presidential landslide of 1972, which resulted in a Republican president but also in a Democratic Congress that was bound to disagree with him. Or consider the following complex sequence. In 1980 Ronald Reagan won comfortably, with Republicans also gaining control of the Senate, but not the House. By 1982 the Democrats had recouped. President Reagan won even more decisively in 1984 but failed to do much of consequence in Congress; two years later the Democrats made a strong comeback and regained control of the Senate. The Clinton era elections are even more difficult to interpret. Bill Clinton won presidential elections twice by decisive margins over his Republican opponents but without achieving a majority of the popular vote. In between those elections, Republicans won a landslide election that gave them control of both houses of Congress. Then, in 1998, Clinton's party bucked history to gain House seats (and broke even in the Senate). Even in a landslide, winners can sensibly claim only a temporary, equivocal mandate. In any case, elections that are clear-cut are rare.

It is easy to be cynical and expect too little from elections or to be euphoric and expect too much from them. A cynical view would hold that the United States was ruled by a power elite—a small group outside the democratic process. Under these circumstances the ballot would be a sham and a delusion. What difference can it make how voting is carried on or who wins if the nation is actually governed by other means? In contrast, a euphoric view, holding that the United States is ruled as a mass democracy with equal control over decisions by all or most citizens, would enormously magnify the importance of the ballot. Through the act of casting a ballot, it could be argued, a majority of citizens would determine major national policies. What happens at the polls would not only decide who occupies public office; it also would determine the content of specific policy decisions. In a way, public office would then be a sham because the power of decision in important matters would be removed from the hands of public officials. A third type of political system, in which numerous minorities compete for shares in policy-making within broad limits provided by free elections, has more complex implications. It suggests that balloting is important but that it often does not and sometimes should not determine individual policy decisions. The ballot guides and constrains public officials, who are free to act within fairly broad limits subject to their anticipations of the responses of the voters and to the desires of other active participants.

It is evident that the American political system is of this third type. Public officials do make major policy decisions, but elections matter in that they determine which of two competing parties holds public office. In a competitive two-party situation such as exists in American presidential politics, the lively possibility of change provides an effective incentive for political leaders to remain in touch with followers.

But voters in presidential elections do not transmit their policy preferences to elected officials with a high degree of reliability. There are few clear mandates in our political system because elections are fought on so many issues and in so many incompletely overlapping constituencies. Often the same voters elect candidates to Congress and to the presidency who disagree on public policies. Thus, even if mandates could be identified, they might well be impossible to enact because of inconsistency in the instructions issued to officials who must agree on legislation.[1]

Presidential elections are not one-issue referendums. The relationship between presidential elections and policies is a great deal subtler than the relations between the outcomes of referendums and the policies to which they pertain. In principle, the American political system is designed to work like this: Two teams of politicians, one in office, the other seeking office, both attempt to get enough votes to win elections. In order to win, they go to various groups of voters and, by offering to pursue policies favored by these groups, or by suggesting policies they might come to favor, hope to attract their votes. If there were only one office-seeking team, its incentive to respond to the policy preferences of groups in the population would diminish; if there were many such teams, the chances that any one of them could achieve a sufficient number of backers to govern would diminish. Hence a two-party system might be regarded as a kind of compromise between the goals of responsiveness and effectiveness.

The proponents of a different theory would say that elections give the winning party a mandate to carry out the policies proposed during the campaign. Only in this way, they maintain, is popular rule through the ballot meaningful. A basic assumption in this argument is that the voters (or at least a majority of them) approve of all or most of the policies advocated by the victorious candidate. No doubt this is plausible, but not in the sense intended because, as we have seen, a vote for a presidential candidate is often an expression of a party habit: particular policy directions are therefore not necessarily meant by the vote. Indeed, citizens may be voting not for but against a candidate or a past president, saying, in effect, no more of this but not necessarily more of the other party's policies. Most voters in the United States are not ideologically oriented. They do not seek to create or to adopt systems of thought in which issues are related to one another in some highly consistent manner. Caring about more than one value, sometimes they prefer a strong government here and a weak one there, or just not to decide at the present time. Thus voters can hardly be said to transmit strong preferences for a uniform stream of particular policies by electing candidates to public office.

Other basic objections to the idea that our elections are designed to confer mandates on specific public policies may also be raised. First, the issues debated in the campaign may not be the ones in which most voters are interested. These issues may be ones that interest the candidates or that, for tactical reasons, they want to stress, or that interest segments of the press. There is no clear reason to believe that any particular issue is of great concern to voters just because it gets publicity. Time and again, voting studies have demonstrated that what appear to be the major issues of a campaign turn out not to be significant for most of the electorate. In 1952, for example, three great Republican themes were communism, Korea, and corruption. It turned out that the communism issue, given perhaps the most publicity, had virtually no impact. Democrats simply would not believe that their party was the party of treason, and Republicans did not need that issue to make them vote the way they usually did. Korea and corruption were noticeable issues.[2] Yet how could anyone know, in the absence of a public opinion poll (and perhaps not even then), which of the three issues was important to the voters and which therefore conferred a mandate? There were, in any event, no significant policy differences between the parties on these issues: Democrats were also against communism and corruption and wanted an end to the war in Korea. A broadly similar story can be told, as we have shown, for more recent elections, in which nobody was for welfare fraud or large budget deficits, everybody was for a strong economy, and nobody favored crime.[3]

A second reason why voting for a candidate does not necessarily signify approval of the candidate's policies is that candidates pursue many policy interests at any one time with widely varying intensity, so that they may collect support from some voters on one issue and from other voters on another. It is possible for a candidate to get 100 percent of the votes and still have every voter opposed to most of the candidate's policies, as well as having every one of those policies opposed by most of the voters.

Assume that there are four major issues in a campaign. Make the further, quite reasonable, assumption that the voting population is distributed in such a way that people who care intensely about one major issue support the victorious candidate for that reason alone, although they differ with that candidate mildly on the other three issues. Thus, voters who are deeply concerned about the problem of defense against nuclear weapons may vote for candidate Jones, who prefers a minimum deterrence position, rather than Smith, who espouses a doctrine that requires huge retaliatory forces. This particular group of voters disagrees with Jones on farm price supports, on the overall size of government, and on national health insurance, but they do not feel strongly about any of these matters. Another group, meanwhile, believes that farmers, the noble yeomanry, are the backbone of the nation, and that if they are prosperous and strong, everything else will turn out all right. So they vote for Jones, too, although they prefer a large defense budget and disagree with Jones's other policies. And so on for other groups of voters. Jones ends up with all the votes, yet each of Jones's policies is preferred by less than a majority of the electorate. Since this is possible in any political system where many issues are debated at election time, it is hard to argue that our presidential elections give unequivocal mandates on specific policies to the candidates who win.[4]

People vote for many reasons not directly connected with issues. They may vote on the basis of party identification alone. Party habits may be joined with a general feeling that Democrats are better for the common citizen or that Republicans will keep us safe, or vice versa—feelings too diffuse to tell us much about specific issues. Some people vote on the basis of a candidate's personality, or "image." Others follow a friend's recommendation. Still others may be thinking about policy issues but may be all wrong in their perception of where the candidates stand. It is ordinarily impossible to distinguish the votes of these people from those who know, care, and differentiate accurately among the candidates on the basis of issues. We do know, however, that issue-oriented persons are usually in a minority, while those who cast their ballots with other things in mind are generally in the majority. Voters, if asked, may say they want to move government in a more liberal or conservative direction, but desires of this sort are so general in character, they imply approval of nearly anything.

Even if there is good reason to believe that a majority of voters do approve of specific policies supported by the victorious candidate, the mandate may be difficult or impossible to carry out. A candidate may get elected for a policy he or she pursued or preferred in the past that has no relevance to present circumstances. Some may have voted Republican in 1956 because Dwight Eisenhower got rid of the rascals in the Truman administration (three years earlier), or Democratic in 1976 in response to Watergate; but this did not point to any future policy that was currently in the realm of presidential discretion. John F. Kennedy promised in 1960 to get the nation moving. This was broad enough to cover a multitude of vague hopes and aspirations. More specifically, as president, Kennedy might have wished to make good his promise by increasing the rate of growth in the national economy, but no one was quite sure how to do this. Lyndon Johnson was able to deliver on many of his 1964 campaign promises on domestic policy, but observers after the election could not readily distinguish his subsequent Vietnam policies from those they may have wanted to reject by voting against Barry Goldwater. The 1980 and 1984 elections can be seen as referendums on the economic performance of the incumbent administrations. Clearly voters thought the economy was doing poorly under Carter and better under Reagan. More than likely, however, it was the monetary policies of the Federal Reserve under the leadership of Paul Volcker, a Republican Carter appointee, that produced the pro-Reagan electoral results. The opposite may have been the case in the 1992 and 1996 elections. Then, voters approved of the economic performance of the Clinton administration but not that of the Bush administration, presumably giving the Democrats credit for success in no small measure designed by Federal Reserve Chair Alan Greenspan—a Republican appointee.

Leaving aside all the difficulties about the content of a mandate, there is no accepted definition of what size electoral victory gives a president special popular sanction to pursue any particular policy. Would a 60 percent victory be sufficient? What about 51 percent or 52 percent, or cases such as 1992 and 1996 in which the winner receives less than half the votes cast? Moreover, is it right to ignore the multitudes who do not vote and whose preferences are not directly registered? We might ignore the nonvoters for the purpose of this analysis if we were sure they were divided in their preferences between candidates in nearly the same proportions as those who do vote. There is now reason to believe that this is, more or less, true.[5] But we cannot be sure this is always the case. In practice, this problem is easily solved. Whoever wins the presidential election is allowed to pursue whatever policies he or she pleases, within the very important constraints imposed by the checks and balances of the rest of the policymaking institutions (notably, Congress) in the political system. This, in the end, is all that a "mandate" is in American politics.

Opinion polls and focus groups may help the politician gauge policy preferences, but there are always lingering doubts as to their reliability. It is not certain in any event that they tell the political leader what that leader needs to know. People who really have no opinion but who care only a little may be counted equally with those who are intensely concerned. Many people giving opinions may have no intention of voting for some of the politicians who heed them, no matter what. The result may be that a politician will get no visible support from a majority that agrees with him or her, but instead will get complaints from an intense minority that disagrees. The people who agree with the politician may not vote, while those who differ may attempt retribution at the ballot box—as single-issue interest groups are reported to do. Those who are pleased may be the ones who would have voted for the public official in any case. Unless the poll is carefully done, it may leave out important groups of voters, overrepresent some, underrepresent others, and otherwise give a misleading impression. The correlations that are made, say, showing that support comes disproportionately from certain economic or social groups, do not explain why some people, often a substantial minority, possessing these self-same characteristics act in the opposite way.

Let us turn the question around for a moment. Suppose a candidate loses office. What does this signify about the policies he or she should have preferred? If one or two key issues were widely debated and universally understood, the election might tell the candidate a great deal. But this is seldom the case. More likely, there were many issues, and it was difficult to separate out those that did from those that did not garner support for the opponent. Perhaps the election was decided on the basis of personal images or some events in the economic cycle or a military engagement—points that were not debated in the campaign and that may not have been within anyone's control. Losing candidates may always feel that if they continue to educate the public to favor the policies they prefer, they will eventually win. Should a candidate lose a series of elections, however, the party would undoubtedly try to change something—policies, candidates, organization, maybe all three—in an effort to improve its fortunes.

How do winning candidates appraise an election? What does this event tell officeholders and their parties about the policies they should prefer when in office? Some policy positions undoubtedly were rather vague, and specific applications of them may turn out quite differently from what the campaign suggested. Others may founder on the rock of practicality; they sounded fine, but they simply cannot be carried out. Conditions change and policies that seemed appropriate a few months before turn out to be irrelevant. Democrats may prefer to spend more on welfare and Republicans to cut taxes, but huge deficits endanger both policies. As the time for putting policies into practice draws near, the new officeholders may discover that the policies generate a lot more opposition than when they were merely campaign oratory. Term limits are a good current example. Those policies that are pursued to the end may have to be compromised considerably in order to get the support of other participants in the policy-making process. Nevertheless, if they have even a minimal policy orientation, newly elected candidates can try to carry out a few of their campaign proposals, seeking to maintain a general direction consonant with the approach that may—they cannot be entirely certain—have contributed to their election.

The practical impossibility in our political system of ascertaining mandates is one important reason it is so difficult for parties to emphasize their function as policy advocates. It is, however, entirely possible for parties to adopt mandates that have little or no support in the general population. It is to the exploration of this possibility that we now turn.

Parties of Advocacy Versus Parties of Intermediation

The presidential election process in the United States has undergone a major transformation. As late as 1952, a president of the United States could, and with good reason, dismiss a prospective Estes Kefauver victory in the New

Hampshire primary as "eye-wash." Now primaries select most convention delegates and, combined with the effects of the media, have an overwhelming impact on the outcome of the nominating process.[6]

Behind the shift in the role of primary elections lie shifts in the roles of political activists, both candidate enthusiasts and party regulars, and changes in the powers and the significance of the news media. We believe that these changes and other changes that we have discussed—the shift to public financing not only of the general election but also of primary elections, the vast increase in the number of primaries, and the new rules for converting votes into delegates—add up to a fundamental redefinition of the place of the national political parties in our public life. One way to characterize this redefinition is to say that the conception of parties as agents of consensus government has begun to fade. If we are right, then more and more we can expect candidates and party leaders to raise divisive issues and to emphasize party differences rather than paper them over.

Activists are now favored by the rules of the game, and officeholders and party officials are comparatively disfavored. In the early days of preprimary activity, the people who become most active are apt to be those who have the most spare time, the most ideological commitment, and the most enthusiasm for one candidate above all others. Since the rules are now written to encourage activity at an earlier and earlier date, as a basis for federal subsidies during the primaries and as a necessary condition for being taken seriously by the news media, it follows that activists will have more to say about the eventual outcome of the nomination process. Party officials in the various states, in contrast, who once preferred to wait until they could see a majority forming, under the new rules of the game must ally themselves with one or another active candidate early in the process or forfeit their influence. This applies even to the Democratic high officeholders who get a free ride to the convention and make up around 15 percent of the total number of delegates. By the time their peculiar skills and interests in majority building might be needed—for instance, at a convention—it is too late for them to get into the process: most of the seats will have been taken by the enthusiasts for particular candidates who won in the various primaries and state conventions.

We can therefore ask how the emerging structure of presidential election politics helps and hinders political parties in performing the tasks customarily allotted to them in the complex scheme of American democracy. In essence, we would argue that the parties have been greatly strengthened in their capacities to provide advocacy and weakened in their abilities to provide intermediation or later to facilitate implementation in the political system. Consensus among party activists has been achieved at the expense of increasing dissension within government. Thus party platforms become ever more internally consistent, while government finds it increasingly difficult to relate revenues to expenditures.

Advocacy is strengthened because the rules of the game offer incentives to party leaders and candidates who are able to attract personal followings on an ideological basis. What is lost, in our view, is a capacity to deliberate, weigh competing demands, and compromise so that a variety of differing interests each gain a little. This loss would not be so great if the promise of policy government—to select efficacious programs and implement them successfully—were likely to be fulfilled in performance. But, on the record so far, this is doubly doubtful.

It is doubtful because for many of the problems that form the basis of political campaign discussion—crime, racism, hostility abroad—there are no known, sure-fire solutions. Second, even if we knew what to do about more of our problems, it is unclear, given the ways in which various forces in our society are arranged, that presidents alone could deliver on their promises.

This last dilemma is especially poignant for candidates who speak to a very wide spectrum of issues. Were they elected, then program implementation would require support in Congress, the bureaucracies, state and city governments, and elsewhere. The ability of such policy-oriented candidates to gain the agreement of others depends on many factors that typically are neither discussed nor understood in election campaigns. Yet gaining the agreement of others is part of making policies work. Policy government might enhance the legitimacy of government if it increased the effectiveness of programs, but the insensitivity of its advocates to the needs for consensus makes that unlikely. Under these circumstances, neither policy nor consensus, advocacy nor intermediation, are likely to be served.

Two factors account for the decline in the vital function of intermediation by parties. First, candidates have far fewer incentives than heretofore to deal with interest groups organized on traditional geographic or occupational lines or with state and local party leaders. These leaders and groups have in the past provided links between national politicians and the people and have focused the hopes and energies of countless citizens on the party organizations as meaningful entities in the nomination process. Nowadays, as we have been told by politicians as varied as Richard Nixon and Jimmy Carter, a candidate for the presidency need no longer build up a mosaic of alliances with interest groups and party leaders. Candidates such as Walter Mondale who do work to secure these alliances are attacked for being beholden to "special interests." Now, through the miracle of the mass media (especially television), through mass mailings to appeal for money, and through federal subsidy if these mass mailings are successful, presidential candidates can reach every home and touch every heart and claim the allegiance of followers based on ideological appeals rather than concrete bargains.

This is the first sense in which parties have been diminished in their capacity to mediate between the desires of ordinary citizens and the policies of government: candidates no longer need parties to reach voters. In a second sense, parties are losing the capacity to mediate between leaders and followers because the formal properties of plebiscitary decision making, such as occurs in primary elections, leave little room for a bargaining process to occur. Contingent choices are impossible to express straightforwardly through the ballot box. Thus a candidate who is acceptable to a sizable majority but is the first choice of only a few systematically loses out under the current primary-driven rules to candidates who might be unacceptable to most voters but secure in their control over a middle-sized fraction (20 to 30 percent, depending on how many play the game) of first-choice votes.

In this sense we can say that "participatory" democracy, as the American party system has begun to practice it, is inimical to "deliberative" democracy. As more and different people have won the right to participate in the nomination process by voting in primaries, the kinds of communications they have been able to send to one another have not correspondingly been enriched. They can vote, but they cannot bargain. They can make and listen to speeches, but they cannot deliberate.

Let us see what happens when a free spirit like George McGovern breaks through the network of old politicians and gets nominated for president, as happened in 1972. A piece of bad luck afflicts his campaign: his vice-presidential candidate, Thomas Eagleton, has concealed a medical history that may weaken the ticket. The *New York Times* writes, "Dump Eagleton." The *Washington Post* writes, "Dump Eagleton."

What does an "old politics" candidate do? Presumably he or she gets on the telephone and asks around among interest-group leaders and state and local party bosses: "Can we stand the flak?" "What do the party workers think?" "What do you think?"

What do "new politics" candidates do? Well, what choice have they? To whom can they place a telephone call other than the far-flung members of their immediate families? There is no negotiating with the editorial board of the *New York Times* in or out of a smoke-filled room. There is no give-and-take with the moderator of *Meet the Press*. The moderator gives. Politicians take. So also in the preprimary process, where bad news can drive candidates out of contention before their candidacies are even tested by primaries or caucus activity, as happened to Gary Hart in 1987, even though he was far and away the Democratic front-runner at the time.

We have no way of knowing whether the democratic paradox of participation swallowing up deliberation has had the net effect of turning citizens away from political parties. It is in any event true that by a variety of measures—nonvoting, propensity of voters to decline to identify with a political party, direct expressions of disapproval of parties—political parties, like so many other institutions of American society, have suffered substantial losses in public confidence. In our view, the most promising way for them to regain public confidence would be to avoid factional candidates and not only to nominate and elect good candidates but also to help them govern.

What is objectionable about policy government? What could be wrong with so intuitively attractive an idea? Governments must make policies. Candidates must be judged, in part at least, on their policy preferences, as well as on indications of their ability to perform when in office. Has there not been, in the recent past, too much obfuscation of issues and too little candor in speaking one's mind? Obviously our society needs more, rather than less, discussion of issues, and greater, rather than less, clarification of alternatives. The problem is that the premises on which policy government is based are false. Most people do not want parties that make extreme appeals by taking issue positions far from the desires of the bulk of the citizenry.[7] Perhaps people feel safer if their parties give them a choice, but they do not want losing to be a catastrophe. This may be why they see no great difficulty in voting for a president of one party and a Congress of another.[8]

Advocates of issue expression have so far managed to control no more than one presidential nominating convention at a time; but suppose they manage in the future to face off a right-wing Republican against a left-wing Democrat? The trends now perceived as products of consensus government—alienation, nonvoting—would, we conjecture, show an alarming increase if the vast majority of citizens discovered that their preferences had been disregarded and that they had nowhere to turn. Indeed, it may well be that the vastly increased participation of activists, by making campaigns distasteful to the majority, has led to the very decline in participation that they deplore.

It is one thing to say that policy options have been insufficiently articulated and quite another to create conflict and develop disagreements where these did not exist before. Political activists in the United States are more ideological and polarized than at any time since studies were first conducted in the 1930s, and possibly since the 1890s or even the Civil War. Should ordinary citizens be compelled to choose from policy alternatives that appeal to these activists, or are they entitled to select from a menu closer to their tastes? The question is not whether there will be issues, for inevitably there must be, but who will set the agenda for discussion and whether this agenda will primarily reflect differences in the population or among elites. Thus one objection to a party of advocacy is that it imposes on the great majority of people preferences to which the majority is largely indifferent or opposed.

The rationale behind parties of advocacy leads to plebiscitary democracy. If it is not only desirable for all citizens to vote in general elections but also for them to choose candidates through preelection primaries, it must be even more desirable for them to select governmental policies directly through referendums. Instead of rule by special interests or congressional cliques, the public's interest would supposedly be expressed by the public.

Experience with referendums in California, however, suggests that this is not quite how things work in practice. Without measures for limiting the number of referendums voters may face at a given election, citizens are swamped by the necessity of voting on dozens of items. Elites, not the people, determine the selection and wording of referendums. How they are worded is, of course, extremely important. Money—to arrange for the signatures on petitions to get referendums on the ballot—becomes more meaningful than ever. The public is faced with a bewildering array of proposals, all sponsored by special interests that want a way around the state legislature. To learn what is involved in a single seemingly innocuous proposal takes hours of study. To understand twenty or more per election is unduly onerous. Are citizens better off guessing or following the advice of the local newspaper instead of trying to choose a legislator or a party to represent their interests?

To take a famous case, were citizens or legislators better qualified to understand that Proposition 13 in California would not only keep property taxes down, which it was supposed to do, but would also, by depriving localities of resources, centralize control at the state level over many areas of public policy, which no one wanted? Were citizens of California, where referendums abound, wise to vote at widely separated intervals for so many mandatory expenditures as to make it difficult for the state legislature to mobilize resources to meet new needs?

A plebiscitary democracy, stressing the direct connection between candidates and voters, could not abide the electoral college. Only direct democracy, mass voting for candidates, would do. Abolishing the electoral college, however, as we have seen, would further decrease the need for forming diverse coalitions. Both the agents of consensus, mediating parties, and the fact of consensus, with political leaders who nurture it, would decline.

After a few decades of severe internal difficulty, when confidence in virtually all national institutions has suffered repeated blows, the need for consensus-building parties seems clear. Ideological parties might be desirable for a people homogeneous in all ways except the economic; but can a multiracial, multiethnic, multireligious, multiregional, multiclass nation such as the United States sustain itself when its main agents of political action—the parties—strive to exclude rather than include, to sharpen rather than dull the edge of controversy?

It is even doubtful that the rise of parties of advocacy leads to a more principled politics. If principles are precepts that must not be violated, when contrary principles are firmly embedded in the programs of opposing parties, one person's principles necessarily become another's fighting words. A few principles, such as those enshrined in the Bill of Rights, may be helpful in establishing boundaries beyond which governmental action may not go. Too many principles stymie the cooperative government required by the design of the Constitution. As being a Democrat increasingly requires adherence to litmus-tested liberal positions and a Republican to litmus-tested conservative positions, cross-cutting cleavages—people who support one another on some issues while opposing on others—will diminish. With officeholders opposing each other on more issues, and with more issues defined as moral issues, political passions are sure to rise. So, we suppose, will negative campaigning and popular disapproval of government and of politicians.

Compromise, of course, can also be a curse. If everything were bargainable, including basic liberties, no one would feel safe, and, indeed, no one would be. Similarly, if candidates cared everything about winning and nothing about how they win, if they were not restrained by internal norms or enforceable external expectations, elections would become outrages.

Parties without policies would be empty; parties fixated on only a narrow band of policies are dangerous. Without the desire to win elections, not at any cost but as a leading motive, politicians have no reason to pay attention to the people who vote. Winning requires a widespread appeal. Thus the desire to win leads to moderation, to appeals to diverse groups in the electorate, and to efforts to bring many varied interests together. This is why we prefer parties of intermediation to parties of advocacy. Parties of advocacy do not sustain themselves well in government. They fail to assist political leaders in mobilizing consent for the policies they adopt, and this widens the gap between campaign promises and the performance of government.

Because so many of the rules of presidential election politics are changing, we cannot say with a high degree of assurance how parties, candidates, and voters will adapt to the new incentives and disabilities that are continuously enacted into law. We are confident only in asserting that the adaptations they make will be of enormous consequence in determining the ultimate capacity of the American political system to sustain the fascinating and noble experiment in self-government begun on this continent more than two hundred years ago.

Notes

CHAPTER 1

1. See Bruce Cain, John Ferejohn, and Morris Fiorina, *The Personal Vote: Constituency Service and Electoral Independence* (Cambridge, Mass.: Harvard University Press, 1987), 13; Leon D. Epstein, *Political Parties in Western Democracies* (New York: Praeger, 1967), 43.
2. Richard Boyd's research suggests that heavy demands on U.S. voters may be depressing participation in any one election. In the Connecticut town he studied, he found that more people voted at some time during the year than voted in any given election: "A system that holds elections as frequently as we do in the United States must expect that even citizens who are attentive to politics and its obligations will not be at the polls every election. I would argue, then, that the frequency of elections in the United States is one explanation of the somewhat lower voting rate we experience in any given election compared to European countries." Boyd, "Decline of U.S. Voter Turnout: Structural Explanations," *American Politics Quarterly* 9 (April 1981): 133–59. Switzerland, the other low turnout democracy, also has frequent elections, and referendums; see David Butler and Austin Ranney, ed., *Referendums around the World: The Growing Use of Direct Democracy* (Washington, D.C.: The AEI Press, 1994). In *Running Scared: Why America's Politicians Campaign Too Much and Govern Too Little* (New York : Free Press, 1997), Anthony King argues that the U.S. pattern of frequent elections has important consequences for governing.
3. See Steven J. Rosenstone and John Mark Hansen, *Mobilization, Participation, and Democracy in America* (New York: Macmillan, 1993), 178–79.
4. Ibid., 146–50. Americans do least well on "trust in government" questions, but respond much more positively to questions of efficacy (rejecting such statements as "people like me have no say in what the government does") and to questions asking if a political party expresses their point of view.
5. Peverill Squire, Raymond E. Wolfinger, and David P. Glass, "Residential Mobility and Voter Turnout," *American Political Science Review* 81 (March 1987): 45–84.
6. U.S. Constitution, Art. I, sec. 2, says: "The House of Representatives shall be composed of members chosen every second year by the people of the several states and the electors in each state shall have the qualifications requisite for electors of the most numerous branch of the state legislature."
7. Paul E. Meehl, "The Selfish Voter Paradox and the Thrown-Away Vote Argument," *American Political Science Review* 71 (March 1971): 11–30.
8. The classic statement of this view is that of Anthony Downs, whose best effort is: "The advantage of voting per se is that it makes democracy possible. If no one votes, then the system collapses because no government is chosen. We assume that the citizens of a democracy subscribe to its principles and therefore derive benefits from its continuance; hence they do not want it to collapse. For this reason they attach value to the act of voting per se and receive a return from it." Downs, *An Economic Theory of Democracy*

(New York: Harper, 1957), 261–62. More recently, see John A. Ferejohn and Morris Fiorina, "The Paradox of Not Voting: A Decision Theoretic Analysis," *American Political Science Review* 68 (1974): 525–46; William H. Riker and Peter C. Ordeshook, "A Theory of the Calculus of Voting," *American Political Science Review* 62 (1968): 25–42. But see Raymond Wolfinger, "The Rational Citizen Faces Election Day," in *Elections at Home and Abroad*, ed. M. Kent Jennings and Thomas Mann (Ann Arbor: University of Michigan Press, 1994), 71–91. Wolfinger quotes Gary Jacobson: "It's the California model; people vote because it makes them feel good" (p. 84).

9. See Rosenstone and Hansen, *Mobilization, Participation, and Democracy,* 23, 156–58.

10. Still an excellent summary of the literature is Raymond E. Wolfinger and Steven J. Rosenstone, *Who Votes?* (New Haven: Yale University Press, 1980). See also Kay Lehman Schlozman, Sidney Verba, and Henry E. Brady, "Participation's Not a Paradox: The View from America's Activists," *British Journal of Political Science* 25 (January 1995): 1–36. This study asks American activists why they participate. The authors conclude: "In an era when surveys show Americans to be disillusioned about politics, distrustful of politicians, and impatient with the level of political debate, we might have expected that activists would either characterize their own political involvement in cynically self-interested terms or see themselves as spectators at an exciting, if sometimes foolish or dirty, sport. On the contrary, their retrospective interpretations of their activity are replete with mentions of civic motivations and a desire to influence policy. Of course, many participants also report selective material or social gratifications. Still, it is striking the extent to which references to doing one's share and making the community or nation a better place to live run as a thread through activists' reports of the concerns that animated their involvement and the number of participants who discuss nothing but civic motivations for their activity" (p. 32).

11. Wolfinger and Rosenstone, *Who Votes?,* 94–101.

12. This is one of the most venerable and most secure generalizations in the entire literature of voting behavior studies. See Angus Campbell, Philip E. Converse, Warren E. Miller, and Donald E. Stokes, *The American Voter* (New York: Wiley, 1960), 120–34. For variations on this interpretation, see Arthur S. Goldberg, "Social Determination and Rationality as a Basis of Party Identification," *American Political Science Review* 63 (1969): 5–25; Morris P. Fiorina, *Retrospective Voting in American Presidential Elections* (New Haven: Yale University Press, 1981), 89–90; Gregory B. Markus and Philip E. Converse, "A Dynamic Simultaneous Model of Electoral Choice," *American Political Science Review* 73 (1979): 1055–70; and Sven Holmberg, "Party Identification Compared across the Atlantic," in Jennings and Mann, Elections at Home and Abroad, 93–121. William H. Flanigan and Nancy H. Zingale, Political Behavior of the American Electorate, 8th ed. (Washington, D.C.: CQ Press, 1994), say, "party identification and retrospective evaluation appear to be … strongly related to vote choice— even when analysis is complicated (as in 1992) by a third candidate" (p. 189).

13. Flanigan and Zingale, *Political Behavior,* give findings on the timing of voters' decisions: "In all recent elections the independents and weak partisans were more likely to make up their minds during the campaign, while strong partisans characteristically made their decisions by the end of the conventions" (p. 162).

14. Earlier research did not differentiate among the various sorts of independents and characterized the entire population of independents as comparatively uninvolved in politics, less interested, less concerned, and less knowledgeable than party identifiers. These generalizations hold better for the truly nonpartisan subset of "pure independents," that is, people who do not "lean" toward one party or the other. See Campbell et al., *American Voter,* 143; Bernard Berelson, Paul F. Lazarsfeld, and William N. McPhee, *Voting* (Chicago: University of Chicago Press, 1954), 25–27; and Bruce E. Keith, David B. Magleby, Candice J. Nelson, Elizabeth Orr, Mark C. Westlye, and Raymond E. Wolfinger, *The Myth of the Independent Voter* (Berkeley: University of California Press, 1992), 65–67. For a somewhat different treatment, see Robert Agger, "Independents and Party Identifiers," in *American Voting Behavior,* ed. Eugene Burdick and Arthur J. Brodbeck (Glencoe, Ill.: Free Press, 1959), chap. 17.

15. Berelson, Lazarsfeld, and McPhee, *Voting,* 215–33. George Belknap and Angus Campbell state that "for many people Democratic or Republican attitudes regarding foreign policy result from conscious or unconscious adherence to a perceived party line rather than from influences independent of party identification." Belknap and Campbell, "Political Party Identification and Attitudes toward Foreign Policy," *Public Opinion Quarterly* 15 (Winter 1951–52): 623.

16. Many voting studies contain substantial discussions of this subject. See Robert E. Lane, "Fathers and Sons: Foundations of Political Belief," *American Sociological Review* 24 (August 1959): 502–11; Campbell et al., *American Voter,* 146–47; and H.H. Remmers, "Early Socialization of Attitudes," in Burdick and Brodbeck, *American Voting Behavior,* 55–67. V.O. Key, *Public Opinion and American Democracy* (New York: Knopf, 1961), 293–314, sums up in these words: "Children acquire early in life a feeling of party identification; they have sensitive antennae and since they are imitative animals, soon take on the political color of their family" (p. 294). See also Fred I. Greenstein, *Children and Politics* (New Haven: Yale University Press, 1965), chap. 4. In a later work, Paul R. Abramson presents an interesting discussion of this familial link and the forces that later play against it; see *Generational Change in American Politics* (Lexington, Mass.: Lexington Books, 1975), esp. chaps. 3 and 4.

17. "People are more likely to associate with people like themselves—alike in political complexion as well as social position." Berelson, Lazarsfeld, and McPhee, *Voting,* 83. See also Robert D. Putnam, "Political Attitudes and the Local Community," *American Political Science Review* 60 (September 1966): 640–54; and Ada W. Finifter, "The Friendship Group as a Protective Environment for Political Deviants," *American Political Science Review* 68 (June 1974): 607–26.

18. Paul Lazarsfeld, Bernard Berelson, and Hazel Gaudet, *The People's Choice* (New York: Duell, Sloan and Pearce, 1944), 16–28.

19. Ibid.; Angus Campbell and Homer C. Cooper, *Group Differences in Attitudes and Votes* (Ann Arbor: University of Michigan Press, 1956); Julian L. Woodward and Elmo Roper, "Political Activities of American Citizens," *American Political Science Review* 44 (December 1950): 872–75; Key, *Public Opinion and American Democracy,* 99–120, 121–81; Berelson, Lazarsfeld, and McPhee, Voting, 54–76; Robert Axelrod, "Where the Votes Come From: An Analysis of Electoral Coalitions, 1952–1968," *American Political Science Review* 66 (March 1972); idem, "Communication," *American Political Science Review* 68 (June 1974): 717–20; idem, "Communication," *American Political Science Review* 72 (June 1978): 622–24; and idem, "Communication," *American Political Science Review* 76 (June 1982): 393–96. See also Robert Axelrod, "Presidential Election Coalitions in 1984," *American Political Science Review* 80 (March 1986): 281–84. See table 3 in chap. 2.

20. V.O. Key Jr., *Southern Politics* (New York: Knopf, 1949), 25, 75–81, 223–28, 280–85. Indeed, conflict over secession was at the root of the formation of the state of West Virginia, which broke away from Virginia and was admitted as a separate state in 1863.

21. See Earl Black and Merle Black, *Politics and Society in the South* (Cambridge, Mass.: Harvard University Press, 1987); and Raymond Wolfinger and Michael Hagen, "Republican Prospects: Southern Comfort," *Public Opinion,* October/November 1985, 8–13.

22. See C. Vann Woodward, *The Strange Career of Jim Crow* (New York: Oxford University Press, 1966); and Woodward, *Origins of the New South* (Baton Rouge: Louisiana State University Press, 1951).

23. Nicholas Lemann says: "In 1940, 77 percent of black Americans still lived in the South—49 percent in the rural South. The invention of the cotton picker was crucial to the great migration by blacks from the Southern countryside to the cities of the South, the West, and the North. Between 1910 and 1970, six and a half million black Americans moved from the South to the North; five million of them moved after 1940, during the time of the mechanization of cotton farming....For blacks, the migration meant leaving what had always been their economic and social base in America and finding a new one." Lemann, *The Promised Land* (New York: Knopf, 1991), 6.

24. Campbell et al., *American Voter,* 160. See, more generally, James Q. Wilson, *Negro Politics* (Glencoe, Ill.: Free Press, 1960), and Nancy Weiss, *Farewell to the Party of Lincoln* (Princeton: Princeton University Press, 1983), esp. 209–35. Barry Goldwater's 1964 candidacy intensified the Democratic loyalties of black voters. For more recent data on the black vote, see Warren E. Miller and J. Merrill Shanks, *The New American Voter* (Cambridge, Mass.: Harvard University Press, 1996), 117–85.

25. George H. Mayer, *The Republican Party,* 1854–1966, 2d ed. (New York: Oxford University Press, 1967), 221–71.

26. Maria de los Angeles Torres says: "In the late 1800s, Cuban workers migrated to the United States in search of employment. Eventually they formed the backbone and the most radical element of the independence movement against Spain. Interestingly, Cuban tobacco workers also participated in the radical wing of the American Federation of Labor....

   "After 1959, Cubans migrated to the United States in great numbers. This time it was not workers, but rather the middle and upper classes.

   "After the revolution, the tradition of the progressive Cuban immigrant changed radically. Since those sectors most affected by the radical programs of the revolution supplied the initial post-revolutionary immigrations from Cuba, most tended to be politically conservative." Torres, "From Exiles to Minorities: The Politics of the Cuban Community in the United States," Ph.D. dissertation, University of Michigan, 1986, 7–8.

27. See David Hackett Fischer, *Albion's Seed* (New York: Oxford University Press, 1989), 17; Steven Erie, *Rainbow's End* (Berkeley: University of California Press, 1988), 25–28; Duane Lockard, *New England State Politics* (Princeton: Princeton University Press, 1959); Robert Dahl, *Who Governs?* (New Haven: Yale University Press, 1961), 33–51, 216–17; Elmer E. Cornwell, "Party Absorption of Ethnic Groups: The Case of Providence, R.I.," *Social Forces* 38 (March 1960): 205–10; J. Joseph Huthmacher, *Massachusetts People and Politics* (Cambridge, Mass.: Harvard University Press, 1959), 118–26.

28. Samuel Lubell, *The Future of American Politics* (New York: Harper, 1951), 129–57; Willi Paul Adams, *The German-Americans: An Ethnic Experience,* Translated and Adapted by LaVern J. Rippley and Eberhard Reichmann (New York: Max Kade German-American Center, 1993).

29. A notable study developing the implications of this notion is Downs's classic, *An Economic Theory of Democracy.*

30. William Lyons and John M. Scheb II, "Ideology and Candidate Evaluation in the 1984 and 1988 Presidential Elections," *Journal of Politics* 54 (May 1992): 573–84.

31. See Aaron Wildavsky, "Choosing Preferences by Constructing Institutions: A Cultural Theory of Preference Formation," *American Political Science Review* 81 (March 1987): 3–21; and Michael Thompson, Richard Ellis, and Aaron Wildavsky, *Cultural Theory* (Boulder, Colo.: Westview Press, 1990).

32. On Eisenhower, see Campbell et al., *American Voter,* 55–57, 525–28, and 537; and Herbert H. Hyman and Paul B. Sheatsley, "The Political Appeal of President Eisenhower," *Public Opinion Quarterly* 17 (Winter 1953): 443–60. On McGovern, see Arthur H. Miller, Warren E. Miller, Alden S. Raine, and Thad A. Brown, "A Majority Party in Disarray: Policy Polarization in the 1972 Election," *American Political Science Review* 70 (September 1976): 753–78; and Samuel L. Popkin, John W. Gorman, Charles Phillips, and Jeffrey A. Smith, "Comment: What Have You Done for Me Lately? Toward an Investment Theory of Voting," *American Political Science Review* 70 (June 1976): 779–805.

33. Martin P. Wattenberg, *The Rise of Candidate-Centered Politics* (Cambridge, Mass.: Harvard University Press, 1991), 45–65. See also Wattenberg, "The Reagan Polarization Phenomenon and the Continuing Downward Slide in Presidential Candidate Popularity," *American Politics Quarterly* 14 (July 1986): 219–45.

34. The portions of this analysis that deal with voters and issues are adapted from chap. 8, "Public Policy and Political Preference," in Campbell et al., *American Voter,* 168–87.

35. See Hazel Gaudet Erskine, "The Polls: The Informed Public," *Public Opinion Quarterly* 26 (Winter 1962): 669–77. This article summarizes questions asked from 1947 to 1960 of national samples of Americans in order to ascertain their information on current news topics. Similar data for 1935–46 are contained in Hadley Cantril and Mildred Strunk, *Public Opinion, 1935–46* (Princeton: Princeton University Press, 1951). In light of this and later work, Philip E. Converse was able to conclude: "Surely the most familiar fact to arise from sample surveys in all countries is that popular levels of information about public affairs are, from the point of view of the informed observer, astonishingly low." Converse, "Public Opinion and Voting Behavior," in *Handbook of Political Science*, ed. F.I. Greenstein and N.W. Polsby (Reading, Mass.: Addison-Wesley, 1975), 4:79.

36. The data on which this conclusion is based refer to issues in rather general categories such as "economic aid to foreign countries," the "influence of big business in government," and "aid to education" (Campbell et al., *American Voter*, 182). It is highly probable that the proportion of people meeting the requirements of having an opinion and differentiating among the parties would be substantially reduced if precise and specific policies within these general issue categories formed the basis of questions in a survey. See also Converse, "Public Opinion and Voting Behavior."

37. Campbell et al., in *American Voter*, tentatively conclude that in the Eisenhower years, covered by their study, "people who paid little attention to politics were contributing very disproportionately to partisan change" (p. 264). John Zaller, *The Nature and Origins of Mass Opinions* (New York: Cambridge University Press, 1992), confirms these findings. He shows that the greater the level of political awareness, the more likely people are to possess "cueing messages" that help them filter out information contrary to their existing viewpoint on a given issue. Thus greater awareness results in an increasing ratio of ideologically consistent to inconsistent considerations governing opinion formation. This means that more aware liberals, for example, are more likely to support liberal positions (pp. 100–1). The implications for partisan change are clear: political awareness leads to stability in issue preferences and discourages change. Political inattentiveness, conversely, leads to unstable issue preferences and is therefore more likely to lead to partisan change.

38. Philip E. Converse, "Information Flow and the Stability of Partisan Attitudes," *Public Opinion Quarterly* 26 (Winter 1962): 578–99. John Zaller says: "When people are exposed to two competing sets of electoral information, they are generally able to choose among them on the basis of their partisanship and values even when they do not score especially well on tests of political awareness. But when individuals are exposed to a one-sided communication flow, as in low-key House and Senate elections, their capacity for critical resistance appears quite limited.

    "The conclusion I draw from this is that the most important source of resistance to dominant campaigns ... is countervalent information carried within the overall stream of political information." Zaller, *Nature and Origins of Mass Opinions*, 252–53.

39. In the 1980 University of Michigan Center for Political Studies postelection survey, 35 percent of the respondents classified themselves as independents; of these respondents, only one-third did not further specify that they leaned either toward the Democratic or Republican Party. See Keith et al., *Myth of the Independent Voter*.

40. Sidney Verba, Richard A. Brody, Edwin B. Parker, Norman H. Nie, Nelson W. Polsby, Paul Eckman, and Gordon S. Black, "Public Opinion and the War in Vietnam," *American Political Science Review* 61 (June 1967): 317–33; and Richard A. Brody et al., "Vietnam, the Urban Crisis and the 1968 Presidential Election: A Preliminary Analysis," paper delivered at the meeting of the American Sociological Association, San Francisco, September 1969.

41. Arthur H. Miller et al., "A Majority Party in Disarray," 760. The issues studied include Vietnam withdrawal, amnesty for draft dodgers, reducing military spending, government health insurance, guaranteed standard of living, urban unrest, campus unrest, protecting the rights of those accused of crime, government aid to minorities, equal rights for women, abortion, legalization of marijuana, busing, and a "liberal-conservative philosophic position." For similar findings, see Jeane J. Kirkpatrick, "Representation in the American National Conventions: The Case of 1972," *British*

Journal of Political Science 5 (July 1975): 265–322; and Kirkpatrick, *The New Presidential Elite* (New York: Russell Sage Foundation, 1976).

42. See David W. Brady, *Critical Elections and Congressional Policy Making* (Stanford: Stanford University Press, 1988), 85–89.

43. Miller, Miller, Raine, and Brown, "Majority Party in Disarray," 761–72.

44. Gary C. Jacobson, *The Electoral Origins of Divided Government* (Boulder, Colo.: Westview Press, 1990), 125. For a detailed discussion of the relationship between presidential popularity and economic performance, see Richard A. Brody, *Assessing the President* (Stanford: Stanford University Press, 1991), 91–103; for 1992, see R. Michael Alvarez and Jonathan Nagler, "Economics, Issues and the Perot Candidacy: Voter Choice in the 1992 Presidential Election," *American Journal of Political Science* 39 (August 1995): 738–40.

45. Paul R. Abramson, John H. Aldrich, and David W. Rohde, *Change and Continuity in the 1992 Elections* (Washington, D.C.: CQ Press, 1994), 242–43.

46. Campbell et al., *American Voter*, 148.

47. V.O. Key Jr., with the assistance of Milton C. Cummings Jr., *The Responsible Electorate: Rationality in Presidential Voting, 1936–1960* (Cambridge, Mass.: Harvard University Press, 1966). This was the finding that led Key to his famous remark: "The perverse and unorthodox argument of this little book is that voters are not fools" (p. 7).

48. Charles H. Franklin, "Issue Preferences, Socialization and the Evaluation of Party Identification," *American Journal of Political Science* 28 (August 1984): 459–75.

49. Ibid., 474.

50. Morris Fiorina, *Retrospective Voting in American National Elections* (New Haven: Yale University Press, 1981), 84.

51. Donald R. Kinder and D. Roderick Kiewiet, "Sociotropic Politics: The American Case," *British Journal of Political Science* 11 (April 1981): 129–61; Douglas Rivers, "The Dynamics of Party Support in the American Electorate, 1952–1976," paper delivered at the annual meeting of the American Political Science Association, Washington, D.C., 28–31 August 1980.

52. Philip E. Converse, "The Nature of Belief Systems in Mass Publics," in *Ideology and Discontent*, ed. David E. Apter (New York: Free Press, 1964), 206–62; and Philip E. Converse and Gregory B. Markus, "Plus Ça Change: The New CPS Election Study Panel," *American Political Science Review* 73 (March 1979): 18–30. In view of the resistance to change of individual voters and the fact that nevertheless in aggregate there are changes, it is worth considering the idea that change occurs through processes by which old voters are replaced by new. This is strongly suggested for Canada by Richard Johnston in "Party Alignment and Realignment in Canada, 1911–1965," Ph.D. dissertation, Stanford University, 1976. V.O. Key also supported a mobilization-of-new-voters interpretation in "A Theory of Critical Elections," *Journal of Politics* 17 (February 1955): 3–18. Arthur S. Goldberg's study of American data finds that children tend to defect from the party identification of their parents when the parents' party identification is atypical for their status and the children are relatively well educated. See Goldberg, "Social Determinism and Rationality as Bases of Party Identification," *American Political Science Review* 63 (March 1969): 5–25. Kristi Andersen, *The Creation of a Democratic Majority 1928–1936* (Chicago: University of Chicago Press, 1979), 69, argues that "the surge in the Democratic vote in 1932 and 1936 came primarily from ... newly mobilized groups": those who came of political age in the 1920s but did not vote until 1928, 1932, or 1936, and those who came of age between 1928 and 1936. On the other side, see the intriguing arguments for opinion change by individual voters in Robert S. Erikson and Kent L. Tedin, "The 1928–1936 Partisan Realignment: The Case for the Conversion Hypothesis," *American Political Science Review* 75 (December 1981): 951–62.

53. Donald R. Kinder, "Enough Already About Ideology: The Many Bases of American Public Opinion," paper delivered at the annual meeting of the American Political Science Association, Denver, September 1982, 31–32.

54. Keith et al., *Myth of the Independent Voter*, 13.

55. Kinder reports that "between 1956 and 1976, Democratically inclined Independents voted 70 percent, on the average, for the Democratic candidate (compared to 64 percent among Weak Democrats), while Independent Republicans gave an average of 88 percent of their votes to the Republican nominee (compared to 85 percent among Weak Republicans)" (p. 27). Kinder, "Enough Already About Ideology," 23–27. See also Keith et al., *Myth of the Independent Voter,* 65–67. Partisan independents—leaners—vote their party preferences less frequently than strong party identifiers but more frequently than weak party identifiers, and pure independents do not vote very much at all. Party identification was considered strong in 1952 at a time when 23 percent of the voting public declared themselves to be independents: 10 percent leaning to the Democrats, 7 percent leaning to the Republicans, and 6 percent pure independents. By 1980 the proportion of self-styled independents had risen to 37 percent: 13 percent pure, 11 percent Democratic, and 13 percent Republican. It has remained more or less stable since: 39 percent in 1992 (12 percent pure, 14 percent Democratic, and 13 percent Republican). Thus, while the number of pure independents has doubled, they are still not a large fraction of the voting population. It is easy to overstate the political impact of the decline in party identifiers, in view of the fact that the increase among independents is divided between two-thirds hidden party supporters and one-third nonvoters. Kinder, "Enough Already About Ideology," 27–29; Keith et al., *Myth of the Independent Voter,* 47–51. We thank Raymond E. Wolfinger for supplying 1992 figures on independents.
56. Kinder, "Enough Already About Ideology," 29–31.
57. Nelson W. Polsby, *Consequences of Party Reform* (New York: Oxford University Press, 1983), 87; Raymond E. Wolfinger, "Dealignment, Realignment, and Mandates in the 1984 Election," in *The American Elections of 1984,* ed. Austin Ranney (Durham, N.C.: Duke University Press, 1985), 281; "Portrait of the Electorate," *New York Times,* 10 November 1996, 28.

CHAPTER 2

1. Some years ago, David R. Mayhew noticed this pattern of difference in the congressional parties. See Mayhew, *Party Loyalty among Congressmen: The Difference between Democrats and Republicans, 1947–1962* (Cambridge, Mass: Harvard University Press, 1966).
2. Nelson W. Polsby and William G. Mayer, "Ideological Cohesion in the American Two Party System," in *On Parties: Essays Honoring Austin Ranney*, ed. Nelson W. Polsby and Raymond Wolfinger (Berkeley: Institute of Governmental Studies Press, 1999).
3. Robert Axelrod, "Where the Votes Come From: An Analysis of Electoral Coalitions, 1952–1968," *American Political Science Review* 66 (March 1972); idem, "Communication," *American Political Science Review* 76 (June 1982): 394; idem, "Communication," *American Political Science Review* 72 (June 1974): 622–24; idem, "Communication," *American Political Science Review* 76 (June 1982): 393–96; and idem, "Presidential Election Coalitions in 1984," *American Political Science Review* 80 (March 1986): 281–84. We wish to thank Ben Highton for updating Axelrod's work for the 1988 and 1992 elections and Samantha Luks for updating Axelrod's work for the 1996 election, working from data supplied by the American National Election Studies, University of Michigan, Center for Political Studies, and the University of California, Berkeley, State Data Program.
4. Harold W. Stanley, William J. Bianco, and Richard G. Niemi, "Partisanship and Group Support over Time: A Multivariate Analysis," *American Political Science Review* 80 (September 1986): 969–76.
5. Raymond Wolfinger and Michael Hagen, "Republican Prospects: Southern Comfort," *Public Opinion* (October/November 1985): 8–13.
6. Raymond Wolfinger, "Dealignment, Realignment, and Mandates in the 1984 Election," in *The American Elections of 1984,* ed. Austin Ranney (Durham, N.C.: Duke University Press, 1985), 290.

7. Axelrod, "Communication," June 1982, 395; and idem, "Presidential Election Coalitions in 1984."
8. See Raymond A. Bauer, Ithiel de Sola Pool, and Lewis Anthony Dexter, *American Business and Public Policy* (New York: Atherton Press, 1963), 323–99, esp. 373. More recently, a similar argument is made in John R. Wright, "PACs, Contributions, and Roll Calls: An Organizational Perspective," *American Political Science Review* 79 (June 1985): 400–14.
9. Richard Berke, "Trade Vote Effect May Ebb over Time," *New York Times,* 23 November 1993, 23; R.W. Apple Jr., "Unions Faltering in Reprisals Against Trade Pact Backers," *New York Times,* 21 February 1994, 1.
10. "The 1994 Elections: Portrait of an Electorate: Who Voted for Whom in the House," *New York Times,* 13 November 1994, 24.
11. Aaron B. Wildavsky, "The Intelligent Citizen's Guide to the Abuses of Statistics: The Kennedy Document and the Catholic Vote," in *Politics and Social Life,* ed. Nelson W. Polsby, Robert Dentler, and Paul Smith (Boston: Houghton Mifflin, 1963), 825–44; and Philip E. Converse, Angus Campbell, Warren E. Miller, and Donald Stokes, "Stability and Change in 1960: A Reinstating Election," *American Political Science Review* 55 (June 1961): 269–80.
12. See Seymour M. Lipset, Paul F. Lazarsfeld, Allen H. Barton, and Juan Linz, "The Psychology of Voting: An Analysis of Political Behavior," in *Handbook of Social Psychology,* ed. Gardner Lindzey (Cambridge, Mass.: Addison-Wesley, 1954).
13. Angus Campbell, Philip E. Converse, Warren E. Miller, and Donald E. Stokes, *The American Voter* (New York: Wiley, 1960), 483–94.
14. CBS News/*New York Times* 1980 exit polls showed men voting 54 percent Reagan to 37 percent Carter and women 46 percent Reagan to 45 percent Carter. Everett Carll Ladd, "The Brittle Mandate: Electoral Dealignment and the 1980 Presidential Election," *Political Science Quarterly* 96 (Spring 1981): 16.
15. See Kathleen Frankovic, "Sex and Politics: New Alignments, Old Issues," *PS: Political Science and Politics* 15 (Summer 1982): 439–48; and "Women and Men: Is a Realignment Under Way?" *Public Opinion* 5 (April/May 1982): 21–32.
16. Adam Clymer, "Polls Show a Married-Single Gap in Last Election," *New York Times,* 6 January 1983.
17. Paul Abramson, John Aldrich, and David Rohde, *Change and Continuity in the 1988 Elections* (Washington, D.C.: CQ Press, 1990), 123–25.
18. Harold W. Stanley and Richard G. Niemi, *Vital Statistics on American Politics 1997–1998* (Washington, D.C.: CQ Press, 1998), 116–18; Peter A. Brown, "Gender Gap: Why Men and Women Vote Differently," *Arizona Republic,* 26 November 1994, A44.
19. See the data in Frankovic, "Sex and Politics."
20. Celinda C. Lake, "Guns, Butter and Equality: The Women's Vote in 1980," paper presented at the annual meeting of the Midwest Political Science Association, 28 April–1 May 1982.
21. Ethel Klein, "The Gender Gap: Different Issues, Different Answers," *Brookings Review* 3 (Winter 1985): 34.
22. Ibid., 37.
23. Indeed, some of the most vocal groups have no membership at all and exist only as lobbying organizations. Jeffrey M. Berry, *Lobbying for the People: The Political Behavior of Public Interest Groups* (Princeton: Princeton University Press, 1977), 186.
24. "Why Americans Are Mad: An Interview with Rush Limbaugh," *Policy Review* 61 (Summer 1992): 47; "Behind the Bestsellers," *Publishers Weekly,* 4 October 1993, 14; Joyce Howard Price, "Scandal Rushes Limbaugh Back into Radio's Top Spot," *Washington Times,* 27 September 1998, A3.
25. Joseph E. Cantor, "PACs: Political Financiers of the '80s," *Congressional Research Service Review* (February 1982): 14–16; Xandra Kayden and Eddie Mahe Jr., *The Party Goes On* (New York: Basic Books, 1985); and Stanley and Niemi, *Vital Statistics on American Politics 1997–1998,* 94.
26. "Corporate Political Action Committees Are Less Oriented to Republicans Than Expected," *Congressional Quarterly,* 8 April 1978, 849–54; and Theodore J. Eismeier

and Philip H. Pollock III, "PACs and the Campaign Environment," in *Business, Money and the Rise of Corporate PACs in American Politics* (New York: Quorum Books, 1988), 79–96.

27. Edwin M. Epstein, "Corporations and Labor Unions in Electoral Politics," *Annals of the American Academy of Political and Social Science* 425 (May 1976): 49.

28. Ibid., 50. For more on PACs, see William Crotty and Gary Jacobson, *American Parties in Decline* (Boston: Little, Brown, 1980), 100–155. An especially complete account is Edwin M. Epstein, "PACs and the Modern Political Process," paper delivered at the conference on "The Impact of the Modern Corporation," Columbia University, New York, 1982. See also Michael J. Malbin, ed., *Parties, Interest Groups, and Campaign Finance Laws* (Washington, D.C.: American Enterprise Institute, 1980); Elizabeth Drew, *Politics and Money* (New York: Macmillan, 1983); and Theodore Eismeier and Philip Pollock, "A Tale of Two Elections," paper delivered at the annual meeting of the Midwest Political Science Association, Chicago, 10–12 April 1986.

29. For example, see *Toward a More Responsible Two-Party System,* Report of the Committee on Political Parties, American Political Science Association, New York, 1950.

30. Frank J. Sorauf, *Money in American Elections* (Glenview, Ill.: Scott, Foresman, 1988), 72–80; Edwin M. Epstein, "Business and Labor Under the Federal Election Campaign Act of 1971," in Malbin, *Parties, Interest Groups, and Campaign Finance Laws,* 107–51.

31. Frank J. Sorauf, "Parties and Political Action Committees in American Politics," in *When Parties Fail,* ed. Kay Lawson and Peter Merkl (Princeton: Princeton University Press, 1988), 16.

32. There are, of course, numerous ways of gaining access to public officials, but participation in their original selection is the primary avenue of access used by political parties. Our interpretation of parties is based largely on E. Pendleton Herring, *The Politics of Democracy* (New York: Norton, 1940); V.O. Key Jr., *Politics, Parties, and Pressure Groups,* 4th ed. (New York: Crowell, 1958); David B. Truman, "Federalism and the Party System," in *Federalism: Mature and Emergent,* ed. Arthur MacMahon (New York: Doubleday, 1955), 115–36; Anthony Downs, *An Economic Theory of Democracy* (New York: Harper, 1957); and a burgeoning literature on state and local political party organizations. See especially David B. Truman, *The Governmental Process* (New York: Knopf, 1971), 262–87; Sarah McCally Morehouse, *State Politics, Parties, and Policy* (New York: Holt, Rinehart and Winston, 1981); and David R. Mayhew, *Placing Parties in American Politics* (Princeton: Princeton University Press, 1986).

33. See Gary Jacobson, *The Politics of Congressional Elections,* 3d ed. (New York: HarperCollins, 1992), 118–21; and Bruce E. Cain, John Ferejohn, and Morris Fiorina, *The Personal Vote* (Cambridge, Mass.: Harvard University Press, 1987).

34. See John F. Bibby, "Party Renewal in the National Republican Party," in *Party Renewal in America,* ed. Gerald M. Pomper (New York: Praeger, 1980), 102–15; and Cornelius P. Cotter and John F. Bibby, "Institutional Development of Parties and the Thesis of Party Decline," *Political Science Quarterly* 95 (Spring 1980): 127.

35. Stanley and Niemi, *Vital Statistics on American Politics 1997–1998,* 91; Anthony Corrado, "Financing the 1996 Elections," in Gerald M. Pomper et al, *The Election of 1996* (Chatham, N.J.: Chatham House, 1997), 145–55.

36. An acutely self-satiric evaluation of the purist mentality is contained in the following excerpt from Richard M. Koster's "Surprise Party," *Harper's,* March 1975, 31, on the Democratic Party conference of that year: "Alan Baron, the sharpest of the young pros, who had coached the liberals brilliantly on the Mikulski and charter commissions, decided that, whatever happened, the conference was a success: we might lose organized labor, but we'd brought in God."

37. Herbert McClosky, Paul J. Hoffman, and Rosemary O'Hara, "Issue Conflict and Consensus Among Party Leaders and Followers," *American Political Science Review* 54 (June 1960): 406–27. The authors compared large samples of Democratic and Republican leaders on twenty-four major public issues and conclude that "the belief that the two American parties are identical in principle and doctrine has little foundation in fact. Examination of the opinions of Democratic and Republican leaders show them to be distinct communities of co-believers who diverge sharply on many

important issues." They add, "little support was found for the belief that deep cleavages exist among the electorate but are ignored by the leaders. One might, indeed, more accurately assert the contrary, to wit: that the natural cleavages between the leaders are largely ignored by the voters" (pp. 425–26). They found in 1956 that on most issues, the Democratic Party elite held positions not only closer to the Democratic rank and file but also closer to the Republican rank and file than those of the Republican elite. While the party elites still differed significantly from each other in 1972, the tables had turned and the "Republican elite held views that were more representative of the views and values of rank and file Democrats than were the views of Democratic delegates." Jeane Kirkpatrick, "Representation in the American National Conventions: The Case of 1972," *British Journal of Political Science* 5 (July 1979): 265–322. Differences between the party elites have increased substantially since 1972; see Kent Jennings and Warren Miller, *Parties in Transition* (New York: Russell Sage Foundation, 1986).

38. Martin Schram, *Running for President, 1976: The Carter Campaign* (New York: Stein and Day, 1977), 92, 93, 114, 150.

39. John F. Bibby, Robert J. Huckshorn, James L. Gibson, and Cornelius P. Cotter, *Party Organization and American Politics* (New York: Praeger, 1984), 314.

40. The structure of American political parties is treated, among other places, in Key, *Politics, Parties and Pressure Groups*. The Supreme Court now gives the national convention the right to regulate standards for admission to it, even overriding enactments of state legislatures on the subject of primary elections, and in this important respect national standards can be imposed on state party organizations. See *Cousins v. Wigoda*, 419 U.S. 477 (1975) and *Democratic Party of the U.S. et al. v. LaFollette et al.*, 450 U.S. 107 (1981). See also Everett Carll Ladd Jr., with Charles D. Hadley, *Transformations of the American Party System* (New York: Norton, 1975); Austin Ranney, *Curing the Mischiefs of Faction: Party Reform in America* (Berkeley: University of California Press, 1975); William Crotty, *Party Reform* (New York: Longman, 1983); James Ceaser, *Reforming the Reforms* (Cambridge, Mass.: Ballinger, 1982); Gary D. Wekkin, *Democrat versus Democrat* (Columbia: University of Missouri Press, 1984); and Nelson W. Polsby, *Consequences of Party Reform* (New York: Oxford University Press, 1983).

41. If the federal government ends up subsidizing the national committees instead of individual candidates, the next phase of party reform could give the national parties much greater leverage.

42. For a good brief account, see Richard Cohen, "Party Help," *National Journal*, 16 August 1986, 1998–2004.

43. Paul S. Herrnson, "Do Parties Make a Difference? The Role of Party Organizations in Congressional Elections," *Journal of Politics* 48 (August 1986): 598.

44. See William S. Livingston, "A Note on the Nature of Federalism," *Political Science Quarterly* 67 (March 1952): 81–95.

45. This seems, more often than not, to be the case with third-party candidates. Seventy-four percent of presidential "third parties" have persisted long enough to contest only two elections and over half contest only one, suggesting that they are built around the easily exhausted presidential aspirations of individuals, rather than longer-term party-building activities. Figures taken from Steven J. Rosenstone, Roy Behr, and Edward Lazarus, *Third Parties in America* (Princeton: Princeton University Press, 1984), 19.

46. In *Timmons v. Twin Cities Area New Party* (117 S. Ct. 1364 (1997), the courts allowed states to prohibit third parties from choosing major party nominees as their own nominees. See Leon D. Epstein, "The American Party Primary," in *On Parties: Essays Honoring Austin Ranney*, ed. Nelson W. Polsby and Raymond E. Wolfinger (Berkeley: Institute of Governmental Studies Press, 1999), 66–67.

47. At least one study demonstrates that Perot took more votes from Bush than he did from Clinton; see R. Michael Alvarez and Jonathan Nagler, "Economics, Issues and the Perot Candidacy: Voter Choice in the 1992 Election," *American Journal of Political Science* 37 (August 1995): 737–38.

48. Robert G. Meadow, "Televised Campaign Debates as Whistle-Stop Speeches," in *Television Coverage of the 1980 Presidential Campaign,* ed. William C. Adams (Norwood, N.J.: Ablex, 1983), 91.

49. John Zaller, *Politics as Usual: Ross Perot and the Popularization of Politics* (Chicago: University of Chicago Press, forthcoming), 21.

50. Herbert F. Weisberg and David C. Kimball, "Attitudinal Correlates of the 1992 Presidential Vote," in *Democracy's Feast: Elections in America,* ed. Herbert F. Weisberg (Chatham, N.J.: Chatham House, 1995), 104.

51. Daniel Mazmanian has shown that third-party candidates do best in years in which there is an intensely conflictual issue on the political agenda, suggesting that focusing discontent and raising issues are, for these candidates, functions most profitably performed in unison. Mazmanian, *Third Parties in Presidential Elections* (Washington, D.C.: Brookings Institution, 1974), 28.

52. See Paul R. Abramson, John H. Aldrich, Phil Paolino, and David W. Rhode, "Third-Party and Independent Candidates: Wallace, Anderson, and Perot," *Political Science Quarterly* 110 (Fall 1995): 349–67.

CHAPTER 3

1. The unit rule is not prescribed in the Constitution or by federal law. Instead, it is the result of individual state action that provides, in all states except Maine and Nebraska, that electors for party nominees are grouped together and elected en bloc on a "general ticket" such that a vote for one elector is a vote for all the electors on that ticket, with the majority vote electing all electors for the state. Missouri Senator Thomas Hart Benton said in 1824: "The general ticket system...was the offspring of policy...It was adopted by the leading men [ten states] to enable them to consolidate the vote of the state..." Thomas Jefferson had earlier pointed out that "while ten states choose either by legislatures or by a general ticket it is folly for the other states not to do it." In short once a few states maximized their impact by using the unit rule, the others followed suit. See Motion for Leave to File Complaint, Complaint and Brief, *Delaware v. New York*, No. 28 Original, U.S. Supreme Court, October term, 1966; and Neal R. Peirce, "The Electoral College Goes to Court," *The Reporter*, 6 October 1966.

   In Maine and Nebraska the electoral vote of each congressional district (two in Maine and three in Nebraska) are determined by the vote within the district, and the two electoral votes that the states have by virtue of their senators are cast according to the overall vote in the state as a whole. Here is a summary of the Maine law, taken from *Nomination and Election of the President and Vice President of the United States Including the Manner of Selecting Delegates to National Political Conventions* (Washington, D.C.: Government Printing Office, 1980), 356: "Electors shall vote by separate ballot for one person for President and one person for Vice President. A presidential elector is elected from each congressional district and two at large. They shall convene in the Senate chamber in Augusta on the first Monday after the second Wednesday of December at 2:00 P.M. following their election. The presidential electors at large shall cast their ballots for President and Vice President of the political party which received the largest number of votes in the State. The presidential electors of each congressional district shall cast their ballots for the candidates for President and Vice President of the political party which received the largest number of votes in each congressional district."

2. Michael Barone and Grant Ujifusa with Richard E. Cohen, *The Almanac of American Politics* 1998 (Washington, D.C.: National Journal, 1997), 82, 140, 969.

3. Further confirmation of this view is provided by Steven J. Brams and Morton D. Davis, "The 3/2's Rule in Presidential Campaigning," *American Political Science Review* 68 (March 1974): 113–34; Claude S. Colatoni, Terrence J. Levesque, and Peter D. Ordeshook, "Campaign Resource Allocations Under the Electoral College," *American Political Science Review* 69 (March 1975): 141–52; and John A. Yunker and Lawrence D. Longley, "The Biases of the Electoral College; Who Is Really Advantaged?" in *Perspectives on Presidential Selection*, ed. Donald R. Matthews (Washington, D.C.: Brookings Institution, 1972), 172–203.

4. Martin Schram, *Running for President, 1976: The Carter Campaign* (New York: Stein and Day, 1977), 298.

5. Our discussion of money in elections owes a great deal to the work of Herbert Alexander who, over the years, has built up an unequaled store of knowledge on this subject. Important legislation affecting money in politics includes the Federal Election Campaign Act of 1971 and the Federal Election Campaign Act Amendments of 1974 (2 USC 431). For a wide-ranging set of materials on election reform up to and including the 1971 act, see *U.S. Senate Select Committee on Presidential Campaign Activities, Election Reform: Basic References* (Washington, D.C.: Government Printing Office, 1973). A compact summary of the state of the law as of 1975 is contained in *U.S. Senate Subcommittee on Privileges and Elections of the Committee on Rules and Administration, Federal Election Campaign Laws* (Washington, D.C.: Government Printing Office, 1975). For a useful discussion of the law's political implications, see the American Bar Association, *Symposium on Campaign Financing Regulation* (Chicago: ABA, 1975); and Jo Freeman, "Political Party Contributions and Expenditures Under the Federal Election Campaign Act: Anomalies and Unfinished Business," *Pace Law Review* 4 (Winter 1984): 267–96. Data about the 1980 election were supplied by Herbert Alexander from his *Financing the 1980 Election* (Lexington, Mass.: Lexington Books, 1983); 1984 data are from Herbert Alexander, *Financing the 1984 Election* (Lexington, Mass.: Lexington Books, 1987). Information for 1988 is from Herbert Alexander and Monica Bauer, *Financing the 1988 Election* (Boulder, Colo.: Westview Press, 1991); 1992 data are taken from the manuscript of Herbert Alexander and Anthony Corrado, *Financing the 1992 Election* (New York: M.E. Sharpe, 1995); 1996 data are from Anthony Corrado, "Financing the 1996 Elections" in Gerald M. Pomper, ed., *The Election of 1996: Reports and Interpretations* (Chatham, N.J: Chatham House, 1997) and from Herbert Alexander, "Financing the 1996 Election" in Regina Dougherty, ed., *America at the Polls 1996* (Storrs, Conn: Roper Center for Public Opinion Research, 1997).

6. For 1960 figures, see Herbert Alexander, *Financing the 1960 Election* (Princeton, N.J.: Citizens Research Foundation, 1962), 10. Figures for 1964 are contained in Herbert E. Alexander and Harold B. Meyers, "The Switch in Campaign Giving," *Fortune,* November 1965, 103–8. Figures for 1968 are contained in Herbert Alexander, "Financing Parties and Campaigns in 1968: A Preliminary Report," Citizens Research Foundation, Princeton, N.J., 1969; mimeographed. Figures for 1972, 1976, and 1980 are contained in Alexander, *Financing the 1980 Election,* 110, table 4-6; 1984 figures are from Alexander, *Financing the 1984 Election,* 81. Figures for 1988 are from Alexander and Bauer, *Financing the 1988 Election,* 3. Figures are not available for 1992. Figures for 1996 are from Corrado, "Financing the 1996 Elections," 151.

7. Alexander Heard, *The Costs of Democracy* (Chapel Hill: University of North Carolina Press, 1960), 7–8; Herbert E. Alexander, "Financing the Parties and Campaigns," in *The Presidential Election and Transition, 1960–61,* ed. Paul T. David (Washington, D.C.: Brookings Institution, 1961), 116–18; Alexander and Meyers, "Switch in Campaign Giving"; Alexander, "Financing Parties and Campaigns in 1968," 2; Herbert Alexander, *Financing the 1972 Election* (Lexington, Mass.: Lexington Books, 1976), 77–78; Herbert Alexander, *Financing the 1976 Election* (Washington, D.C.: CQ Press, 1979), 166; Alexander, *Financing the 1980 Election,* 103; Alexander, *Financing the 1984 Election,* 82; Alexander and Bauer, *Financing the 1988 Election,* 7; Alexander and Corrado, *Financing the 1992 Election,* 12; Alexander, "Financing the 1996 Election," 142.

8. Frank J. Sorauf, *Money in American Politics* (Glenview, Ill.: Scott, Foresman, 1988), 192.

9. Ibid., 191.

10. Federal Election Commission data in Corrado, "Financing the 1996 Elections," 139.

11. Alexander, *Financing the 1992 Election,* 191.

12. Changes to the primary and caucus timetable, whereby many states have moved their delegate-selection procedures forward, have increased the importance of early money. Because of the shortened primary season, candidates can no longer plan to rely on early

victories to boost fund raising, since there will be insufficient time in between primaries to campaign and raise funds. This poses a special problem for candidates of the party without an incumbent president seeking reelection. In 1996 most Republicans supposed that candidates needed to amass at least $20 million by the start of the season in order to be even barely credible. James A. Barnes, "A Doozy of a First Step for Candidates," *National Journal*, 18 February 1995, 431. For 2000, Republicans estimated $22 million would be needed. Jill Abramson, "Unregulated Cash Flows into Hands of P.A.C.'s for 2000," *New York Times*, 29 November 1998, A1.

13. Alexander and Corrado, *Financing the 1992 Election*, 89.
14. For political operatives such as these, according to Robert Farmer, one of their Democratic counterparts, "the issue is simply this: Is this guy going to win?" What do they want if their guy should win? "A lot of them want to change their first name to 'Ambassador' or 'Secretary.' A lot of them want the candidate's attention. A lot of them would like to sleep in the Lincoln bedroom, or be on the board of the Kennedy Center, or go to a state dinner at the White House, or ride on Air Force One. Some of them want to be appointed to Federal positions in their state. Some of them just want to know the candidates on a first name basis." Sorauf, *Money in American Politics*, 195.
15. Alison Mitchell, "Building a Bulging War Chest: How Clinton Financed His Run," *New York Times*, 27 December 1996, A12.
16. Alexander and Corrado, *Financing the 1992 Election*, 44–46.
17. Ibid., 54.
18. Leslie Wayne, "Hunting Cash, Candidates Follow the Bright Lights," *New York Times*, 20 October 1996, E5.
19. Patrick Anderson, *Electing Jimmy Carter* (Baton Rouge: Louisiana State University Press, 1994), 89.
20. Ibid., 41–42, 62–63, 74, 80. A detailed historical account of the relationship between Hollywood and Washington is given by Ronald Brownstein in *The Power and the Glitter* (New York: Pantheon, 1990).
21. Sorauf, *Money in American Politics*, 128–30.
22. Alexander and Bauer, *Financing the 1988 Election*, 22.
23. Alexander and Corrado, *Financing the 1992 Election*, 99–100.
24. Ibid., 71.
25. Ibid., 81–86.
26. For a more detailed description, see the FEC website, "Citizens Guide to Contributions and the Law," www.fec.gov/pages/citnlist.htm.
27. Corrado, *Creative Campaigning: PAC's and the Presidential Selection Process* (Boulder, Colo.: Westview Press, 1992), 35. For example, while the consumer price index increased by 40 percent between 1976 and 1980, direct-mail costs increased by 50 percent, television time by 100 percent, and air fares by 300 percent over the same period.
28. Ibid., 35.
29. Evan Thomas and Peter Goldman, "Victory March: The Inside Story," *Newsweek Special Election Issue*, 18 November 1996, 66–72, 80–82; Corrado, "Financing the 1996 Elections," 146–50.
30. Ibid., 36–39. Alexander and Bauer point out that if the state limits were aggregated, the resulting total would be almost three times the national spending limit (Alexander and Bauer, *Financing the 1992 Election*, 18). Thus the national limit serves also to restrict the number of states in which a candidate can spend close to the state limit.
31. Sorauf, *Money in American Politics*, 201.
32. Alexander and Bauer, *Financing the 1988 Election*, 18. The FEC has since tried to remove some of the need for subterfuge by ruling that certain kinds of expenditures do not apply to the state limits, for example, placing fees for advertisements, salaries of staff while they are in the state, and their travel expenses. Alexander and Corrado, *Financing the 1992 Elections*, 26.
33. For a full discussion of the regulatory history of this loophole, see Corrado, *Creative Campaigning*, 43–70. FEC rulings on precandidacy PACs have upheld rather

than struck down their activities, despite the fact that they seem to undermine much of the logic of the FECA.

34. Democrats Bruce Babbitt, Richard Gephardt, Joseph Biden, and Paul Simon; and Republicans George Bush, Robert Dole, Jack Kemp, Alexander Haig, and Pat Robertson. Ibid., 74.
35. Alexander and Corrado, *Financing the 1992 Election,* 19–23.
36. Abramson, "Unregulated Cash Flows into Hands of P.A.C.'s for 2000."
37. Ibid., 69. See also Charles T. Royer, ed., *Campaign for President: The Managers Look at '92* (Hollis, N.H.: Hollis Publishing Company, 1994), 83–84.
38. Alexander and Corrado, *Financing the 1992 Election,* 57.
39. Corrado, "Financing the 1996 Elections," 144–45.
40. Ibid., 150.
41. Sorauf, *Money in American Politics,* 211.
42. Corrado, "Financing the 1996 Elections," 145–50.
43. Alexander and Corrado, *Financing the 1992 Election,* 144.
44. Corrado, "Financing the 1996 Elections," 151–55.
45. Ibid., 144–46.
46. See Edwin M. Epstein, "Corporations and Labor Unions in Electoral Politics," *Annals of the American Academy of Political and Social Science* 425 (May 1976): 33–58.
47. Heard, *Costs of Democracy,* 18–22, 39; Alexander, "Financing Parties and Campaigns," 118; Alexander and Meyers, "Switch in Campaign Giving"; Alexander, *Financing the 1972 Elections.*
48. Alexander and Meyers, "Switch in Campaign Giving."
49. Alexander, *Financing the 1972 Election.*
50. Alexander and Bauer, *Financing the 1988 Election,* 73; see table accompanying note 43.
51. For expenditure figures, see ibid., 17–24, and for 1956 on, see Alexander, *Financing the 1976 Election.*
52. Alexander, "Financing Parties and Campaigns," 119.
53. Alexander, *Financing the 1972 Election,* 98; and Alexander, *Financing the 1976 Election,* 169.
54. Alexander, *Financing the 1976 Election,* 246; Alexander, *Financing the 1980 Election; FEC Reports on Financial Activities 1979–1980,* Final Report, Presidential Pre-nomination Campaign (Washington, D.C.: Government Printing Office, October 1981).
55. Alexander, *Financing the 1984 Election,* 149, table 4-2.
56. Alexander and Bauer, *Financing the 1988 Election,* 37–38.
57. Ibid., 34; Bruce Babbitt's 1988 attempts to cope with the high-tech requirements of a modern campaign without front-runner money are described in Maxwell Glen, "Running on a Shoestring," *National Journal,* 25 April 1988, 998–1002.
58. Michael J. Robinson, "Where's the Beef? Media and Media Elites in 1984," in *The American Elections of 1984,* ed. Austin Ranney (Durham, N.C.: Duke University Press, 1985), 173–77.
59. Ibid., 175.
60. Schram, *Running for President,* 55.
61. Ibid., 16.
62. Jack Kemp, for example, on withdrawing from the race, said of the nomination campaign, "There are a lot of grotesqueries, not the least of which is the fund-raising side of it. I have no passion for that." Similarly, Bill Bennett declared, "I sat down and looked at reality. How am I going to raise enough money to win in the New York media market?" Richard L. Berke, "To Campaign (v): to Beg, to Borrow, to Endure," *New York Times,* 5 February 1995, sec. 4, 1. Phil Gramm, by contrast, was a candidate who seemed actually to enjoy raising money. Gramm boasted of spending two hours each day asking for money on the telephone. "I don't have trouble asking people for support," says Gramm, "I believe in what I am doing." John Harwood, "Cash Machine: Candidate Gramm Rarely Skips a Chance to Raise More Money," *Wall Street Journal,* 17 February 1995, 7.

63. Alexander and Bauer, *Financing the 1988 Election*, 37–40.

64. For the details on the Forbes campaign, see Corrado, "Financing the 1996 Elections," 143–45; and William G. Mayer, "The Presidential Nominations," also in Gerald M. Pomper et al., *The Elections of 1996: Reports and Interpretations* (Chatham, N.J.: Chatham House, 1997), 36–56.

65. Mayer, "The Presidential Nominations," 55.

66. Thomas and Goldman, "Victory March: The Inside Story," 64.

67. *1972 Congressional Campaign Finances*, 10 vols. (Washington, D.C.: Government Printing Office, 1973).

68. *Buckley et al. v. Valeo et al.*, 424 U.S. I (1976). See also Daniel D. Polsby, "*Buckley v. Valeo:* The Special Nature of Political Speech," *Supreme Court Review*, 1976, 1–43.

69. Howard R. Penniman, "U.S. Elections: Really a Bargain?" *Public Opinion* 7 (June/July 1984), 51–53; see also Herbert Alexander, "Do the Presidential Candidates Need Even More Funds?" *San Diego Union*, 9 October 1988, C4. For an analysis of media biases in reporting on PACs and campaign spending, see Frank J. Sorauf, "Campaign Money and the Press: Three Soundings," *Political Science Quarterly* 102 (Spring 1987): 25–42.

70. In a *per curiam* opinion, the Court wrote: "The ceiling on personal expenditures, like the limitations on independent expenditures…, imposes a substantial restraint on the ability of persons to engage in protected First Amendment expression. The candidate, no less than any other person, has a First Amendment right to engage in the discussion of public issues and vigorously and tirelessly to advocate his own election and the election of other candidates. Indeed, it is of particular importance that candidates have unfettered opportunity to make their views known so that the electorate may intelligently evaluate the candidates' personal qualities and their positions on vital public issues before choosing among them on election day….Section 608(a)'s ceiling on personal expenditures by a candidate in furtherance of his own candidacy thus clearly and directly interferes with constitutionally protected freedoms." *Buckley* v. *Valeo* 424 U.S. I (1976), 53.

71. Bill Keller and Irwin B. Arieff, "Special Report: Washington Fund Raisers," *Congressional Quarterly*, 17 May 1980, 1335.

72. In October 1968, for example, multimillionaire Stewart Mott offered to raise a million dollars for Hubert Humphrey, then in desperate need of cash. Mott "made it clear that the Presidential candidate would have to modify his views on Vietnam." Humphrey refused Mott's offer. Herbert Alexander and H.B. Meyers, "A Financial Landslide for the GOP," *Fortune*, March 1970, 187.

73. Quoted in Jasper B. Shannon, *Money and Politics* (New York: Random House, 1959), 35.

74. See Mark V. Nadel, *Corporations and Political Accountability* (Lexington, Mass.: Heath, 1976), 27–28, 32, on American Airlines' sense of being a victim of virtual extortion by the Nixon campaign.

75. The provision of the Communications Act that focuses the attention of broadcasters so efficiently is section 315, which says, in part: "If any licensee shall permit any person who is a legally qualified candidate for any public office to use a broadcasting station, he shall afford equal opportunities to all other such candidates for that office in the use of such broadcasting station" (U.S. Code Annotated Title 47, sec. 315). Broadcast television stations have few programs of news commentary and these are not usually overtly partisan. (To be sure, the wealthier party may buy more television time for its candidate, but we have already discussed the limitations of this resource.) Cable television and radio news commentary is more ubiquitous, and lately more right-wing, but only those who initially agree with the more highly opinionated commentators are likely to tune in regularly. Consider, however, the impact of television coverage of the 1968 convention in Chicago. Two incidents will suffice to give a sense of the options open to television news directors under special circumstances:

> [San Francisco Mayor Joseph] Alioto rose on screen to nominate [Humphrey]; back and forth the cameras swung from Alioto to pudgy, cigar-smoking politicians, to Daley, with his undershot, angry jaw, painting

visually without words the nomination of the Warrior of Joy as a puppet of the old machines.

Carl Stokes, the black mayor of Cleveland, was next—to second Humphrey's nomination—and then, at 9:55, NBC's film of the bloodshed had finally been edited, and Stokes was wiped from the nation's vision to show the violence in living color.

The Humphrey staff was furious—Stokes is their signature on the Humphrey civil-rights commitment; and Stokes's dark face is being wiped from the nations' view to show blood—Hubert Humphrey being nominated in a sea of blood. (Theodore H. White, *The Making of the President, 1968* [New York: Atheneum, 1969], 300–302).

On the evening of 28 August 1968, according to Richard Pride and Barbara Richards, "NBC showed the same violent event, which lasted less than five minutes, from three different camera angles with three separate reporters and led viewers to believe it was one continuous battle lasting several hours." Pride and Richards, "Denigration of Authority? Television News Coverage of the Student Movement," *Journal of Politics* 36 (August 1974): 640.

76. See Nathan B. Blumberg, *One-Party Press? Coverage of the 1952 Presidential Campaign in 35 Daily Newspapers* (Lincoln: University of Nebraska Press, 1954); Edwin Emery and Henry L. Smith, *The Press and America* (Englewood Cliffs, N.J.: Prentice Hall, 1954), 714ff.; Arthur Edward Rowse, *Slanted News: A Case Study of the Nixon and Stevenson Fund Stories* (Boston: Beacon Press, 1975); George Garneau, "Clinton's the Choice," *Editor and Publisher* 125 (24 October 1992), 9; and Dorothy Giobbe, "Dole Wins...in Endorsements," *Editor and Publisher* 129 (26 October 1996), 7. Garneau says: "Since 1940, newspapers have endorsed Republicans by overwhelming margins—except when Johnson edged Goldwater, 440 endorsements to 359. A larger proportion of newspapers than ever before—66.7%—have not endorsed a candidate....In 1988, 62.8% of papers had not endorsed."

77. The classic formulation by A.J. Liebling is: "With the years, the quantity of news in newspaper is bound to diminish from its present low. The proprietor, as Chairman of the Board, will increasingly often say that he would like to spend 75 cents now and then on news coverage, but that he must be fair to his shareholders." Liebling, *The Press* (New York: Ballantine Books, 1961), 5. Occasionally, there is evidence of an improvement in the news coverage in some communities when the papers have been taken over by the more responsible chains. Cases in point include Philadelphia and San Jose, where the Knight-Ridder chain upgraded newspapers they purchased.

78. Bernard C. Cohen, *The Press and Foreign Policy* (Princeton: Princeton University Press, 1963), presents figures from a variety of sources on foreign affairs news (chap. 4). His conclusion: "The volume of coverage is low." See also Elie Abel, ed., *What's News: The Media in American Society* (San Francisco: Institute for Contemporary Studies, 1981).

79. Here is an example, atypical but illuminating, of this aimlessness at work. Former House Speaker Joseph Martin in his memoirs describes the appearance of an editorial mildly critical of presidential candidate Thomas E. Dewey in Martin's own newspaper (Martin was nominally editor and publisher) on the day of Dewey's arrival in Martin's hometown during the 1948 campaign. "Behind all this fuss was a very simple explanation. Having a small staff, the *Evening Chronicle* bought 'boilerplate' editorials prepared by a syndicate. The day of Dewey's visit, the editorial in question happened to be on the top of the pile, and a man in the composing room slapped it into the paper. Ironically, I never read the editorial until it was well on its way to fame." Joseph W. Martin Jr., *My First Fifty Years in Politics,* as told to Robert J. Donovan (New York: McGraw-Hill, 1960), 196–97.

80. This issue is carefully studied and evaluated by Edwin Bayley, *Joe McCarthy and the Press* (Madison: University of Wisconsin Press, 1981). See also Richard Rovere, *Senator Joe McCarthy* (New York: Harcourt, Brace, 1959), 137, 162–69.

81. See Frank Luther Mott, *The News in America* (Cambridge: Harvard University Press, 1952), 110; and Emery and Smith, *The Press and America*, 541ff.

82. See William L. Rivers, "The Correspondents after 25 Years," *Columbia Journalism Review* 1 (Spring 1962). On p. 5 he says, "In 1960, 57 percent of the daily newspapers reporting to the *Editor and Publisher* poll supported Nixon, and 16 percent supported Kennedy. In contrast, there are more than three times as many Democrats as there are Republicans among the Washington newspaper correspondents; slightly more than 32 percent are Democrats, and fewer than 10 percent are Republicans."

83. Michael J. Robinson, "Just How Liberal Is the News? 1980 Revisited," *Public Opinion*, February/March 1983, 55–60.

84. For a definitive, though fictitious, commentary, see Nathanael West, *Miss Lonelyhearts* (New York: Harcourt, Brace, 1933).

85. See Richard Brody and Catherine R. Shapiro, "A Reconsideration of the Rally Phenomenon in Public Opinion," in *Political Behavior Annual,* ed. Samuel Long, vol. 2 (Boulder, Colo.: Westview Press, 1989). See also John E. Mueller, "Presidential Popularity from Truman to Johnson," *American Political Science Review* 64 (March 1970): 18–34; and Kenneth N. Waltz, "Electoral Punishment and Foreign Policy Crises," in *Domestic Sources of Foreign Policy,* ed. James N. Rosenau (New York: Free Press, 1967), 263–93.

86. Amos Tversky and Daniel Kahneman, "Rational Choice and the Framing of Decisions," *Journal of Business* 59 (1986): S251–78.

87. Aaron Wildavsky and Karl Dake, "Theories of Risk Perception: Who Fears What and Why," *Daedalus* 119 (Fall 1990): 41–60.

88. John R. Zaller, *The Nature and Origins of Mass Opinion* (New York: Cambridge University Press, 1992), 6–16. Zaller's main work in this area remains unpublished: "The Role of Elites in Shaping Public Opinion," Ph.D. dissertation, University of California, Berkeley, 1984.

89. Shanto Iyengar and Donald R. Kinder, *News That Matters* (Chicago: University of Chicago Press, 1986); Stephen Ansolabehere and Shanto Iyengar, *Going Negative: How Attack Ads Shrink and Polarize the Electorate* (New York: Free Press, 1995).

90. See Theodore H. White, *The Making of the President, 1960* (New York: Atheneum, 1965), 333–38. Corroborative testimony is given by Benjamin C. Bradlee, *Conversations with Kennedy* (New York: Norton, 1975). On Barry Goldwater's press relations, see Charles Mohr, "Requiem for a Lightweight," *Esquire*, August 1968, 67–71, 121–22.

91. Jules Witcover, *The Resurrection of Richard Nixon* (New York: Putnam, 1970), 173; see also 188–92.

92. Timothy Crouse, *The Boys on the Bus* (New York: Random House, 1973), 189–90; Theodore H. White, *The Making of the President, 1972* (New York: Atheneum, 1973), 251–68; Witcover, *Resurrection of Richard Nixon;* and Joe McGinniss, *The Selling of the President, 1968* (New York: Trident Press, 1969).

93. Robinson, "Where's the Beef?" Unfavorable reporting may still diminish a candidate's support from the higher levels it otherwise might achieve. See Michael J. Robinson, "News Media Myths and Realities: What the Network News Didn't Do in the 1984 General Election," in *Elections in America*, ed. Kay Lehman Schlozman (Boston: Allen and Unwin, 1987), 143–77.

94. Elmo Roper observed that "on the civil rights issue [in 1948], Mr. Dewey draws the support of voters favoring exactly opposite things, and more than that, each side thinks Dewey agrees with them." Hugh A. Bone, *American Politics and the Party System* (New York: McGraw-Hill, 1955), 477. In 1968 the bulk of those voting for Eugene McCarthy in the New Hampshire primary were not Vietnam "doves," as McCarthy was, but were even more belligerent about the war than Lyndon Johnson. See Philip E. Converse, "Public Opinion and Voting Behavior," in *Handbook of Political Science,* ed. F.I. Greenstein and N.W. Polsby (Reading, Mass.: Addison-Wesley, 1975), 4:81.

95. When asked by the Gallup poll in 1979 to gauge how much confidence they had in newspapers, among other institutions, 51 percent of the respondents said "a great deal or quite a lot," 47 percent said "some or very little," 1 percent said "none," and

1 percent had no opinion. *The Gallup Poll: Public Opinion 1979* (Wilmington, Del.: Scholarly Resources, 1980), 159. In 1980 only 42 percent said "a great deal or quite a lot." *The Gallup Poll: Public Opinion 1980* (Wilmington, Del.: Scholarly Resources, 1981), 247. By 1986, the number of respondents saying "a great deal or quite a lot" had shrunk to 37 percent. Since then, reported confidence has remained fairly steady, falling as low as 29 percent in 1994 and rising as high as 39 percent in 1990. It stood at 35 percent in 1997. Frank Newport, "Small Business and Military Generate Most Confidence in Americans," *The Galllup Poll Monthly* no. 383 (August 1997), 21–24.

96. This paragraph summarizes the major findings of researchers on what has come to be called the "two-step flow" of information. See Elihu Katz and Paul F. Lazarsfeld, *Personal Influence* (Glencoe, Ill.: Free Press, 1955).

97. V. O. Key Jr., *Public Opinion and American Democracy* (New York: Knopf, 1961).

98. Preponderant academic opinion argues that the media have little effect on candidate and issue preferences. See Benjamin I. Page, Robert Y. Shapiro, and Glenn R. Dempsey, "What Moves Public Opinion?" *American Political Science Review* 81 (March 1987): 23–44, and Zaller, *The Nature and Origins of Mass Opinion.*

99. David W. Moore, "The *Manchester Union Leader* in the New Hampshire Primary," in *Media and Momentum,* ed. Gary R. Orren and Nelson W. Polsby (Chatham, N.J.: Chatham House, 1987), 104–26.

100. Research documents the growing preference for television over newspapers as a primary source of news from the early days of television until it became the dominent source. Asked their usual source of news about what's going on in the world, 51 percent of those polled in 1959 said television, 57 percent said newspapers, and 34 percent said radio. By 1978, of those polled, 67 percent said television, 49 percent said newspapers, and 20 percent said radio. See *Public Opinion* 2 (August/September, 1979): 30. Since 1978, television has continued a gradual climb, at the expense of newspapers and radio; see Karlyn Bowman, "The Reach of Television," *The American Enterprise* (September/October 1997), 92.

101. Examples would be instances where candidates are not known to voters before the campaign or where they run without benefit of party labels, as in local nonpartisan elections. See Charles R. Adrian, "Some General Characteristics of Nonpartisan Elections," *American Political Science Review* 46 (September 1952): 766–76; Charles E. Gilbert and Christopher Clague, "Electoral Competition and Electoral Systems in Large Cities," *Journal of Politics* 24 (May 1962): 323–49, esp. 344; and Raymond E. Wolfinger and Fred I. Greenstein, "The Repeal of Fair Housing in California: An Analysis of Referendum Voting," *American Political Science Review* 62 (September 1968): 753–69.

102. Robert S. Erikson, "The Impact of Newspaper Endorsements in Presidential Elections: The Case of 1964" *American Journal of Political Science* 20 (May, 1976): 207–33.

103. Angus Campbell, Philip E. Converse, Warren E. Miller, and Donald E. Stokes, *The American Voter* (New York: Wiley, 1960), 58, 530.

104. See Nelson W. Polsby, "The Iowa Caucuses in a Front-Loaded System: A Few Historical Lessons" in *The Iowa Caucuses and the Presidential Nominating Process,* ed. Peverill Squire (Boulder, Colo.: Westview Press, 1989), 149–62.

105. C. Anthony Broh, "Horse Race Journalism," *Public Opinion Quarterly* 44 (Winter 1980): 514–29.

106. Gary R. Orren, "The Nominating Process," in Ranney, *American Elections of 1984,* 53–54; for an analysis of network news and the 1984 campaign, see Allan R. Gutkin, "Network Coverage of the 1984 Campaign: From Iowa to New Hampshire," unpublished paper, Stanford University, 1984.

107. See Richard L. Rubin, *Press, Party and Presidency* (New York: Norton, 1981), 191–96. "Not only was [television journalists'] affirmation of primaries clear from the vastly disproportionate air time given primaries compared to other selection methods, but also numerous phrases attributing inherent democratic values to primaries appeared, sprinkled liberally throughout network news" (p. 193).

108. Nelson W. Polsby, *Consequences of Party Reform* (New York: Oxford University Press, 1983).

109. For an early discussion of this phenomenon, see Stanley Kelley, *Professional Public Relations and Political Power* (Baltimore: Johns Hopkins University Press, 1956). See also Larry J. Sabato, *The Rise of Political Consultants: New Ways of Winning Elections* (New York: Basic Books, 1981); Jonathan Bernstein, "The *New* New Presidential Elite," in *In Pursuit of the White House 2000*, ed. William G. Mayer (Chatham, N.J.: Chatham House, 1999).

110. Lichter and Rothman, "Media and Business Elites."

111. Orren, "Nominating Process," 53–54.

112. See, for example, Jules Witcover's comments about reporters' attempts to deny Gerald Ford the advantage of the White House. Witcover, *Marathon* (New York: Viking Press, 1977), 528–56.

113. Nelson W. Polsby, "The Democratic Nomination," in Ranney, *American Elections of 1980* (Washington, D.C.: American Enterprise Institute, 1981), 37–60; and *The Gallup Opinion Index*, Report No. 183, December 1980, 51. Another example occurred during the 1964 campaign, when United States vessels in the Gulf of Tonkin were fired upon and President Johnson took to the airwaves to promise vigorous defensive measures. In late July, just before the incident, he received favorable ratings from 59 percent of the voters, to 31 percent for Goldwater; in early August, just after the incident, the president's score went up to 65 percent, and Goldwater's declined to 29 percent. American Institute of Public Opinion Survey, released 18 October 1964. For other examples, see Nelson W. Polsby, *Congress and the Presidency*, 4th ed. (Englewood Cliffs, N.J.: Prentice Hall, 1986), 73; and Richard Brody, *Assessing the President: The Media, Elite Opinion, and Public Support* (Stanford, Calif.: Stanford University Press, 1991).

114. Howard S. Bloom and H. Douglas Price, "Voter Response to Short-Run Economic Conditions: The Asymmetric Effect of Prosperity and Recession," *American Political Science Review* 69 (December 1975): 1240–54. For more recent discussions of the relationship between economic performance, other events, and presidential popularity, see Brody, *Assessing the President*, 91–132; and Sam Kernell, *Going Public: New Strategies of Presidential Leadership* (Washington: CQ Press, 1997).

115. A good indicator of whether or not people were better off in 1980 is real disposable income per capita, which increased by about 10 percent in constant dollars between 1976 and 1980: from $5,477 to $8,176 in current dollars ($4,158 to $4,571 in 1972 dollars), according to the U.S. Department of Commerce, Bureau of Economic Analysis, *Survey of Current Business* 61 (March 1981): 10; and *Survey of Current Business* 62 (July 1982): 37.

116. Much of the material in this section is adapted from Nelson W. Polsby, *Political Promises: Essays and Commentary on American Politics* (New York: Oxford University Press, 1974), 156–59.

117. The following discussion draws from Nelson W. Polsby, "The American Election of 1988: Outcome, Process, and Aftermath," Ernst Fraenkel Lectures, Free University of Berlin, 1989, 1–23.

118. Ray C. Fair, "The Effect of Economic Events on Votes for President: 1984 Update," *Political Behavior* 10, no. 2 (1988): 168–79; Larry Bartels, "Economic Consequences of Retrospective Voting," manuscript, July 1988; Alan Abramowitz, "An Improved Model for Predicting Presidential Election Outcomes," *PS* 21 (Fall 1988): 843–47.

119. Jerry Roberts, "What Dukakis Did Wrong," *San Francisco Chronicle*, 10 November 1988, A3.

120. Polsby, *Consequences of Party Reform;* Nelson W. Polsby and William Mayer, "Ideological Cohesion in the American Two-Party System," in *On Parties: Essays Honoring Austin Ranney*, ed. Nelson W. Polsby and Raymond Wolfinger (Berkeley: Institute of Governmental Studies Press, 1999), 219–55.

121. Finley Peter Dunne, *Dissertations by Mr. Dooley* (New York: Harper & Brothers, 1906), 118.

122. Harry S Truman, *Memoirs: Year of Decisions* (Garden City, N.Y.: Doubleday, 1955), 19, 53.

123. Elizabeth Drew, *On the Edge: The Clinton Presidency* (New York: Simon and Schuster, 1994), 227–29. Drew describes Gore as "the most influential Vice President in history."

124. Ross Baker, "The Second Reagan Term," in *The Election of 1984: Reports and Interpretations,* ed. Gerald Pomper (Chatham, N.J.: Chatham House, 1985), 150.

125. Howard Reiter, *Selecting the President* (Philadelphia: University of Pennsylvania Press, 1985), 119–20.

CHAPTER 4

1. Much of the discussion of the nomination process in this chapter is drawn from our own observations via the mass media, the personal observations of one of us who attended the Democratic National Conventions of 1960, 1968, 1972, and 1980 and the Republican National Conventions of 1964 and 1980, and from a classic set of basic texts on American parties and elections, including Moisei Ostrogorski, *Democracy and the Party System in the United States* (New York: Macmillan, 1910); C.E. Merriman and H. Gosnell, *The American Party System* (New York: Macmillan, 1929); Peter H. Odegard and E.A. Helms, *American Politics* (New York: Harper & Brothers, 1938); Pendleton Herring, *The Politics of Democracy* (New York: Norton, 1940); E.E. Schattschneider, *Party Government* (New York: Farrar and Rinehart, 1942); D.D. McKean, *Party and Pressure Politics* (Boston: Houghton Mifflin, 1949); V.O. Key Jr., *Politics, Parties and Pressure Groups,* 4th ed. (New York: Crowell, 1958); H.R. Penniman, *Sait's Parties and Elections* (New York: Appleton-Century-Crofts, 1952); Austin Ranney and Willmoore Kendall, *Democracy and the American Party System* (New York: Harcourt Brace, 1956); William Goodman, *The Two-Party System in the United States* (Princeton: Van Nostrand, 1960); and Gerald Pomper, *Nominating the President: The Politics of Convention Choice,* 2d ed. (Evanston, Ill.: Northwestern University Press, 1966). We also found quite useful a more specialized literature on nominations, including Paul T. David, Malcolm C. Moos, and Ralph M. Goldman, *Presidential Nominating Politics in 1952,* vols. 1–5 (Baltimore: Johns Hopkins University Press, 1954); Paul T. David, Ralph M. Goldman, and Richard C. Bain, *The Politics of National Party Conventions* (Washington, D.C.: Brookings Institution, 1960); and Richard C. Bain, *Convention Decisions and Voting Records* (Washington, D.C.: Brookings Institution, 1960). More recent texts on party organization and presidential nominations that a student might find useful include Samuel J. Eldersveld, *Political Parties in American Society* (New York: Basic Books, 1982); Joel L. Fleishman, ed., *The Future of American Political Parties* (Englewood Cliffs, N.J.: Prentice Hall, 1982); Howard Reiter, *Selecting the President* (Philadelphia: University of Pennsylvania Press, 1985); William J. Crotty and Gary C. Jacobson, *American Parties in Decline* (Boston: Little, Brown, 1980); Gerald M. Pomper, *Elections in America: Control and Influence in Democratic Politics,* rev. ed. (New York: Longman, 1980); Nelson W. Polsby, *Consequences of Party Reform* (New York: Oxford University Press, 1983); Everett Carll Ladd Jr., with Charles D. Hadley, *Transformations of the American Party System,* 2d ed. (New York: Norton, 1978); and William G. Mayer, ed., *In Pursuit of the White House: How We Choose Our Presidential Nominees* (Chatham, N.J.: Chatham House, 1996).

2. See Democratic National Committee (Charles T. Manatt, chairman), *Delegate Selection Rules for the 1984 Democratic National Convention* (Washington, D.C., 26 March 1982). For a discussion of some of the consequences of the rules in the case of the 1980 convention, see Rhodes Cook, "Democrats Adopt New Rules for Picking Nominee in 1980," *Congressional Quarterly Weekly Report,* 17 June 1978, 1571–72.

3. Democrats have resisted "open" primaries in which any citizen can participate; the national Democratic Party has fought to prohibit Republicans from voting in Democratic presidential primaries. See Gary D. Wekkin, *Democrat versus Democrat* (Columbia: University of Missouri Press, 1984); see also *Tashjian v. Republican Party of Connecticut,* 107 S. 544 (1986). The results of these cases suggest that the state of California, which adopted blanket primaries (open to all) in 1998, would have a hard time defending against challenges to their delegation's right to be seated

at the national conventions. Since Democrats wish to expand rather than narrow the primary electorate, they do allow independents, whose support they seek at election time, to vote in their primaries. Changes in state law, such as requiring states to hold primaries, generally apply to both parties; thus state responses to the post-1968 Democratic rules helped transform the Republican nominating process as well. See, for example, Rhodes Cook, "In '88 Contest, It's What's Up Front That Counts," *Congressional Quarterly Weekly Report,* 23 August 1986, 2882.

4. As the *New York Times* mused:

> Now, a full year before the first 1984 delegate selection, the competition for attention among hopefuls is so intense that a new device has been introduced into national politics: the announcement of the announcement.
>
> In mid-January, campaign planners for Senator Alan Cranston let it be known that the California Democrat would announce his candidacy 2 February. The result: a small story, followed by a bigger one—more prominence than would have resulted otherwise. Planners for Senator Gary Hart observed this gambit and promptly let it be known that he would announce 17 February. Planners for Walter F. Mondale said, not for attribution, that their man would do his thing on 21 February; off the record, they said the event would be in St. Paul. Later they distributed a schedule confirming these rumors.
>
> Representative Morris K. Udall handled his different problem differently. His staff let it be known that he would announce his presidential decision in a speech at the National Press Club. The day before, too late to affect attendance materially, a few reporters were told the Arizonan had reluctantly decided not to run after all.
>
> Planners for Senator John Glenn, who is generally regarded as a little slower off the mark than the other Democratic competitors, have been willing to say only that they will not have an announcement about his announcement until March or April. Come to think of it, maybe that's a story. (Phil Gailey and Warren Weaver Jr., "The New Announcement," *New York Times,* 14 February 1983)

5. The Republican candidates in June 1987 were Vice President George Bush, Senator Robert Dole of Kansas, former Delaware Governor Pierre du Pont IV, the Reverend Pat Robertson, Representative Jack Kemp of New York, ex-Senator Paul Laxalt of Nevada, and former Secretary of State Alexander Haig. The Democrats were Massachusetts Governor Michael Dukakis, Senator Joseph Biden of Delaware, the Reverend Jesse Jackson, former Arizona Governor Bruce Babbitt, Representative Richard Gephardt of Missouri, Senator Paul Simon of Illinois, and Tennessee Senator Al Gore.

6. Tom Fiedler, "Sex Lives Become an Issue for Presidential Hopefuls," *Miami Herald,* 27 April 1987, 1.

7. See Rhodes Cook, "Buchanan to Reprise '92 Bid; Wilson Tests the Waters," *Congressional Quarterly Weekly Report,* 18 March 1995, 882.

8. Richard L. Berke, "Shorter Season Is Already Molding 2000 Race," *New York Times,* 19 January 1999, A12; "Quayle Hits the Campaign Trail," *San Francisco Chronicle,* 23 January 1999, A8; *The Hotline,* 16 August 1999, item 2.

   The other Republicans running in March 1999 included former Vice President Dan Quayle, New Hampshire Senator Bob Smith, Arizona Senator John McCain, John Kasich, a member of the House from Ohio, and Gary Bauer and Pat Buchanan, both of whom had worked in the Reagan White House.

9. Ronald Brownstein, "Getting an Early Start," *National Journal,* 29 November 1986, 2880.

10. Carroll J. Doherty, "Dole Takes a Political Risk in Crusade to Aid Bosnia," *Congressional Quarterly Weekly Report,* 11 March 1995, 761; see also Juliana Gruenwald, "Candidates' Voting Records Match Their Reputations," *Congressional Quarterly Weekly Report,* 25 March 1995, 882.

11. Citizens and politicians in these states seem to care deeply about their status as first in the nation and guard it jealously. Indeed, when Arizona began to consider challenging New Hampshire by scheduling an early primary for 1996, Senator Phil Gramm was widely criticized in New Hampshire for seeming to approve of that attempt; see "Rocky Start in Granite State Knocks Gramm Off Balance," *Washing-

ton Post, 26 February 1995, A18. Our discussion of Iowa and New Hampshire borrows freely from Nelson W. Polsby, "The Iowa Caucuses in a Front-Loaded System: A Few Historical Lessons," in *The Iowa Caucuses and the Presidential Nominating Process,* ed. Peverill Squire (Boulder, Colo.: Westview Press, 1989). See also Squire, *The Iowa Caucuses;* Gary R. Orren and Nelson W. Polsby, eds., *Media and Momentum* (Chatham, N.J.: Chatham House, 1987); "Special Report: Political Odd Couple," W. John Moore, "Rural Prospecting," and Burt Solomon, "Where America Is At," all *National Journal,* 26 September 1987, 2394–2409; "When Iowa Becomes Brigadoon," *The Economist,* 9 January 1988, 21–22; "Iowa," *Congressional Quarterly Weekly Report,* 29 August 1987, 1994–97; and "The Iowa Democratic Caucuses: How They Work," *New York Times,* 7 February 1988, 14.

12. On the Republican side in 1988, the numbers breathlessly reported on the networks were the outcome of a straw poll ballot, conducted at the precinct caucuses, and phoned into the networks just like the real delegate divisions on the Democratic side. After the straw poll was conducted, Republican delegates to the next level up were selected in each precinct, without any necessary connection to the straw poll. As David Oman, co-chair of the Iowa Republican Party, described the process the week before:

> Essentially we have one very large straw poll taken in 2500 different locations simultaneously....Those at the caucus will be given small cards and will mark on these cards their choice for president. The cards will be tallied. ...Our straw poll is not tied to the process of choosing delegates. After the poll is taken and reported, the caucus will then pick its precinct committeeman and committeewoman, then pick the men and women who will go to the Republican county convention, and then discuss the platform. (*Presidential Campaign Hotline,* 4 January 1988, 15–16.)

> The county conventions met in March and picked delegates to district conventions, which met in June on the eve of the state convention. The district conventions selected three national convention delegates for each district and then the state convention selected the rest. Thus the straw poll might or might not predict the results of the delegate selection process accurately in any given year. In 1988, the preferences of the eventual delegates were 16 for Dole, 12 for Bush, 2 each for Robertson and Kemp, and 5 uncommitted. (*Congressional Quarterly,* 6 August 1988, 2161)

13. William C. Adams, "As New Hampshire Goes," in Orren and Polsby, *Media and Momentum,* 42–59, esp. 43.

14. Indeed, Henry Brady and Richard Johnston argue that the main educational effect of the entire primary process for voters is to inform them about candidate viability. See "What's the Primary Message? Horse Race or Issue Journalism," in Orren and Polsby, *Media and Momentum,* 127–86.

15. See Polsby, *Consequences of Party Reform,* for the full argument to this effect, and, for copious evidence, Byron Shafer, *Quiet Revolution: The Struggle for the Democratic Party and the Shaping of Post-Reform Politics* (New York: Russell Sage Foundation, 1983).

16. See R. W. Apple Jr., "Iowa's Weighty Caucuses: Significance by Accident," *New York Times,* 25 January 1988, 1. In 1976 the Iowa caucuses were held on 19 January; in 1980 on 21 January; in 1984 on 20 February.

17. As Muskie told Theodore H. White: "That previous week ... I'd been down to Florida, then I flew to Idaho, then I flew to California, then I flew back to Washington to vote in the Senate, and I flew back to California, and then I flew into Manchester and I was hit with this 'Canuck' story. I'm tough physically, but no one could do that." White, *The Making of the President 1972* (New York: Atheneum, 1973), 81–82.

18. R. W. Apple Jr., "Carter Defeats Bayh by 2–1 in Iowa Vote," *New York Times,* 20 January 1976, 1.

19. "Ford's 1976 Campaign for the GOP Nomination," 1976 *Congressional Quarterly Almanac* (Washington, DC: CQ Press, 1976), 900.

20. Elizabeth Drew writes of Carter: "Early successes and surprises were big elements in Carter's plan....The basic idea was to show early that the southerner could do well in the North and could best Wallace in the South....He visited a hundred and fourteen

towns in Iowa, beginning in 1975 (and his family made countless other visits)."
Drew, *American Journal: The Events of 1976* (New York: Random House, 1977),
143–44, 466–67. See also Jules Witcover, *Marathon: The Pursuit of the Presidency
1972–1976* (New York: Viking Press, 1977), 14.

21. See ibid., passim.
22. See Witcover, *Marathon,* 202–5; Drew, *American Journal,* passim; Martin Schram,
    Running for President 1976 (New York: Stein and Day, 1977), 13–15.
23. Apple, "Carter Defeats Bayh." This was not the first time in 1976 that Apple had
    puffed Carter. Elizabeth Drew's diary of 27 January 1976 reported: "A story by R.
    W. Apple Jr., in the *Times* last October saying that Carter was doing well in Iowa
    was itself a political event, prompting other newspaper stories that Carter was doing
    well in Iowa, and then more news magazine and television coverage for Carter than
    might otherwise have been his share." Drew, *American Journal,* 6.
24. Ibid., 16.
25. Nelson W. Polsby, "The Democratic Nomination," in *The American Elections of 1980,*
    ed. Austin Ranney (Washington, D.C.: American Enterprise Institute, 1981), 47–48.
26. Ibid., 49.
27. Jack Germond and Jules Witcover, *Blue Smoke and Mirrors* (New York: Viking
    Press, 1981), 96.
28. David W. Moore, "The *Manchester Union Leader* in the New Hampshire Primary"
    in Orren and Polsby, *Media and Momentum,* 104–26, esp. 116, 123.
29. Nelson W. Polsby, "The Democratic Nomination and the Evolution of the Party
    System," in *The American Elections of 1984,* ed. Austin Ranney (Durham, N.C.:
    Duke University Press, 1985), 36–65. In the eight-day gap between Iowa and New
    Hampshire, Gary Hart went from 10 percent in the public opinion polls to a 41 per-
    cent vote in the New Hampshire primary itself. See Peter Hart's comments in the
    Presidential Campaign Hotline, 25 January 1988, 19.
30. Mickey Kaus et al., "Yes We Have a Front-Runner," *Newsweek,* 20 July 1987;
    Richard Berke, "Iowa Eclipsing New Hampshire among Hopefuls," *New York
    Times,* 6 September 1987; Thomas B. Edsall and David S. Broder, "Dukakis' New
    Hampshire Campaign Not Unraveled by Biden Videotape," *Washington Post,* 3
    October 1987; Mickey Kaus et al., "Now, a Dukakis Fiasco," *Newsweek,* 12 October
    1987; Maralee Schwartz, "Dukakis Still a Top Fund-Raiser," *Washington Post,* 11
    November 1987; Gwen Ifill, "Bush and Dukakis Far Ahead in Poll," *Washington
    Post,* 20 November 1987.
31. See Polsby, "The Democratic Nomination and the Evolution of the Party System."
32. Monica Langley, "In Pre-New Hampshire Flurry, Images Prevail, and TV Coverage
    May be Pivotal to Candidates," *Wall Street Journal,* 16 February 1988, 64.
33. Charles T. Royer, ed., *Campaign for President: The Managers Look at '92* (Hollis,
    N.H.: Hollis Publishing, 1994), 75–76. Several candidates considered attempting to
    score an easy coup by spending a little money in Iowa in order to finish second. The
    only candidate who actually did it, Paul Tsongas, indeed finished second (with less
    than 5 percent of the vote); the Tsongas campaign believed this took some pressure off
    of Tsongas in New Hampshire, where he had been identified as a regional candidate.
34. For the timetable of these events, see Royer, *Campaign for President,* 305–9.
35. Ibid., 327.
36. *The Hotline,* 13 February 1996, items 3 and 9; *The Hotline,* 14 February 1996, item 4.
37. *The Hotline,* 15 February 1996, item 1.
38. *The Hotline,* 21 February 1996, items 1 and 4.
39. The one extremely mild exception to this rule occured in the uncontested Iowa cau-
    cuses for Democrats in 1992. Far behind favorite son Senator Tom Harkin, Bill Clin-
    ton finished fourth, a handful of votes behind the second- and third-place candidates.
    Since the national media had accepted that Iowa was uncontested, this did no harm
    to his campaign.
40. Richard M. Scammon and Alice V. McGillivray, *America at the Polls* (Washington,
    D.C.: Elections Research Center, Congressional Quarterly, 1988), 585.
41. Alice V. McGillivray, *Presidential Primaries and Caucuses 1992* (Washington, D.C.:
    CQ Press, 1992), 8–9.

42. Delegate counts vary between the parties, but to get a general idea, here are the electoral vote totals of states holding primaries or first-round caucuses in each month in 1992 and 1996 and those likely to hold those procedures in each month in 2000 (District of Columbia unavailable):

	1992	1996	2000
February	18	25	74
March	258	332	372
April	94	63	49
May	79	75	40
June	86	40	0

Sources: "Election Calendar," *Campaigns & Elections*, February 1995, 6; "Elections '92," *Campaigns & Elections*, October–November 1991, 56.

43. Maxwell Glen, "Front-Loading the Race: Because of the Accelerated Timetable for the 1988 Presidential Nominating Contest, Ample Financial Resources Will Be More Important Than Ever to Candidates," *National Journal*, 29 November 1986, 2882.
44. Charles D. Hadley and Harold W. Stanley, "Super Tuesday 1988: Regional Results and National Implications," *Publius* 19 (Summer 1989): 19–37; Linda Wertheimer, "The Stubborn Triumph of Michael Dukakis," *Washington Post*, 12 June 1988, C1–2.
45. Cook, "In '88 Contest, It's What's Up Front That Counts," 1997–2002.
46. B. Drummond Ayres Jr., "War Between States For Nominating Glory," *New York Times*, 7 February 1999, A20; *The Hotline*, 23 February 1996, item 12.
47. Barbara Norrander, *Super Tuesday: Regional Politics and Presidential Primaries* (Lexington: University Press of Kentucky, 1992).
48. Bruce E. Cain, I.A. Lewis, and Douglas Rivers, "Strategy and Choice in the 1988 Presidential Primaries," *Electoral Studies* 8 (1988): 23–48; see also Charles D. Hadley and Harold W. Stanley, "The Southern Super Tuesday: Southern Democrats Seeking Relief from Rising Republicanism," in Mayer, ed., *In Pursuit of the White House*, 158–89.
49. B. Drummond Ayres Jr., "McCain Rethinks the Arizona Primary," *New York Times*, 7 February 1999, A20.
50. Cook, "In '88 Contest, It's What's Up Front That Counts," 1999.
51. Ibid., 2002.
52. Further discussion can be found in F. Christopher Arterton, *Media Politics: The News Strategies of Presidential Campaigns* (Lexington, Mass.: Lexington Books, 1984).
53. See Harry W. Ernst, *The Primary That Made a President: West Virginia* (New York: McGraw-Hill, 1962), and Theodore H. White, *The Making of the President, 1960* (New York: Atheneum, 1961).
54. See Theodore H. White, *The Making of the President, 1968* (New York: Atheneum, 1969), 89; Lewis Chester, Godfrey Hodgson, and Bruce Page, *An American Melodrama* (New York: Viking Press, 1969), 79–99; Arthur Herzog, *McCarthy for President* (New York: Viking Press, 1969), 97; Jack Newfield, *Robert Kennedy: A Memoir* (New York: Dutton, 1969), 218.
55. Royer, *Campaign for President*, 79–80; Peter Goldman, Thomas M. DeFrank, Mark Miller, Andrew Murr, and Tom Mathews, *Quest for the Presidency* (College Station: Texas A&M University Press, 1994), 132–35, 144–49.
56. See Tom Rosensteil, *Strange Bedfellows* (New York: Hyperion, 1993), 136.
57. Henry E. Brady and Michael C. Hagen, "The 'Horse-Race' or the Issues: What Do Voters Learn From Presidential Primaries?" manuscript, Harvard University, Center for American Political Studies, 1986. See also Brady and Johnston, "What's the Primary Message?" in Orren and Polsby, *Media and Momentum*, 127–86.
58. John G. Geer, "Voting in Presidential Primaries," paper delivered at the annual meeting of the American Political Science Association, Washington, D.C., 30 August–2 September 1984, 6.
59. Cited in ibid., 15.

60. Ibid., 15–21.

61. Brady and Hagen, "The 'Horse-Race' or the Issues," 38–39.

62. Larry M. Bartels, "Ideology and Momentum in Presidential Primaries," paper delivered at the annual meeting of the American Political Science Association, Denver, Colorado, September 1982. See also Larry Bartels, *Presidential Parties and the Dynamics of Public Choice* (Princeton: Princeton University Press, 1988).

63. Larry Rothenberg and Richard Brody, "Participation in Presidential Primaries," *Western Political Quarterly* 41 (June 1988): 253–72.

64. See Austin Ranney, "Turnout and Representation in Presidential Primary Elections," *American Political Science Review* 66 (March 1972): 21–37, for the years 1948 to 1968. The same held true in 1976, when turnout averaged 28 percent in the primaries versus 54 percent in the general election. See Austin Ranney, *Participation in American Presidential Nominations 1976* (Washington, D.C.: American Enterprise Institute, 1977), 20; and James Lengle, Representation in Presidential Primaries: The Democratic Party in the Post Reform Era (Westport, Conn.: Greenwood Press, 1981), 10. In 1980 the figures were 25 percent in primaries and 54 percent in the general election. Ranney, *American Elections of 1980*, 353, 364.

65. For an interesting argument along these lines, see Malcolm E. Jewell, "A Caveat on the Expanding Use of Presidential Primaries," *Policy Studies Journal* 2 (Summer 1974): 279–84.

66. James Lengle and Byron Shafer, "Primary Rules, Political Power and Social Change," *American Political Science Review* 70 (March 1976): 35.

67. Thomas E. Mann, "Elected Officials and the Politics of Presidential Selection," in Ranney, *American Elections of 1984,* 103–5. See also David Price, *Bringing Back the Parties* (Washington, D.C.: CQ Press, 1984); Glenn, "Front-Loading the Race," 333; and Dennis W. Gleiber and James D. King, "Party Rules and Equitable Representation: The 1984 Democratic National Convention," *American Politics Quarterly* 15 (January 1987): 107–21.

68. Mann, "Elected Officials," 105–6. For evidence that caucuses, and not primaries, have yielded the "best" proportional representation results, see Stephen Ansolabehere and Gary King, "Measuring the Consequences of Delegate Selection Rules in Presidential Nominations," *Journal of Politics,* 52 (May 1990): 609–21.

69. Mann, "Elected Officials," 119ff.

70. Elizabeth Drew, *Election Journal: Political Events of 1987–1988* (New York: Morrow, 1989), 243–49.

71. Anthony L. Teasdale, "The Paradox of the Primaries," *Electoral Studies* 1 (1982): 43–63; quotes from 43–44, 49.

72. See Brownstein, "Getting an Early Start," 2876ff.

73. Harold W. Stanley and Richard C. Niemi, *Vital Statistics on American Politics 1997–1998* (Washington, D.C.: CQ Press, 1998), 86.

74. Michael Granberry, "San Diego Falls Short in Bid to Be GOP Host," *Los Angeles Times,* 9 January 1991, A3.

75. *National Journal Convention Special,* 21 July 1983, 38. Dianne Feinstein, a Democrat, was elected on a nonpartisan ballot, as California law requires for local elections.

76. William Schneider, "Both Parties Embark on a Southern Strategy," *National Journal,* 21 February 1987, 436.

77. This is the number that White (*The Making of the President, 1968,* 259) estimates the Democrats needed for their convention. For a more recent example, see Eric Pianin, "Democrats Pick San Francisco as Site of '84 National Convention," *Washington Post,* 22 April 1983.

78. Richard Reeves, *Convention* (New York: Harcourt Brace Jovanovich, 1977), 32.

79. Material on the Kennedy organization in 1960 is drawn from Fred G. Burke, "Senator Kennedy's Convention Organization," in *Inside Politics: The National Conventions, 1960,* ed. Paul Tillett (Dobbs Ferry, N.Y.: Oceana Publications, 1962), 25–39.

80. Ibid., 39.

81. Recognizing the importance of communication at the Republican convention of 1860, a supporter of Abraham Lincoln carefully seated all the solid Seward states close together and as far as possible from the states whose delegates were in some doubt

about whom to support. Glyndon G. Van Deusen, *Thurlow Weed: Wizard of the Lobby* (Boston: Little, Brown, 1947), 253. Mayor Daley arranged for something similar at the Democratic National Convention in 1968, but the level of protest about excessive security procedures and the lack of communication facilities reached such a pitch that whatever strategic advantages Daley might have hoped for evaporated.

82. See David, Moos, and Goldman, *Presidential Nominating Politics in 1952,* vol. 1; Robert Elson, "A Question for Democrats: If Not Truman, Who?" *Life,* 24 March 1952, 118–33; Albert Votaw, "The Pros Put Adlai Over," *New Leader,* 4 August 1952, 3–5; Douglass Cater, "How the Democrats Got Together," *The Reporter,* 19 August 1952, 6–8; J.M. Arvey, as told to John Madigan, "The Reluctant Candidate: An Inside Story," *The Reporter,* 24 November 1953; and Walter Johnson, *How We Drafted Adlai Stevenson* (New York: Knopf, 1955).

83. F. Christopher Arterton, "Exploring the 1976 Republican Convention: Strategies and Tactics of Candidate Organizations," *Political Science Quarterly* 92 (Winter 1977–78): 664.

84. Jo Freeman, "The Political Culture of the Democratic and Republican Parties," *Political Science Quarterly* 101 (Fall 1986): 327–56; quote on 328. See also Byron Shafer, "Republicans and Democrats as Social Types: or, Notes Toward an Ethnography of the Political Parties," *Journal of American Studies* 20 (1986): 341–54.

85. Freeman, "Political Culture," 329.

86. Ibid.

87. For extensive documentation, see Ladd, *Transformations of the American Party System.* See also Everett Carll Ladd Jr. and Charles D. Hadley, "Political Parties and Political Issues: Patterns in Differentiation Since the New Deal," Sage Professional Paper, American Politics Series, Beverly Hills, Calif., 1973, 4–11; Herbert McClosky, Paul J. Hoffman, and Rosemary O'Hara, "Issue Conflict and Consensus Among Party Leaders and Followers," *American Political Science Review* 54 (June 1960): 406–27; and Jeane J. Kirkpatrick, "Representation in the American National Conventions: The Case of 1972," *British Journal of Political Science* 5 (July 1975): 304.

88. Kirkpatrick, "Representation in the American National Conventions," 285.

89. Barbara G. Farah, "Delegate Polls: 1944 to 1984," *Public Opinion,* August/September 1984, 43–45.

90. M. Kent Jennings, "Women in Party Politics," prepared for the Russell Sage Foundation Women in Twentieth-Century American Politics Project, Beverly Hills, Calif., January 1987, 11–12.

91. Jo Freeman, "Who You Know versus Who You Represent," in *The Women's Movements of The United States and Western Europe: Consciousness, Political Opportunity and Public Policy,* ed. Mary Fainsod Katzenstein and Carol McClurg Mueller (Philadelphia: Temple University Press, 1987), 231–32.

92. Ibid., 242.

93. John D. Huber and G. Bingham Powell Jr., "Congruence Between Citizens and Policymakers in Two Visions of Liberal Democracy, *World Politics* (April 1994): 291–326; Torben Iversen, "Political Leadership and Representation in West European Democracies: A Test of Three Models of Voting," *American Journal of Political Science* 38 (February 1994): 45–74. An important early work is Maurice Duverger, *Political Parties: Their Organization and Activity in the Modern State* (London: Methuen, 1954).

94. Peter Begans, "The ABC News/*Washington Post* Poll," 1984 survey numbers 0122–25, 4–5.

95. Center for Political Studies, Institute for Social Research, "Convention Delegate Study: Report to Respondents," University of Michigan, Ann Arbor, 1985, 2.

96. Warren Miller, *Without Consent: Mass-Elite Linkages in Presidential Politics* (Lexington: University Press of Kentucky, 1988), chap. 2.

97. See Polsby, "Democratic Nomination and Evolution of the Party System," and Raymond E. Wolfinger, "Dealignment, Realignment, and Mandates in the 1984 Election," in Ranney, *American Elections of 1984,* 38, 289.

98. For the best description of the role of the modern convention, see Byron E. Shafer, *Bifurcated Politics* (Cambridge, Mass.: Harvard University Press, 1988); see also Polsby, *Consequences of Party Reform,* 75–78.

99. The three big broadcast networks, in the days when they were the only sources of immediate coverage, featured "gavel-to-gavel" reporting, which meant that whenever the conventions were in session, the networks would switch from normal entertainment programming to the convention. It did not mean that the networks necessarily broadcast whatever was happening at the podium, although they did spend plenty of time transmitting live speeches; in addition, the news teams supplied analysis, interviews with party leaders and rank-and-file delegates, and other stories of interest. For the gradual end of the "gavel-to-gavel" standard, see Shafer, *Bifurcated Politics,* 226–89. On cable television, CNN comes close to the old gavel-to-gavel coverage, while C-SPAN offers full coverage of the official proceedings, which the networks never did even in the days of gavel to gavel. C-SPAN, with its seemingly endless supply of airtime, also airs hours of viewer call-ins, interviews with party elites and rank-and-file delegates, and feature stories in which their cameras follow individual delegates from their hometowns to the convention floor, including in 1992 a trip to the laundromat with a delegate before she boarded the bus to the Democratic convention in New York City.

100. The focus on disunity during the coverage of the 1980 convention (see Joe Foote and Tony Rimmer, "The Ritual of Convention Coverage in 1980," in *Television Coverage of the 1980 Presidential Campaign,* ed. William C. Adams [Norwood, N.J.: Ablex, 1983]) did not seem to affect the public, at least immediately; Carter's convention "bounce" was a historically large 10 points (Shafer, *Bifurcated Politics,* 234).

101. These wrap-up shows may go "late," thereby extending the time on the air, especially if a speech shown live (typically, the presidential nominee's acceptance speech) runs long. On the other hand, in 1992 the second day of the Democratic convention coincided with baseball's All-Star Game. CBS chose baseball over politics and did not even have a wrap-up show from the convention that night. "Media Coverage: Take Me Out to the Ballgame," *The Hotline,* 15 July 1992. See also Rosenstiel, *Strange Bedfellows,* 201–33; Edwin Diamond, "Scaling Back the TV Coverage," *National Journal Convention Preview,* 16 June 1992, 19.

102. Rosenstiel, *Strange Bedfellows,* 214.

103. The withdrawal of Ross Perot from the race during the convention makes it very difficult to measure exactly how big the bounce attributable to convention advertising was. A typical result was the change in the *Newsweek*/Gallup poll. A preconvention poll taken on 9–10 July (the convention ran from 13 July through 16 July) put Clinton in second place in a three-way race: Bush, 32 percent; Clinton, 31 percent; Perot, 28 percent. The *Newsweek*/Gallup poll taken the day after the convention gave Clinton a large lead in a two-way race, leading Bush 59 percent to 32 percent. The *L.A. Times* poll taken just after the convention reported 57 percent of those polled looked "favorably" on the Democratic nominee, compared to only 41 percent before the convention. According to Rosenstiel, *Strange Bedfellows,* most of the gain was early in the week, with Clinton moving into a clear lead "after only one night of the convention" (p. 212); a *New York Daily News/Hotline* tracking poll shows a growing gap as the convention went on. See *The Hotline,* 13 July 1992 and 20 July 1992. *Newsweek* only measured a three-point bounce for Bush after the Republican convention, although other polls indicated larger movement to the Bush ticket. See *The Hotline,* 24 August 1992. For bounces after conventions from 1964–1984, see Shafer, *Bifurcated Politics,* 234.

104. Evan Thomas and Peter Goldman, "Victory March: The Inside Story," *Newsweek Special Election Issue,* 18 November 1996, 88–90, 97–98.

105. Christopher Madison, "The Convention Hall and the TV Screen," *National Journal Convention Special,* 23 July 1988, 1950.

106. Rosenstiel, *Strange Bedfellows,* 224.

107. Unfortunately for the Republicans' efforts, losing candidate Pat Buchanan won the right to give a speech without prior vetting and promptly violated GOP plans to avoid some kinds of personal attacks on the Democratic nominee. Others who were not vetted included former President Ronald Reagan and the candidates. Christopher Madison, "Scripting a Scripted GOP Convention," *National Journal Convention Daily,* 19 August 1992, 10.

108. Rosenstiel, *Strange Bedfellows,* 205–6. At the Democratic convention, Al Gore was told to pause fifteen minutes before beginning his acceptance speech so that NBC's *Cheers,* the top-rated show in America at the time, could double as the perfect lead-in to his speech.

109. In 1992 Republicans running for lower offices were dissatisfied with their allotment of time from the convention; see Richard E. Cohen, "No Showcase for Rest of Ticket," *National Journal Convention Daily,* 20 August 1992, 34. Unlike the Democrats, who had one long session each day beginning in the evening, the Republicans divided into a prime-time session and a daytime session, thus (in the eyes of the daytime speakers) clearly signaling to reporters that only the prime-time session was newsworthy.

110. See Andrew Mollison, "Maestro of the Democrats," *New Leader,* 27 June 1988, 3–4. On the other hand, the leader of a too-united party may need to create excitement, as George Bush apparently intended to do in 1988 by refusing to reveal his choice for vice president until the eve of the convention. James M. Perry and Ellen Hume, "Bush Aiming for Suspense as GOP Starts Convention," *Wall Street Journal,* 15 August 1988, 40.

111. Robert S. Boyd and Tom Fiedler, "Dukakis Hopes for Party Unity at Convention," *Philadelphia Inquirer,* 18 July 1988, 1A, 4A.

112. "Dukakis-Jackson Accord May Avert Floor Fight," *Los Angeles Times,* 26 June 1988, 36. See also E. J. Dionne Jr., "Harmonious Convention Closes with Jackson Hugging Nominee," *New York Times,* 22 July 1988, A9.

113. For the complete story, see Shafer, *Quiet Revolution.*

114. See Irving G. Williams, *The American Vice-Presidency: New Look* (New York: Doubleday, 1954); and Joel K. Goldstein, *The Modern American Vice Presidency* (Princeton: Princeton University Press, 1982).

115. David Broder and Robert Woodward, *The Man Who Would Be President: Dan Quayle* (New York: Simon and Schuster, 1992), 13–30; and "Bush Takes Command but Quayle Draws Fire," *Congressional Quarterly Weekly Report,* 20 August 1988, 2307–9.

116. Thomas Goldman, "Victory March," 85–88.

117. Richard Brookhiser, *The Outside Story* (Garden City, N.Y.: Doubleday, 1986), 155. In the event, Representative Ferraro's candidacy was mildly detrimental to the ticket. See Polsby, "Democratic Nomination and Evolution of the Party System," 36–65.

118. Most of the 130-odd Goldwater delegates we interviewed at the 1964 Republican convention were prepared to sacrifice victory if victory meant becoming a "me-too" party or "going against principles" by adopting what they termed the "devious and corrupt" balanced tickets of the past.

119. Quoted in Ross K. Baker, "Outlook for the Reagan Administration," in *The Election of 1980,* ed. Gerald Pomper (Chatham, N.J.: Chatham House, 1981), 167.

120. Rhodes Cook, "Dispute over Convention's Role: Brushing Aside Complaints, DNC Approves Rules for 1988," *Congressional Quarterly Weekly Report,* 15 March 1986, 627.

121. Mann, "Elected Officials."

CHAPTER 5

1. See Seymour M. Lipset, Paul F. Lazarsfeld, Allen H. Barton, and Juan Linz, "The Psychology of Voting: An Analysis of Political Behavior," in *Handbook of Social Psychology,* ed. Gardner Lindzey (Reading, Mass.: Addison-Wesley, 1954), 1124–75; Paul Lazarsfeld, Bernard Berelson, and Hazel Gaudet, *The People's Choice* (New York: Columbia University Press, 1948), 87–93; Bernard Berelson, Paul Lazarsfeld, and William N. McPhee, *Voting* (Chicago: University of Chicago Press, 1954), 16–17; and Richard A. Brody, "Change and Stability in Partisan Identification: A Note of Caution," paper delivered at the annual meeting of the American Political Science Association, Chicago, September 1974.

2. Nicholas von Hoffman, "Campaign Craziness," *New Republic,* 5 November 1984, 17–19; quote on 17.

3. Ibid., 17.

4. Patrick Anderson, *Electing Jimmy Carter: The Campaign of 1976* (Baton Rouge: Louisiana State University Press, 1994), 134.

5. "Election Billboard," *Economist,* 5 October 1996, 28.

6. Jules Witcover, *Marathon* (New York: Viking, 1977), 132–37.

7. Garry Abrams, "See How They Run: Why Do Candidates Dash Madly Across the Map? Blame It on a Special Breed Called the Scheduler," *Los Angeles Times,* 29 September 1988, pt. 5, p. 1.

8. Ibid.

9. Ibid.

10. "A Day in the Life of the Campaign," *Washington Post,* 23 October 1992.

11. Witcover, *Resurrection of Richard Nixon* (New York: Putnam, 1970), 237–39.

12. One study has found at least small effects from campaign visits; see Jeffrey M. Jones, "Does Bringing Out the Candidate Bring Out the Votes?" *American Politics Quarterly* 26 (October 1998): 395–419. Campaigns may allocate a variety of resources, including candidate visits and paid advertising in a coordinated way, making it impossible for outside researchers or the campaign managers to know which affected the voters.

13. Evan Thomas and Peter Goldman, "Victory March: The Inside Story," *Newsweek Special Election Issue,* 18 November 1996, 124.

14. Dom Bonafede, "Hey, Look Me Over," *National Journal,* 21 November 1987.

15. Ibid., 2967.

16. Peter Goldman, Thomas M. DeFrank, Mark Miller, Andrew Murr, and Thomas Mathews, *Quest for the Presidency, 1992* (College Station: Texas A&M University Press, 1994), 551.

17. See Jonathan Bernstein, "Candidate Campaign Organizations in House Elections," paper delivered at the meeting of the American Political Science Association, Washington, D.C., 28–31 August 1997.

18. See, for an early survey, Stanley Kelley Jr., *Professional Public Relations and Political Power* (Baltimore: Johns Hopkins University Press, 1956).

19. *Campaigns and Elections* 19 (March 1998): 4. Opposition research is the fastest-growing subfield in political consulting. For more information, see Ruth Shalit, "The Oppo Boom," *New Republic,* 3 January 1994, 16–20.

20. Frank I. Luntz, *Candidates, Campaigns, and Consultants* (Oxford: Basil Blackwell, 1988), 52.

21. Ibid.

22. Ibid., 49.

23. Andrew Rosenthal, "Politicians Yield to Computers," *New York Times,* 9 May 1988, 21, 23.

24. Mark Petracca, "Political Consultants and Democratic Governance," *PS: Political Science and Politics* 22 (March 1989): 13.

25. Ibid.

26. Luntz, *Candidates, Campaigns, and Consultants,* 57.

27. Larry J. Sabato, *The Rise of Political Consultants: New Ways of Winning Elections* (New York: Basic Books, 1981), 13.

28. Luntz, *Candidates, Campaigns, and Consultants,* 51.

29. Sabato, *Rise of Political Consultants,* 26.

30. Dick Kirschten and James A. Barnes, "Itching for Action," *National Journal,* 4 June 1988, 1478.

31. Luntz, *Candidates, Campaigns, and Consultants,* 72.

32. Ibid., 112.

33. Occasionally the roles are reversed and consultants find themselves more "dovish" than their employers. In the 1972 general campaign, McGovern ditched Charles Guggenheim, his media adviser, because the latter refused (on pragmatic grounds) to produce negatives. See Sabato, *Rise of Political Consultants,* 121.

34. See Jonathan Bernstein, "The *New* New Presidential Elite," in *In Pursuit of the White House 2000,* ed. William G. Mayer (Chatham, N.J.: Chatham House, 1999); Robin Kolodny and Angela Logan, "Political Consultants and the Extension of Party Goals," *PS: Political Science and Politics* 31 (June 1998): 155–59.

35. Luntz, *Candidates, Campaigns and Consultants,* 50.

36. Katharine Q. Seelye, "Politics; The Manager; Dole Campaign Chief Relying on Determnination, and Luck." *New York Times,* 3 June 1996, A1. For several such profiles, see Bernstein, "The *New* New Presidential Elite."

37. Kirk Victor, "The Braintrusters," *National Journal,* 13 February 1988, 392–97.
38. Ibid., 397.
39. Ibid.
40. Ibid.
41. Ibid., 393.
42. Ibid., 392.
43. Ibid., 393.
44. See, for example, the Gallup poll for 25–28 June 1982, in which 43 percent of a national sample said that the Democrats were the party best able to keep the country prosperous. Only 34 percent picked the Republicans. *The Gallup Report,* no. 204 (September 1982): 45. See also Campbell et al., *American Voter,* 44–59.
45. Transcript of presidential debates, *New York Times,* 16 October 1976. See also Campbell et al., *American Voter,* 44–59; and Angus Campbell, Gerald Gurin, and Warren E. Miller, *The Voter Decides* (Evanston, Ill.: Row, Peterson, 1954), 44–45, esp. table 4-3.
46. See Henry A. Plotkin, "Issues in the Campaign," in *The Election of 1984,* ed. Gerald Pomper (Chatham, N.J.: Chatham House, 1985), 48–52; Albert R. Hunt, "The Campaign and the Issues," in Ranney, *American Elections of 1984,* 142–44; William Schneider, "The November 6 Vote for President: What Did It Mean?" in Ranney, *American Elections of 1984,* 239–42; Benjamin Ginsberg and Martin Shefter, "A Critical Realignment? The New Politics, the Reconstituted Right, and the Election of 1984," in *The Elections of 1984,* ed. Michael Nelson (Washington, D.C.: CQ Press, 1985), 5–24.
47. Richard Scammon and Ben Wattenberg, *The Real Majority* (New York: Coward-McCann, 1970), 39; see also 37–43.
48. *The People, Press, and Politics: A Times Mirror Study of The American Electorate,* Conducted by the Gallup Organization (Los Angeles: Times Mirror Company, 1987).
49. Nelson W. Polsby and William G. Mayer, "Ideological Cohesion in the American Two-Party System," in *On Parties: Essays Honoring Austin Ranney,* ed. Nelson W. Polsby and Raymond Wolfinger (Berkeley: Institute of Governmental Studies Press, 1999), 232.
50. See Richard Nixon, *Six Crises* (New York: Doubleday, 1962), and especially Theodore H. White, *The Making of the President, 1960* (New York: Atheneum, 1961), for a discussion of two candidates' contrasting attitudes toward their "camp" of reporters. For the 1964 election, see Theodore H. White, *The Making of the President, 1964* (New York: Atheneum, 1965). For 1968, see Theodore H. White, *The Making of the President, 1968* (New York: Atheneum, 1969), 327ff. For 1972, see Timothy Crouse, *The Boys on the Bus* (New York: Random House, 1973). For 1976, see Witcover, *Marathon.* For 1980, see Jack W. Germond and Jules Witcover, *Blue Smoke and Mirrors* (New York: Viking, 1981), 213–15, 260–64. On 1984, see Martin Schram, *The Great American Video Game: Presidential Politics in the Television Age* (New York: Morrow, 1987).
51. In 1984 Mondale's backers felt President Reagan was avoiding the issues in a campaign that stuck to broad, patriotic themes. The "great communicator," they argued, was exploiting the media with his carefully staged events. Many in the media agreed and did negative stories about the Reagan campaign's manipulative tactics. Negative coverage of this sort gave the Reagan camp grounds for complaints of their own concerning an anti-Republican "spin" to nightly newscasts. See Michael J. Robinson, "Where's the Beef? Media and Media Elites in 1984," in Ranney, *American Elections of 1984.* Allegations of bias in the ABC newsroom tainted the 1992 campaign. They were fueled in part by the decision of anchor Peter Jennings to invite Clinton to respond to a speech President Bush gave after the Los Angeles riots. Jennings was called into the network's executive offices. ABC Vice President Richard Wald was concerned that Jennings was deliberately undermining President Bush.

Tom Rosenstiel reports: "This is wrong," he [Wald] yelled at Jennings. "This is a presidential occasion. A state of emergency, and the President has a right to go to the nation and speak to the people without making it a political occasion." Jennings disagreed, arguing that had Bush made the speech at the beginning of the crisis, then it would have been "presidential." Since he had waited a day after responding (Bush sent troops to Los Angeles the day before the speech), Jennings believed that the timing of Bush's comment was purely political. Although Wald disagreed, he did not order Jennings to change his plans, but the incident caused ABC's objectivity to be questioned throughout the rest of the campaign. (Tom Rosenstiel, *Strange Bedfellows* [New York: Hyperion, 1993], 141).

52. Ibid., 139.
53. See Stephen Hess, *The Washington Reporters* (Washington, D.C.: Brookings Institution, 1981); S. Robert Lichter and Stanley Rothman, "Media and Business Elites," *Public Opinion* 4 (October/November 1981): 42–46, 59–60; and William Schneider and I.A. Lewis, "Views on the News," *Public Opinion* 8 (August/September 1985): 6–11, 58.
54. Howard Kurtz, "Out There; It's 10 Past Monica, America. Do You Know Where Matt Drudge Is?" *Washington Post*, 28 March 1999, F1; William Powers, "Punctured Franchise," *National Journal*, 27 March 1999, 843.
55. Jack Germond and Jules Witcover, *Whose Broad Stripes and Bright Stars?* (New York: Warner Books, 1989), 403.
56. 27 April 1992 memorandum from Mandy Grunwald to Bill Clinton, "Free Media Scheduling," reprinted in Goldman et al., *Quest for the Presidency*, 665.
57. Ibid., 240–41. This is consistent with the public opinion polls—largely in support of Clinton—when his private life became more public during his impeachment crisis. See "Clinton's Popularity Up Despite His Plight," *CQ Weekly* 13 February 1999, 356–57.
58. Goldman et al., *Quest for the Presidency*, 422–23.
59. Howard Kurtz, "Second Honeymoon with Press Didn't Last," *Washington Post*, 4 October 1992, A21.
60. Goldman et al., *Quest for the Presidency*, 551–52.
61. *Larry King Live*, CNN Transcript, "The New Media Politics," 9 November 1992.
62. Sabato, *Rise of Political Consultants*, 69.
63. Quoted in Scott C. Ratzan, "The Real Agenda Setters: Pollsters in the 1988 Presidential Campaign," *American Behavioral Scientist* 32 (March/April 1989): 451.
64. Quoted in Paul Simon, *Winners and Losers* (New York: Continuum, 1989), 165.
65. Sabato, *Rise of Political Consultants*, 71.
66. Ibid., 21.
67. Gerald M. Goldhaber, "A Pollster's Sampler," *Public Opinion* (June/July 1984): 50.
68. Mark Levy, "Polling and the Presidential Election," in *Annals of the American Academy of Political and Social Science: Polling and the Democratic Consensus* (Beverly Hills, Calif.: Sage, 1984), 88; and Jerry Hagstrom and Robert Guskind, "Calling the Races," *National Journal*, 30 July 1988, 1974.
69. Hagstrom and Guskind, "Calling the Races," 1974.
70. Kathleen Hall Jamieson, *Packaging the Presidency: A History and Criticism of Presidential Campaign Advertising* (New York: Oxford University Press, 1984), 429.

   In primaries, candidates can use polls to detect opportunities to surpass the media's expectations. Louis Harris analyzed 1960 polls in West Virginia and discovered that although conventional wisdom considered the primary a sure loss for Kennedy, JFK in fact had considerable support. Thus the Kennedy campaign targeted the state for a critical "upset" victory. In 1988 the Dukakis campaign used the same strategy in the Wisconsin primary against Jesse Jackson. In its preprimary polls, the press showed a tight race, but Dukakis pollster Tubby Harrison's numbers revealed a double-digit lead for Dukakis. According to Christine Black and Thomas Oliphant, "Dukakis' aides ... privately reasoned that the bigger Jackson became in the press, the harder he would fall, and Dukakis would rise if Harrison's data were accurate." As it turned out, the Wisconsin results were as Harrison had foreseen: 48 percent for Dukakis, 28 percent for Jackson, and 17 percent for Gore. The surprisingly large margin—actually not a surprise for Dukakis—deflated Jackson's support, and Dukakis went on to win all subsequent primaries. See Sabato, *Rise of Political Consultants*, 69–70; Christine M. Black and Thomas Oliphant, *All by Myself: The Unmaking of a Presidential Campaign* (Chester, Conn.: Globe Pequot Press, 1989), 128.

71. See Memorandum from Tubby Harrison, Clifford Brown, and Lynda Powell, "Re: Target Voters and the Debate," 19 September 1988; also, Memorandum from Dukakis's pollsters, 4 September 1988. These memorandums are part of a set of unpublished internal campaign memos and other reports from Dukakis's pollsters to the candidate.
72. Goldman et al., *Quest for the Presidency*, 292.
73. See April memo from Fred Steeper to Bush reprinted in ibid., 666–75.
74. Ibid, 531.
75. "Face Off: A Conversation with the Presidents' Pollsters Patrick Caddell and Richard Wirthlin," *Public Opinion* 3 (December/January 1981): 5.
76. "Pollsters on the Polls: An Interview with Vincent Breglio," *Public Opinion* 11 (January/February 1989): 4.
77. Germond and Witcover, *Whose Broad Stripes and Bright Stars?*, 416.
78. Ibid.
79. Rosenstiel, *Strange Bedfellows*, 279–80, and Goldman et al. *Quest for the Presidency*, 504–5.
80. Danny N. Bellenger, Kenneth L. Bernhardt, and Jac L. Goldstucker, *Qualitative Research in Marketing* (Chicago: American Marketing Association, 1976), 8.
81. Myril Axelrod, "10 Essentials for Good Qualitative Research," *Marketing News* 8 (14 March 1975): 10.
82. Elizabeth Kolbert, "Test-Marketing a President," *New York Times Magazine*, 30 August 1992, 21.
83. William D. Wells, "Group Interviewing," in *Focus Group Interviews* (Chicago: American Marketing Association, 1979), 2.
84. Hagstrom and Guskind, "Calling the Races," 1974.
85. Peter Goldman and Tom Mathews, *Quest for the Presidency, 1988* (New York: Simon and Schuster, 1989), 358.
86. David R. Runkel, ed., *Campaign for the President: The Managers Look at '88* (Dover, Mass.: Auburn House, 1989), 157.
87. Ibid.
88. "Pollsters on the Polls: An Interview with Irwin 'Tubby' Harrison," *Public Opinion* 11 (January/February 1989): 5.
89. Nicholas Mitropoulos and Nelson W. Polsby, "Retrospective Analysis of Campaign '88: Process and Politics," audiotape, Institute of Governmental Studies, 1989.
90. "Pollsters on the Polls," 51.
91. See 27 April memorandum from Stan Greenberg, James Carville, and Frank Greer to Bill Clinton on "The General Election Project," reprinted in Goldman et al., *Quest for the Presidency*, 657–64.
92. Thomas and Goldman, "Victory March," 45.
93. Hagstrom and Guskind, "Calling the Races," 1975.
94. Levy, "Polling and the Presidential Election," 91.
95. Goldman and Mathews, *Quest for the Presidency, 1988*, 358.
96. Goldman et al., *Quest for the Presidency*, 257–58.
97. Ibid., 563–64.
98. 13 October memorandum from Fred Steeper to George Bush on "Voter Reactions to the First Debate," reprinted in ibid., 729–30.
99. Hagstrom and Guskind, "Calling the Races," 1974.
100. Goldman and Mathews, *Quest for the Presidency, 1988*, 400.
101. Rosenstiel, *Strange Bedfellows*, 327–31.
102. Ibid., 302.
103. Levy, "Polling and the Presidential Election," 86.
104. Ibid., 89.
105. Sabato, *Rise of the Political Consultants*, 112.
106. Jerry Hagstrom, "Peddling a President," *National Journal*, 10 September 1988, 2250.
107. Sabato, *Rise of Political Consultants*, 113.
108. Hagstrom, "Peddling a President," 2250.

109. Longer ads are occasionally produced, especially for small, low-cost media markets, but prime-time is dominated by ten- and thirty-second spots.

110. Luntz, *Candidates, Consultants, and Campaigns,* 83–88.

111. Rosenstiel, *Strange Bedfellows,* 285–88. For one of the newspaper critiques of the Bush ad, see Howard Kurtz, "30-Second Politics," *Washington Post,* 24 September 1992, A10.

112. David Chagall, *The New Kingmakers* (New York: Harcourt Brace Jovanovich, 1981), 218.

113. Sabato, *Rise of the Political Consultants,* 182.

114. Luntz, *Candidates, Campaigns, and Consultants,* 210.

115. John Power, "Plug in to Cable TV," *Campaigns and Elections* 8 (September/October 1987): 54–57.

116. Luntz, *Candidates, Campaigns, and Consultants,* 210.

117. Rosenstiel, *Strange Bedfellows,* 165–66, 174–75; Goldman et al., *Quest for the Presidency,* 665.

118. Rosenstiel, *Strange Bedfellows,* 316–17.

119. Rosenstiel, *Strange Bedfellows,* 164–65.

120. Luntz, *Candidates, Campaigns, and Consultants,* 107.

121. Ibid., 109–10.

122. Ibid., 211–12.

123. Dan Koeppel, "A Race to the Finish Line: Election Fundraising Blends Old Standards with High-Tech Appeals," *Direct* (November 1992): 20.

124. Richard Armstrong, *The Next Hurrah: The Communications Revolution in American Politics* (New York: Beech Tree Books, 1988), 197.

125. Ibid., 198.

126. Goldman et al., *Quest for the Presidency,* 209–10.

127. Occasionally, inducements of a less savory kind may be offered. For example, the Kennedy organization was alleged to have used bribes in the 1960 West Virginia primary. On the Republican side, in 1993 consultant Ed Rollins claimed, and later denied, that he had paid clergymen in the community $500,000 to depress the African American vote during the New Jersey gubernatorial election. See Harry W. Ernst, *The Primary That Made a President: West Virginia, 1960* (New York: McGraw-Hill, 1962), 31; and Jerry Gray, "Whitman Denies Report by Aide That Campaign Paid Off Blacks," *New York Times,* 11 November 1993.

128. There is another possibility: voters who turn out only by being dinned at by the media are likely to be less stable in their political orientations and will therefore vote less for the party and more for the candidate whose name or personality seems more familiar to them. This, in a year when an Eisenhower is on the ticket, might well mean Republican votes. The most thoroughly documented research on the question suggests that increasing turnout by relaxing registration rules would have little or no effect on the partisan distribution of the vote. See Steven J. Rosenstone and Raymond E. Wolfinger, "The Effect of Registration Laws on Voter Turnout," *American Political Science Review* 72 (March 1978): 22–48; and John R. Petrocik, "Voter Turnout and Electoral Preference: The Anomalous Reagan Elections," in *Elections in America,* ed. Kay L. Schlozman (Boston: Allen and Unwin, 1987), 239–59. Petrocik argues that the 1980 election did not fit the general pattern. Low turnout, he claims, seriously hurt Jimmy Carter.

129. See Philip E. Converse, Angus Campbell, Warren E. Miller, and Donald E. Stokes, "Stability and Change in 1960: A Reinstating Election," *American Political Science Review* 55 (June 1961): 269–80, esp. 274. This is roughly what Stanley Greenberg, President Clinton's poll taker, calculated Clinton would have received in 1992 had Ross Perot not been a candidate. Stanley B. Greenberg, *Middle Class Dreams* (New York: Times Books, 1995), 13.

130. Raymond E. Wolfinger, "Dealignment, Realignment, and Mandates," in *The American Elections of 1984,* ed. Austin Ranney (Durham, N.C.: Duke University Press, 1985), 277–96.

131. See I.M. Destler, "The Myth of the 'Electoral Lock,'" *PS: Political Science and Politics* 29 (September 1996): 491–94.
132. See Angus Campbell, Philip E. Converse, Warren E. Miller, and Donald E. Stokes, *The American Voter* (New York: Wiley, 1960), 537–38; and Herbert H. Hyman and Paul B. Sheatsley, "The Political Appeal of President Eisenhower," *Public Opinion Quarterly* 19 (Winter 1955–56): 26–39.
133. In 1962 Raymond E. Wolfinger and his associates administered a questionnaire to 308 "students" at an anticommunism school conducted by Dr. Fred Schwarz's Christian Anti-Communism Crusade in Oakland, California. Among the findings of this study were that 278 of the 302 persons in this sample who voted in 1960 (or 92 percent of those who voted) had voted for Nixon and that 58 percent of those who answered the question chose Goldwater over Nixon for 1964. At about the same time, a nationwide Gallup poll showed Goldwater the choice of only 13 percent of Republicans. Raymond E. Wolfinger, Barbara Kaye Wolfinger, Kenneth Prewitt, and Sheilah Rosenhack, "America's Radical Right: Politics and Ideology," in *Ideology and Discontent,* ed. David E. Apter (New York: Free Press, 1964), 267–69. Analysis of various election returns and of a 1954 Gallup poll suggests that support for the late Senator Joseph McCarthy was importantly determined by party affiliation, with Republicans far exceeding Democrats or independents in the ranks of his supporters. See Nelson W. Polsby, "Towards an Explanation of McCarthyism," *Political Studies* 8 (October 1960): 250–71.
134. Louis Harris Survey News Releases, New York, 13 July 1964, and 14 September 1964. Some of the Harris survey findings on foreign affairs are shown here:

TABLE 5-6—ISSUE DIFFERENCES BETWEEN VOTERS AND GOLDWATER, 1964

Issues	Voters describe Goldwater position		Voters describe own position	
	July	September	July	September
Go to war over Cuba				
Percentage for	78	71	29	29
Percentage against	22	29	71	71
Use atomic bombs in Asia				
Percentage for	72	58	18	18
Percentage against	28	42	82	82
United Nations				
Percentage for	42	50	82	83
Percentage against	58	50	18	17

135. "Our Cheesy Democracy," *New Republic,* 3 November 1986, 8–9.
136. Sabato, *Rise of Political Consultants,* 169–70. One writer claims that the height of negativity was reached in that year when Johnson's campaign, along with the Daisy ad, included an "ad (never aired) that tied Goldwater to the Ku Klux Klan, a third that featured the eastern seaboard being sawed off and cast out to sea, ... and a fourth that showed a little girl eating an ice cream cone laced with strontium 90 and cesium 137, the presumed result of Goldwater's commitment to nuclear testing." Armstrong, *The Next Hurrah,* 17.
137. Ibid., 170–71.
138. Rich Galen, "Nail the Opposition," *Campaigns and Elections* 9 (May– June 1988): 45. See also Rich Galen, "The Best Defense Is a Good Offense," *Campaigns and Elections* 9 (October/November 1988): 29–34.
139. Sabato, *Rise of Political Consultants,* 166.
140. Galen, "The Best Defense Is a Good Offense," 30.
141. Jamieson, *Packaging the Presidency,* 436.

142. Steven W. Colford, "Ailes: What He Wants Next: Bush Adman Aims Attack at Madison Ave.," *Advertising Age,* 14 November 1988, 1, 67.
143. "In elections at home, which Muskie contests vigorously and wins by handsome margins despite the state's strong Republican orientation, he rarely mentions his opponent's name, let alone attack him. He dwells instead on his own positive (and pragmatic) approach to problems....Throughout the campaign he waits hopefully for his opponent to strike, in desperation, some more or less low blow in response to which Muskie can become magnificently outraged. Then, voice trembling with indignation but still without mentioning the opponent's name, he chastises the opposition for stooping to such levels, and thus manages to introduce a little color into the campaign. Usually the opposition obliges him: 'I can always count on the Republicans doing something stupid,' he once said with satisfaction." David Nevin, *Muskie of Maine* (New York: Random House, 1972), 27.
144. Robert E. Sherwood, *Roosevelt and Hopkins* (New York: Harper, 1948), 821. The effectiveness of underhanded tactics remains unknown. Dan Nimmo, *The Political Persuaders* (Englewood Cliffs, N.J.: Prentice Hall, 1970), 50, argues that deviating from a vague sense of "fairness" that exists in the electorate may backfire. There is plenty of evidence on the other side as well. For a treasure trove of such material, see Kelley, *Professional Public Relations and Political Power.*
145. Ibid., 362–63.
146. The best description of these events is found in Fred Emery, *Watergate: The Corruption of American Politics and the Fall of Richard Nixon* (New York: Times Books, 1994); see especially 21-137. See also Stanley Kutler, ed., *Abuse of Power* (New York: The Free Press, 1997); Carl Bernstein and Bob Woodward, *All The President's Men* (New York: Simon and Schuster, 1974), 112–62, 197, 199, 251–53, 285–86, 328; and Senate Select Committee on Presidential Campaign Activities, *The Senate Watergate Report* (Washington, D.C.: Government Printing Office, 1974).
147. Thomas and Goldman, "Victory March," 65.
148. Lloyd Grove, "When They Ask If Dukakis Has a Heart, They Mean It," *Washington Post Weekly Edition,* 17–23 October 1988, 24–25.
149. Curt Suplee, "Bush's Candidacy Is Being Cooled Off by His Warmth Index," *Washington Post National Weekly Edition,* 25–31 July 1988, 23–24.
150. Goldman et al., *Quest for the Presidency,* 657–58.
151. See White, *Making of the President, 1960,* 269–75; White, *Making of the President, 1964,* passim; and Crouse, *Boys on the Bus.*
152. Thomas and Goldman, "Victory March," 63.
153. Department of Marketing, Miami University, Oxford Research Associates, *The Influence of Television on the Election of 1952* (Oxford, Ohio, 1954), 151–60.
154. See White, *Making of the President, 1960,* 282–83; and Herbert A. Selz and Richard D. Yoakum, "Production Diary of the Debates," in *The Great Debates: Kennedy versus Nixon, 1960,* ed. Sidney Kraus (Bloomington: Indiana University Press, 1977), 73–126.
155. Ibid.; see also Nixon, *Six Crises,* 346–86.
156. Earl Mazo, *Richard Nixon* (New York: Harper, 1959), 21–22, 362–69.
157. See Elihu Katz and Jacob J. Feldman, "The Debates in the Light of Research: A Survey of Surveys, " in Kraus, *Great Debates,* 173–223.
158. See Charles Mohr, "President Tells Polish-Americans He Regrets Remark on East Europe," *New York Times,* 9 October 1976; and R.W. Apple Jr., "Economy Is Stressed by Dole and Mondale During Sharp Debate," *New York Times,* 16 October 1976.
159. See Hedrick Smith, "No Clear Winner Apparent; Scene Is Simple and Stark," *New York Times,* 29 October 1980. After the election, Terence Smith of the *Times* wrote: "The continual emphasis on Mr. Reagan's image as a hair-triggered proponent of American military intervention—the war and peace issue as it came to be called—may have been overdone, in the opinion of some Carter aides. In June, Mr. [Jody] Powell [Carter's Press Secretary] was telling reporters that Mr. Reagan was 'too benign' a figure to be painted as a warmonger, a la Barry Goldwater in 1964. 'It wouldn't be believable,' he said then.

"But beginning with his Middle Western swing the day after Labor Day, Mr. Carter stressed this point above all others, warning that the election was a choice between war and peace. He did so because of private polls taken by Mr. Caddell that showed this to be the public's greatest hidden fear about the Republican candidate. The President was hoist by his own hyperbole, in the view of some Carter aides, who feel the President grossly overstated Mr. Reagan's record and aroused the public's skepticism about his argument. In the end, they feel, Mr. Reagan's cool, collected, nonthreatening performance in the debate defused the issue." See "Carter Post-Mortem: Debate Hurt but Wasn't Only Cause for Defeat," *New York Times,* 9 November 1980.

160. Gerald M. Pomper, "The Presidential Election," in *The Election of 1984,* ed. Gerald Pomper (Chatham, N.J.: Chatham House, 1985), 76.
161. Richard Brookhiser, *The Outside Story* (Garden City, N.Y.: Doubleday, 1986), 272.
162. Hunt, "The Campaign and the Issues," 149–58.
163. Goldman et al., *Quest for the Presidency,* 559.
164. Ibid., 563–64.
165. Ibid., 562.
166. Ibid., 572–73.
167. Ibid., 577.
168. Thomas and Goldman, "Victory March," 112–17.
169. See Austin Ranney, ed., *The Past and Future of Presidential Debates* (Washington, D.C.: American Enterprise Institute, 1977).
170. Steve Gostel, "Argument Begins over Presidential Debates," *Oakland Tribune,* 19 February 1987. See also James A. Barnes, "Debating the Debates," *National Journal,* 28 February 1987, 527; and Newton Minow and Clifford M. Sloan, *For Great Debates: A New Plan for Future Presidential TV Debates* (New York: Priority Press, 1987).
171. Goldman et al., *Quest for the Presidency,* 534–36, 554.
172. See Jules Abels, *Out of the Jaws of Victory* (New York: Holt, 1959).
173. Robert Alford, "The Role of Social Class in American Voting Behavior," *Western Political Quarterly* 16 (March 1963): 180–94; and Campbell et al., *American Voter,* chap. 13.
174. White, *Making of the President, 1960,* 203–4.
175. Ibid., 315.
176. White, *Making of the President, 1968,* 331.
177. David Shribman and James M. Perry, "Self-Inflicted Injury: Dukakis's Campaign Was Marred by a Series of Lost Opportunities," *Wall Street Journal,* 8 November 1988, 1.
178. "'Liberal' Tag Hurts Dukakis, Times Mirror Survey Finds," *Times Mirror News Interest Index,* 22 September 1988.
179. Ibid.
180. For extensive recital of these critiques, see Black and Oliphant, *All by Myself.*
181. Shribman and Perry, "Self-Inflicted Injury," 1.
182. Karen M. Paget, "Afterthoughts on the Dukakis/Bentsen Campaign," *Public Affairs Report* 30 (January 1989): 1, 4.
183. John Jacobs, "Dukakis Admits Campaign 'Mistakes,'" *San Francisco Examiner,* 14 October 1989.
184. Michael J. Robinson, "Can Values Save George Bush?" *Public Opinion* (July/August 1988): 11. This was a *Times Mirror* poll conducted by the Gallup organization.
185. John Dillon, "Mood of America: Shifting to Bush?" *Christian Science Monitor,* 29 September 1988, 1, reporting on a *Times Mirror* survey.
186. Ibid., 28.
187. Rosenstiel, *Strange Bedfellows,* 94.
188. Ibid., 246–49.
189. Ibid., 283.
190. Thomas and Goldman, "Victory March," 56–68, 80–90, 106–14.
191. Ibid., 93–98, 120–25.

CHAPTER 6

1. There are many examples of the party reform school of thought. See, for example, Woodrow Wilson, *Congressional Government* (Boston: Houghton Mifflin, 1889); Henry Jones Ford, *The Rise and Growth of American Politics* (New York: Macmillan, 1898); A. Lawrence Lowell, *Public Opinion and Popular Government* (New York: Longmans, Green, 1913); William MacDonald, *A New Constitution for a New America* (New York: B.W. Huebsch, 1921); William Y. Elliott, *The Need for Constitutional Reform* (New York: McGraw-Hill, 1935); E.E. Schattschneider, *Party Government* (New York: Farrar and Rinehart, 1940); Henry Hazlitt, *A New Constitution Now* (New York: McGraw-Hill, 1942); Thomas K. Finletter, *Can Representative Government Do the Job?* (New York: Reynal and Hitchcock, 1945); James M. Burns, *Congress on Trial* (New York: Harper, 1949); Committee on Political Parties, American Political Science Association, *Toward a More Responsible Two-Party System* (New York: APSA, 1950); Stephen K. Bailey, *The Condition of Our National Political Parties* (New York: Fund for the Republic, 1959); James M. Burns, *The Deadlock of Democracy* (Englewood Cliffs, N.J.: Prentice Hall, 1963); Lloyd N. Cutler and C. Douglas Dillon, "Can We Improve on Our Constitutional System?" *Wall Street Journal,* 15 February 1983; and Lloyd N. Cutler, "To Form a Government," *Foreign Affairs* 59 (Fall 1980): 126–43. The work of the Committee on Political Parties, representing the collective judgment of a panel of distinguished political scientists in 1950, is the statement we refer to most often. In 1971 a member of the committee published a thoughtful reconsideration of its main ideas. See Evron M. Kirkpatrick, "Toward a More Responsible Two-Party System: Political Science, Policy Science, or Pseudo Science?" *American Political Science Review* 65 (December 1971): 965–90.
2. Committee on Political Parties, *Toward a More Responsible Two-Party System,* 1.
3. Ibid., 66.
4. Ibid., 15.
5. A sample of this literature might include E. Pendleton Herring, *The Politics of Democracy* (New York: Norton, 1940); Herbert Agar, *The Price of Union* (Boston: Houghton Mifflin, 1950); Malcolm C. Moos, *Politics, Presidents, and Coattails* (Baltimore: Johns Hopkins University Press, 1952); Austin Ranney and Willmoore Kendall, *Democracy and the American Party System* (New York: Harcourt, Brace, 1956); David B. Truman, *The Governmental Process* (New York: Knopf, 1953); John Fischer, "Unwritten Rules of American Politics," *Harper's,* November 1948, 27–36; Peter Drucker, "A Key to American Politics: Calhoun's Pluralism," *Review of Politics* 10 (October 1948): 412–26; Ernest F. Griffith, *Congress: Its Contemporary Role* (New York: New York University Press, 1951); Murray Stedman and Herbert Sonthoff, "Party Responsibility: A Critical Inquiry," *Western Political Quarterly* 4 (September 1951): 454–86; Julius Turner, "Responsible Parties: A Dissent from the Floor," *American Political Science Review* 45 (March 1951): 143–52; William Goodman, "How Much Political Party Centralization Do We Want?" *Journal of Politics* 13 (November 1961): 536–61; and Austin Ranney, *The Doctrine of Responsible Party Government* (Urbana: University of Illinois Press, 1954).
6. Herring, *Politics of Democracy,* 327.
7. Ibid., 420.
8. Committee on Political Parties, *Toward a More Responsible Two-Party System,* 19.
9. Bailey, *Condition of Our National Political Parties,* 20.
10. See David B. Truman, "Federalism and the Party System," in *Federalism: Mature and Emergent,* ed. Arthur W. MacMahon (New York: Russell and Russell, 1962), 115–36. This situation is deplored in Cutler and Dillon, "Can We Improve on Our Constitutional System?" One remedy, changing the terms of office of representatives and senators to coincide exactly with presidential elections, is analyzed in Nelson W. Polsby, "A Note on the President's Modest Proposal," in Polsby, *Political Promises* (New York: Oxford University Press, 1974), 101–7.

11. Members of Congress with local strength not based on ideology are not at all uncommon. See, for instance, examples in Raymond A. Bauer, Ithiel de Sola Pool, and Lewis Anthony Dexter, *American Business and Public Policy* (New York: Atherton Press, 1963), chaps. 16, 18, and 19; Richard F. Fenno, *Home Style* (Boston: Little, Brown, 1978); and Bruce Cain, John Ferejohn, and Morris Fiorina, *The Personal Vote* (Cambridge, Mass.: Harvard University Press, 1987).

12. The near removal in 1987 of Les Aspin as chair of the House Armed Services Committee, however, was clearly based on policy differences, and so were several other threats to Democratic committee chairs over the past decade.

13. For strong evidence on this point, see Samuel Stouffer, *Communism, Conformity and Civil Liberties* (Garden City, N.Y.: Doubleday, 1955), passim; and Julian L. Woodward and Elmo Roper, "Political Activity of American Citizens," *American Political Science Review* 44 (December 1950): 872–75. Two more recent studies have examined the voters' desire not to be interfered with by the government as well as the importance of their private lives to them as compared with national issues. See Paul M. Sniderman and Richard A. Brody, "Coping: The Ethic of Self-Reliance," *American Journal of Political Science* 21 (August 1977): 501–21; and Richard A. Brody and Paul M. Sniderman, "From Life Space to Polling Place: The Relevance of Personal Concerns for Voting Behavior," *British Journal of Political Science* 7 (July 1977): 337–60.

14. See, for example, Jack Citrin, Herbert McClosky, J. Merrill Shanks, and Paul M. Sniderman, "Personal and Political Sources of Alienation," *British Journal of Political Science* 5 (January 1975): 1–31; and Arthur H. Miller, "Political Issues and Trust in Government: 1964–70," along with the "Comment" by Jack Citrin, both in *American Political Science Review* 68 (September 1974): 951–1001.

15. Jürgen Habermas, *Legitimation Crisis* (Boston: Beacon Press, 1975).

16. An earlier statement of main themes in this section is Aaron B. Wildavsky's "On the Superiority of National Conventions," *Review of Politics* 24 (July 1962): 307–19.

17. Everett Carll Ladd, "Party Reform and the Public Interest," paper delivered at the Brookings Conference on Party and Electoral Renewal, Washington, D.C., 6–7 April 1987. See, more generally, Gary R. Orren and Nelson W. Polsby, eds., *Media and Momentum: The New Hampshire Primary and Nomination Politics* (Chatham, N.J.: Chatham House, 1987).

18. See V.O. Key Jr., *American State Politics* (New York: Knopf, 1956), chap. 6.

19. V.O. Key Jr., *Southern Politics* (New York: Knopf, 1950), for example, chap. 3 (Alabama) and chap. 9 (Arkansas).

20. Key, *American State Politics*, 216.

21. Nelson W. Polsby, "Was Hart's Life Unfairly Probed?" *New York Times*, 6 May 1987.

22. See Austin Ranney, *The Federalization of Presidential Primaries* (Washington, D.C.: American Enterprise Institute, 1978), 507; see also Commission on Presidential Nomination and Party Structure (Morley Winograd, chair), *Openness, Participation and Party Building: Reforms for a Stronger Democratic Party* (Washington, D.C.: The Commission, 1979), 32–37.

23. A classic statement is Moisei Ostrogorski, *Democracy and the Party System in the United States* (New York: Macmillan, 1910), 158–60. See also Elmo Roper, "What Price Conventions?" *Saturday Review*, 3 September 1960, 26.

24. The most famous account is still Ostrogorski, *Democracy and the Party System in the United States*, 141–42.

25. At least one notable from the world of television news apparently feels as we do about this problem. Walter Cronkite argues that "it is not necessary that we be admitted to the actual floor of the convention. There is a better way (such as the use of immediate off-floor interview booths) to cover the non-podium action in order to permit a more orderly convention procedure." Cronkite, *The Challenges of Change* (Washington, D.C.: Public Affairs Press, 1971), 75.

26. See Herbert McClosky, Paul J. Hoffman, and Rosemary O'Hara, "Issue Conflict and Consensus Among Party Leaders and Followers," *American Political Science Review*

54 (June 1960): 406–27; Jeane Kirkpatrick, *The New Presidential Elite: Men and Women in National Politics* (New York: Russell Sage Foundation, 1976); and John S. Jackson III et al., "Political Party Leaders and the Mass Public: 1980–1984," paper presented at the annual meeting of the Midwest Political Science Association, Chicago, 19 April 1987.

27. John Morris, "Negro Delegates Drop Plans to Walk Out as a Demonstration against Goldwater," *New York Times,* 16 July 1964.

28. Gerald M. Pomper, *Elections in America: Control and Influence in Democratic Politics,* rev. ed. (New York: Longman, 1980), 185–87.

29. Alan D. Monroe, "American Party Platforms and Public Opinion," *American Journal of Political Science* 27 (February 1983): 38.

30. Ibid., 27–42.

31. There were, of course, many other plans for "reform," involving almost all possible combinations of these three alternatives. For example, President Nixon at one point recommended that the 40 percent plurality plank that usually goes with the direct election proposal be applied instead to the present electoral college setup. See David S. Broder, "Mitchell Recommends Electoral Compromise," *Washington Post,* 14 March 1969. A second example is the "federal system plan" of Senators Dole and Eagleton, which stated the following:

1.   A president would be elected if he (a) won a plurality of the national vote and (b) won either pluralities in more than 50 percent of the states and D.C., or pluralities in states with 50 percent of the voters in the election.

2.   If no candidate qualified, the election would go to an electoral college where the states would be represented as they are today, and each candidate would automatically receive the electoral votes of the states he won.

3.   In the unlikely event that no candidate received a majority of the electoral votes, the electoral votes of states that went for third-party candidates would be divided between the two leading national candidates in proportion to their share of the popular votes in those states. *Congressional Record,* 5 March 1970, S3026.

   These plans had the following characteristics: (1) they were too complicated to solve any problems of public confusion or public perception that they are not "democratic," and (2) they had no significant body of congressional support.

32. This argument roughly corresponds to one of the main approaches to calculating the strategic advantage of members of a coalition, pioneered by Irwin Mann and Lloyd Shapley. The argument proceeds as follows: "the Shapley value defines the power of actor A as the number of permutations (orderings) in which A occupies the pivotal position (that is, orderings in which A can cast the deciding vote) divided by the total number of possible permutations." See George Rabinowitz and Stuart MacDonald, "The Power of the States in U.S. Presidential Elections," *American Political Science Review* 80 (March 1986): 66. This approach shows the large states to be the winners. Their influence is more than proportional to their size. This model is often supplemented by an analysis that attempts to determine the influence of the average voter within each state. Along these lines, Lawrence Longley and James Dana Jr., conclude that residents of California (the most advantaged state) have more than twice the "relative voting power" of the inhabitants of Arkansas (the least advantaged state). See Longley and Dana, "New Empirical Estimates of the Biases of the Electoral College for the 1980s," *Western Political Quarterly* 37 (March 1984): 157–75.

   Yet these calculations assume that all patterns of state voting are equally likely. This obviously is not a realistic assumption. Some states lean strongly toward one party. Building on this insight, Rabinowitz and MacDonald utilize the results of recent elections to identify likely pivotal states and make their own calculation of relative voting power. Once again, the large states are the winners. There are differences, however, from the results of the previous model. Most large states are even more influential, but the power of the states that lean strongly toward one party is diminished. Strongly Democratic Massachusetts is the biggest loser, dropping to a mere one-seventh of its influence as determined by the Shapley model.

Which model of state electoral power is more accurate? The second, which takes into account likely voting patterns, would appear more complete. Yet pivot patterns are an imperfect guide to future behavior. With Jimmy Carter at the head of the ticket in 1980, Georgia was one of the most strongly Democratic states in the nation. In 1984 Walter Mondale lost Georgia by an even larger margin than the nation as a whole. Predicting future swing states from past behavior may lead to serious errors.

One might also question the emphasis on the importance of swing states. Is a state that provides a loyal and consistent base of support for one party necessarily unimportant? Is not a solid base as important to a winning coalition as more volatile swing states? In recent years, the Republicans have started presidential campaigns with a very strong position in the mountain states. Since the outcome in these states has not been in doubt, neither campaign expends much effort on them. Thus it could be said that one-party states are less important. On the other hand, a safe base is valuable. The Republicans start ahead and are able to focus their resources on other areas. Democrats would love to have such a safe base of their own (besides D.C.). In short, calculations of state influence depend heavily on the assumptions one begins with.

33. For example, Ed Gossett, original cosponsor of the district plan, asked: "Is it fair, is it honest, is it democratic, is it to the best interests of anyone in fact to place such a premium on a few thousand labor votes or Italian votes or Irish votes or Negro votes or Jewish votes or Polish votes, or Communist votes or big city machine votes, simply because they happen to be located in two or three industrial pivotal states? Can anything but evil come from placing such temptation and power in the hands of political parties and political bosses? Both said groups and said politicians are computed as a nation suffers." Cited in David Brook, "Proposed Electoral College Reforms and Urban Minorities," paper delivered at the annual meeting of the American Political Science Association, New York, August 1969, 6.

34. Eric R.A.N. Smith and Peverill Squire argue, following Shapley's logic, that the importance of states should be calculated according to the ease with which undecided voters can be influenced. While this method differs from ours, it also leads to the conclusion that southern states would gain in influence if the electoral college was abolished. See Eric R.A.N. Smith and Peverill Squire, "Direct Election of the President and Power of the States," *Western Political Quarterly* 40 (March 1987): 31–44.

35. In "The South Will Not Rise Again Through Direct Election of the President, Polsby and Wildavsky Notwithstanding," *Journal of Politics* 31 (August 1969): 808–11, Professor Harvey Zeidenstein shows that the winner's margin of victory in eight large northern urban states, taken together, was greater than in the eleven states of the old Confederacy, taken together, in four of the six presidential elections between 1948 and 1968. From this he concludes that the influence of northern urban states, where the votes are, is likely to be very great under a system of direct elections. We agree, but we argue in the text that direct elections improve the strategic position of one-party states (including some southern states), as compared with the electoral college winner-take-all system. On this issue, Zeidenstein is silent.

36. On 18 September 1969, by a vote of 339 to 70, a direct-election plan with a 40 percent plurality runoff provision was passed by the U.S. House of Representatives. See *Congressional Record*, 18 September 1969, H8142–43; for the content of the bill, see *Congressional Record*, 10 September 1969, H7745–46. For more recent discussion of proposed reforms, see Committee on the Judiciary, U.S. Senate, *Hearings on the Electoral College and Direct Election*, 95th Cong. (Washington, D.C., 1977).

37. Harold W. Stanley and Richard G. Niemi, *Vital Statistics on American Politics*, 4th ed. (Washington, D.C.: CQ Press, 1994), 90. In 1968, the figures were similar when George Wallace ran a strong third-party campaign in the race between Richard Nixon and Hubert Humphrey. As in 1992, a fourth candidate would have needed only 6 or 7 percent of the national total to keep either major-party candidate from having the required 40 percent (Nixon won with only 43 percent, although he had 56.2 percent of the electoral vote). The Michigan Survey Research Center finds that only 1.5 percent of the voters in 1968 felt that Senator Eugene McCarthy was the

best man for president in the spring and still felt that way after the election. If all participants in the system had known that he was not going to be defeated and disappear but would be a serious candidate at least through the first election, it is at least possible to conjecture that he could have picked up an additional 4 or 5 percent. Philip E. Converse, Warren E. Miller, Jerrold G. Rusk, and Arthur C. Wolfe, "Continuity and Change in American Politics: Parties and Issues in the 1968 Election," *American Political Science Review* 63 (December 1969): 1092.

38. The article that deals most clearly with the electoral college in terms of its virtues of conciliation and broad coalition building is John Wildenthal, "Consensus After L.B.J.," *Southwest Review* 53 (Spring 1968): 113–30. Wildenthal argues in part, "rather than complain about being deprived of a choice when both parties wage 'me too' campaigns, the American people should be thankful that the interests of a wide variety of Americans can be reconciled by both parties with similar programs."

39. One summary of this position was given by Representative Thomas Kleppe of North Dakota in the *Congressional Record,* 3 February 1969, H648. An interesting sidelight is his citation of Senator John F. Kennedy, who in 1956 had said, "After all, the states came into the Union as units. Electoral votes are not given out on the basis of voting numbers, but on the basis of population. The electoral votes belong to each state. The way the system works now is that we carry on a campaign in fifty states, and the electoral votes of that state belong to that party which carries each state. If we are going to change that system, it seems to me it would strike a blow at states' rights in major proportions. It would probably end states' rights and make this country one great unit."

40. Roscoe Drummond, "Perils of the Electoral System," *Washington Post,* 14 November 1960. An argument in some ways parallel to our own is contained in Anthony Lewis, "The Case Against Electoral Reform," *The Reporter,* 8 December 1960, 31–33. See also Allan Sindler, "Presidential Election Methods and Urban-Ethnic Interests," *Law and Contemporary Problems* 27 (Spring 1962): 213–33.

41. See Estes Kefauver, "The Electoral College: Old Reforms Take a New Look," *Law and Contemporary Problems* 27 (Spring 1962): 197.

42. See Arthur Schlesinger Jr., "A One-for-All Electoral College," *Wall Street Journal,* 19 August 1988, 16.

43. Despite popular misconceptions, even the 1964 Republican platform, written by supporters of Barry Goldwater, contained explicit promises to preserve these programs.

44. See Kirk H. Porter and Donald Bruce Johnson, *National Party Platforms, 1840–1956* (Urbana: University of Illinois Press, 1956). There are immense differences in both party platforms between 1932 and 1952. Note, for example, the subheadings under domestic policy in the 1952 platforms dealing with a range of topics entirely missing in 1932. The 1952 Democratic platform includes subheadings on full employment, price supports, farm credit, crop insurance, rural electrification, the physically handicapped, migratory workers, river basin development, arid areas, wildlife, recreation, Social Security, unemployment insurance, public assistance, needs of our aging citizens, health, medical education, hospitals and health centers, costs of medical care, public housing, slum clearance, urban redevelopment, aid to education, school lunches, day-care facilities, specific steps under civil rights, and many other subjects completely absent in 1932. Most of these worthy causes were also supported in the 1952 Republican platform and were missing from the 1932 Republican platform. Nevertheless, there are differences between the parties in 1952 in regard to use of the public lands, public housing, labor legislation, farm legislation, public power, aid to education, and much more. In regard to education, for example, the 1952 Republican platform reads: "The tradition of popular education, tax-supported and free to all, is strong with our people. The responsibility for sustaining this system of popular education has always rested upon the local communities and the states. We subscribe fully to this principle." The corresponding Democratic plank reads in part: "Local, State, and Federal government have shared responsibility to contribute appropriately to the pressing needs of our education system....We pledge immediate consideration

for those school systems which need further legislation to provide Federal aid for new school construction, teachers' salaries and school maintenance and repair." Porter and Johnson, 485, 504. See also Gerald M. Pomper, *Elections in America* (New York: Dodd, Mead, 1968), 149–78.

45. David R. Mayhew argues in *Divided We Govern: Party Control, Lawmaking and Investigations* (New Haven: Yale University Press, 1991) that sheer legislative productivity is not harmed by divided government, with its constraints on party responsibility.

Chapter 7

1. This parallels in many respects an argument to be found in Robert A. Dahl, *A Preface to Democratic Theory* (Chicago: University of Chicago Press, 1956).
2. Angus Campbell, Philip E. Converse, Warren E. Miller, and Donald E. Stokes, *The American Voter* (New York: Wiley, 1960), 525–27.
3. Richard A. Brody and Benjamin I. Page, "Policy Voting and the Electoral Process: The Vietnam War Issue," *American Political Science Review* 66 (September, 1972): 979. See also William Schneider, "The November 4 Vote for President: What Did It Mean?" in *The American Elections of 1980*, ed. Austin Ranney (Washington, D.C.: American Enterprise Institute, 1981), 212–62; and Nelson W. Polsby, "Party Realignment in the 1980 Election," *Yale Review* 72 (Autumn 1982): 43–54.
4. See Dahl, *Preface to Democratic Theory*, 124–31. The famous general statement from which this application is derived is Kenneth Arrow, *Social Choice and Individual Values* (New York: Wiley, 1951).
5. Raymond E. Wolfinger and Steven J. Rosenstone, *Who Votes?* (New Haven: Yale University Press, 1980), 83.
6. See Nelson W. Polsby, *Consequences of Party Reform* (New York: Oxford University Press, 1983).
7. See Jack Dennis, "Trends in Public Support for the American Political Party System," *British Journal of Political Science* (April 1975): 187–230.
8. For the story on split-ticket voting and its effects, see Gary C. Jacobson, *The Electoral Origins of Divided Government* (Boulder, Colo.: Westview Press, 1990).

Appendixes

CONTENTS

TABLE A.1—VOTE BY GROUPS IN PRESIDENTIAL ELECTIONS SINCE 1952

	1952		*1956*	
	Stevenson	Eisenhower	Stevenson	Eisenhower
National	44.6%	55.4%	42.2%	57.8%
Sex				
Men	47	53	45	55
Women	42	58	39	61
Race				
White	43	57	41	59
Nonwhite	79	21	61	39
Education				
College	34	66	31	69
High school	45	55	42	58
Grade school	52	48	50	50
Occupation				
Professional and business	36	64	32	68
White collar	40	60	37	63
Manual	55	45	50	50
Members of labor union families	61	39	57	43
Age				
Under 30 years	51	49	43	57
30–49 years	47	53	45	55
50 years and older	39	61	39	61
Religion				
Protestants	37	63	37	63
Catholics	56	44	51	49
Politics				
Republicans	8	92	4	96
Democrats	77	23	85	15
Independents	35	65	30	70
Region				
East	45	55	40	60
Midwest	42	58	41	59
South	51	49	49	51
West	42	58	43	57

TABLE A.1—(CONTINUED)

	1960		1964	
	Kennedy	Nixon	Johnson	Goldwater
National	50.1%	49.9%	61.3%	38.7%
Sex				
Men	52	48	60	40
Women	49	51	62	38
Race				
White	49	51	59	41
Nonwhite	68	32	94	6
Education				
College	39	61	52	48
High school	52	48	62	38
Grade school	55	45	66	34
Occupation				
Professional and business	42	58	54	46
White collar	48	52	57	43
Manual	60	40	71	29
Members of labor union families	65	35	73	27
Age				
Under 30 years	54	46	64	36
30–49 years	54	46	63	37
50 years and older	46	54	59	41
Religion				
Protestants	38	62	55	45
Catholics	78	22	76	24
Politics				
Republicans	5	95	20	80
Democrats	84	16	87	13
Independents	43	57	56	44
Region				
East	53	47	68	32
Midwest	48	52	61	39
South	51	49	52	48
West	49	51	60	40

TABLE A.1—(CONTINUED)

	1968			1972	
	Humphrey	Nixon	Wallace	McGovern	Nixon
National	43.0%	43.4%	13.6%	38%	62%
Sex					
Men	41	43	16	37	63
Women	45	43	12	38	62
Race					
White	38	47	15	32	68
Nonwhite	85	12	3	87	13
Education					
College	37	54	9	37	63
High school	42	43	15	34	66
Grade school	52	33	15	49	51
Occupation					
Professional and business	34	56	10	31	69
White collar	41	47	12	36	64
Manual	50	35	15	43	57
Members of labor union families	56	29	15	46	54
Age					
Under 30 years	47	38	15	48	52
30–49 years	44	41	15	33	67
50 years and older	41	47	12	36	64
Religion					
Protestants	35	49	16	30	70
Catholics	59	33	8	48	52
Politics					
Republicans	9	86	5	5	95
Democrats	74	12	14	67	33
Independents	31	44	25	31	69
Region					
East	50	43	7	42	58
Midwest	44	47	9	40	60
South	31	36	33	29	71
West	44	49	7	41	59

Table A.1—(continued)

	1976			1980		
	Carter	Ford	McCarthy	Carter	Reagan	Anderson
National	50%	48%	1%	41%	51%	7%
Sex						
Men	53	45	1	38	53	7
Women	48	51	*	44	49	6
Race						
White	46	52	1	36	56	7
Nonwhite	85	15	1	86	10	2
Education						
College	42	55	2	35	53	10
High school	54	46	*	43	51	5
Grade school	58	41	1	54	42	3
Occupation						
Professional and business	42	56	1	33	55	10
White collar	50	48	2	40	51	9
Manual	58	41	1	48	46	5
Members of labor union families	63	36	1	50	43	5
Age						
Under 30 years	53	45	1	47	41	11
30–49 years	48	49	2	38	52	8
50 years and older	52	48	*	41	54	4
Religion						
Protestants	46	53	*	39	54	6
Catholics	57	42	1	46	47	6
Politics						
Republicans	9	91	*	8	86	5
Democrats	82	18	*	69	26	4
Independents	38	57	4	29	55	14
Region						
East	51	47	1	43	47	9
Midwest	48	50	1	41	51	7
South	54	45	*	44	52	3
West	46	51	1	35	54	9

TABLE A.1—(CONTINUED)

	1984		*1988*	
	Mondale	Reagan	Dukakis	Bush
National	41%	59%	46%	54%
Sex				
Men	36	64	44	56
Women	45	55	48	52
Race				
White	34	66	41	59
Nonwhite	87	13	82	18
Education				
College	39	61	42	58
High school	43	57	46	54
Grade school	51	49	55	45
Occupation				
Professional and				
business	34	66		
White collar	47	53	NA	NA
Manual	46	54		
Members of labor				
union families	52	48	63	37
Age				
Under 30 years	40	60	37	63
30–49 years	40	60	45	55
50 years and older	41	59	49	51
Religion				
Protestants	39	61	42	58
Catholics	39	61	51	49
Politics				
Republicans	4	96	7	93
Democrats	79	21	85	15
Independents	33	67	43	57
Region				
East	46	54	51	49
Midwest	42	58	47	53
South	37	63	40	60
West	40	60	46	54

SOURCE: Gallup Monthly Opinion Index, December 1976, December 1980; *Gallup Poll,* 7 November 1984, November 1988, Report No. 278.
*Less than one percent.
*Nonunion.
NA = Not available.

TABLE A.2—VOTE BY GROUPS IN PRESIDENTIAL ELECTIONS, 1992

	1992		
	Clinton	Bush	Perot
National	44%	37%	14%
Sex			
Men	39	37	19
Women	48	36	10
Race			
White	40	40	15
Nonwhite	76	12	4
Education			
College graduate	43	39	14
High school	45	37	12
Grade school	43	35	15
Occupation			
Professional white collar	NA	NA	NA
Manual			
Union			
Income			
$50,000 +	35	42	18
$30,000–49,999	43	38	14
$20,000–29,999	46	36	12
Under $20,000	57	29	9
Age			
Under 30 years	38	44	14
30–49 years	43	35	17
50 years and older	46	37	11
Religion			
Protestants	41	41	18
Catholics	47	35	18
Politics			
Republicans	7	77	13
Democrats	82	8	7
Independents	38	28	23
Region			
East	47	33	15
Midwest	45	35	13
South	40	42	13
West	43	36	15

SOURCE: *Gallup Poll Monthly*, November 1992, 9.

NOTE: The information on occupation and religion is no longer asked and the categories for education have changed. Instead of the information on occupation, we have included for 1992 data on income.

TABLE A.3—VOTE BY GROUPS IN PRESIDENTIAL ELECTIONS, 1996

	1996		
	Clinton	Dole	Perot
National	50%	41%	9%
Sex			
Men	45	44	11
Women	54	39	7
Race			
White	46	45	9
Nonwhite	82	12	6
Education			
College graduate	47	45	8
High school	52	34	14
Grade school	58	27	15
Occupation			
Professional white collar	NA	NA	NA
Manual			
Union			
Income			
$50,000 +	45	47	8
$30,000–49,999	45	46	9
$20,000–29,999	57	36	7
Under $20,000	64	25	11
Age			
Under 30 years	54	30	16
30–49 years	49	44	10
50 years and older	50	45	5
Religion			
Protestants	44	50	6
Catholics	55	35	10
Politics			
Republicans	10	85	5
Democrats	90	6	4
Independents	48	33	19
Region			
East	60	31	9
Midwest	46	45	9
South	44	46	10
West	51	43	6

SOURCE: *Gallup Poll Monthly,* November 1992, 20.

TABLE B.1—PARTICIPATION IN NATIONAL ELECTIONS, BY POPULATION
CHARACTERISTICS, 1968–1996

| Characteristic | Persons of voting age | 1968 Persons reporting they voted | | Percent reporting they did not vote |
		Total	Percent	
Total	116,535	78,964	67.8	30.0
Male	54,464	38,014	69.8	27.6
Female	62,071	40,951	66.0	32.1
White	104,521	72,213	69.1	28.9
Black	10,935	6,300	57.6	38.5
18–20 years old	432	144	33.3	64.1
21–24 years old	11,170	5,707	51.1	45.6
25–34 years old	23,198	14,501	62.5	35.8
35–44 years old	22,905	16,223	70.8	27.1
45–64 years old	40,362	30,238	74.9	22.8
65 years and older	18,468	12,150	65.8	31.9
Median age (years)	45.2	46.7	(x)	(x)
Metropolitan residence	40,778	27,461	67.3	32.7
Nonmetropolitan residence	40,778	27,461	67.3	32.7
North and West residence	81,594	57,970	71.0	29.0
South residence	34,941	20,994	60.1	39.9
Years of school completed:				
8 years or less	30,430	16,592	54.4	45.5
9–11 years	20,429	12,519	61.3	38.7
12 years	39,704	28,768	72.5	27.5
More than 12 years	25,971	21,086	81.2	18.8
Employed	70,002	49,772	71.1	28.9
Unemployed	1,875	977	52.1	47.9
Not in labor force	44,657	28,215	63.2	36.8

SOURCE: U.S. Bureau of the Census, *Current Population Reports*, Series p-20, no. 192; *Statistical Abstract* 1970, 369.

NOTE: Persons in thousands, as of November. Covers civilian noninstitutional population. For 1968, persons 18 years and over in Georgia and Kentucky, 19 and over in Alaska, 20 and over in Hawaii, and 21 and over elsewhere.

TABLE B.2—PARTICIPATION IN NATIONAL ELECTIONS, BY POPULATION
CHARACTERISTICS, 1968–1996

		1972		
	Persons of	Persons reporting they voted		Percent reporting
Characteristic	voting age	Total	Percent	they did not vote
Total	136,203	85,766	63.0	37.0
Male	63,833	40,908	64.1	35.9
Female	72,370	44,858	62.0	38.0
White	121,243	78,166	64.5	35.5
Black	13,493	7,032	52.1	47.9
18–20 years old	11,022	5,318	48.3	51.7
21–24 years old	13,590	6,896	50.7	49.3
25–34 years old	26,933	16,072	59.7	40.3
35–44 years old	22,240	14,747	66.3	33.7
45–64 years old	42,344	29,991	70.8	29.2
65 years and older	20,274	12,741	63.5	36.5
Median age (years)	42.4	44.9	(x)	(x)
Metropolitan residence	99,248	63,799	64.3	35.7
Nonmetropolitan residence	36,855	21,976	59.4	49.6
North and West residence	93,653	62,193	66.4	33.6
South residence	42,550	23,573	55.4	44.6
Years of school completed:				
8 years or less	28,065	13,311	47.4	52.6
9–11 years	22,277	11,587	52.0	48.0
12 years	50,749	33,193	65.4	34.6
More than 12 years	35,113	27,675	78.8	21.2
Employed	80,164	52,899	66.0	34.0
Unemployed	3,735	1,863	49.9	50.1
Not in labor force	52,305	31,001	59.3	40.7

SOURCE: U.S. Bureau of the Census, *Current Population Reports*, Series p-20, no. 253; *Statistical Abstract* 1974, 437.

NOTE: For 1972–1984, persons 18 years old and over in all states. Includes aliens. Figures are based on a populations sample. Differences in percentages may also be due to over-reporting of voting persons in the sample. Excludes persons who did not report whether or not they had voted.

TABLE B.3—PARTICIPATION IN NATIONAL ELECTIONS, BY POPULATION
CHARACTERISTICS, 1968–1996

		1976		
	Persons of	Persons reporting they voted		Percent reporting
Characteristic	voting age	Total	Percent	they did not vote
Total	146,500	86,700	59.2	40.8
Male	69,000	41,100	59.6	40.4
Female	77,600	45,600	58.8	41.2
White	129,300	78,800	60.9	39.1
Black	14,900	7,300	48.7	51.3
18–20 years old	12,100	4,600	38.0	62.0
21–24 years old	14,800	6,800	45.6	54.4
25–34 years old	31,500	17,500	55.4	44.6
35–44 years old	22,800	14,400	63.3	36.7
45–64 years old	43,300	29,800	68.7	31.1
65 years and older	22,000	13,700	62.2	37.8
Median age (years)	41.5	45.1	(x)	(x)
Metropolitan residence	99,600	58,900	59.2	40.8
Nonmetropolitan residence	47,000	27,800	59.1	40.9
North and West residence	99,400	60,800	61.2	38.8
South residence	47,100	25,900	54.9	45.1
Years of school completed:				
8 years or less	24,900	11,000	44.1	55.9
9–11 years	22,200	10,500	47.2	52.8
12 years	55,700	33,100	59.4	40.6
More than 12 years	43,700	32,200	73.5	26.5
Employed	86,000	53,300	62.0	38.0
Unemployed	6,400	2,800	43.7	56.3
Not in labor force	54,100	36,000	56.5	43.5

SOURCE: U.S. Bureau of the Census, *Current Population Reports*, Series p-20, no. 322;
Statistical Abstract 1977, 491.

NOTE: Persons in thousands, as of November. Covers civilian noninstitutional population.
For 1968, persons 18 years and over in Georgia and Kentucky, 19 and over in Alaska, 20
and over in Hawaii, and 21 and over elsewhere.

TABLE B.4—PARTICIPATION IN NATIONAL ELECTIONS, BY POPULATION
CHARACTERISTICS, 1968–1996

Characteristic	Persons of voting age	*1980* Persons reporting they voted		Percent reporting they did not vote
		Total	Percent	
Total	157,100	93,100	59.2	40.8
Male	74,100	43,800	59.1	40.9
Female	83,000	49,300	59.4	40.6
White	137,700	83,900	60.9	39.1
Black	16,400	8,300	50.5	49.5
18–20 years old	12,300	4,400	35.7	64.3
21–24 years old	15,900	6,800	43.1	56.9
25–34 years old	35,700	19,500	54.6	45.4
35–44 years old	25,600	16,500	64.4	35.6
45–64 years old	43,600	30,200	69.3	30.7
65 years and older	24,100	15,700	65.1	34.9
Median age (years)	40.7	44.6	(x)	(x)
Metropolitan residence	106,700	62,700	58.8	41.2
Nonmetropolitan residence	50,500	30,400	60.2	39.8
North and West residence	106,500	65,000	61.0	39.0
South residence	50,600	28,100	55.6	44.4
Years of school completed:				
8 years or less	22,700	9,600	42.6	57.4
9–11 years	22,500	10,200	45.6	54.4
12 years	61,200	36,000	58.9	41.1
More than 12 years	50,800	37,200	73.2	26.8
Employed	95,000	58,800	61.8	38.2
Unemployed	6,900	2,800	41.2	58.8
Not in labor force	55,200	31,400	57.0	43.0

SOURCE: U.S. Bureau of the Census, *Current Population Reports*, Series p-20, no. 359; *Statistical Abstract* 1981, 499.

NOTE: Persons in thousands, as of November. Covers civilian noninstitutional population. For 1968, persons 18 years and over in Georgia and Kentucky, 19 and over in Alaska, 20 and over in Hawaii, and 21 and over elsewhere.

TABLE B.5—PARTICIPATION IN NATIONAL ELECTIONS, BY POPULATION
CHARACTERISTICS, 1968–1996

Characteristic	Persons of voting age	1984 Persons reporting they voted		Percent reporting they did not vote
		Total	Percent	
Total	170,000	101,800	59.9	41.1
Male	80,300	44,400	59.0	41.0
Female	89,600	54,500	60.8	39.2
White	146,800	90,100	61.4	38.6
Black	18,400	10,300	55.8	44.2
18–20 years old	11,200	4,100	36.7	63.3
21–24 years old	16,700	7,300	43.5	56.5
25–34 years old	40,300	22,000	54.5	45.5
35–44 years old	30,700	19,500	63.5	36.5
45–64 years old	44,300	30,900	69.8	30.2
65 years and older	26,700	18,000	67.7	32.3
Metropolitan residence*				
Nonmetropolitan residence*				
North and West residence	112,400	69,200	61.6	38.4
South residence	57,600	32,700	56.8	43.2
Years of school completed:				
8 years or less	20,600	8,800	42.9	57.1
9–11 years	22,100	9,800	44.4	55.6
12 years	67,800	39,800	58.7	41.3
More than 12 years	59,500	40,200	67.5**	32.5
			79.1**	20.9
Employed	104,200	64,200	61.6	38.4
Unemployed	7,400	3,300	44.0	56.0
Not in labor force	58,400	34,400	58.9	41.1

SOURCE: U.S. Bureau of the Census, *Current Population Reports*, Series p-20, no. 405;
Statistical Abstract 1986, 256.

*Census Bureau has changed its definitions, and these data are no longer available. In past
years there was little difference in turnout between these two categories.

TABLE B.6—PARTICIPATION IN NATIONAL ELECTIONS, BY POPULATION
CHARACTERISTICS, 1968–1996

Characteristic	Persons of voting age	1988 Persons reporting they voted Total	Percent	Percent reporting they did not vote
Total	178,100	48,500	57.4	42.6
Male	84,500	47,700	56.4	43.6
Female	93,600	54,600	58.3	41.7
White	152,000	90,400	59.1	40.9
Black	19,700	10,100	51.5	48.5
18–20 years old	10,700	3,600	33.2	66.8
21–24 years old	14,800	5,700	38.3	61.7
25–34 years old	42,700	20,500	48.0	52.0
35–44 years old	35,200	21,600	61.3	38.7
45–64 years old	45,900	31,200	67.9	32.1
65 years and older	28,800	19,800	68.8	31.2
Metropolitan residence	139,134	79,505	57.1	42.9
Nonmetropolitan residence*	38,964	22,719	58.3	41.7
North and West residence	117,400	69,100	58.9	41.1
South residence	60,700	33,000	54.5	45.5
Years of school completed:				
8 years or less	19,100	7,000	36.7	63.3
9–11 years	21,100	8,700	41.3	58.7
12 years	70,000	38,300	54.7	45.3
More than 12 years	67,900	43,800	64.5**	35.5
			77.6**	22.4
Employed	113,800	66,500	58.4	41.6
Unemployed	5,800	2,200	38.6	61.4
Not in labor force	58,500	33,500	57.3	42.7

SOURCE: U.S. Bureau of the Census, *Current Population Reports*, Series p-20, no. 440; *Statistical Abstract* 1990, 262.

TABLE B.7—PARTICIPATION IN NATIONAL ELECTIONS, BY POPULATION CHARACTERISTICS, 1968–1996

Characteristic	Persons of voting age	Persons reporting they voted		Percent reporting they did not vote
		1992		
		Total	Percent	
Total	185,700	113,866	61.3	42.6
Male	88,557	53,312	60.2	39.8
Female	97,126	60,554	62.3	37.7
White	157,837	100,405	63.6	36.4
Black	27,863	13,461	48.3	46.0
18–20 years old	9,728	3,749	38.5	61.5
21–24 years old	14,644	6,693	45.7	54.3
25–34 years old	41,603	22,120	53.2	46.8
35–44 years old	39,716	25,269	63.6	36.4
45–64 years old	49,147	34,399	70.0	30.0
65 years and older	30,846	21,637	70.1	29.9
Median age (years)	NA	NA		
Metropolitan residence	144,593	88,222	61.0	39.0
Nonmetropolitan residence	41,091	25,644	62.4	37.6
North and West residence	122,025	76,275	62.5	37.5
South residence	63,659	37,590	29.0	41.0
Years of school completed:				
8 years or less	15,391	5,406	35.1	64.9
9–11 years	20,970	8,638	41.2	58.8
12 years	65,281	37,517	57.5	42.5
More than 12 years	84,042	62,305	68.7*	31.3
			81.0**	29.0
Employed	116,290	74,138	63.8	36.2
Unemployed	8,263	3,820	46.2	53.8
Not in labor force	61,131	35,908	58.7	41.3

SOURCE: U.S. Bureau of the Census, *Current Population Reports*, Series p-20, no. 466; *Statistical Abstract* 1994, 288.

NOTE: Persons in thousands, as of November. Covers civilian noninstitutional population. For 1968, persons 18 years and over in Georgia and Kentucky, 19 and over in Alaska, 20 and over in Hawaii, and 21 and over elsewhere.

*One to three years in college
**Four years or more in college
NA=Not applicable

Table B.8—Participation in National Elections, by Population Characteristics, 1968–1996

Characteristic	Persons of voting age	1996 Persons reporting they voted	
		Total	Percent
Total	193,700	104,985	54.2
Male	92,600	48,893	52.8
Female	101,000	56,055	55.5
White	162,800	91,168	56.0
Black	30,900	13,817	44.7
18–20 years old	10,800	3,370	31.2
21–24 years old	13,900	4,643	33.4
25–34 years old	40,100	17,283	43.1
35–44 years old	43,300	23,722	54.9
45–64 years old	53,700	NA	NA
65 years and older	31,900	NA	NA
Median age (years)		NA	
Metropolitan residence	NA	NA	NA
Nonmetropolitan residence	NA	69,457	NA
North and West residence	125,600	35,548	55.3
South residence	68,100		53.2
Years of school completed:			
8 years or less	14,100	3,962	28.1
9–11 years	2,100	7,098	33.8
12 years	65,200	32,013	49.1
More than 12 years	93,400	61,820	60.5*
			73.0**
Employed	125,600	68,331	55.2
Unemployed	6,400	2,381	37.2
Not in labor force	61,600	33,326	54.1

Source: U.S. Bureau of the Census, *Current Population Reports,* Series P-20, no. 453 and P-20, no. 466. *Statistical Abstract* 1997, 288.

*One to three years in college
**Four years or more in college
NA=Not applicable

Index